WHERE TO LIVE

Society of Biblical Literature

Academia Biblica

Saul M. Olyan,
Old Testament Editor

Mark Allan Powell,
New Testament Editor

Number 14

WHERE TO LIVE
The Hermeneutical Significance of
Paul's Citations from Scripture in
Galatians 3:1–14

WHERE TO LIVE
The Hermeneutical Significance of Paul's Citations from Scripture in Galatians 3:1–14

Andrew H. Wakefield

Society of Biblical Literature
Atlanta

WHERE TO LIVE

Copyright © 2003 by the Society of Biblical Literature

All rights reserved. No part of this work may be reproduced or transmitted in any form or by any means, electronic or mechanical, including photocopying and recording, or by means of any information storage or retrieval system, except as may be expressly permitted by the 1976 Copyright Act or in writing from the publisher. Requests for permission should be addressed in writing to the Rights and Permissions Office, Society of Biblical Literature, 825 Houston Mill Road, Atlanta, GA 30329, USA.

Library of Congress Cataloging-in-Publication Data

Wakefield, Andrew Hollis, 1960-
  Where to live : the hermeneutical significance of Paul's citations from Scripture in Galatians 3:1–14 / by Andrew H. Wakefield.
    p. cm. — (Academia Biblica ; no. 14)
  Includes bibliographical references and index.
  ISBN 1-58983-084-9 (pbk. : alk. paper)
  1. Bible. N.T. Galatians III, 1–14—Relation to the Old Testament. 2. Bible. O.T.—Quotations in the New Testament. 3. Bible. O.T.—Relation to Galatians. 4. Paul, the Apostle, Saint —Views on Jewish law. 5. Law and gospel—Biblical teaching. I. Title. II. Series: Academia Biblica (Series) (Society of Biblical Literature) ; no. 14.
  BS2685.6.L34 W35 2003
  227'.406—dc22
                        2003014915

07 06 05 04 03 02   5 4 3 2 1

Printed in the United States of America
on acid-free paper

TABLE OF CONTENTS

ACKNOWLEDGEMENTS ix

CHAPTER 1. INTRODUCTION 1
  STATEMENT OF THE PROBLEM 1
  INTERTEXTUALITY: A POSSIBLE WAY FORWARD 7
  PROCEDURE 9

CHAPTER 2. SUMMARY AND ANALYSIS OF RECENT SCHOLARSHIP:
  PAUL AND THE LAW 11
  LUTHER AND THE "TRADITIONAL" POSITION 13
    Luther 13
    Sinful Self-Righteousness: Bultmann 16
    The "Missing Premise": No One Can Keep the Law 18
    Summary 20
  THE "NEW PERSPECTIVE ON PAUL": AN EMERGING CONSENSUS? 23
    E. P. Sanders 23
    Response to Sanders 28
      James D. G. Dunn: "Works of Law" and "Boundary Markers" 30
      Response from the Traditional Reformation Position: Gundry,
        Westerholm, Thielman 33
    Summary: Problems Remaining 39
  ALTERNATIVES 45
    John M. G. Barclay: Identity and Behavior 46
    J. Louis Martyn: Apocalyptic Antinomies 49

CHAPTER 3. SUMMARY AND ANALYSIS OF RECENT SCHOLARSHIP:
  PAUL'S USE OF SCRIPTURE 57
  GENERAL APPROACHES TO PAUL'S USE OF SCRIPTURE 57
    The Mechanics of Citation: Paul as Quoter of Scripture 58
    The Hermeneutics of Citation: Paul as Interpreter of Scripture 61

EFFORTS TO DEAL WITH TENSIONS: PAUL'S USE OF SCRIPTURE IN
　　　GALATIANS 3:1–14 65
　　　Tension Between Paul's Argument and the Citations 66
　　　　Two "Standard" Solutions 67
　　　　Other Solutions 74
　　　Tension Between Citations 79
　　　　The Problem: Contradictory Citations 79
　　　　Two "Standard" Solutions 80
　　　　Solutions from Historical/Cultural Antecedents 89
　　　The Citations as Evidence for Pauline Inconsistency? 93
　　CONCLUSIONS 94

CHAPTER 4. INTERTEXTUALITY 97
　　A BRIEF SYNOPSIS OF INTERTEXTUALITY 98
　　　Theory 98
　　　Practice: Problems and Limitations 102
　　　　Limiting the Scope 102
　　　　Observations 110
　　　Intertextuality in Biblical Studies 112
　　　　Echoes of Scripture: Richard Hays 112
　　　　Intertextuality and Midrash: Daniel Boyarin 115
　　　　Short Intertextual Studies on Paul: Keesmat, Jervis, Jobes 117
　　　　Analysis 119
　　INTERTEXTUALITY AND GALATIANS 3: SELECTED INSIGHTS AND
　　　METHODS 120
　　　Limiting the Scope of the Investigation 120
　　　Selected Methods 122

CHAPTER 5. UNGRAMMATICALITIES AND PRESUPPOSITIONS IN
　　GALATIANS 3:1–14 131
　　STRUCTURE AND FORM 132
　　　The Chiastic Structure of the Citations 132
　　　Significance of the Chiastic Structure 137
　　　　The Citations as the Framework of Paul's Argument 137
　　　　Metaleptic Ungrammaticality: Blessing, Curse, Life, and . . . ? 142
　　　Summary 144
　　PRESUPPOSED INTERTEXTS 145
　　　The Role of Scripture in Paul's Argument 146
　　　　Authority and Applicability 147
　　　　Citation as Proof, Premise, or Conclusion 151
　　　Presuppositions of Contrast: Ζήσεται as the "Hinge-Point" of the
　　　　Argument 167
　　　Summary 171

"Ungrammaticalities" and the Matrix of Meaning 172
    Leviticus 18:5 and Habakkuk 2:4: Scripture Against Scripture 174
    Deuteronomy 27:26: The Threat of the Curse 177
    Loose Ends and Implications: Redemption and Righteousness 180
Summary: A Reading of Gal 3:1–14 184

Chapter 6. Conclusion: Implications for Issues in Pauline Theology 189
    Paul and the Law 190
        What Is Wrong with the Law? 190
        What Is the Place of the Law in the Ongoing Life of the Christian? 194
        Law in General, or the Torah Specifically? 197
    Living in the Spirit: A Practical Ethic? 199
        Living by the Spirit: Inadequate Answers 199
        Living *in* the Spirit 202
    Tasks Remaining 204
    Conclusion 206

Appendix. ὍΤΙ . . . ΔΗΛΟΝ . . . ὍΤΙ in Hellenistic Literature 207

Bibliography 215

Index of Modern Authors 225

ACKNOWLEDGEMENTS

Far more people than I can name have fulfilled the law of Christ by helping me bear the burden of the writing of this dissertation (Gal 6:2). My advisor, Richard B. Hays, has provided invaluable insight and feedback all along the way. The members of churches where I have served as interim pastor (Page Road Baptist Church and Park View Baptist Church of Durham, NC; Live Oak Baptist Church of Selma, NC; and First Baptist Church of Lumberton, NC), the students in my classes at Campbell University Divinity School, and many friends have offered much support and encouragement. The administration of Campbell University and the Divinity School have been patient and supportive throughout the process, and my colleagues on the faculty have helped with feedback and proofreading. As I prepared this dissertation for publication, David R. Vinson has been especially helpful in offering feedback and pointing out errors. In addition to their support and encouragement, my parents have modeled life in the Spirit more than anyone else I know. Most of all, I want to thank my wife, Olivia; without her love and support I never would have succeeded.

Chapter 1
INTRODUCTION

STATEMENT OF THE PROBLEM

It is of course impossible to know whether the author of 2 Peter had any particular passages especially in mind when he declared that Paul's letters contain "some things hard to understand" (2 Pet 3:16), but if one were to speculate, the third chapter of Galatians must surely present itself as a serious candidate. Especially with regard to Gal 3:1–14, exegetes regularly note the complexity of the task before plunging in to try once more to untangle Paul's thought. Indeed, while there is often little agreement among scholars as to the interpretation of the passage, there is universal accord as to its difficulty.[1]

No small part of this difficulty stems from the density and interplay of Paul's citation of scripture in this passage.[2] In the space of nine verses, Paul explicitly cites six texts: Gen 15:6 in Gal 3:6, Gen 12:3 in 3:8, Dt 27:26 in 3:10, Hab 2:4 in 3:11, Lev 18:5 in 3:12, and Dt 21:23 in 3:13.[3] While it might seem

---

[1] So, for example, H. D. Betz, *Galatians: A Commentary on Paul's Letter to the Churches in Galatia*, Hermeneia (Philadelphia: Fortress Press, 1979), 137: "There is agreement among exegetes that Paul's argument is extremely difficult to follow." Cf. J. Christiaan Beker, *Paul the Apostle: The Triumph of God in Life and Thought* (Philadelphia: Fortress Press, 1980), 58; referring primarily to the problems of Gal 3, he states, "All this makes Galatians one of Paul's most difficult letters, as the history of interpretation shows."

[2] For the purposes of the current investigation, the issue of which text Paul cites is of little significance (see below, 59n4). To avoid anachronism, we will speak of Paul's citation of "scripture(s)," resorting to the term "Old Testament" only when it is needed to draw a distinction with the New Testament.

[3] In only one other letter (Romans) do we see a density of citation similar to that which occurs here in Galatians. It is surely no coincidence that Paul's explicit use of scripture greatly increases in the two letters in which he is most directly dealing with issues concerning the Law and the relationship of Gentiles to that Law, as many scholars have noted; cf. Adolf von Harnack, "Das Alte Testament in den Paulinischen Briefen und

reasonable to suppose (or at least hope) that these citations would help illuminate Paul's thinking, they do more to exacerbate the problems of this passage. Two of the six citations, for example, seem to be exactly at odds with the argument in support of which Paul apparently quotes them. According to Dt 27:26, the curse of the law falls on those who do *not* keep the law, not those who do, while Lev 18:5 seems to promote the law as a valid means to life. Moreover, one of these same citations (Lev 18:5) appears to be directly contradicted by another citation (Hab 2:4). Only in one other place in Paul's letters does such an apparent contradiction between citations occur, and then in rather a different manner.[4] In short, the citations in Gal 3:1–14 have only added to the problems posed by this passage.

That Paul's thinking is so hard to untangle in this passage is especially unfortunate, given the key position it occupies in his letter to the Galatians. Gal 3:1–14 is something of a "crossroads" in the text. In this passage, Paul begins to draw together the autobiographical and historical material of the first two chapters with all that he goes on to say about Abraham, the Law, the covenant(s), the Spirit and its fruit, and so on. Having set the stage with a scathing attack, a personal defense, and a carefully presented account of the events at Antioch, Paul now begins to lay out his arguments in support of his vision of the gospel, the gospel to which he is calling the Galatians to return.

As a result, scholars regularly point to the importance of Gal 3:1–14 for understanding the letter as a whole. Drawing on insights derived from Hellenistic rhetoric, for example, Hans Dieter Betz identifies Gal 3:1–14 as the beginning of Paul's *probatio*, his proof of the thesis laid out in the preceding chapter—the section which is "most decisive of all," the part which "determines whether or not the speech as a whole will succeed."[5] Charles H. Cosgrove goes even further, arguing that 3:1–14 is where Paul first begins "directly" and "specifically" to address the problem in Galatia, and that therefore this is the passage with

---

in den Paulinischen Gemeinden," *Sitzungsberichte der Preussischen Akademie der Wissenschaften*, Philosophisch-historische Klasse (1928): 124–41; Rudolf Bultmann, "The Significance of the Old Testament for Christian Faith," in *The Old Testament and Christian Faith*, ed. Bernhard W. Anderson (New York: Harper & Row, 1963), 8–35. I am indebted to Richard B. Hays, *Echoes of Scripture in the Letters of Paul* (New Haven: Yale University Press, 1989), 7–8, for these references.

[4]It comes as no surprise that this other occurrence is also in Romans (Rom 10:5–10), and also involves—again, surely no coincidence—Lev 18:5. Here, however, Paul does not introduce the same sort of tightly coupled, highly structured set of citations that play off of each other as we find in Gal 3; instead, there is the short citation of Lev 18:5 contrasted with a sort of running commentary on Dt 9 & 30. It is also more open to debate whether Paul is actually setting up the citations in Rom 10:5–10 as contradictory; cf. Alain Gignac, "Citation de Lévitique 18,5 en Romains 10,5 et Galates 3,12," *Église et Théologie* 25 (1994): 367–403.

[5]Betz, *Galatians*, 14ff, 128ff.

which interpreters must begin, rather than with the actual beginning of the letter, in order to arrive at a correct understanding of the letter as a whole.[6]

Not only is Gal 3:1–14 a key passage in the development of and for the understanding of Paul's argument in Galatians, however, but it has also proved to be a key passage in scholarly debates about Pauline theology. In particular, this passage plays a prominent role in discussions about Paul's view of the law.[7] Rightly or wrongly, Paul's view of the law tends to assume a central role in discussions of Pauline theology, with significant implications for issues such as Pauline soteriology (including atonement and the so-called doctrine of justification), Paul's continuity or discontinuity with Judaism, Paul's understanding and use of covenant, and so on. Thus, two scholars who are diametrically opposed in their understanding of Paul can nevertheless describe the importance of his view of the law in similar terms:

> Paul's theology of the law constitutes an essential part of his gospel, for we cannot grasp Pauline theology without explaining his understanding of the law and justification . . . . Grasping Paul's theology in this area is essential for understanding his soteriology, the death of Jesus, Christian ethics, the relationship between Jews and Gentiles in the new community, and the continuity and discontinuity between the Testaments.[8]

> The difficulty of the topic, however, is matched by its importance, and it merits the effort that has been expended. It is a subject which must be penetrated if one is to understand Paul's thought, and it is no less crucial for understanding an important moment in the divorce of Christianity from Judaism.[9]

Given the importance of this passage, it is unfortunate—though not surprising, in light of its notorious difficulty—that scholars have come to little consensus on how to interpret it. To be sure, there is widespread agreement on the most basic description of the point of Gal 3:1–14: Paul is urging the Galatians not to take up the law. The details of the argument, however, are not so clear. Exactly *why* is Paul so vehemently rejecting the law? Why would the Galatians be tempted to take up the law? In what manner and to what extent are

---

[6]Charles H. Cosgrove, *The Cross and the Spirit: A Study in the Argument and Theology of Galatians* (Macon, GA: Mercer University Press, 1988), 23–38.

[7]See chapters 2 and 3 below. While I have not taken a formal survey, I would expect that Gal 3:1–14 may be the *most* heavily discussed passage, or at least one the most heavily discussed passages, in the debates concerning Paul and the law.

[8]Thomas R. Schreiner, *The Law and Its Fulfillment: A Pauline Theology of the Law* (Grand Rapids: Baker Books, 1993), 13.

[9]E. P. Sanders, *Paul, the Law, and the Jewish People* (Minneapolis: Fortress, 1983), 3. (Hereafter, this work will be cited as *PLJP*.) Sanders's comment is especially interesting, in that Sanders identifies participation in Christ, rather than justification by faith (vs. works of law), as the central feature of Paul's thought; see below, 25.

they dabbling with the law? And how, exactly, is Paul attempting to persuade them not to do so?

It is this last question that particularly highlights the differences between various interpretations of Gal 3:1–14.[10] Many scholars, following the lead of Luther, understand Paul's argument as a proof that the law is a false road to salvation because it depends on works:[11] Either the law cannot be satisfied, because no one can obey it perfectly,[12] or the effort to achieve salvation by works inevitably leads to self-righteousness rather than dependence on God.[13] Other scholars, however, understand Paul's argument to rest on the question of who is to be counted among Abraham's children.[14] Yet others would point to the historical background of Israel's failure with the law and subsequent experience of curse,[15] or to the sociological significance of certain works of law which divided Jews and Gentiles,[16] or to Paul's christological understanding of salvation, that salvation is available to all peoples only through Christ.[17] At least one scholar

---

[10] See below, chap. 2, for a survey of these positions.

[11] The standard English translation of Luther's writings on Galatians is found in Martin Luther, *Luther's Works*, ed. J. Pelikan, vols. 26–27 (St. Louis: Concordia, 1963–1964). Luther's lectures on Galatians given in 1516–1517 (published 1519) are contained in vol. 27, while his lectures from 1531 (published 1535) span both volumes. Also useful is idem, *A Commentary on St. Paul's Epistle to the Galatians: Based on Lectures Delivered by Martin Luther at the University of Wittenberg in the year 1531 and First Published in 1535*, trans. P. W. Watson (London: James Clarke, 1953). Despite its title, this translation is based on the 1538 revised edition of Luther's 1531 lectures; it thus contains some material not found in *Works*.

[12] E.g., Thomas Schreiner, *The Law and Its Fulfillment*; idem, "Is Perfect Obedience to the Law Possible? A Re-Examination of Galatians 3:10," *JETS* 27 (1984): 151–60; idem, "Paul and Perfect Obedience to the Law: An Evaluation of the View of E. P. Sanders," *WTJ* 47 (1985): 245–78.

[13] E.g., Rudolf Bultmann, *Theology of the New Testament*, vol. 1, trans. K. Grobel (New York: Charles Scribner's Sons, 1951).

[14] A number of scholars have given varying degrees of emphasis to the question of who is to be counted among Abraham's descendents, e.g., Beker, *Paul the Apostle*, 48. For an in-depth investigation focused on the importance of Abraham in Paul's argument in Galatians, see G. Walter Hansen, *Abraham in Galatians: Epistolary and Rhetorical Contexts*, JSNTSS 29 (Sheffield: JSOT Press, 1989).

[15] E.g., Frank Thielman, *From Plight to Solution: A Jewish Framework for Understanding Paul's View of the Law in Galatians and Romans* (Leiden: E. J. Brill, 1989); Martin Noth, "'For all who rely on works of the law are under a curse,'" in *The Laws of the Pentateuch and Other Studies*, trans. D. R. Ap-Thomas (Edinburgh: Oliver & Boyd, 1966), 108–117.

[16] E.g., James D. G. Dunn, *Jesus, Paul, and the Law: Studies in Mark and Galatians* (Louisville: John Knox, 1990).

[17] E.g., E. P. Sanders, *PLJP*; idem, *Paul and Palestinian Judaism* (Philadelphia: Fortress Press, 1977) (hereafter cited as *PPJ*).

would suggest that the key to the passage lies in Paul's discussion of the Spirit, and that the key issue is how the Galatians should continue to experience the Spirit.[18]

Given the lack of consensus on the one hand, and the wide-ranging issues on which the passage potentially bears on the other, it is clear that a better understanding of Gal 3:1–14 would be of great benefit. What is at stake here is not simply a better understanding of how Paul argues his case before the Galatians, but also a better understanding of Paul himself. This passage offers insight both into what Paul thought about the various issues of law, continuity with Judaism, and so on, and also into *how* he thought—whether Paul was a coherent thinker to any degree at all, how he used and viewed scripture, and so on.[19]

Unfortunately, there has been a tendency among many scholars to leap too quickly ahead to these larger issues without thoroughly exploring the details of this passage or adequately resolving the problems it presents. This is not necessarily unexpected, of course, in an investigation that is topical rather than exegetical.[20] Even in many exegetical investigations, however, scholars often have a tendency to bypass the problems of the text in pursuit of the big picture. Thus, for example, even after acknowledging some of the problems posed by the passage, one commentator justifies skipping over them as follows:

> The details of Paul's argument (3:6–14) are, frankly, difficult to follow. The texts from the Old Testament do not appear to say exactly what he concludes from them, and in the case of the citation from Habakkuk, Paul quotes a verse which differs significantly in meaning from both the Septuagint and the Masoretic text. Still, the direction of Paul's thinking is clear. One must be careful in treating a passage like this not to miss the forest for the trees. It is easy to get bogged down in the details and never see the whole.[21]

As Cousar's comments illustrate, very often the problems which scholars skip over have specifically to do with the citations. In fact, in spite of the prominence of the citations in this passage, and in spite of the obvious problems they cause, very little attention has been given to a systematic examination of all of these citations as an integral component of Paul's argument. This is not to say that the citations have not received a good bit of attention in certain ways. The citations have been examined to discover Paul's text or his citation technique; they have been the subject of debate concerning Paul's exegetical practice; they

---

[18]Cosgrove, *The Cross and the Spirit*.

[19]To be sure, it may be too much to claim, in light of the hermeneutical circle, to have grasped Paul or his thinking *per se*, but at the very least we can hope to explore the contours and implications of the text which his thinking produced. Cf. Richard Hays's "common-sense" approach described below, 113.

[20]E.g., Sanders, *PLJP*.

[21]Charles B. Cousar, *Galatians*, Interpretation (Louisville: John Knox, 1982), 72.

have featured in discussions of Paul's attitude towards the Old Testament scriptures.[22] From time to time, scholars *have* focused on *certain* citations as a key for understanding Paul's argument—but generally only one or at most two of the citations, rather than all of them together. Most often, the citations have been treated as no more than a secondary feature of Paul's argument, as little more than scriptural proof-texts to back up the case Paul is building.[23] Thus, according to E. P. Sanders, one need not even ask what the citations themselves mean or what they contribute to Paul's argument; they mean only what Paul says and uses them to mean.[24]

What is lacking in any of these treatments of the citations is an approach that takes seriously the possibility that the citations may function together—all together—to provide something more than exemplars of Paul's citation technique on the one hand, or tenuous scriptural proof-texts in support of Paul's assertions on the other.[25] Rather than treating the citations as semi-optional adjuncts to Paul's argument, might one profit from viewing them instead as intrinsic components of that argument? If the density and complexity of Paul's thought in this passage is matched by and indeed linked to the density and complexity of the citations, is it not possible that the texts Paul cites might have played a role in shaping his thought? Even if Paul's thought or its development is not directly accessible, certainly it seems reasonable to suspect that the citations play a significant role in shaping one's reading of the text.

It is worth exploring, therefore, whether an approach that takes seriously and looks carefully at the way(s) the citations function within Gal 3:1–14 to contribute to its meaning might be helpful in opening up new insights into this difficult passage. What is needed is an approach that deals with the interrelation-

---

[22] See chap. 3 below for a survey of various treatments of the citations in Gal 3:1–14.

[23] Cf. Betz, *Galatians*, 137ff.

[24] Sanders, *PLJP*, 21–22.

[25] Gerhard Ebeling, *The Truth of the Gospel: An Exposition of Galatians*, trans. David Green (Philadelphia: Fortress, 1985), 167–69, represents another alternative. He uses the structure of the citations to determine the proper divisions of the passage. In 3:6–9, the citations come first, thus functioning as premises leading to Paul's conclusions; in 3:10–12, the citations come last, thus functioning as proof for Paul's assertions; in 3:13–14, the citation comes in the middle. Ironically, Ebeling's attention to the citations merely proves the point. Though he discusses the arrangement of the citations as a way to determine the structure of Paul's argument, he eschews any close examination of what they actually say: "So far our interpretation of vv. 6–14 has dealt with the passage as a whole. This does not make exegesis unnecessary but does free us from the need to examine each detail in order to pave the way for a general interpretation. Therefore, we shall be content with a few remarks focusing on specific points of the three component sections" (ibid., 175). It should be noted also that Ebeling's description of the function of the citations rests on assertion rather than investigation; see the investigation of the function of the citations below, 158–69.

ship of texts within and with other texts, not from the perspective of tracing sources or exposing alterations, but rather from the perspective of hermeneutical significance. Fortunately, such an approach is readily available by way of the phenomenon known as intertextuality.[26]

INTERTEXTUALITY: A POSSIBLE WAY FORWARD

Though intertextuality as a discipline in the field of literary studies has been developing for several decades, it is a relative newcomer to the field of biblical studies.[27] As it has been practiced both in its newer and in its more mature settings, intertextuality has taken on a surprisingly wide variety of forms, with differing specific methodologies and sometimes even differing assumptions. At the heart of all intertextual studies, however, is a common understanding about meaning in texts. Meaning emerges in a text as a function of (and cannot be separated from) the interaction of the text with a potentially unlimited number of "intertexts." These intertexts are potentially unlimited, because they include not only written texts cited or alluded to in the text, but also any sort of encoded message drawn from the context of the author or the reader (or both), whether literary, social, cultural, historical, political, or so on, with which the author or reader makes any sort of connection. In other words, neither authors nor readers handle texts in isolation; they cannot avoid interacting with a text in the context of all of these potential intertexts. Therefore, to interpret a text, one must look carefully at these intertextual interactions.

Even so brief a description of intertextuality as is given above raises an important question. How can an intertextual investigation of a text actually be conducted in a practical way, given the potentially unlimited number of intertexts? Obviously, intertextual practitioners must somehow limit the scope of the investigation, finding some way to limit the number of intertexts to be considered and some sort of method for exploring the kinds of interactions that ensue.[28] In the case of the current investigation, both the relevance of an intertextual approach and the way to limit the scope seems obvious. One should undertake an intertextual investigation focused on the explicit citations in Gal 3:1–14. Obvious though it may seem, however, intertextual practitioners have tended to neglect or even to reject explicit citations as worthy objects of intertextual investigation.[29]

---

[26]In many ways, it might be better to describe intertextuality as a phenomenon rather than a discipline; see below, 111. For convenience, however, we will describe that approach to interpreting texts which gives conscious attention to intertextual phenomena as the "discipline" (or "approach") of intertextuality.

[27]See below, chap. 4, for a thorough discussion of intertextuality.

[28]See below, 102–110, for further discussion of this key issue.

[29]See below, 110n43.

One of the primary tasks of the current investigation, therefore, is to sort through the claims and theories of intertextuality to evaluate whether and how an intertextual investigation focused on the citations in Gal 3:1–14 might be possible. In anticipation of the results realized below, two observations can be made. First, Paul's use of citations in Gal 3:1–14 simply makes explicit what was already obvious. One of the most significant intertextual contexts in which his discussion unfolds is the context of scripture—both in terms of the content of the particular scriptures that he cites (and others that they may call to mind), and in terms of the use of scripture as a tool for argument and interpretation. It is certainly appropriate, therefore, to examine how this highly significant intertextual context informs our understanding of the passage; indeed, the presence of explicit citations not only calls for an intertextual investigation, but also provides a clear way to focus its scope.

Second, while it is true that many specific methodologies used by various intertextual practitioners may not be well suited to an investigation of explicit citations, there are at least two approaches which seem very promising for this passage. The first of these is Michael Riffaterre's focus on "ungrammaticalities"—inconsistencies or tensions within the text—as a key for moving beyond the surface, "heuristic" reading of a text to discover its true unity and significance (the "hermeneutical" reading).[30] Certainly in Gal 3:1–14, several of the citations stand out as "ungrammatical"; rather than simply treating them as problems to be resolved, Riffaterre's approach suggests that these tensions may offer a key to interpretation. The second approach that seems very promising is Jonathan Culler's discussion of "presuppositions," anonymous intertexts that inform the way we understand a text, which can be deduced from the way a text is constructed.[31] Here again, Culler's approach seems tailor-made for the problems presented by the citations in Gal 3:1–14, because of the need to explore how the citations really do function within Paul's argument, and to see what really is and is not presupposed by his use of explicit citations.

As will be explored in detail in chapter 5 below, using these approaches to investigate the citations in Gal 3:1–14 does lead to new insights about this difficult passage. In particular, a key insight that arises from this investigation is that the "matrix" which resolves the ungrammaticalities and provides significance to the passage as a whole is the phrase, "where to live." Rather than dealing with what might be described as primarily soteriological issues—how to gain life, how to maintain one's status among the saved, who is to be counted among the saved, and so on—this passage revolves around the eschatological issue of

---

[30] See below, 123–30.
[31] See below, 128–32.

where one lives, in the old age which includes the law, or in the new age in Christ.[32]

This eschatological matrix not only provides insight into Gal 3:1–14, helping to resolve the problems created by the citations and offering a new understanding of the passage as a whole, but also it provides insight into some larger issues. For example, a focus on "where to live" helps to draw together the discussion of Gal 3–4 with the parenetic material that follows in Gal 5–6. While "where to live" does speak to one's soteriological status, it also and more importantly speaks to the issue of how one lives righteously, or rather *where* one lives righteously. Righteousness is a matter of where one lives. One lives righteously by living in the new age, apart from either sin or the law; in other words, to paraphrase Gal 5:16, one walks not just by, but *in* the Spirit (the new age), and thus one is free from the desires of the flesh (the old age).

Likewise, this matrix has important implications for the issue of Paul and the law. Paul rejects the law not because of any defect within it, but rather because it is a feature of the old age—it was given as a response to sin (Gal 3:19); it is locked up (or locks us up) together with sin (Gal 3:22–23); it is our pedagogue until the new age comes (Gal 3:24–25); it has no power to produce the new age by way of resurrection (Gal 3:21). To turn to (or return to) the law, therefore, is to step out of the new age in Christ and return to the old age. Again, the basic issue is where to live. Either we live in the new age in Christ, or in the old age together with the law.

Procedure

The procedure which this investigation will follow has already largely been suggested in the remarks above. First, in chapters 2 and 3, we will conduct a selective survey of the history of scholarship related to Gal 3:1–14. In chapter 2, the primary focus of the survey will be on the most significant issue related to the study of Gal 3: "What, if anything, does Paul see as wrong with the law, vis-à-vis the Galatian situation?"[33] In chapter 3, the primary focus will be on schol-

---

[32] Certainly soteriology is an eschatological issue (or at least has eschatological implications), and certainly the question of where one lives has soteriological implications. The distinction that is made above, however, points to the primary focus of the discussion. Are questions about whether (or how) one is saved the best way to understand the points Paul is making and the distinctions he is drawing, particularly with his use of citations? As will be argued below, though scholars almost always assume a soteriological focus for Gal 3:1–14, that assumption contributes significantly to some of the problems of the passage.

[33] It should be noted that the current investigation is *not* intended to be a study of Paul and the law as such. This investigation is much more narrowly focused on a specific passage (Gal 3:1–14) and even on a specific feature of that passage (the citations). Because Gal 3:1–14 is a key passage in the study of Paul and the law, a significant part of

arly treatments of the citations in Gal 3:1–14, both in terms of Paul's use of scripture in general, and in terms of the specific problems posed by these citations in particular. In chapter 4, we will examine the discipline of intertextuality, looking in particular at whether and how intertextual insights might be applied to the problems of this passage, especially those having to do with the citations. In chapter 5, we will use selected intertextual insights to conduct a thorough investigation of the way the citations function within and contribute to the meaning of Gal 3:1–14, culminating in a fresh reading of the passage. Chapter 6 will then provide some summarizing and concluding remarks, suggesting how the results of this investigation might be extended to address other concerns in the study of Pauline theology.

---

this investigation will inevitably be concerned with Paul's understanding of the law—but only as expressed and developed in *this* passage. The primary focus will be on understanding what Gal 3:1–14 has to say, and on how the citations help to shape that understanding.

Chapter 2
SUMMARY AND ANALYSIS OF RECENT SCHOLARSHIP: PAUL AND THE LAW

Any investigation of Paul's letter to the Galatians, and in particular the third chapter of that letter, must be prepared to grapple with one crucial question. From Paul's perspective, particularly as it pertained to the Galatian situation, what, if anything, is wrong with the law? Paul's understanding of the law is, of course, a broad concern in Pauline studies, far too broad and complex to deal with comprehensively in a brief chapter. On the one hand, this topic has generated innumerable monographs and articles; on the other hand, a full treatment of the topic demands attention not only to Galatians but also to Romans at the very least (if not the entire Pauline corpus), not to mention considerable attention to rabbinic writings, and possibly also to Hellenistic rhetoric as well. Since the current investigation is narrowly focused on the hermeneutical significance of Paul's use of citations in Galatians 3:1–14, it is more than a little tempting to bypass such a potentially overwhelming topic as Paul's understanding of the law.[1]

---

[1] Fortunately, we can bypass the concerns of a traditional historical introduction. For our purposes, it matters not at all whether the Galatian churches were located in the northern or southern portion of the province, nor does it make much difference when Paul wrote the letter, or even exactly who the opponents were against whom Paul so fiercely defends his gospel. Though a clear understanding of any of these issues would no doubt be helpful in understanding the hermeneutical significance of the letter, the only primary source for any of these is the letter itself. Rather than getting bogged down in the hermeneutical circle—reconstructing what the letter means on the basis of a reconstruction of the historical background of the letter, which itself is based on an understanding of what the letter means, and so on—it seems better to rely on the general historical background that is available apart from the letter, and within that context, to take the letter as it stands.

For those who wish to pursue the historical issues, ample investigation of such issues is available in any of the major commentaries on Galatians, including H. D. Betz, *Galatians: A*

Tempting though it may be, it is not possible to bypass the question of Paul and the law. Virtually all scholars, even those who do not view Paul's understanding of the law as a central concern of his theology, would readily admit that it is a central concern of his letter to the Galatians.[2] Moreover, the citations in Galatians 3:1–14, while certainly not the only focal point for this discussion, have certainly played a major role in the ongoing scholarly discussion.[3] All in all, it would not be too much of an overstatement to say that virtually every exegetical discussion of Galatians 3:1–14 in the past 300 years has at least touched on the topic of Paul and the law, even when that topic is not the primary focus of the investigation. It is imperative, therefore, that we survey at least the major trends of scholarship on the issue as it pertains to Paul's letter to the Galatians, and in particular to the citations in Galatians 3:1–14.[4]

Commentary on Paul's Letter to the Churches in Galatia, Hermeneia (Philadelphia: Fortress Press, 1979); F. F. Bruce, *The Epistle to the Galatians*, NIGTC (Grand Rapids: Eerdmans, 1982); Richard N. Longenecker, *Galatians*, WBC 41 (Dallas: Word Books, 1990); and J. Louis Martyn, *Galatians*, AB 33A (New York: Doubleday, 1997).

[2]The foremost modern scholar to argue that the law and/or the doctrine of justification are *not* central to Paul's theology is of course E. P. Sanders, especially in *Paul and Palestinian Judaism* (Philadelphia: Fortress Press, 1977), hereafter cited as *PPJ*, and idem, *Paul, the Law, and the Jewish People* (Minneapolis: Fortress, 1983), hereafter cited as *PLJP*. In this regard, Sanders, whom we will discuss below, draws on the views of Albert Schweitzer, *Paul and His Interpreters* (London: Adam & Charles Black, 1950 [1912]) and idem, *The Mysticism of Paul the Apostle* (New York: Seabury, 1931). Schweitzer, in turn, built to some degree on Wilhelm Wrede, *Paul* (Lexington: American Library Association Committee on Reprinting, 1962 [1908]). In response to a prepublication version of this book, David R. Vinson pointed out to me that N. T. Wright has similarly displaced justification by faith from the center of Paul's thought; see *What Saint Paul Really Said: Was Paul of Tarsus the Real Founder of Christianity?* (Grand Rapids: Eerdmans, 1997).

Though Sanders argues that the law and/or the doctrine of justification by faith are not central to Paul's theology, he does acknowledge the importance of the topic for understanding Paul (Sanders, *PLJP*, 3), and it requires only a brief glance at the table of contents of *PLJP*, v-vi, to see that Galatians (along with Romans) provides most of the basis for his discussion of Paul's view of the law.

[3]See, for example, the importance of Gal 3:10 in the argument of Thomas Schreiner described below, 18; see also the survey of scholarly treatments of the citations in chap. 3 below.

[4]For a more thorough survey of scholarly treatments of Paul and the law in general (i.e., not limited to the letter to the Galatians), see Stephen Westerholm, *Israel's Law and the Church's Faith: Paul and His Recent Interpreters* (Grand Rapids: Eerdmans, 1988). As the title suggests, Westerholm's very useful summary and analysis of scholarship on Paul and the law focuses on more recent scholarship, with the notable exception of Martin Luther—a pattern which I will follow below, although with a somewhat different selection of scholars and a very different way of organizing and analyzing the summary.

In order to keep the survey that follows to a manageable scope, it is limited in two ways. First, it focuses on the issue of Paul and the law primarily as it relates to his letter to the Galatians. This limitation cannot be absolutely maintained, since so much of the scholarly discussion has involved Romans, Philippians 3, and other portions of Paul's writings, but where possible the emphasis is given to the portion of the discussion involving Galatians. Second, the survey focuses primarily on recent trends and issues in scholarship on Paul and the law. Though the survey begins with a brief summary of Luther—since Luther set the stage for so much of the modern discussion[5]—most of the emphasis is given to scholarship of the last few decades.[6]

LUTHER AND THE "TRADITIONAL" POSITION

LUTHER

According to Luther, what Paul thought was wrong with the law can be summed up in a single word: "works."[7] In his letter to the Galatians, of course, Paul uses "works" repeatedly in connection with "law"; in particular, Paul insists that justification is to be found by faith, and not through "works of law." What precisely Paul means by this phrase (and what he means when he uses the word "works" by itself) is very much a point of dispute in modern scholarship, as we will see below. For Luther, though, there is no question of where the emphasis is to be laid. It is not so much that there is a problem with the law as such; indeed, the law has had and continues to have its proper place even in the lives

---

See also Frank Thielman's chapter, "Paul, Torah, and Judaism in Recent Debate" in *From Plight to Solution: A Jewish Framework for Understanding Paul's View of the Law in Galatians and Romans* (Leiden: E. J. Brill, 1989), 1–27. Thielman's survey is oriented primarily to the issue of Paul's relationship with Judaism as it is expressed in his views of the law; while his research is thorough and excellently presented, this orientation makes his survey less useful for the current investigation.

[5]Cf. Westerholm, *Israel's Law*, 12: ". . . without Luther the current debate is inconceivable."

[6]It should be noted that the survey is not given in strictly chronological order; following the discussion of Luther, other scholars who have taken the same or slightly modified views are discussed; then challenges to the traditional view are discussed.

[7]Note, for example, what Luther says in his introductory remarks in 1531: ". . . this we have to fear as the greatest and nearest danger, lest Satan take from us the pure doctrine of faith, and bring into the church again the doctrine of works . . ." (Martin Luther, *A Commentary on St. Paul's Epistle to the Galatians: Based on Lectures Delivered by Martin Luther at the University of Wittenberg in the year 1531 and First Published in 1535*, trans. P. W. Watson [London: James Clarke, 1953], 21).

of believers.[8] Instead, the problem is with works, not just "works of law," but works of any sort:

> ... even as the Turks do other works than the Papists, and the Papists than the Jews, &c. But albeit that some do works more splendid, great, and difficult by far than others, notwithstanding the substance is the same, the quality only is different: that is to say, the works do differ in appearance and name only, and not in very deed, for they are works notwithstanding, and they which do them are and remain, not Christians, but hirelings, whether they be called Jews, Mahometists, Papists, &c.[9]

What Paul is rejecting throughout the book of Galatians is, for Luther, not so much the law as such, but rather any attempt to achieve self-righteousness by one's own efforts, rather than receiving the righteousness of faith. This includes, but is not limited to, efforts to achieve self-righteousness by keeping the law.

What distinguishes the righteousness of works from the righteousness of faith? Of foremost importance for Luther is that the former is an *active* righteousness—it involves *doing*—while the latter is a *passive* righteousness, given by the grace of God, without any hint of merit on our part; it consists not in *doing* but in *believing*.[10] But why is a passive righteousness better than an active one? Luther suggests several answers, which we might boil down to two of particular significance.[11] First, the "active righteousness" is hopeless, not just because it involves doing, but because it is more than we can do; the demands of the law cannot be met:

> Of course, the Law says: "He who does them shall live by them." But where is the one who does them? Where is the one who loves God with all his heart, etc., and his neighbor as himself? Therefore there is no one who keeps the Law.[12]

---

[8]Not only does the law play a necessary role in the humbling of persons in order to lead them to faith (Martin Luther, *Luther's Works*, ed. J. Pelikan, [St. Louis: Concordia, 1963], 26:6–7), but Luther can even say of believers and the law, "By it we perform good works" (ibid., 26:8).

[9]Luther, *Commentary*, 26–27; cf. idem, *Works*, 26:333, 396–98. In the preface to the 1535 edition of his lectures (Luther, *Works*, 27:145–49), Luther describes the successful efforts of Satan from the Garden of Eden up through the present day to deceive humanity with the "doctrine of works"; even the works of the idolater are done "in the hope of placating a god or goddess or gods or goddesses by his own works" (ibid., 27:146).

[10]Luther, *Works*, 26:5–7, 208, 271–72.

[11]Westerholm, *Israel's Law*, 6–8, extracts six points from what Luther says about the inadequacy of works, all of which are, at least to some degree, an elaboration of one or the other of the two points sketched out above.

[12]Luther, *Works*, 26:273.

"There is no one who keeps the law," because, according to Luther's reading of Paul, the law requires *perfect* obedience:

> If we loved God with all our heart, etc., then, of course, we would be justified and would live on account of that obedience, according to the statement (Lev. 18:5): "By doing this a man shall live." But the Gospel says: "You are not doing this; therefore you shall not live on account of it." For the statement, "You shall love the Lord," requires *perfect* obedience, *perfect* fear, trust, and love toward God. In the corruption of their nature men neither do nor can produce this.[13]

Second, the "active righteousness" is hopeless because even to make the attempt to secure righteousness by works is to spurn the grace of God and to usurp his glory by substituting our own human efforts in place of God's gracious offer of "passive righteousness" through faith.[14] Indeed, even if we *could* keep the law perfectly, it would be of no avail, because it would constitute merely the righteousness of the flesh rather than the righteousness of God:

> Therefore "flesh" means the entire nature of man, with reason and all his powers. This flesh, he says, is not justified by works, *not even by those of the Law*. He is not saying: "The flesh is not justified by works *against* the Law, such as debauchery, drunkenness, etc." But he is saying: "It is not justified by works done *in accordance with* the Law, works that are *good*. For Paul, therefore, "flesh" means the highest righteousness, wisdom, worship, religion, understanding, and will of which the world is capable.[15]

It is no secret, of course, that Luther's exegesis of Paul owes a great deal to his identification of the "works of law" against which Paul writes in Galatians with his own experience of the "works" of the Church.[16] Luther accordingly read Paul through the eyes of a formerly very troubled, and now very relieved, conscience; indeed, throughout his writing on Galatians, it is clear that the conscience, guilty under the law, but now freed by grace through faith, is central to his thinking.[17] Nor is it any secret that Luther's reading of Paul determined his

---

[13] Ibid., 26:398; emphasis added.

[14] Ibid., 26:127, 227–29, 253–54.

[15] Ibid., 26:139–40; emphasis added. Cf. ibid., 26:216.

[16] See for example ibid., 26:126: "For every monk imagines as follows to himself: 'By the observance of my holy rule I am able to merit grace "by congruity." And by the works I perform after receiving this grace I am able to accumulate such a treasure of merit that it will not only be enough for me to obtain eternal life but can also be given or sold to others.' This is how all the monks have taught and lived."

[17] For example, in describing what is wrong with the law, Luther says, "For although the Law is the best of all things in the world, it still cannot bring peace to a terrified conscience but makes it even sadder and drives it to despair" (ibid., 26:5).

highly negative understanding of Judaism as a religion of self-righteous legalism, though it certainly bears repeating that Luther saw *all* humanity apart from faith under the same heading, most notably and most culpably the "Church of the Gentiles."[18]

In recent years, both of these aspects of Luther's thought have been questioned and largely discarded by the mainstream of New Testament scholarship.[19] Even where these features of Luther's thought have been discarded, however, it must not be supposed that the basic thrust of Luther's understanding of Paul has fallen by the wayside.[20] On the contrary, in spite of significant challenges, many scholars continue to defend Luther's understanding of Paul's problem with the law, emphasizing either or both the impossibility of keeping all the law, or the invalidity of the self-righteousness that would be gained even if we could keep the law perfectly.

SINFUL SELF-RIGHTEOUSNESS: BULTMANN

Chief among those who emphasize the invalidity of self-righteousness is Rudolf Bultmann.[21] The real problem with the law, according to Bultmann's understanding of Paul, is not so much that we cannot keep it—though of course

---

[18] Cf. the quote from Luther above, 14. In Luther's preface to the 1535 edition, after detailing the failings of the Jewish people in regards to self-righteousness, Luther goes on to say, "In the Church of the Gentiles, however, things have been and are even worse, so that the madness of the Synagogue may well seem mere child's play in comparison" (Luther, *Commentary*, 17).

[19] Those who have done the most to challenge Luther's reading of Paul in terms of a guilty Pauline conscience are Werner Georg Kümmel, *Römer 7 und die Bekehrung des Paulus* (Leipzig: J. G. Hinrichs, 1929) and Krister Stendahl, "The Apostle Paul and the Introspective Conscience of the West," in *Paul among Jews and Gentiles* (Philadelphia: Fortress, 1976), 78–96. With regard to rethinking the description of Judaism as a religion of self-righteous legalism, see C. G. Montefiore, *Judaism and St. Paul* (London: Max Goschen, 1914); George Foot Moore, "Christian Writers on Judaism," *HTR* 14 (1921): 197–254; H. J. Schoeps, *Paul: The Theology of the Apostle in the Light of Jewish Religious History* (Philadelphia: Westminster, 1961); and especially E. P. Sanders, *PPJ* and *PLJP*.

[20] Cf. the qualified but strong affirmation of Luther's reading of Paul given by Westerholm, *Israel's Law*, 173: "Students who want to know how a rabbinic Jew perceived humanity's place in God's world will read Paul with caution and Luther not at all. On the other hand, students who want to understand Paul but feel they have nothing to learn from a Martin Luther should consider a career in metallurgy. Exegesis is learned from the masters."

[21] In addition to various articles and essays, the most systematic expression of Bultmann's thought about Paul and the law is to be found vol. 1 of Rudolf Bultmann, *Theology of the New Testament*, 2 vols., trans. K. Grobel (New York: Charles Scribner's Sons, 1951, 1955).

we cannot—but rather that keeping the law was never intended as a means of salvation:

> ... no man *can* procure his own 'rightwising' by works of the Law. He cannot because he cannot exhibit 'the works of the Law' in their entirety.... The reason why man under the Law does not achieve 'rightwising' and life is that he is a transgressor of the Law, that he is guilty before God. But Paul goes much further still; he says not only that man *can* not achieve salvation by works of the Law, but also that he is not even *intended* to do so.[22]

We were never intended to find salvation through works of the law, because the effort to do so leads to inauthentic existence: "Man's effort to achieve his salvation by keeping the law only leads him into sin, indeed this effort itself in the end *is already sin*."[23] The attempt to keep the law is already sin because in it we fail to recognize ourselves as creatures, substituting self-reliance in place of utter dependence on the Creator: "Sin is man's self-powered striving to undergird his own existence in forgetfulness of his creaturely existence, to procure his salvation by his own strength, that striving which finds its extreme expression in 'boasting' and 'trusting in the "flesh"'."[24]

In spite of the enormous influence Bultmann has had in New Testament scholarship, relatively few commentators have followed his lead in placing primary emphasis on this aspect of Luther's thought, at least with regard to Galatians.[25] Heinrich Schlier is perhaps the most similar to Bultmann in this regard. According to Schlier, the curse which Paul pronounces in Gal 3:10 falls, not so much on those who fail to do the law, but precisely on those who *do* the law (rather than believing in Christ).[26] Slightly different, but certainly related, is

---

[22]Bultmann, *Theology*, 1:263 (emphases are original).

[23]Ibid., 1:264; some emphasis removed. Cf. Rudolf Bultmann, "Christ the End of the Law," in *Essays, Philosophical and Theological* (London: SCM, 1955), 46: "According to Paul the person who fulfils the law needs grace as much as the one who trespasses against it—indeed it is he most of all who needs it! For in seeking to establish his own righteousness, he is acting *fundamentally* against God."

[24]Bultmann, *Theology*, 1:264; cf. 1:283.

[25]Hans Hübner, *Das Gesetz bei Paulus: Ein Beitrag zum Werden der paulinischen Theologie* (Göttingen: Vandenoeck & Ruprecht, 1978); ET *Law in Paul's Thought: A Contribution to the Development of Pauline Theology*, trans. J. C. G. Greig, Studies of the New Testament and Its World (Edinburgh: T & T Clark, 1984), argues that this more "qualitative" view of the problem with the law is found in Romans, but not in Galatians. Heikki Räisänen, "Legalism and Salvation by the Law," in *The Pauline Literature and Theology*, ed. S. Pedersen, Teologiske Studier 7 (Göttingen: Vandenhoeck & Ruprecht, 1980), 68, points out that the key texts for Bultmann's view actually come from Romans and Philippians, not Galatians.

[26]Heinrich Schlier, *Der Brief an die Galater*, 5th ed., Meyers Kommentar 7 (Göttingen: Vandenhoeck & Ruprecht, 1971), 132–33.

the view of Ragnar Bring and others. It is not so much the doing of the law which is the problem, but rather the misapprehension that the law offers a means to salvation based on human merit; properly understood, the *whole* law points to God's action in Christ rather than to human effort.[27]

THE "MISSING PREMISE": NO ONE CAN KEEP THE LAW

Even when they acknowledge a contrast between *doing* and *believing* (especially in Gal 3:11–12), the majority of scholars who take up Luther's position put the primary emphasis on human inability to keep all the law.[28] One of the most outspoken proponents of this position in recent years is Thomas Schreiner.[29] While agreeing with Luther that Paul saw his opponents as legalists

---

[27]Ragnar Bring, *Commentary on Galatians*, trans. E. Wahlstrom (Philadelphia: Muhlenberg Press, 1961), 120–25; cf. Charles B. Cousar, *Galatians*, Interpretation (Atlanta: John Knox, 1982), 74–75; Daniel P. Fuller, "Paul and 'The Works of the Law,'" *WTJ* 38 (1975), 33. Cf. similarly Gerhard Ebeling, *The Truth of the Gospel: An Exposition of Galatians*, trans. David Green (Philadelphia: Fortress, 1985), 178–79. There are, of course, innumerable variations. Bruce, *Galatians*, seems to accept that Paul thinks "no one can keep [the law] in its entirety" (159); at the same time, based on Phil 3:6, he acknowledges the possibility that someone might keep it, but on the basis of Gal 3:11–12 he argues that "even for one who does persevere in doing all things written in the book of the law justification is not thereby assured" (160). Vincent M. Smiles, "The Gospel and the Law in Galatia: Paul's Response to Christian Separatism and the Threat of Galatian Apostasy," (Ph.D. diss., Fordham University, 1988), 238ff, attempts to take a "mediating position" between the "extremes" of Bultmann and Wilckens, but winds up sounding more like Bultmann: "Accordingly, the obedient, no less than the lawless Gentiles, are exposed by the gospel to be sinners . . . . In this regard their 'sin' has nothing to do with moral evil but simply with a failure to know their true standing before God, and thus to recognize their absolute need of grace."

[28]Donald Guthrie, *Galatians*, NCBC (Grand Rapids: Eerdmans, 1973), is typical. While noting that "A man is not called upon to believe the law but to do it" (97), he finds the real problem with the law in Paul's assuming, "without the necessity to prove, that no-one is able to do, and therefore no-one is able to live by, the law" (98); cf. Ernest De Witt Burton, *A Critical and Exegetical Commentary on the Epistle to the Galatians*, ICC (Edinburgh: T & T Clark, 1921), 164; G. Walter Hansen, *Galatians* (Downers Grove, IL: InterVarsity Press, 1994), 92–93; John F. MacArthur, *Galatians* (Chicago: Moody, 1987); Albrecht Oepke, *Der Brief des Paulus an die Galater*, THKNT 9 (Berlin: Evangelische Verlagsanstalt, 1964), 72; etc. Even many who do not take up Luther's position *per se* would agree that Paul is arguing that no one can do all the law; cf. Schoeps, *Paul*, 175–77; Heikki Räisänen, *Paul and the Law* (Philadelphia: Fortress, 1983), 94.

[29]Thomas Schreiner, "Is Perfect Obedience to the Law Possible? A Re-Examination of Galatians 3:10," *JETS* 27 (1984): 151–60; idem, "Paul and Perfect Obedience to the Law: An Evaluation of the View of E. P. Sanders," *WTJ* 47 (1985): 245–78; idem, *The Law and Its Fulfillment: A Pauline Theology of Law* (Grand Rapids: Baker Books, 1993).

who were trying to gain self-righteousness by doing rather than by depending on God for righteousness by faith, Schreiner insists that self-righteousness is not the primary reason Paul rejects the law; rather, "Paul rejected the law as a way of salvation because of human inability to obey it."[30] Of key importance in this reading of Paul is Galatians 3:10–13. When Paul tells the Galatians that all who are of the law are under a curse because everyone who does *not* do *all* the law is cursed (citing Dt 27:26), the "implied premise" is "obvious." No one can do all the law.[31]

While Schreiner's position is very much a conscious re-statement of the traditional Reformation position—even to the point of continuing to insist on Jewish legalism as the backdrop for what Paul says about the law![32]—other scholars have proposed more carefully nuanced views that nevertheless maintain the emphasis on the impossibility of doing all the law.[33] Ulrich Wilckens, for example, agrees that the reason Paul rejects justification by the law is that *all* have sinned.[34] Wilckens' reasoning, however, is considerably more subtle than the typical "one-strike-and-you're-out," quantitative understanding. The reason even a single transgression disables any possibility of justification by law, even in spite of the law's provision for atonement and repentance, is that once one has sinned, the curse of the law is activated and must be carried out, one way or an-

---

As the title of one of his articles suggests, Schreiner frames his position as a response to E. P. Sanders (see discussion of Sanders below); in reality, however, Schreiner's work is less a rebuttal of Sanders *per se*, and more a restatement of the traditional position. In other words, his work functions more effectively as a clear statement of the view that Sanders rebuts rather than the reverse; hence, we will discuss Schreiner before rather than after Sanders.

[30]Schreiner, *Law*, 44; cf. ibid., 60: "Paul's fundamental objection, though, is not with doing *per se* but with inability to 'do' perfectly."; cf. idem, "Re-Examination," 156.

[31]Ibid., 156; Schreiner, *Law*, 44–45. Likewise, when Paul cites Lev 18:5 in Gal 3:12, he indicates that perfect obedience of the law *would* lead to life; therefore it is obvious that the real problem is that no one can render perfect obedience (Schreiner, *Law*, 59–61). For several arguments raised against Schreiner's position, see Michael Cranford, "The Possibility of Perfect Obedience: Paul and an Implied Premise in Galatians 3:10 and 5:3," *NovT* 36 (1994): 242–58.

[32]Schreiner, *Law*, 93–121.

[33]Again, it should be noted that this survey is arranged not chronologically but thematically; Wilckens' work preceded that of Schreiner. Because Schreiner represents the most unadulterated and even blunt statement of the traditional position in recent years, however, I have used his work first to illustrate the position from which others, such as Wilckens, have taken their departure.

[34]Ulrich Wilckens, "Was heißt bei Paulus: 'Aus Werken des Gesetzes wird kein Mensch gerecht'?" in *Rechtfertigung als Freiheit: Paulusstudien* (Neukirchen-Vluyn: Neukirchener, 1974), 77–109; see especially 79–94.

other.³⁵ There is nothing one can do, no work of law, that can recall that curse or put it back in the bottle, as it were, because the law has only the power to curse, but not the power to give life.³⁶ It is therefore only when the curse is expended in the death of Christ that sinners can be justified.³⁷

Summary

It is clear from the preceding sketches that there have been and continue to be many variations on Luther's understanding of Paul's problem with the law in Galatians, including many more variations than we have been able to cover above. Nevertheless, in spite of the variations, the basic thrust of this traditional Reformation position is well-defined and simply stated: Paul rejects the false doctrine of justification by works of law in favor of the true doctrine of justification by faith. As simple and familiar as this statement is, however, it potentially obscures two important issues:³⁸ First, does "works of law" refer to any works of any law, or only to certain works of the Torah specifically? Second, does the rejection of "works of law" apply only to salvation, or does it apply also or instead to Christian living?³⁹

As we have seen above, proponents of the traditional Reformation position have differed on where to place the emphasis concerning the exact meaning of "works of law." For some the stress lies on the *doing* of works, self-effort which

---

³⁵Ibid., 108.

³⁶Ulrich Wilckens, "Zur Entwicklung des paulinischen Gesetzesverständnisses," *NTS* 28 (1982): 172–73; cf. ibid., "Was heißt bei Paulus," 92, 104

³⁷Ibid., 108. It should be noted that, while Wilckens essentially agrees with the typical Reformation view that one cannot keep all the law, his argument is much more focused on the law as Torah, rather than on works in general.

³⁸Cf. Schweitzer, *Mysticism*, 177–204, who uses two key questions to analyze Paul's view of the law; cf. Sanders' summary of these questions in *PPJ*, 477. Schweitzer's first question more or less amounts to "What is wrong with the law"; his second question is essentially identical to the second question above.

³⁹It might be tempting to formulate the second question in terms of "justification" vs. "righteousness" (i.e., in terms of which is the appropriate translation of δικαιοσύνη). This is a temptation which should be resisted. To be sure, the meaning(s) or nuance(s) of δικαιοσύνη are not without relevance to our discussion, but the issues surrounding the translation of this word go well beyond the scope of the current inquiry. For a thorough investigation of δικαιοσύνη and related words in Paul, see J. A. Ziesler, *The Meaning of Righteousness in Paul: A Linguistic and Theological Inquiry*, SNTSMS 20 (Cambridge: Cambridge University Press, 1972); cf. also Manfred T. Brauch, "Perspectives on 'God's righteousness' in recent German discussion" in E. P. Sanders, *PPJ*, 523–42. For our purposes, however, the point of the second question above is not so much the meaning of δικαιοσύνη, but rather the status of the law for the believer. Does Paul object to the law only as a (false) means of entry into salvation, or does he reject it also as a guide for Christian practice?

leads to boasting in one's human accomplishments rather than dependence on God; for others the stress belongs on the *quantity* of works, the demand of the law for perfect obedience. Behind these differences, however, there is a common perspective. In either case, what is rejected is any attempt to earn salvation by self-righteous merit. What is in view in either case, therefore, is a more general sense of law as law, rather than specifically the Jewish Torah in its historical, sociological, covenantal context. It is not so much this particular law, the Torah, to which Paul objects; he would object equally to *any* attempt to gain salvation through *any* works of *any* law. We are, in other words, back where we started with Luther. The problem with the law—both law in general and Torah in particular—is *works*.[40]

Richard Longenecker's treatment of Gal 2:16 and 3:12 provides a good illustration of this point. First, he distinguishes between the Mosaic law as a "revelational standard" and as a "religious system," noting that here the issue "has to do with Paul's view of the Mosaic Law as a religious system."[41] He then distinguishes those scholars who think Paul's objection is to "the law itself" from those who think the problem is "a particular attitude toward the law that sees the law as a means of winning favor with God (i.e., 'legalism')." For Longenecker, it is the former: "Paul directs his attack not just against legalism . . . but against even the Mosaic religious system."[42] Thus far, it would seem that Longenecker sees the issue in terms of the Torah in particular—the "Mosaic Law"—rather than in terms of law in general and certainly not in terms of a legalistic attitude. But when he discusses "works of law," he describes the phrase as "a catch phrase to signal the whole legalistic complex of ideas having to do with winning God's favor by a merit-amassing observance of Torah."[43] Later on he says, "His point in quoting Lev 18:5 is obvious: the law has to do with 'doing' and 'living by its prescriptions' and not with faith."[44] If the real problem with "works of law" is doing, living by prescriptions, and legalistic amassing of merit, then it seems clear that the problem has more to do with *works* (of any law) than with the Torah specifically.

Concerning the ongoing role of the law in the life of the believer, supporters of the traditional Reformation view have typically held one of two positions:[45]

---

[40]Cf. Westerholm, *Israel's Law*, 141.

[41]Longenecker, *Galatians*, 85.

[42]Ibid. Longenecker goes on to concede that Judaism was and is *not* a legalistic religion as such.

[43]Ibid., 86.

[44]Ibid., 120. He also agrees with the traditional view that in 3:10 we should supply Paul's understood premise, that "no one is capable of keeping all the law" (ibid., 118).

[45]Schreiner traces these two positions back to Calvin and Luther, respectively (Schreiner, *Law*, 16). I am not completely convinced; Luther certainly speaks about the ongoing use of the law in the life of the believer, so long as it is kept in its proper sphere

Some insist that Paul's rejection of the law refers only to the misguided attempt to use it to earn one's salvation, but for believers the law continues in force; others argue that Paul's rejection of the law applies even to the ongoing life of the believer.[46] With respect to Galatians, the key verse is 5:14. As is frequently noted in the commentaries, after arguing vociferously *against* the law throughout chapters 3 and 4, Paul now paradoxically affirms its fulfillment in the life of the believer. For those who argue that the law continues in force, the resolution of this paradox generally depends on a reduction of that law—only the moral norms of the law continue in force, not the ceremonial or ritual requirements—and on the assertion that believers are now enabled to keep the law by the power of the Spirit.[47] For those who argue that the law is abolished even for believers, the issue often turns on the distinction between "doing" the law and "fulfilling" the law. A believer *fulfills* the law in a different way than simply *doing* it; Paul's call to fulfill the law does not mean that the law as such continues in force.[48]

Once again, however, it is not so much the differences which are important for the current investigation, but rather the underlying agreement: though proponents of the traditional Reformation view disagree about the ongoing role of the law in the life of the believer, they are unanimous that Paul rejects the law as a means to salvation. In particular, the point of Paul's argument in Galatians 3, according to virtually all scholars who hold the traditional Reformation position, has to do with salvation; Paul is rejecting a false understanding of how to be saved (works of law) and arguing instead for the correct understanding (faith). These two points of agreement in the traditional Reformation position—that Paul in Galatians 3 is primarily concerned with the issue of salvation, and that his rejection of the law, though obviously formulated in terms of the Torah, is nevertheless a rejection of law in general—take on particular significance as we turn our attention to recent trends in scholarship that have challenged the traditional Reformation understanding of Paul's rejection of the law.

(Luther, *Commentary*, 24–25). Perhaps it is this qualification ("so long as it is kept in its proper sphere") that leads Schreiner to the conclusion that Luther rejects the law even in the life of the believer. According to Luther, the law continues to be of use in the life of the believer only to the extent that believers are not yet fully redeemed, that is to say, in the believer's earthly existence; in the spiritual existence of the believer, law has no place (ibid., 26–29).

[46]Representatives of the former position include C. E. B. Cranfield, "St. Paul and the Law," *SJT* 17 (1964): 42–68, and Schreiner, *Law*, 145–78. Representatives of the latter position include Betz, *Galatians*, 275; Westerholm, *Israel's Law*, 198–218, and Longenecker, *Galatians*, 241–43. Burton, *Commentary*, 294–97, offers a variation based on seeing Paul's rejection of "works of law" in terms of the legalistic distortion of the law; thus, a believer keeps the law as it was *intended* to be kept, not in a legalistic fashion.

[47]See e.g. Schreiner, *Law*, 145–78.

[48]See e.g. Westerholm, *Israel's Law*, 198–218.

The "New Perspective on Paul": An Emerging Consensus?[49]

E. P. Sanders

The most significant challenge (and impetus for ongoing challenges) to the traditional Reformation understanding of Paul's view of the law comes from E. P. Sanders.[50] The scope of Sanders' work precludes a full review and analysis, particularly in connection with his detailed investigation of Jewish sources.[51] Instead, we will sketch out an outline of the main points of Sanders' argument, with particular attention to those points which have to do with Paul's rejection of the law in Galatians.

Patterns of Religion: Getting In and Staying In

One of the important features of Sanders' comparison of Paul and Palestinian Judaism is his methodology: he sets out to compare them *holistically*.[52] By a holistic comparison, Sanders does not mean a comparison of every element, motif, proposition or concept, but rather a comparison based on the pattern of each religion:[53]

> A pattern of religion, defined positively, is the description of how a religion is perceived by its adherents to *function*. 'Perceived to function' has the sense not of what an adherent does on a day-to-day basis, but of *how getting in and staying in are understood*: the way in which a religion is understood to admit and retain members is considered to be the way it 'functions.'[54]

---

[49] The title for this section comes from James D. G. Dunn, "The New Perspective on Paul," *BJRL* 65 (1983): 95–122. This article has recently been reprinted in idem, *Jesus, Paul, and the Law: Studies in Mark and Galatians* (Louisville: John Knox, 1990), 183–214; all citations from this article will be drawn from the latter source.

[50] Of particular importance are two previously cited works, *PPJ* and *PLJP*. Much of what Sanders says had been anticipated to some degree by various scholars (see above, nn. 2 and 19), but it was not until the publication of *PPJ* that the mainstream of scholarship begin seriously to re-examine its understanding of and assumptions about Judaism and about Paul and the law; cf. Dunn, "New Perspective," 184.

[51] Like many other scholars—including many who disagree with Sanders' conclusions!—we can only gratefully acknowledge the service Sanders' has rendered to New Testament scholarship in analyzing and clarifying a vast array of contemporary Jewish sources.

[52] The groundwork for Sanders' holistic method is laid out in E. P. Sanders, "Patterns of Religion in Paul and Rabbinic Judaism: A Holistic Method of Comparison," *HTR* 66 (1973): 455–78, and reiterated in idem, *PPJ*, 12–24.

[53] Sanders, *PPJ*, 16–17.

[54] Ibid., 17.

This is, of course, the basis for the now famous terminology of "getting in" and "staying in," but it is important to note carefully the sphere in which *both* of these terms operate for Sanders. They *both* have to do with *defining membership*. In terms of a religion that anticipates "salvation" as its end, one can be even more precise: "A pattern of religion thus has largely to do with the items which a systematic theology classifies under 'soteriology,'" i.e., defining membership in the group of those who will be saved.[55] It is therefore *not* the case that only "getting in" describes soteriology, while "staying in" describes "what an adherent does on a day-to-day basis"; *both* terms specifically *exclude* "day-to-day" activity, except to the extent that such activity is integral to maintaining one's membership status.[56]

Judaism: Covenantal Nomism

As alluded to above, no small part of the challenge Sanders has raised against the traditional Reformation view of Paul and the law has to do with its understanding (or rather, misunderstanding) of Judaism. Contrary to Luther's depiction, the Judaism of Paul's day was *not* characterized by the attempt to earn salvation by works, but rather by *covenantal nomism*.[57] "Covenantal nomism" sums up the pattern of Jewish religion. One "gets in" *by grace*, i.e., by the gracious act of God in establishing a covenant with his people; one "stays in" *by observing the law*—which does *not* mean perfect obedience to the law, nor does it involve the amassing or weighing of merit, but rather it means the *acceptance* of the law and therefore the *intention* to obey it, including the practice of sincere repentance and atonement for transgressions:

---

[55]Ibid. Sanders qualifies this comparison, noting that "pattern of religion" includes both more ("it includes the logical beginning-point of the religious life as well as its end, and it includes the steps in betweeen") and less ("the word soteriology has certain connotations which may not always be entirely appropriate") than "soteriology" normally does. Nevertheless, it is clear that the terms "pattern of religion," "getting in," and "staying in" operate within approximately the same sphere as "soteriology," or perhaps better, "defining membership."

[56]Ibid. The full significance of this point will emerge below; for the moment, however, it is enough to observe that there is less distinction between "getting in" and "staying in" than has sometimes been thought or implied—including, perhaps, by Sanders himself—since *both* terms operate within the sphere of "defining membership."

[57]The first 400+ pages of *PPJ* are devoted to establishing and developing this point on the basis of all the available Jewish sources representing Palestinian Judaism (Rabbinic writings, Dead Sea scrolls, Apocrypha and Pseudepigrapha). Despite their differences, Sanders concludes that all forms of Palestinian Judaism represented in these sources shared the same basic pattern of covenantal nomism (Sanders, *PPJ*, 419–28).

The universally held view was rather this: those who accept the covenant, which carries with it God's promise of salvation, accept also the obligation to obey the commandments given by God in connection with the covenant. One who accepts the covenant and remains within it is 'righteous', and that title applies to him *both* as one who obeys God *and* as one who has a 'share in the world to come,' but the former does not earn the latter.... Being righteous in the sense of obeying the law to the best of one's ability and repenting and atoning for transgression *preserves* one's place in the covenant (it is the opposite of rebelling), but it does not *earn* it.... Being righteous is not the goal of a religious quest; it is the behavior proper to one who has accepted the covenant offered at Sinai and the commandments which followed the acceptance of God's kingship.[58]

It is important to note what Sanders is and is not claiming in his characterization of Judaism. It should be perfectly obvious that Sanders *is* affirming the "nomism" in covenantal nomism. Judaism *is* characterized by law observance. Indeed, given the way he has defined "staying in," one can even say that, in covenantal nomism, law observance is a necessary condition for salvation.[59] What Sanders is emphatically denying, however, is that this characteristic law observance has anything to do either with *earning* salvation—that is, by amassing merit—or with a necessarily self-righteous, grace-denying attitude.[60]

Paul: Participationist Eschatology

Just as Sanders has challenged the traditional understanding of Judaism, so too has he challenged the traditional understanding of Paul. Rather than "justification by faith and not by works of law," Sanders argues that Paul's "pattern of religion" is summed up in the phrase, "participationist eschatology":

One enters by becoming one with Christ Jesus and one stays in by remaining 'pure and blameless' and by not engaging in unions which are destructive of the union with Christ.... The sequence of thought, and thus the pattern of Paul's religious thought, is this: God has sent Christ to be the saviour of all, both Jew and Gentile (and has called Paul to be the apostle to the Gentiles); one participates in salvation by becoming one person with Christ, dying with him to sin and sharing the promise of his resurrection; the transformation, however, will not be completed until the Lord returns; meanwhile one who is in Christ

---

[58] Sanders, *PPJ*, 204–205.
[59] Sanders, *PLJP*, 18–19, 51n16; idem, *PPJ*, 180, 320, 517, 543. This is precisely the basis on which Sanders responds to Robert H. Gundry, "Grace, Works, and Staying Saved in Paul," *Biblica* 66 (1985): 8, who argues that the issue in Galatians 3 is more about staying in than about getting in. Sanders, *PLJP*, 52n20, agrees that "staying in" is one way of describing the issue, but since "staying in" concerns conditions for membership in the people of God, this remains effectively a discussion about entry requirements.
[60] See esp. Sanders, *PPJ*, 33–59, 233–38; cf. idem, *PLJP*, 20, 32ff, 154ff.

has been freed from the power of sin and the uncleanness of transgression, and his behaviour should be determined by his new situation; since Christ died to save all, all men must have been under the dominion of sin, 'in the flesh' as opposed to being in the Spirit. It seems reasonable to call this way of thinking 'participationist eschatology'.[61]

In *Paul, the Law, and the Jewish People*, Sanders has further clarified his position. By describing the pattern of Paul's religion as "participationist eschatology," he does not intend to suggest that "participation in Christ" is the *center* of Paul's thought; rather, at the center of Paul's thinking are a series of "primary convictions" (essentially corresponding to the "sequence of thought" described in the quotation above):

> ... that God had sent Jesus Christ to provide for the salvation of all; that salvation is thus available for all, whether Jew or Greek, on the same basis ("faith in Christ," "dying with Christ"); that the Lord would soon return; that he, Paul, was called by God to be the apostle to the Gentiles; and that Christians should live in accordance with the will of God.[62]

"Participation in Christ" is therefore not the center of Paul's thought but rather the "central *terminology* by which he discusses the transfer from the unsaved to the saved state."[63] But if "participation" is the central terminology, that means that "justification by faith" (or "righteousness by faith") is *not* the central terminology. Though Paul uses this terminology in the polemical debate over the law, that is the only place he uses it; in particular, he does *not* use it to derive or explain other features of his thought.[64] Likewise, if "justification by faith" is not central to Paul's thought or terminology, neither is the other half of the formula, "not by works of law."

---

[61]Sanders, *PPJ*, 548–49.

[62]Sanders, *PLJP*, 5. Cf. idem, *PPJ*, 441–42: "There appear to me to be two readily identifiable and primary convictions which governed Paul's Christian life: (1) that Jesus Christ is Lord, that in him God has provided for the salvation of all who believe (in the general sense of 'be converted'), and that he will soon return to bring all things to an end; (2) that he, Paul, was called to be the apostle to the Gentiles."

[63]Sanders, *PLJP*, 5. Though here he seems to be referring only to "getting in"—"the transfer from the unsaved to the saved state"—it is clear that "participation" is the central terminology also for "staying in"; cf. idem, *PPJ*, 439, 450–63, esp. 456: "[the general theme of participation] *is the theme, above all, to which Paul appeals both in parenesis and polemic*."

[64]Sanders, *PPJ*, 439ff. Here especially Sanders draws heavily on Schweitzer (see n. 2 above).

What is Wrong with the Law?

We can now address the guiding question for this part of our investigation, which in short is, "What is wrong with the law?" Sanders' answer is rather startling: nothing! Nothing, that is, except only that it is not faith in Christ:

> The fundamental critique of the law is that following the law does not result in being found in Christ; for salvation and the gift of the Spirit come only by faith (Rom 10:10; Gal. 3:1–5). Doing the law, in short, is wrong only because it is not faith.[65]

The essential point that Sanders is making is that Paul's thought proceeded *from solution to plight*: "Paul did not, while 'under the law', perceive himself to have a 'plight' from which he needed salvation."[66] Rather, when he came to the conviction that salvation for all people was only through Christ, he *then* concluded that it was not through the law.[67] Paul's rejection of the law is therefore based on both the exclusive *and* the universal aspects of his soteriology. On the one hand, if Christ is the *only* means of salvation, then salvation cannot come through the law apart from Christ; on the other hand, if salvation comes to *all* through Christ, Jew and Gentile alike, the law cannot be added to Christ, because that would effectively force Gentiles to become Jews:

> (1) The promise *cannot* be inherited on the basis of keeping the law, because that would exclude Gentiles. But Gentiles *cannot* be excluded, for God has appointed Christ as Lord of the whole world and as saviour of all who believe, and has especially called and appointed Paul as apostle to the Gentiles. 2. If it is necessary and sufficient to keep the law in order to inherit the promises of God, Christ died in vain and faith is in vain.[68]

Once again, we must be clear about what Sanders is and is not claiming. Sanders is *not* claiming that Paul, having started from the solution, did not go on

---

[65] Ibid., 550; cf. idem, *PLJP*, 47.

[66] Sanders, *PPJ*, 443. The most extensive challenge to Sanders' contention that Paul worked from solution to plight comes from Thielman, *From Plight to Solution*.

[67] Sanders, *PPJ*, 442–47, 474ff; idem, *PLJP*, 27, 46–47, 150–54.

[68] Sanders, *PPJ*, 489–90 (the non-parallel numbering is original to the 1977 edition); cf. idem, *PLJP*, 47, 27: "In the midst of a sometimes bewildering series of arguments, quotations, and appeals, there seem to be two sentences in Galatians in which Paul states unambiguously not only what his position is (which is never in doubt), but *why* he holds it.... Put in propositional terms, they say this: God sent Christ; he did so in order to offer righteousness; this would have been pointless if righteousness were already available by the law (2:21); the law was not given to bring righteousness (3:21). That the positive statement about righteousness through Christ grounds the negative one about the law seems to me self-evident."

to consider the plight; on the contrary, not only does Sanders assert that Paul "obviously reflected deeply on man's plight," but also Sanders can even go so far as to give an overwhelmingly positive affirmation of Bultmann's description of Paul's understanding of the human plight, so long as one corrects Bultmann's overly individualistic focus and above all his misapprehension that this plight led Paul to his rejection of the law in favor of Christ.[69] Likewise, Sanders does not claim that Paul advances no *arguments* against the law, but by their very number and variety, these arguments are seen to be supporting an already held position; they do *not* describe Paul's real reason for rejecting the law.[70]

What Sanders *is* claiming is that, since Paul works from solution to plight, he must not perceive any particular "defect" in the law as such. For example, Paul did *not* have a problem with the law because it was impossible to keep. Not only does he claim to have been blameless in the law prior to his conversion (Phil 3:6), but also for him to suggest that a single infraction of the law invokes its curse would require a severe distortion or misunderstanding of the Judaism from which Paul came.[71] Likewise Paul did not reject the law because it involved works rather than grace, "doing" rather than "believing." On the contrary, Paul is not actually so different from contemporary Judaism on the issue of grace and works. *Both*, according to Sanders, thought in terms of salvation by grace and judgment by works.[72] In short, Paul's only objection to the law is when it is used as an entrance requirement, one which necessarily excludes Gentiles; if, on the other hand, he addresses the topic of Christian behavior, he not only requires "doing," but can even effectively say, "do the law."[73]

Response to Sanders

The impact of Sanders' work on the study of Paul has been enormous, as is evident from the way scholars nearly always find it necessary, if not to agree with, at the very least to respond to Sanders. We will sketch out a few representative responses below, using them in part to point out possible problems with Sanders' view of Paul and the law. To help focus our discussion, both in terms of drawing together Sanders' work into some sort of summary, and in terms of organizing and providing a springboard for responses to Sanders, we need to

---

[69] Sanders, *PPJ*, 508–509; cf. ibid., 481, 508–511.

[70] Sanders, *PLJP*, 4, 65–86, 151–52.

[71] Ibid., 20ff. It is interesting to note that James 2:10 *does* reflect the explicit claim that a single infraction of the law is equivalent to breaking all of it. The point that James is making, of course, is not that one thereby becomes cursed and ineligible for salvation, but rather than one must be diligent in keeping all the law, without overlooking any portion of it.

[72] Sanders, *PPJ*, 515–18; idem, *PLJP*, 93–114.

[73] Sanders, *PLJP*, 93–114.

consider again the two questions raised previously in connection with the traditional Reformation view: 1) Is Paul rejecting the law in general, or the Torah specifically? 2) Does Paul's rejection of the law, particularly in Galatians 3, focus primarily on the issue of salvation?

With respect to the first question, it seems clear that Sanders' understanding is exactly opposite that of the traditional Reformation view. Paul's rejection of the law is not a rejection of law-in-general, but rather is a rejection of the Jewish law, the Torah, specifically. On the one hand, there is a certain irony at this point, since no small part of Sanders' agenda has been to eliminate the traditional Reformation misunderstanding that Paul rejects the law because of a characteristic assumed to be specific to Judaism, i.e., legalistic, merit-amassing self-righteousness. On the other hand, not only does Sanders show that such an understanding of Judaism is completely erroneous, but also he argues that "legalistic, merit-amassing self-righteousness" is not at all what Paul rejects about the law. Paul rejects the law not because of the general problem of legalism, or the impossibility of perfect obedience—neither of which, after all, would be limited to the Torah specifically, since any law can, presumably, be legalistically (mis)used, and any law can set standards higher than humans can perfectly maintain—but rather because of the inclusion of the Gentiles. The problem is whether Gentiles have to become Jews, as indicated by taking up *this specific law* with its *specific* requirements concerning circumcision, food, and so on:[74]

> In the phrase "not by works of law" the emphasis is not on *works* abstractly conceived but on *law*, that is, the Mosaic law. The argument is that one need not be Jewish to be "righteous" and is thus against the standard Jewish view that accepting and living by the law is a sign and condition of favored status. *This is both the position which, independently of Paul, we can know to have characterized Judaism and the position which Paul attacks.*[75]

---

[74] At the risk of misrepresenting Sanders, one might in some sense say that he has changed the focus from a doctrinal issue to a sociological one. To be sure, Sanders sees the issue as primarily *theological*, based on Paul's Christological convictions; moreover Sanders specifically denies that Paul is operating only from practical considerations, i.e., to make Gentile conversion easier; cf. Sanders, *PLJP*, 102. Nevertheless, the focus of the problem, according to Sanders, is not a false doctrine of works vs. the true doctrine of faith; *all* parties undoubtedly agreed that one had to have faith in Christ, and all agreed that works were expected of members. Rather the focus of the problem is whether Gentiles have to become Jews by taking on the *Jewish* law; cf. ibid., 158–59. In this sense, the question becomes one of sociological status, Jew vs. Gentile, rather than of doctrine. Cf. John M. G. Barclay, *Obeying the Truth: A Study of Paul's Ethics in Galatians* (Edinburgh: T & T Clark, 1988), 4–6.

[75] Sanders, *PLJP*, 46.

With respect to the second question raised above, Sanders appears to be much more in agreement with the traditional Reformation position. Paul's rejection of the law has to do primarily with the issue of salvation.[76] In fact, Sanders draws the distinction very sharply indeed, so much so that he is regularly criticized in this regard. According to Sanders, anywhere that Paul speaks negatively of the law, it is *always* and *only* in the context of "getting in." This sharp distinction lets Sanders accommodate Paul's seemingly contradictory statements about the law as different answers to different questions:[77] When Paul is asked about the law in connection with "getting in," he emphatically says, "not by works of law"; when he is asked about the law in connection with "staying in," he can say, "fulfill the law."[78] As Sanders himself admits, this explanation leaves Paul with a certain lack of "inner unity" in the various things that he says about the law, which is perhaps the reason so many have criticized Sanders at this point.[79]

James D. G. Dunn: "Works of Law" and "Boundary Markers"[80]

James D. G. Dunn is one of the scholars who have criticized Sanders for making too sharp a distinction between getting in and staying in. Part of the reason for his critique is, as suggested above, that it leads to a picture of Paul with too many inconsistencies and tensions.[81] Oddly enough, however, the main thing that leads Dunn to this critique is his enthusiastic embrace of the "new perspective" which Sanders has provided for the study of Paul. Dunn contends that Sanders has not sufficiently applied his own insights concerning the Judaism

---

[76]In a sense, though Sanders differs sharply from the traditional view in other respects, his position in this regard is not all that different from those of the traditional view who see Paul rejecting the law for salvation but maintaining an ongoing role for the law in the life of the believer.

[77]Cf. Sanders, *PLJP*, 3–10, 143ff.

[78]Ibid. Note that "when Paul is asked about the law" is an essential qualification. Part of Sanders' point is that Paul's thought does not *begin* from or center on an understanding of law. Cf. n. 79 below.

[79]Sanders, *PLJP*, 147. For Sanders, the tensions that remain between Paul's positive and negative statements about the law reflect the fact that the coherence of Paul's thought lies elsewhere, namely in his "primary convictions."

[80]Dunn's position is worked out in a series of articles: James D. G. Dunn, "The New Perspective on Paul"; idem, "Works of Law and the Curse of the Law (Galatians 3.10–14)," *NTS* 31 (1985): 523–42; idem, "The Theology of Galatians: The Issue of Covenantal Nomism," in *Pauline Theology*, vol. 1, ed. J. M. Bassler (Minneapolis: Fortress, 1991), 125–46. These articles have now been collected, with additional comments, in idem, *Jesus, Paul, and the Law*. Though less immediately relevant to our investigation in Galatians, see also idem, *Romans*, WBC 38A&B (Dallas: Word, 1988).

[81]Dunn, "The New Perspective," 187, 202, 211–12.

from which Paul comes to his portrayal of Paul himself.[82] On the one hand, Sanders has failed to understand the limited scope of Paul's attack on the law, or rather, the way in which the scope is limited; on the other hand, Sanders has not adequately accounted for Paul's rejection of the law. According to Sanders, Paul rejects the whole law, but only when the topic is "getting in," and only because the law is not Christ; according to Dunn, however, Paul rejects the law, both for getting in and for staying in, but only in terms of, *and because of*, the misuse of one aspect of the law, namely the law in its *social function*.[83]

A key element in Dunn's position, particularly with respect to Galatians, has to do with the phrase, "works of law." When Paul refers to "works of law," he is using a phrase "already familiar to his readers or self-evident to them in its significance"—a phrase which refers to those works, especially circumcision, food laws, and sabbath observance, which define and reinforce the *boundaries* between those who are "in" the covenant and those who are not.[84] Dunn therefore agrees with Sanders that Paul is not rejecting works in the sense of merit-amassing, legalistic self-righteousness, or works as doing versus believing, but Dunn goes a step farther. Paul rejects the law not just because it is not Christ, but rather because of and in terms of its nationalistic exclusivism.[85] Likewise, Dunn agrees with Sanders that the "curse of the law" in Galatians 3:10 does not come because it is impossible to keep the law, but again Dunn goes a step further. Rather than simply being a rhetorical "threat," the curse comes because those who are "of works of law" are actually falling short of what the law really requires, precisely because they are emphasizing only the nationalistic and exclusive aspects of the law.[86]

In actuality, the differences between Dunn and Sanders are not as great as Dunn suggests.[87] For example, even though Sanders insists that Paul rejects the law only because it is not Christ, we have seen above that a significant part of the logic that leads to this exclusive either/or between Christ and the law is the law's role in excluding Gentiles. Because Jesus Christ is God's universal solution for all people, Jew and Gentile alike, the law which distinguishes Jew from Gentile *cannot* be part of God's solution.[88] Thus, though Sanders does not make

---

[82]Ibid., 183–86.

[83]Concerning the "social function" of the law, see esp. Dunn, "Works of Law," 524ff.

[84]Ibid., 527ff; idem, "The New Perspective," 191–93.

[85]Dunn, "The New Perspective," 197–98.

[86]Dunn, "Works of Law," 533–34.

[87]As Dunn seems to hint in his remarks concerning his correspondence with Sanders in his "Additional Note" following "The New Perspective" in *Jesus, Paul, and the Law*, 211–12.

[88]Especially in *PLJP*, Sanders comes very close to saying that what is wrong with the law, or at least part of what is wrong with the law, is that it excludes Gentiles; see esp.

the point quite so explicitly as Dunn, he has certainly set the stage for Dunn's emphasis on social factors as the grounds for Paul's rejection of the law.

Even when it comes to the distinction between getting in and staying in, Dunn is not as different from Sanders as he claims, *given the way Sanders has defined these terms*. Dunn is quite right to point out that Paul's urgent call in Galatians 3 to continue in the path they have already begun is better described in terms of staying in than getting in. Paul is urging them to maintain their righteous status not by faithful practice of the covenant "works," but rather by continuing in the faith in which they began.[89] It is clear, however, that Dunn sees this as a soteriological issue. The question is on what basis the Gentiles will be counted as righteous, not just now (getting in), but also and especially *at the final judgment* (staying in).[90] This is precisely the sense in which Sanders insists that the discussion is one of "entry requirements" (or, to say it another way, that "righteousness" and its cognates in this passage are strictly transfer terminology). Even though they phrase it differently, the question for both Dunn and Sanders is the same, and it is the question of soteriological membership: what does it take to be truly in—whether in terms of getting in or staying in is almost irrelevant—the group of those who will be saved?[91]

The similarities between Dunn and Sanders become most obvious in light of the two questions which we have used above. On the one hand, both Dunn and

---

Sanders, *PLJP*, 47, 152–53, 155. I suspect that Sanders' more typical formulation, that Paul saw nothing wrong with the law except that it is not Christ, is driven to some degree by his polemical stance against the traditional reformation position.

[89] Dunn, "Theology," 129–31; idem, "Works of Law," 532–33.

[90] Cf. Dunn, "The New Perspective," 207–208. Here Dunn is actually responding to Heikki Räisänen, but on a point that Räisänen shares with Sanders, namely that "righteousness" and its cognates are strictly transfer terminology in this passage. Dunn rejects this point because there is clearly a future element in view, i.e. being found righteous at the final judgment (Gal 2:16–17). But this simply makes clear that for Dunn, "righteousness" and its cognates are *soteriological* terms. They have to do with whether or not one is truly "in." It is precisely in this sense, if I understand him correctly, that Sanders refers to "righteousness" and its cognates as transfer terminology. They have to do, not with how you are behaving, but with whether or not you are really "in." See further in the section below, "Summary: Problems Remaining."

[91] Sanders' response to Gundry (Sanders, *PLJP*, 52n20) could just as well be directed to Dunn at this point: "Robert Gundry argued that, from Paul's point of view, the question in Galatians is how one *stays* in, not how one gets in. There is a sense in which that is entirely correct. Those who accept the law will be cut off from Christ (Gal. 5:4). But that does not change the fact that the argument is about a membership requirement: how to be righteoused or how to be a true descendant of Abraham. Paul argues that the Galatian Christians already have that status and must not accept the law, represented by circumcision, in order truly to be 'in.' Accepting another membership requirement besides faith in Christ means rejecting the one which, in Paul's view, really counts."

Sanders see Paul rejecting the law only when it comes to the issue of salvation, while affirming the law, correctly understood, in the ongoing life of the believer: "Paul's negative remarks had a more limited thrust . . . so long as the law is not similarly misunderstood as defining and defending the prerogatives of a particular group, it still has a positive role to play in the expression of God's purpose and will."[92] On the other hand, both Dunn and Sanders understand Paul to be rejecting the Torah specifically, not law-in-general: "Paul is not arguing here for a concept of faith which is totally passive because it fears to become a 'work' . . . . What he is concerned to exclude is the *racial* not the *ritual* expression of faith; it is *nationalism* which he denies not *activism*."[93]

In a sense, what Dunn is doing on both of these points is taking Sanders' position to its logical conclusion. If, according to Sanders, Paul effectively says "do the law" in response to the question of staying in, then Dunn arrives at the logical conclusion: "[Paul] still believes in a kind of 'covenantal nomism'!"—simply one with different boundary markers.[94] Likewise, if for Sanders Paul rejected the law not for any inherent defect (such as legalism or impossible demands) but rather simply because it was not Christ, through whom God saves Jews and Gentiles without distinction, then Dunn again reaches the logical conclusion: the law is wrong to the extent that it promotes or is used to promote ethnic distinctions, specifically by means of those "works" which identify Jews as Jews.

Response from the Traditional Reformation Position: Gundry, Westerholm, Thielman

Not everyone, of course, has received Sanders' views quite so enthusiastically as Dunn, nor have many scholars gone as far in embracing and developing the implications of Sanders' arguments. There are of course a few scholars—but only a few—who have rejected Sanders' arguments altogether.[95] More typically, a number of scholars have acknowledged that Sanders has offered some needed correctives (particularly with respect to the traditional Reformation misrepresen-

---

[92] Dunn, "Theology," 137. Cf. ibid., 131–32, 136n41; idem, "Works of Law," 538.

[93] Dunn, "The New Perspective," 198.

[94] Dunn, "Theology," 131. Dunn would of course object to drawing the distinction based on "staying in," and Sanders is not altogether willing to use "covenantal nomism" to describe Paul (cf. Sanders, *PPJ*, 511–15; idem, *PLJP*, 207–10), but as we have seen, these differences are more a matter of semantics than substance. Cf. Morna D. Hooker, "Paul and 'Covenantal Nomism'" in *Paul and Paulinism: Essays in Honour of C. K. Barrett*, ed. M. D. Hooker and S. G. Wilson (London: SPCK, 1982), 47–56.

[95] Schreiner would be an example; as noted above, though he responds to Sanders, his response is less successful as an attempt to wrestle with the insights Sanders presents than as simply a restatement of the traditional Reformation position.

tation of Judaism), but in varying degrees they ultimately have not been persuaded to discard the traditional Reformation position.

Robert H. Gundry is one such scholar who represents the "less persuaded" end of the spectrum. On the one hand, he commends Sanders for his impressive investigation of Jewish sources, both primary and secondary, and even counters some of the objections that have been raised against Sanders' methodology and results.[96] On the other hand, he finds Sanders' explanation for Paul's rejection of the law inadequate, and much of his argument from that point on seems at first glance to be little more than a restatement of the traditional Reformation position:[97]

> Where in past human experience does the incompatibility of the law with faith lie? We are forced back to an answer Sanders rejects: for Paul, the incompatibility lies in the self-righteousness to which unbelievers who try to keep the law succumb . . . . The use of the law to establish one's own righteousness is what Paul finds wrong in Palestinian Judaism, including his past life . . . . Paul is not content to argue that trying to keep the law is incompatible with faith. He takes unbelieving Jews and Christian Judaizers on their own terms and argues also that trying to keep the law never turns out to be successful . . . . Since according to [Gal 3] v. 10 the curse falls on the one who fails to abide by everything in the law, Paul's statement 'Christ redeemed us from the curse of the law' clearly implies that it is failure to abide by everything in the law which necessitates faith in Christ's redemptive work.[98]

Two points in particular show that Gundry is not merely rehashing the traditional Reformation position, however, but rather is seriously grappling with the issues Sanders has raised. First, Gundry argues that Sanders' analysis of the sources falls short, particularly with respect to the agreement between Paul and Judaism on salvation by grace and judgment by works. When one analyzes the sources, not just "formally," but "*materially*—i.e., if we weigh their emphases— quite a different impression may be gained, an impression of Palestinian Judaism as centered on works-righteousness and of Paul's theology as centered on grace":[99]

> In view of Sanders' discussion, it may be too much to say that in Palestinian Judaism good works were always thought to earn God's favor according to a bookish weighing of merits. But in view of the many passages in Palestinian Jewish literature that Sanders cites concerning atonement by good works, it is not too much to say that in Paul's presentation of Palestinian Judaism good

---

[96] Gundry, "Grace," 1–5.
[97] Ibid., 12ff.
[98] Ibid., 13, 16, 20, 25.
[99] Ibid., 5–6.

works constitute a righteousness necessary at least to activate God's grace for the forgiveness of sins.[100]

Second, like Dunn, Gundry argues that Sanders has failed to realize that Paul's argument, both in Romans and in Galatians, is primarily about *staying* in rather than *getting* in.[101] But also like Dunn, Gundry implicitly accepts Sanders' definition of staying in in soteriological terms, i.e., in terms of the conditions one must satisfy in order to prevent "falling from grace."[102] Thus, he too does not differ from Sanders on this point as much as he may think; indeed, he even agrees that Paul expects believers to do the law, empowered by faith and the Spirit.[103] Where the difference between Gundry and Sanders is much sharper is their understanding of "judgment by works." For Gundry, Paul expects good works, but only as *evidence* that one is in, not as a *condition* for staying in.[104]

In general, Stephen Westerholm is more persuaded by Sanders than Gundry is. For example, Westerholm largely accepts and defends Sanders' depiction of Palestinian Judaism. It is *not* properly described as a religion of works-righteousness or merit-amassing legalism, but rather as covenantal nomism, in which grace and works are balanced.[105] In addition, Westerholm is fully persuaded that Paul's thought runs from solution to plight, and that "Paul harbored no serious misgivings about the 'righteousness based on law' before he encountered the risen Christ."[106]

However, Westerholm is by no means persuaded to abandon the traditional Reformation position altogether. That Paul thought from solution to plight, for example, does not mean that he did not develop an understanding of the problem with the law: "Paul's exclusivist soteriology provokes, but does not answer, the question of the law's inadequacy."[107] Nor does the fact that Judaism balanced grace and works, or the fact that Paul does not see works or law as bad in and of themselves, mean that Paul does not understand the problem with the law in terms of works.[108] In fact, it is *because* Paul accepts the law's promise of life to

---

[100]Ibid., 19.

[101]Ibid., 8–12.

[102]Ibid., 11 (emphasis removed); cf. ibid., 8.

[103]Ibid., 12, 19. Gundry seems to accept the traditional view that one could not do the law apart from faith, but now in the power of the Spirit, one can and does fulfill the law. While Sanders rejects the idea that the problem before faith was inability to do the law (Sanders, *PLJP*, 146–47), he too seems to agree that faith now empowers law-keeping: "When discussing behavior, [Paul] emphasized that faith resulted in fulfilling the law" (ibid., 114).

[104]Gundry, "Grace," 11, 35.

[105]Westerholm, *Israel's Law*, 142ff.

[106]Ibid., 151–52; cf. ibid., 153.

[107]Ibid., 155.

[108]Cf. Ibid., 149–50, 162.

those who do it, and *because* he now sees Christ as God's exclusive means of salvation, which God must have intended from the beginning, that Paul *must* develop his understanding of the problem with the law in terms of an *exclusive* either-or between grace/faith and works/law.[109] Furthermore, the problem with works, with doing the law, must be that no one *can* do it, that humans inevitably transgress it. The law promises life; only in Christ is life available; therefore either the law's promise is false—which is unacceptable to Paul—or, no one actually fulfills the law—which is what Paul concludes.[110]

Westerholm differs from Sanders in one other respect: according to Westerholm, Paul rejects the law, not just as a means of salvation, but also as a guide for the ongoing life of the believer.[111] Westerholm advances several arguments to support this position, some general and some exegetical: 1) Though the behavior which Paul expects of his converts largely *coincides* with the moral demands of the law, that does not necessarily mean that Paul sees them as subject to the law.[112] 2) Paul expects Christians to *fulfill* the law, but "fulfilling" is not necessarily the same as "doing"; Paul is *describing* their behavior, not *prescribing* it.[113] 3) Paul routinely describes Christians as *free* from the law.[114] 4) Paul explicitly contrasts life in the Spirit (which *is* the basis for moral behavior) with obligation to the law.[115] 5) Paul does not see the law as a general expression of God's will, valid for all times and peoples, but rather as a specific feature of the covenant.[116]

With this last point, it might seem that Westerholm understands the issue of Paul and the law not in terms of law in general, but rather in terms of the Torah specifically. Certainly in one sense this is true: it is the Torah in particular, not law in general, which is the specific feature of the covenant; it is the Torah spe-

---

[109]Ibid., 150, 153, 163; cf. ibid., 106ff. Westerholm is careful to note that the difference between Paul and Judaism is *not* that Judaism promotes only works and Paul only grace, but rather that Paul sees an *exclusivity* to grace vs. works which Judaism does not.

[110]Ibid., 156.

[111]Ibid., 198ff.

[112]Ibid., 199–201.

[113]Ibid., 201–205.

[114]Ibid., 205–209.

[115]Ibid., 209–16.

[116]Ibid., 217–22; cf. ibid., 199: "Torah is, for [Paul], not a statement of God's will for people of every age and place, but the covenantal obligations imposed on Israel with sanctions of life and death, blessing and curse. Since the Sinaitic covenant proved unable to convey life, Christians had to be delivered from both its demands and its sanctions to serve God under a new covenant." In effect, even though Westerholm takes the opposite position from Dunn and Gundry with respect to the ongoing validity of the law in the life of the believer, he too raises questions about Sanders' over-sharp distinction between getting in and staying in; in fact, precisely because he does *not* agree with Sanders on this point, his challenge is more effective than Gundry's or Dunn's.

cifically which seemed to offer a promise of life for those who do it; it is the Torah in particular which raises the issue of circumcision. But when it comes to the *problem* with the law—the plight at which Paul arrived once he understood Christ to be the exclusive solution—it is clear that Westerholm understands the issue in terms of law in general. The basic problem with the law is that it is based on the doing of deeds, rather than on faith.[117] More specifically, it is based on the doing of deeds which humans do not and cannot satisfy: "Paul thus believes that humans do not and (apparently) cannot obey God's commandments in a way that satisfies divine requirements."[118]

Frank Thielman offers yet another sort of response to Sanders.[119] Unlike Westerholm, Thielman challenges Sanders' contention that Paul's thought runs from solution to plight. Using a wide variety of sources drawn from the Old Testament and from Second Temple Jewish literature, Thielman traces a pattern within Jewish thought that runs from plight to solution.[120] The plight which Thielman identifies in Jewish thought is a pessimistic theme concerning "humanity's inability to avoid rebellion against God" which begins the Pentateuch,[121] comes to full expression in the prophets, is occasionally manifested in the Psalms and other writings, and also finds expression in the Dead Sea Scrolls and other Second Temple Jewish literature, primarily of the apocalyptic variety. This plight is, according to Thielman, specifically understood and expressed in terms of failure to keep the law.[122] The solution which Thielman identifies, on the other hand, is the eschatological expectation that God will someday make it possible for his people to keep the law.[123]

---

[117]Ibid., 111ff

[118]Ibid., 143.

[119]Thielman's argument is not just a response to Sanders; rather, he is responding to what he calls the "Christological approach" to Paul and the law, of which Sanders is the foremost representative (Thielman, *From Plight to Solution*, 13–27).

[120]Ibid., 28–45.

[121]Ibid., 29.

[122]Ibid., 33–34.

[123]Ibid., 34–36. At times it seems to me that Thielman has overstated the case for the solution as an eschatological action of God. To be sure, Thielman does describe some expressions of eschatological expectation (e.g., "Jeremiah 31:31–34 says that one day God will write his law upon the hearts of his people," ibid., 35), but he has not dealt adequately with an important note in many of the examples he cites, in which there is also (or instead) the expectation that God's people will first repent and seek to obey: "Even in the middle of his warning of impending doom because of Israel's incessant sin, Amos extends the possibility that if Israel seeks 'good, and not evil . . . it may be that the Lord, the God of hosts will be gracious to the remnant of Joseph' (5:14–15)" (ibid., 35). While this example does illustrate an ideal in which redemption is linked with keeping the law, it does not seem to offer much of a "solution" other than for the people to try harder.

Paul's discussion of the law in Galatians and in Romans is therefore best understood in terms of this Jewish framework, often going a step beyond it, but essentially reflecting the same pattern of plight (human inability to keep the law) to solution (God's eschatological provision of the Spirit, whereby Christians can fulfill the law).[124] Thielman's investigation of Galatians begins with 5:14, which he understands as Paul's command to keep the law: "In summary, Paul clearly reserves a place for obedience to the law in his eschatological scheme."[125] Thielman goes on to argue that Paul's understanding of the "boundaries" of the law, in which circumcision (and food laws, etc.) can be understood as optional, is based on a view not uncommon among Hellenistic Jews.[126] He then argues that Paul's major emphasis is on urging the Galatians not to accept circumcision, because to accept circumcision is to step away from the eschatological solution which God has provided through faith in Christ, back into the old aeon with its plight of human inability to keep the law.[127] Unfortunately, Thielman never explains why Paul should understand circumcision to entail a step back into the old aeon.

It is interesting to note that, even though Thielman and Westerholm hold opposite views concerning the direction of Paul's thought—from plight to solution, or from solution to plight—they both arrive at essentially the same understanding of the plight. Ultimately, what is wrong with the law is that humans cannot do it. On the other hand, since Thielman describes the plight as a historical feature of Jewish self-understanding, he understands the problem with the law as primarily a problem with the Torah specifically, not with law in general. The problem as Thielman sees it, in other words, is not with doing (versus believing), but rather is found in Israel's own history, its own repeated experience of failure to keep the law.[128]

---

[124] Thielman traces the pattern of plight to solution in Galatians (ibid., 47–86) and in Romans (ibid., 87–116).

[125] Ibid., 54.

[126] Ibid., 54–59. This part of Thielman's discussion falls short of being totally convincing; as he himself acknowledges, "It must be admitted immediately that few scholars have been willing to see behind this [Hellenistic Jewish] literature a group of Jews who actually abandoned circumcision, food laws, and Sabbath observance" (ibid., 57).

[127] Ibid., 59ff.

[128] Cf. Martin Noth, "'For All Who Rely on Works of the Law are Under a Curse'," in *The Laws of the Pentateuch and Other Studies*, trans. D. R. Ap-Thomas (Edinburgh: Oliver & Boyd, 1966), 108–17; In-Gyu Hong, *The Law in Galatians*, JSNTSS 81 (Sheffield: JSOT, 1993); idem, "Does Paul Misrepresent the Jewish Law? Law and Covenant in Gal. 3:1–14," *NovT* 36 (1994): 164–82. Noth, followed by Hong, argues that the Israelite people had already invoked the curse of the law by their disobedience throughout their history.

Summary: Problems Remaining

It is evident that Sanders has changed the landscape of Pauline scholarship. One can speak not only of a "new perspective," but even perhaps of an emerging consensus—certainly with respect to a revised understanding of the nature of Judaism, if nowhere else. But it is equally evident that Sanders' understanding of Paul has not been entirely satisfactory, even for those who embrace the bulk of his views; certainly he has not succeeded in eliminating support for the traditional answers to the questions raised by Paul and the law. At the same time, it is not clear that those who have critiqued Sanders, particularly those who reiterate the traditional position, have overcome the weight of Sanders' arguments. In short, in spite of the impact Sanders has had, in spite of some level of emerging consensus, in spite of an enormous amount of dialogue and debate, problems remain, problems that neither Sanders nor his critics have fully resolved. We can address these problems under two headings: 1) Why not the law? 2) Getting in or staying in?

Why Not the Law?

Has Sanders adequately accounted for Paul's rejection of the law? Certainly he has mounted a massive attack against the traditional position, that Paul rejects the law either because of human inability or because of self-righteous legalism.[129] In spite of numerous attempts, it is not at all clear that anyone has adequately countered Sanders' critique of the problems in the traditional position. The fact remains that Paul *does* seem confident that humans can keep the law perfectly (Phil 3:6); whatever else the citation of Dt 27:26 means in Gal 3:10, it certainly does *not* indicate that one is cursed for *attempting* to do the law (i.e., that the problem lies in *doing*); and so on. When scholars do return to the traditional view, it is not so much that they can overcome these objections, but more because of a nagging sense that Sanders' own explanation is even less satisfactory.[130]

Even Dunn feels that Sanders has failed adequately to account for the vehemence of Paul's rejection of the law. To say that Paul rejected the law only because it was not Christ results in a picture of an "odd," "idiosyncratic," and "arbitrary" Paul, a picture that is "little more convincing (and much less attractive) than the Lutheran Paul."[131] As we have seen, however, Dunn's own answer

---

[129] For the most part, this represents an attack against the view that Paul rejects the idea of law in general, as opposed to the Torah in particular. As we have seen above, however, Thielman and certain other scholars have maintained the traditional answer of human inability to keep the law, but with respect to the Torah specifically, not law in general.

[130] Cf. Gundry, "Grace," 13: "We are forced back to an answer Sanders rejects...."

[131] Dunn, "The New Perspective," 187–88.

is really only a logical extension of Sanders' view, making explicit what was already implicit. Paul rejects the law not just because it is not Christ, but also and especially because of the law's role in excluding the Gentiles. It is not law-in-general that Paul rejects, but rather the Torah specifically, to the extent that it functions as an entry requirement imposed on Gentiles, an entry requirement other than faith in Christ, without which they cannot be counted as truly "in."

Unfortunately, Dunn has only succeeded in clarifying what it is in Sanders' view that seems inadequate. The more that Paul rejects the Torah-in-particular rather than law-in-general—the more he rejects the Torah because of its ethnic exclusivity, rather than because it requires doing or leads to legalism, etc.—the more difficult it becomes to explain Paul's rejection *of the whole law*. If Paul's problem with the law is limited to the specific features of the Torah that exclude the Gentiles, *why does he not say that*? Why does he reject the whole law?[132]

We can illustrate this point in a couple of ways. First, consider Paul's well-known "threat" in Gal 5:3, "I testify again to every person being circumcised that he is obligated to do the whole law."[133] If we accept the position taken by Dunn and Sanders, this "threat" makes no sense. Paul is trying to keep them from being circumcised by threatening them with the *rest* of the law[134]—but the rest of the law is precisely that "part" of the law which, it would seem, Dunn and Sanders think Paul *wants* them to do![135] Dunn and Sanders make the point that

---

[132] The obvious answer is that Paul sees the Torah as a seamless whole, so that rejecting one part of the law *is* to reject all of it. This answer, however, puts pressure on Sanders' and Dunn's (and many other scholars') insistence that Paul sees the law having ongoing validity in the life of the believer. See further discussion below.

[133] The description of Gal 5:3 as a "threat" comes from Sanders, *PLJP*, 27: "[It is] a kind of threat: if you start it *must* all be kept."

[134] In response to an earlier draft of this investigation, Richard Hays pointed out that this may not be a "threat," but rather an accusation against the advocates of circumcision, that they are "eclectic fly-by-night types who are not presenting Torah in its integrity." In the context, however, it seems clear that 5:3 is directed, not at those who are advocating circumcision, but rather at those who are flirting with the idea. It may be that Paul is making the point that the Galatians cannot take up *just* circumcision, i.e., that to take on circumcision necessarily involves the attempt to become righteous by the law (cf. Gal 5:4). If so, however, this does not relieve the problem inherent in Sanders' and Dunn's approach; once again, they are suggesting that Paul *does* want the Galatians to adopt the "rest" of the law.

[135] Both Dunn and Sanders would, I suspect, object to the implied dividing-up of the law into "parts," some of which should be done, and some which should not, but this is in effect what their portrayal of Paul amounts to: do not do circumcision; do not do those laws which promote ethnic exclusivity; but do the rest of the law. Cf. esp. Sanders, *PLJP*, 93ff. Cf. also Heikki Räisänen, "Galatians 2.16 and Paul's Break with Judaism," *NTS* 31 (1985): 544: "Dunn thus presents a new version of an old thesis: what Paul attacks is not

circumcision, food laws, and the like were seen both as specific identity markers of Judaism and as stumbling blocks for Gentiles; thus these practices created a barrier between Jews and Gentiles.[136] Paul's rejection of the law, however, does not stop with or even especially focus on these practices; it extends to the whole law.[137] He does not say, "By all means take up the rest of the law, but by no means be circumcised"; he does not say, "Be careful that you observe the law only in the right manner, not as a means of nationalistic exclusion"; he does not even say, "Do the law, so long as you understand that it has no bearing on whether or not you are really 'in.'" What he does say is, "Do not start with circumcision, because then you are stuck with all the rest of the law."[138]

Second, it is not at all clear that Paul's objection to the law is actually based on its ethnic exclusivity. Does Paul really object to Gentiles becoming Jews, and if so, why? Even if we suppose that Paul had a keen sense of social egalitarianism, whereby he objected to the degradation and patronization associated with nationalistic exclusivism—admittedly, this is something of a caricature of the

---

the law *as such* or *as a whole*, but just the law as viewed in some particular perspective, a particular *attitude* to the law, or some specific (mis-)*understanding* of it."

[136]Cf. Sanders, *PLJP*, 29: "There is good reason to think that, although observing the law was not burdensome to Jews, it appeared onerous and inconvenient to Gentiles. Paul's opponents may have adopted a policy of gradualism, requiring first some of the major commandments (circumcision, food, days), a policy which was probably not unique among Jewish missionaries." What is odd about this statement in the context of Sanders' argument is this: once these "major commandments" had been required, what was left—except the very part of the law to which Paul had no objections, which he continued to uphold?

[137]Dunn is highly critical of Sanders for equating "works of law" with "law," insisting that it has a much narrower focus only on the nationalistic misuse of the law as expressed in covenant works such as circumcision, etc. (Dunn, "The New Perspective," 200–202). Once again, however, Dunn and Sanders are not actually so far apart. On the one hand, one could certainly argue that Dunn's description of "works of law" essentially takes in all that is included by "law": "'works of the law' . . . denotes those obligations prescribed by the law which show the individual concerned to belong to the law . . . 'works of the law' then is another way of saying 'covenantal nomism'—that which characterizes 'being in' the covenant and not simply 'getting into' the covenant" (idem, "Works of Law," 527–28). On the other hand, Sanders acknowledges that Paul functionally, if not explicitly, distinguishes between those parts of the law which are still binding and those which should be discarded; in the latter category are precisely those laws which "created a social distinction between Jews and other races in the Greco-Roman world" (Sanders, *PLJP*, 102). Cf. Westerholm, *Israel's Law*, 117–18, who argues that Paul uses "works of law" and "law" interchangeably.

[138]Alternately, he warns them that to start with circumcision is to enter into the attempt to be righteous by way of the whole law; cf. n. 134 above.

position represented by Dunn and Sanders[139]—it is nonetheless clear that Paul talks about the real status of the Gentile Christians *in terms of becoming or being Jewish*, that is, being true children of Abraham, true children of Sarah, children of "Jerusalem above" (Gal 3:6–8, 4:22–31), and so on.[140] Nor, as the same passages make clear, is Paul hesitant about being exclusive. He not only excludes, but urges the Galatians to drive out, those who are "children of the slave woman."

In short, we have not yet arrived at a satisfactory answer for the question, "What is wrong with the law?" Sanders has made an effective case *against* the traditional position, and he may well have described the *process* by which Paul thought about the law (from solution to plight), but his explanation for *why* Paul thought as he did about the law remains less than satisfying. Indeed, Sanders himself more or less admits as much. When he asks *why* Paul would arrive at a position so different from his Jewish Christian contemporaries, Sanders can only say, "This will, as far as I see, always remain a question; there are only speculative answers."[141]

Getting In, or Staying In?

It is striking that so many scholars have felt the need to criticize Sanders for his over-sharp distinction between getting in and staying in, particularly when he locates the focus of Paul's rejection of the law solely in terms of getting in. As we have seen above, however, the way such critique is generally developed presents no real problem for Sanders' position.[142] As long as the issue remains one of soteriology—as long as Paul's argument in Galatians 3, for example, has to do with defining the basis on which one is truly in the group of those who will be saved—then whether the law is being imposed in order to *get* in or in order to *stay* in, it effectively remains an entry requirement with respect to the Gentile converts. Gentiles must take on the law in order to be counted truly as "in." In essence, those who criticize Sanders on this point wind up effectively saying the same thing that he does; one wonders therefore if the problem is more a matter of semantics than substance.

Is there any basis for the widespread intuition that there is some sort of problem with Sanders' distinction? I believe there is, and in a sense the problem

---

[139]Something of a caricature, but not entirely off base; cf. e.g. Sanders, *PLJP*, 152–53; Dunn, "The New Perspective," 197–98; idem, "Theology," 132, 137; idem, "Works of Law," 534ff.

[140]The point could be made even stronger with the use of Romans, e.g., 2:28–29, 4:1ff, 11:16ff. Cf. Sanders' discussion of the way in which Paul effectively thought of the church as the "true Israel" (Sanders, *PLJP*, 171–79).

[141]Sanders, *PLJP*, 153–54.

[142]Cf. the discussion of Dunn and Gundry above.

is one of semantics, but in a very substantial way. Sanders does not use his own definitions of getting in and staying in consistently. When the issue has to do with Paul's rejection of the law, he emphasizes the soteriological aspect of the definition of staying in; when the issue has to do with Paul's affirmation of the law, however, he speaks about staying in in terms of *expected behavior*:

> I propose that the negative statements [about the law] arise from the discussion of membership requirements, first of all for Gentiles and then also for Jews. The positive statements arise from questions of *behavior* within the Christian community.[143]

To put the point another way, sometimes Sanders uses both "getting in" and "staying in" to define *identity*, while at other times he uses "staying in" (but *not* "getting in") to refer to *behavior*.[144]

The difference between these uses of "staying in" is subtle and yet profound. On the one hand, it certainly is the case that identity and behavior cannot be neatly separated.[145] Behavior arises out of and defines identity, and vice versa. For one who is "in," there are certain expectations about behavior, expectations that not only define how one should live day-to-day, but also which, when violated, jeopardize one's membership. On the other hand, there is a difference between identity and behavior, a profound difference in terms of assumptions and the focus of attention. If one uses "staying in" in terms of *identity*, the question is whether or not one is really "in"; if one uses "staying in" in terms of *behavior*, whether or not one is in is *not* in question—*it is simply assumed*.

In effect, Sanders exploits this subtle but profound difference when he discusses the ongoing role of the law in the life of the believer. According to Sanders, Paul effectively requires Christians to obey the law when the question has to do with *staying* in—which at this point, Sanders explicitly says, has to do with Christian *behavior*.[146] But what if we press the definition that Sanders started with, which he has used to relegate all of Paul's *negative* statements

---

[143] Sanders, *PLJP*, 84 (emphasis added).

[144] The useful categories of "identity" and "behavior" come from Barclay, who prefers these terms to "getting in" and "staying in" (to which he finds them roughly comparable) in part because of his insistence that behavior and identity are inseparable (Barclay, *Obeying the Truth*, 73–74). Barclay either does not notice or does not address the way in which Sanders uses his own terminology inconsistently.

[145] This is a major thesis of Barclay's work; see further discussion below.

[146] Sanders, *PLJP*, 84; cf. ibid., 95ff. Sanders affirms that Paul thinks of Christian behavior as "springing from life in the Spirit," but denies that that is in tension with requiring obedience to the law: "Living in the Spirit results in obeying the law"; furthermore, Paul's instructions are to be considered binding *as law*—law continues to function "in the standard Jewish way" (ibid., 105).

about the law under the category of "entrance requirement"—what if we insist, as he earlier insists, that "staying in" is a soteriological term? We wind up with a capriciously inconsistent Paul, who denounces his opponents for making something other than faith in Christ a necessary condition for membership, but then turns around and does the very same thing. *The only way Sanders avoids an incoherent Paul is by shifting the meaning of "staying in" part way through his discussion.*[147]

One further question remains: does Paul actually require Christians to *do* the law? Certainly Sanders advances a vigorous argument in support of his contention that Paul expects *deeds* from his converts, that he shares with Judaism the conviction that judgment is by *works*. Here again, however, there is a certain semantic slipperiness. Even if we grant that Paul expects *deeds*, is that equivalent to saying that he upholds the ongoing validity of the *law*? Sanders himself concedes that Paul shows little interest in generating commandments or working out a detailed *halakah*; moreover, the moral instruction he does give is almost never grounded by an appeal to the law, even when such an appeal would be obvious and natural.[148] Nevertheless Sanders insists that Paul upholds the law as law because he believes in judgment by works.[149] It would seem that Sanders has now made in reverse the mistake which he points out in the traditional position. He denies that Paul's rejection of the law is a rejection of works, i.e., that law in this respect is to be equated with works; in demonstrating that Paul also requires works, however, he too quickly assumes that the requirement of works is equivalent to a requirement of the law as law.

Once again we are left with some unresolved problems. In a sense, there does seem to be universal agreement that Paul's rejection of the law has primarily to do with soteriology, or in other words, identity rather than behavior. Though many have questioned Sanders' distinction between getting in and staying in, none of the responses we have surveyed above have had much success in

---

[147]Sanders is not unaware of the tensions in his portrait of Paul; cf. ibid., 99. I would suggest, however, that the tension is considerably greater than he allows. One is left either with an incoherent Paul (as Räisänen, following Sanders, has alleged; see below, 93), or one must say that Paul refuses to allow *some* laws to be required—e.g., circumcision—while requiring others; that, however, only intensifies our question, "Why *not* the law?"

[148]Sanders, *PLJP*, 95–96, 106; cf. idem, *PPJ*, 513. Sanders points to Paul's warnings against idolatry in 1 Cor 10, where "he goes to considerable length to show that idolatry is wrong on typological and christological grounds" and even appeals to the scriptures, but never mentions the first commandment. As pointed out to me by Richard Hays, Sanders is not quite accurate in identifying the issue in 1 Cor 10 as idol worship; the immediate issue is eating eating meat sacrificed to idols. Nevertheless, Sanders' point is well taken; it would not have come as a surprise for Paul to refer to the first commandment at some point in the discussion in 1 Cor 8 and 10—but he does not.

[149]Sanders, *PLJP*, 105ff.

moving the discussion of Paul's rejection of the law out of the category of soteriology, especially with respect to Galatians 3.[150] As we have seen, however, much of this de facto agreement with Sanders arises out of the hidden range of meanings in the term "staying in"; we therefore need, at the very least, to question whether scholars are right to see Paul's rejection of the law (especially in Galatians 3) only or primarily in terms of soteriology.

That raises a further question: what should we do with Paul's positive statements about the law—what is the ongoing role of the law in the life of the believer? If Sanders has gone too far in equating Paul's moral instruction and warnings about judgment by works with the requirement that Christians should obey the law, it does not seem any more satisfactory to say that Paul believes Christians can *now* do the law only because they are empowered by faith or the Spirit; Judaism already understood law observance to be possible only with God's help.[151] Likewise, to suggest that Christians now fulfill the law by observing its essence, i.e., the love command, seems on the one hand to ignore the common Jewish pattern of summarizing the law in terms of love,[152] and on the other to fail to explain why this portion of the law applies, but other portions do not. In short, we need to explore further whether and how Paul rejects or accepts the law with respect to behavior.

One final, related observation is that, while those who understand the issue in terms of law in general have taken differing positions on the role of the law in the ongoing life of the believer, those who understand the issue in terms of the Torah specifically tend to share in common the view that Paul does see the law as having ongoing validity. This is no accident: one of the major advantages of and motivations for understanding the problem in terms of the Torah specifically is that it avoids the difficulties of explaining how Paul can seemingly require deeds of the Christian if he rejects the law because it involves doing, or in other words, law in general. Unfortunately, as we have seen, understanding the problem in terms of the Torah specifically brings with it disadvantages and difficulties of its own.

ALTERNATIVES

We are left with what seem to be divergent options for understanding the background of Galatians in terms of Paul's rejection of the law. Either the problem has to do with law in general, or it is really about the Torah in particular and the specific sociological and historical situation involving conditions for inclusion of the Gentiles (and/or Israel's history of disobedience); either it has to do

---

[150]Westerholm comes closest to moving beyond soteriology, precisely because he argues that Paul's rejection of the law extends even to the ongoing life of the believer.

[151]Martyn, *Galatians*, 262.

[152]Thielman, *From Plight to Solution*, 52–53.

with getting in or with staying in; either Paul requires Christians to obey the law, or he rejects the principle of law as law. As we have seen above, none of these options is entirely free from problems. It seems that we need to explore some alternatives for understanding Paul's problem with the law in Galatians.

JOHN M. G. BARCLAY: IDENTITY AND BEHAVIOR

A recent monograph by John M. G. Barclay, *Obeying the Truth: A Study of Paul's Ethics in Galatians*, suggests one promising alternative. What sets Barclay's wide-ranging and insightful investigation apart is the way it incorporates ethics as an essential rather than peripheral issue throughout the book of Galatians.[153] Barclay's key thesis is that *identity* and *behavior* are inextricably bound together; thus, Paul's ethical exhortations in Galatians 5–6 are not only integral to the letter, but in fact are intimately bound up with his defense of justification by faith in the earlier chapters: "[Paul's] discussion of ethics in terms of faith, love, and walking in the spirit is intended to draw out the implications of justification by faith, and to describe what it means to continue as they had begun, in the Spirit."[154] Paul's efforts to define the identity of the Galatian Christians both necessitates and is necessitated by his efforts to define their behavior.[155]

A key element in Barclay's argument is his exploration of *why* the Galatians would want to embrace the law. Following the lead of Betz and others, Barclay takes seriously the possibility that the Galatians sought out the law as an answer to moral uncertainty.[156] In Paul's absence, and left with little in the way of specific instruction, they had been struggling with the problem of inappropriate behavior, a problem for which the agitators have what seems to be the perfect—or perhaps we might say, perfecting—solution.[157] In addition to the moral dimension, however, Barclay suggests that there is also a sociological dimension. As converts from their pagan society, they would experience a social dislocation that would be intensified with Paul's departure; by accepting the law, they would be regularizing their social status not only with other Christians, but also with respect to their society.[158] By becoming Jewish, in other words, they would become part of a recognized social group.

---

[153] Cf. Barclay, *Obeying the Truth*, 6–8.
[154] Ibid., 217.
[155] Ibid., 73ff.
[156] Ibid., 19–22. Barclay cites Betz, *Galatians*, 8–9, 273–74, 295–96, as well as two articles by Betz, "Spirit, Freedom and Law: Paul's Message to the Galatian Churches," *SEÅ* 39 (1974): 145–60, and idem, "In Defense of the Spirit: Paul's Letter to the Galatians as a Document of Early Christian Apologetics," in *Aspects of Religious Propaganda in Judaism and Early Christianity*, ed. E. Schüssler-Fiorenza (Notre Dame, Ind: University of Notre Dame, 1976), 99–114.
[157] Barclay, *Obeying the Truth*, 20–21, 70–71, 218
[158] Ibid., 56ff.

If the Galatians' acceptance of the law has moral *behavior* as one of its prime motivations, then clearly Paul's rejection of the law cannot be limited to a rejection of the law as entry requirement. In denying that the law defines the identity of the Galatians as Christians, Paul is also denying that the law defines their behavior.[159] Thus, Barclay joins the many scholars who critique Sanders for making too sharp a distinction between getting in and staying in, but with far greater success.[160] Even though he does not address Sanders' inconsistent use of his own terminology, Barclay nevertheless demonstrates the problem inherent in Sanders' claim that Paul approves the law for staying in, even where staying in is understood in terms of behavior rather than identity.

What of Paul's admonitions to fulfill the law? Barclay follows Westerholm's lead in arguing, on the one hand, that Paul refers to the law only in *describing*—but not *prescribing*—Christian behavior, and on the other hand, that "fulfilling" the law means, for Paul, something very different than using it to define one's behavior.[161] Paul describes Christians as "fulfilling the law"—terminology never found in the LXX, and never used by Paul to speak of Jewish observance of the law—precisely because the word "fulfill" is sufficiently ambiguous; it allows him to avoid the charge of antinomianism without actually requiring obedience to the law as such.[162]

Barclay's approach to Galatians goes a long way towards demonstrating and explaining the way the whole letter, specifically including the parenesis of chapters 5–6, is tightly integrated in Paul's argument. His analysis of the structure and significance of that parenetic material and his investigation of the significance of the Spirit/flesh duality is helpful and persuasive. His approach is not without problems, however, two of which in particular are significant for our investigation of Galatians 3.

Barclay has done an excellent job of explaining why the Galatians might want to *embrace* the law; what he fails adequately to address is why Paul so vehemently *rejects* it. To a large degree, Barclay never even considers the question; he merely assumes that Paul sees an incompatibility between the law and faith.[163] To the extent that he does address the issue, Barclay follows the road

---

[159]Ibid., 73ff.

[160]Ibid., 33, 74.

[161]Ibid., 135ff.

[162]Ibid., 140–42.

[163]So, for example, in his overview of Galatians 2–4 (ibid., 75–105), Barclay demonstrates that taking up a Jewish lifestyle means taking on a Jewish identity, and vice versa, but he never addresses *why* it should be a problem to take on either; he merely assumes that this is contrary to the "truth of the gospel." Similarly, Barclay assumes that "the triumphant declaration that 'with the coming of faith we are no longer under a παιδαγωγός' (3.25)" would be "liberating to Paul" (ibid., 107)—but he never establishes that (or explores why) Paul would feel any need for liberation from the law. Interestingly,

paved by Sanders and others. The problem with the law is not works as such, or self-righteousness as such, but rather is primarily the sociological problem of nationalistic exclusivism.[164] As we have seen above, however, the farther one travels down this road, the harder it is to explain why and in what way Paul did not share the assumptions of his opponents, that the Gentile Christians should become Jews.[165]

An even more serious concern, for the purposes of our investigation, is that in spite of his basic insight into the intertwined relationship of identity and behavior, Barclay describes the bulk of Paul's argument in Galatians 2–4 as an argument about *identity*.[166] To be sure, this argument about identity points ahead to the implications for behavior. In Galatians 3:1–5, for example, Paul speaks not only of how they began, but how they must continue.[167] But other than this brief "hint," Barclay seems to assume that the rest of the chapter revolves around the issue of identity.[168]

Though he rejects it in theory, therefore, in practice Barclay seems to grant Sanders' point. Where Paul speaks negatively about the law, the issue is primarily soteriological, i.e., having to do with identity. To be sure, Barclay argues that

---

Barclay notes that Paul's persecution of the church reveals his prior awareness of the incompatibility between faith and law-observance (ibid., 239)—but again, he does not adequately explore the basis for that incompatibility.

[164]Ibid., 168–69, 232–33, 239–40. In his discussion of Paul's use of the Spirit/flesh duality, Barclay does suggest a further reason for Paul's rejection of the law, one which arises out of his apocalyptic perspective: "to commit themselves to Judaism was to enmesh themselves in what had now been shown to be *a merely human religion* ... one is born a Jew by mere human parentage, but made a Christian by the creative work of the Spirit of God" (ibid., 207). Unfortunately, Barclay does not follow up this idea, but rather subsumes it under the sociological issues of nationalism and exclusion. In particular, Barclay does not explore the implications of claiming that Paul saw the law and Judaism as "merely human." Did Paul no longer think that *God* gave the law? Cf. Sanders, *PLJP*, 67.

[165]See above, 40–42. The only explanation that seems to make sense is that Paul rejected the Torah as a matter of expediency, to make it easier to bring in converts. As we have seen, this is an answer that Sanders explicitly rejects, and so, apparently, does Barclay (see e.g. his critique of F. Watson; Barclay, *Obeying the Truth*, 237–39). If one were to accept this answer, it would only intensify the problem. The Galatians were apparently *ready* to take the step of circumcision; it did *not* pose a barrier to their conversion—so why not go for it?

[166]Ibid., 75–105. In Gal 2:11–21, Barclay sees the Antioch episode as primarily about the way the identity of *Jewish* believers is to be defined; in Galatians 3–4, the primary issue is the basis for defining the identity of Gentiles believers as children of Abraham. In each case, Barclay insists that identity has *implications* for behavior, but the primary focus of the discussion has to do with identity.

[167]Ibid., 83–86.
[168]Ibid., 86–94.

Sanders is wrong in saying that Paul accepts or requires the law for staying in (in the sense of behavior), but curiously it is only in connection with Paul's *positive* remarks, both about law and when giving ethical instruction, that Barclay makes this point. Rather than arguing that Paul's *negative* statements against the law directly concern *behavior*, he argues only that the negative statements *imply* a rejection of the law for behavior; where that rejection is directly addressed is in Paul's *positive* statements, in which Paul redefines appropriate Christian behavior apart from the law.

In short, it seems that Barclay has not taken his own insights far enough when it comes to Paul's arguments against the law. If identity and behavior are two sides of the same coin, then it would seem that we need to investigate Paul's negative statements about the law in Galatians 3 with a readiness to not only how they speak against using the law to *maintain identity* ("staying in" in the soteriological sense), but also to what extent they may also have in view *behavior*.

J. LOUIS MARTYN: APOCALYPTIC ANTINOMIES

Another promising alternative for understanding Paul's problem with the law in Galatians arises from the apocalyptic approach of J. Louis Martyn.[169] According to Martyn, Galatians is far from being the least apocalyptic of Paul's writings, as has usually been supposed.[170] On the contrary, not only does Galatians contain apocalyptic themes and motifs, but from start to finish the letter is grounded and structured by Paul's apocalyptic understanding of the significance of Christ. To understand Paul's problem with the law in Galatians, therefore, we must first come to an understanding of Paul's apocalyptic framework, and then explore the way in which the law fits within it.

Martyn begins his case for understanding the nature of Paul's apocalyptic in Galatians with a key passage from the end of the letter (6:13–15):

> ... they wish you to be circumcised, in order that they might boast with regard to your flesh. I, on the contrary, boast in one thing only, the cross of our Lord Jesus Christ, by which the world has been crucified to me, and I to the world.

---

[169] J. Louis Martyn, "Apocalyptic Antinomies in Paul's Letter to the Galatians," *NTS* 31 (1985): 410–24; idem, "Events in Galatia: Modified Covenantal Nomism versus God's Invasion of the Cosmos in the Singular Gospel: A Response to J. D. G. Dunn and B. R. Gaventa," in *Pauline Theology*, vol. 1, ed. J. M. Bassler (Minneapolis: Fortress, 1991), 160–79; see also idem, *Galatians*.

[170] As Martyn points out, the view that Galatians is non-apocalyptic is primarily based on the fact that it contains no explicit reference to an imminent parousia; thus, even a scholar like Beker—whose thesis is that the coherent center of Paul's theology is found in apocalyptic—finds Galatians to be the exception ("Apocalyptic Antinomies," 410–11).

For neither is circumcision anything, nor is uncircumcision anything, but rather what is something is the New Creation.[171]

Martyn identifies two key features of this passage. First, what Paul has announced is not "a choice between two ways of life," but rather "two different worlds," an old world which has been destroyed by a triple death (Christ's, the world's, and his own), and a new creation.[172] Second, and particularly important for our purposes, what has been negated in the passing of the old world is not simply law-observance, but also its opposite, non-law-observance. *Neither* circumcision nor uncircumcision have any real existence in the new creation.[173]

What Paul is presupposing, according to Martyn, is the idea common throughout the ancient world, that "the fundamental building blocks of the cosmos are pairs of opposites."[174] Martyn finds evidence of this presupposition throughout Galatians. In Gal 3:27–28, for example, Paul negates familiar pairs of opposites: male/female, Jew/Gentile, slave/free.[175] In Gal 4:21–5:1, Paul takes over the "table of opposites" presented by the Teachers and "corrects" it. Hagar and Sarah are indeed representative of pairs of opposites, characterized by the opposition slave/free, but the pairs of opposites presented by the Teachers have passed away with the old cosmos; now, the law and the present Jerusalem stand in the *same* column with Hagar.[176] In denying existence to these pairs of opposites, Paul is announcing not only "the horrifying death of the cosmos," but also the freedom, in the new creation, from such divisions.[177] In short, what Paul seeks in the letter to the Galatians is not to get them to covert to a new religion, that is, not to choose between any of the pairs of opposites of the old cosmos, but rather to leave religion behind, to understand themselves as dead to the old world, with all of its pairs of opposites, and alive to a new cosmos.[178]

---

[171] The translation is Martyn's, "Apocalyptic Antinomies," 412.

[172] Ibid.

[173] Ibid., 413.

[174] Ibid., 413–14.

[175] Ibid., 414–15.

[176] Ibid., 418–20. Martyn sees Paul's use of συστοιχέω in 4:25 as a deliberate reference to the technical term for a table of opposites, συστοιχίαι τῶν ἐναντιότων. I find this interesting but by no means conclusive. While this is the only use of συστοιχέω in Paul (for that matter, in the New Testament), Paul does make use of related words (στοιχέω, στοιχεῖα) several times in Galatians, in ways that do not immediately suggest such a table of opposites (e.g., 4:3, 9; 5:25; 6:16; cf. elsewhere in Paul, Rom 4:12; Phil 3:16). Similarly, I am not overly persuaded that Paul's use of ἀντίκειμαι in 5:17 is a technical term (ibid., 416). This is the only occurrence of the term in Galatians; where it occurs elsewhere in Paul's writings, it occurs as a participle with the meaning, "opponent" (1 Cor 16:9; Phil 1:28; 2 Thess 2:4).

[177] Ibid., 414–15.

[178] Cf. Martyn, "Events," 167–68; idem, *Galatians*, 37, 39.

One might be tempted to add to the previous sentence the phrase, "in which opposition is no more, in which unity reigns."[179] Not all of the opposites of which Paul speaks, however, are done away with in the passing of the old cosmos. In fact, some oppositions *emerge* with the dawning of the new creation, including in particular the opposition between Spirit and Flesh and the opposition between the present Jerusalem and the Jerusalem above.[180] These "apocalyptic antinomies" emerge as transformations or realignments of old oppositions.[181] In the old cosmos, the law was in opposition to the "Evil Impulse" of the flesh; no doubt it is largely on this basis that the Teachers are promoting the law in the Galatian churches, as an "antidote" to the desires of the flesh.[182] With the dawning of the new creation, however, law stands not in opposition to but rather as the ally of the flesh; now it is the Spirit which emerges to wage war against the desires of the flesh.[183]

---

[179] At times, this seems to be the direction Martyn wants to go; cf. Martyn, "Apocalyptic Antinomies," 415. Clearly, however, he cannot sustain the idea that the new creation is devoid of oppositions, since he contends that the new creation brings with it *new* oppositions. At most, he can claim that *certain* oppositions—especially the opposition between Jew and Gentile, circumcised and uncircumcised—are done away, without showing clearly why that *must* be so (i.e., why some oppositions emerge, some disappear, and at least one, the divine/human opposition, remains).

[180] Martyn, "Apocalyptic Antinomies," 415–20. In idem, "Events," 170, Martyn hints of another antinomy which has emerged—or perhaps has simply now been revealed—within scripture; he clarifies what that is in idem, "The Textual Contradiction Between Habakkuk 2:4 and Leviticus 18:5," in *Theological Issues in the Letters of Paul* (Nashville: Abingdon, 1997), 183–90; cf. idem, *Galatians*, 37, 300, 320ff: there is within scripture an antinomy between law and scripture, or in other words, between the cursing voice of the law and the promissory and guiding voice of God. Since this issue specifically has to do with the citations in Galatians 3, it will be discussed further in chap. 3, below.

[181] It is not entirely clear whether Martyn intends to reserve the term "antinomies" (or "apocalyptic antinomies") only for the *new* pairs of opposites that emerge with the dawning of the new cosmos. He does not introduce the term until he begins to discuss the new oppositions (Martyn, "Apocalyptic Antinomies," 415ff), but at times he seems to use the term more generally to refer to any pair of opposites, whether characteristic of the new cosmos or the old (cf. ibid., 421).

[182] Ibid., 416; idem, "Events," 177; idem, *Galatians*, 126, 284–85, 291–93; cf. idem, "A Law-Observant Mission to Gentiles: The Background of Galatians," *Scottish Journal of Theology* 38 (1985): 307–24; now reprinted and revised in idem, *Theological Issues in the Letters of Paul*, 7–24. As noted above, Barclay is very much in step with Martyn at this point.

[183] Martyn, "Apocalyptic Antinomies," 416–17. The theme of warfare is of particular significance for Martyn's contention that Galatians is thoroughly apocalyptic; cf. ibid., 417, 420; idem, "Events," 178–79.

What is particularly significant about Martyn's approach for our purposes is the new answers it offers to the questions which have aided our discussion throughout this survey, "Why not the law?" and "What is the ongoing role of the law in the life of believers?" To a certain degree, Martyn sees Paul's rejection of the law as a rejection of the Torah specifically, because of its exclusion of Gentiles. In Galatians, the antinomy of the old cosmos which Paul has especially in view, the passing of which he particularly wants to emphasize, is that of circumcision/uncircumcision, representing the division between Jews and Gentiles.[184] At the same time, there is a sense in which Martyn sees Paul's problem with the law as a problem with law in general, because of works. A key point in Paul's apocalyptic understanding is that the new creation is brought about by *God's* act rather than by any human effort or action.[185] Ultimately, however, neither of these is really the reason Paul rejects the law, according to Martyn's scheme; ultimately, Paul rejects the law not because of a problem with law-in-general or with the Torah-in-particular, but rather because law (in either/both senses) is part of the old cosmos.

At first glance, this may not seem significantly different from Sanders' answer, that Paul rejects the law because it is not Christ—and there are similarities.[186] But there is also a vast difference in how Martyn and Sanders understand the nature of Paul's argument. For Sanders, the issue is the basis on which people "get in" and "stay in"; Paul rejects the law because he is convinced that faith in Christ (participation in Christ) is the sole and universal basis for inclusion in the people of God. For Martyn, how one gets in or stays in is the concern of the Teachers, but *it is not Paul's concern*; what Paul focuses on is God's act in Christ.[187] There is, in other words, a completely different movement

---

[184]Martyn, "Apocalyptic Antinomies," 414; cf. idem, *Galatians*, 256: "What Law was it, specifically, from which Paul was separated by dying? The context provides the answer: It was the Law that distinguishes holy from profane, Jew from Gentile, thus enabling members of the holy people justly to exclude from their company those who are not holy (so the Antioch incident)." Cf. also ibid., 327: ". . . the universal power of the Law's curse consists precisely in its act in differentiating and separating observant from nonobservant, pious from the godless, Jew from Gentile."

[185]To say it the other way around, the old cosmos—which includes observance of the law—equates to what is "merely human" (Martyn, "Events," 165, 168; cf. idem, *Galatians*, 258, 263, 271). This certainly resonates with Luther's view, especially as filtered through Bultmann and Käsemann, though of course with significant differences.

[186]For example, Martyn and Sanders would agree that justification and law are *not* the central categories for understanding Paul, and that Paul's thought did not *begin* with a problem with the law.

[187]Cf. Martyn, "Events," 164–65. According to Martyn, Paul does not simply reject the Teacher's insistence on the law for "getting in," nor does he offer an alternative method of entry as such (i.e., faith). On the contrary, what Paul rejects is their whole frame of reference, their "cosmos." His argument "silences the Teacher's themes not by

in view. Rather than the movement of humans into the people of God—thus focusing on human deeds and human choices—Paul is describing God's invasion of the cosmos.[188] Rather than disputing the conditions for membership, Paul is announcing a new reality.[189] Rather than debating the role of the law, Paul sets law aside as a feature of the old cosmos, which God has brought to an end.[190]

If the law has been set aside along with the old cosmos, it should follow that the law *cannot* play any role in the ongoing life of the believer. At times, this is exactly what Martyn seems to say:[191] To take up the law as the antidote to the flesh (as the Teachers have urged) is to step back into the *old* cosmos, to "abandon life in the Creation that has now been made what it is by the advent of Christ and of his Spirit."[192] With the dawning of the new creation, the law is shown to be not the antidote to, but rather the ally of sin; it is in fact an inimical power which enslaves and from which we need release.[193] It is rather the Spirit which effectively opposes the flesh, having emerged in the new creation to wage

---

contradicting them, properly speaking, but rather by being composed, as it were, on a radically different musical scale" (ibid., 162; cf. idem, *Galatians*, 22–23).

[188]Martyn, "Events," 167–68, esp. n. 18.

[189]Note that according to Martyn, Paul is not even arguing that *faith*—in the sense of human faith in God—is the condition for membership. Though Paul obviously speaks about humans having faith, his main concern is God's action in Christ's faithful death (ibid., 168–69). Here Martyn is following George Howard, "On the Faith of Christ," *HTR* 60 (1967): 459–84; Richard B. Hays, *The Faith of Jesus Christ: An Investigation of the Narrative Substructure of Galatians 3:1–4:11*, SBLDS 56 (Chico, CA: Scholars Press, 1983); Sam K. Williams, "Again *Pistis Christou*," *CBQ* 49 (1987): 431–47; Morna D. Hooker, "ΠΙΣΤΙΣ ΧΡΙΣΤΟΥ," *NTS* 35 (1989): 321–42; *pace* Dunn, "The Theology of Galatians."

[190]Again it should be emphasized that it is not just law-observance which Paul sets aside, but also non-law-observance. One might say that in the new creation, the term "law" has ceased to have any meaning.

[191]Cf. Martyn, "Events," 164: "Gaventa charts a helpful course when she finds in Paul's christology the major clue to his insistence on the singularity of the gospel, *devoid of even the most "reasonable" admixture of Law observance*" (emphasis added). Martyn's reference is to Beverly R. Gaventa, "The Singularity of the Gospel: A Reading of Galatians," in *Pauline Theology*, vol. 1, ed. J. M. Bassler (Minneapolis: Fortress, 1991), 147–59. Gaventa hypothetically asks of Paul, "Why *not* observe the law—even if it is not obligatory? . . . It surely cannot adversely affect their Christian lives, and it might help to restrain their enthusiastic or libertinistic tendencies" (ibid., 151). Gaventa argues (and Martyn seems to agree) that Paul sets up an exclusive antithesis between Christ and the law, such that even "reasonable" law observance, carried out for the sake of controlling behavior, is out of the question.

[192]Martyn, "Apocalyptic Antinomies," 418; cf. idem, *Galatians*, 39.

[193]Ibid., 28, 272–73, 311, 327; idem, "Apocalyptic Antinomies," 416.

war against it; Christian behavior must therefore arise out of life in the power of the Spirit.[194]

Martyn's apocalyptic framework would thus seem to leave no room for the law to have any positive role whatsoever—and yet it does: "There is indeed a positive relationship between the Law and daily life in the church."[195] The tension arises, of course, from the tension within Galatians itself. How can one reconcile Paul's *positive* statements about the law with his scathing rejection of it? The main answer that Martyn gives is based on another "apocalyptic antinomy" that has come to light with the dawning of the new creation:[196] Paul has come to the realization that there is an antinomy within the law itself, an antinomy between its *cursing* voice and its *promissory and guiding* voice, and that the voice which curses is not the voice of God.[197] It is therefore only the promissory and guiding voice which has ongoing relevance for the believer:[198] "Whereas Paul refers in 5:3 to the voice of the Sinaitic Law that curses and enslaves ... he speaks in 5:14 of the voice of the original, pre-Sinaitic Law that articulates God's own mind."[199]

Martyn's approach is not without some problems, not the least of which concerns the plausibility of a Paul who holds the sort of "fractured" view of the law described above.[200] Whether or not one is persuaded that Paul has divided

---

[194] Martyn, "Events," 176–77; idem, *Galatians*, 479ff.

[195] Martyn, *Galatians*, 27.

[196] Martyn hints of some other answers: the law now provides only "an indicative portrait" of Christian behavior, not prescription and exhortation (Martyn, *Galatians*, 27); to "fulfill" the law is not the same as to "do" the law (ibid., 487–88); Christ has completed the law, bringing it to fulfillment in the love commandment (ibid., 489–91). All of these, however, seem to be secondary to the intra-law antinomy. It must be supposed that what is descriptive, what is fulfilled, what is completed is the law in its *positive* sense, i.e., the promissory and guiding voice rather than the cursing voice; cf. ibid., 504–14.

[197] Martyn's understanding of this antinomy is based almost entirely on Galatians 3. For example, Paul sets one scripture against another in 3:11–12, not to reconcile them, but to *emphasize* their contradiction. Lev 18:5 and Hab 2:4 are not both part of the same monolithic structure of scripture, as the Teachers supposed, but represent different voices (Martyn, "Textual Contradiction," 183–190; idem, *Galatians*, 328–34). In Gal 3:13 and 3:19, Paul expresses the crucial realization that the cursing voice of the law is not God's voice—that the law which curses has its origin, not with God, but from angels (idem, *Galatians*, 300, 320ff, 354–58). We will examine this issue in greater detail in chapter 3.

[198] Martyn, *Galatians*, 37, 504–14.

[199] Ibid., 504.

[200] Cf. the critique of Hübner by Sanders, *PLJP*, 67–68: "We would have to suppose that, when he wrote Galatians, Paul was prepared to deny what he had been taught and believed all his life, that God gave the law; that he structured the argument of Galatians 3 around the premise that God did not give the law, but rather 'saved' the situation after it was given; that he reverted to the view that God gave the law when he wrote Romans;

the law into two voices, however, there is a more serious and yet more subtle issue of division at work in Martyn's depiction of Paul's view of the law. Martyn, along with virtually every other scholar, separates soteriology and behavior. Throughout his discussion of Galatians 2–4, Martyn focuses on the theme of "rectification." Paul is rejecting the law *as a means of setting things right*, announcing instead that it is God who has set things right in Christ.[201] In effect, Martyn, like Barclay, concedes Sanders' point. Paul's negative remarks about the law concern its attempted *soteriological* use; his positive remarks about the law concern its application to Christian behavior.[202]

A more general problem with Martyn's approach has to do with the thoroughness with which he applies apocalyptic to the letter. Everything Paul says seems to be forced through an apocalyptic sieve.[203] Moreover, even though it includes some general apocalyptic elements (notably "antinomies" and warfare), this particular apocalyptic sieve, as depicted by Martyn, has a shape peculiar to Paul alone (especially when it comes to the "fractured" view of scripture). As a result, Martyn has difficulty recognizing or accounting for any element of continuity in Paul's thought. On the one hand, he vigorously denies any sense of salvation history in Paul's thinking, not only in Galatians, but even in Ro-

---

and that he had even changed his mind about who gave the law when he wrote the Corinthian correspondence, which most scholars date at approximately the same time as Galatians." (Though Hübner's understanding of Paul and the law differs significantly from Martyn's, Sanders' critique attacks the point at which Martyn and Hübner agree, namely that God did *not* give the Sinaitic law.) A further concern with Martyn's position is whether Paul is really using "law" in such different ways. Though Martyn certainly proposes a different distinction than those traditionally advanced, such as ceremonial vs. moral or law that is "legalistically applied" vs. law that is not, it is not clear how his distinction escapes the same problems; cf. Sanders, *PLJP*, 96ff.

[201] See esp. Martyn, *Galatians*, 249–51, 271–73, 301, 310, 314. Martyn offers an understanding of rectification that differs from the traditional understanding of "justification"; it is not forgiveness or atonement of sins, but rather redemption from enslaving powers that Paul has in view (ibid., 272–73). Nevertheless, this remains a *soteriological* focus.

[202] Cf. ibid., 251: "On the contrary, *as regards salvation*, observance of the Law and the faith of Jesus Christ constitute a genuine antinomy"; likewise, ibid., 261n50: ". . . one of Paul's basic convictions: When considered *salvific*, observance of the Law belongs on the human side of the divine/human antinomy" (emphasis added to both quotations). Ironically, though Martyn rejects the whole scheme of "getting in" and "staying in," he effectively makes very nearly the same distinction here. On the other hand, by speaking of the "promissory voice" of the law, Martyn does leave room for the law, or at least some parts of it, to point ahead to Christ.

[203] Cf., e.g., the comments above, n. 176, concerning his interpretation of συστοιχέω and ἀντίκειμαι.

mans.[204] On the other hand, he can offer little in the way of explanation for how Paul could have arrived at views so remarkably divergent not only from Judaism, but even from his Jewish-Christian contemporaries.[205]

In spite of these and various other problems,[206] however, Martyn's approach has much to offer our investigation. Together with Barclay's insights concerning identity and behavior, we begin to see some promising alternatives for understanding the background of Galatians in general and Paul's rejection of the law in particular. What remains to be seen, of course, is to what extent any of these alternatives are supported by and/or help to explain the features of the text; in particular, we need to see how they contribute to our understanding of Paul's use of the citations in Galatians 3. Accordingly, we now turn our attention to a survey of approaches to these citations.

---

[204]Cf. Martyn, "Events," 172ff; cf. the much more balanced approach of Barclay, *Obeying the Truth*, 96ff, who sees in Paul elements of both continuity (salvation history) and discontinuity (apocalyptic), and indeed, finds in the tension between these an explanation for the tension in some of what Paul says about the law.

[205]Martyn does not directly engage the question of how Paul arrived at his unique apocalyptic understanding of Christ. He does seem to suggest that the key event in the process was, not surprisingly, the cross and resurrection: "Paul takes his bearings from the conviction that in the event of the crucifixion there was a collision between the Law and God's Christ (3:13)" (Martyn, "Events," 170). When Jesus was cursed by the law as one crucified, but vindicated as Messiah by God's resurrection, the "cursing voice" of the law was shown not to be God's voice (idem, *Galatians*, 257, 275, 307, 320, 325–26). This goes some ways towards explaining Paul's rejection of the law, but not very far towards explaining the extremity of his apocalyptic. Cf. Sanders, *PLJP*, 25–26, who critiques similar ideas from Beker, Schweitzer, Harvey, and Hooker, calling it "plausible as a line of reasoning" but arguing that Paul does not actually reason this way.

[206]Not directly relevant to the current investigation, but still troubling, is Martyn's methodological confidence (overconfidence?) in his ability to reconstruct and imaginatively participate in not only the Galatians' hearing of the letter, but also Paul's writing of it—even to the point of knowing Paul's intentions in writing; cf. Martyn, "Events," 160–61. This methodological issue particularly surfaces with a statement such as the following: "The Galatians will have sensed his doing that; he will have anticipated their doing so; he will have intended them to do so" (ibid., 166).

Chapter 3
SUMMARY AND ANALYSIS OF RECENT SCHOLARSHIP: PAUL'S USE OF SCRIPTURE

In comparison to the history of investigation on Paul and the Law, investigations of Paul's use of scripture seem to be few and far between—but only in comparison. There has been no lack of interest in the subject through the years, and in recent times that interest has greatly increased.[1] What was true of our survey of Paul and the law must therefore also be true of our survey of Paul's use of scripture. Rather than attempting to describe the history of scholarship in detail, we will limit our survey to those aspects which have particular relevance to the current investigation. Accordingly, though the first section below sketches out an overview of issues concerning Paul's use of scripture in general, it does so with particular attention to how these issues play out in Galatians 3, especially in recent investigations. Meanwhile, the second section below focuses specifically on ways that scholars have addressed particular problems raised by the citations in Galatians 3.

GENERAL APPROACHES TO PAUL'S USE OF SCRIPTURE

The task of the following section is very briefly to sketch out some of the concerns and approaches scholars have brought to the investigation of Paul's use

---

[1] Recent monographs on Paul's use of scripture include E. Earle Ellis, *Paul's Use of the Old Testament* (Edinburgh: Oliver & Boyd, 1957); Otto Michel, *Paulus und seine Bibel* (Darmstadt: Wissenschaftliche Buchgesellschaft, 1972); A. T. Hanson, *Studies in Paul's Technique and Theology* (London: SPCK, 1974); Dietrich-Alex Koch, *Die Schrift als Zeuge des Evangeliums: Untersuchungen zur Verwendung und zum Verständnis der Schrift bei Paulus*, BHT 69 (Tübingen: J. C. B. Mohr; Paul Siebeck, 1986); Richard B. Hays, *Echoes of Scripture in the Letters of Paul* (New Haven: Yale University Press, 1989); Christopher D. Stanley, *Paul and the Language of Scripture: Citation Technique in the Pauline Epistles and Contemporary Literature*, SNTS 74 (Cambridge: Cambridge University Press, 1992).

of scripture in general, but with particular interest in how these general investigations touch on Galatians 3. A general investigation into Paul's use of scripture must obviously extend far beyond Galatians 3, but at the same time Galatians 3 provides a convenient focus, a convenient example, for illustrating the concerns of such an investigation, since any such investigation must take into account the concentration of scripture in Galatians 3. (Conversely, any investigation which includes Galatians 3 is likely to give at least some attention to the question of Paul's use of scripture, as we will see in the second section below.) As a way of organizing these general investigations of Paul's use of scripture, we will undertake this survey under two headings: Paul as *quoter* of scripture, and Paul as *interpreter* of scripture.

THE MECHANICS OF CITATION: PAUL AS QUOTER OF SCRIPTURE

To investigate Paul as *quoter* of scripture is to be concerned primarily with what might be called "essentially technical" issues:[2] Where and how often does Paul cite scripture? What source(s) does he use in citation—does he cite from a Hebrew or Greek *Vorlage*, or from some other written source, or from memory? How can we identify a citation, as opposed to an allusion or simply a use of common language—how does Paul signal or introduce citations? These are the sorts of questions that have dominated many of the investigations of Paul's use of scripture, particularly those of earlier decades.[3]

What particularly gives rise to this sort of question is what we might call Paul's consistently inconsistent citation of scripture. At times, he scarcely mentions scripture at all, much less cites it; at other times his citation of scripture is so full and frequent that it threatens to overwhelm the reader. At times, his citations are in strict agreement with the texts known to us in extant Greek versions of the Old Testament; once or twice his citations agree instead with the text of

---

[2]This description comes from Hays, *Echoes*, 9, though he includes within the "essentially technical tasks of scholarship" the comparison of Paul's exegetical methods with other Christian and non-Christian interpreters of his day; I have reserved this task for the discussion of Paul as interpreter of scripture below. This distinction is somewhat artificial, as most investigations of Paul's use of scripture in this century have given at least some attention to Paul's interpretation of scripture. For example, even Stanley, who carefully limits his focus to Paul's "citation technique," which he describes as the "mechanics" of the citation process (Stanley, *Paul and the Language of Scripture*, 3–5), also touches on the extent to which Paul's technique reveals and is influenced by his interpretive strategy.

[3]Koch, *Schrift*, and Stanley, *Paul and the Language of Scripture*, represent the culmination of this sort of investigation. Also very helpful is D. Moody Smith, "The Pauline Literature," in *It is Written: Scripture Citing Scripture. Essays in Honour of Barnabas Lindars, SSF*, ed. D. A. Carson and H. G. M. Williamson (Cambridge: Cambridge University Press, 1988), 265–91.

the Masoretes; quite often, his citations vary to a greater or lesser degree from every known text, Greek or Hebrew.[4] Frequently Paul marks off his citations with clearly distinguishing formulae (for example, "as it is written"), but from time to time he incorporates a citation so smoothly into his own composition that the unwary reader is apt to pass over it without recognition. Furthermore, these different citation practices may all occur within a single letter, even with respect to citations drawn from a single book of scripture.[5] As with the Synoptic Problem in the study of the gospels, it is the tantalizing inconsistency—the combination of agreements and disagreements, the nagging discrepancies and exceptions to every model—that gives rise to the puzzle.[6]

Certainly no small part of the difficulties posed by the citations in Gal 3:1–14 can be described along these lines. Galatians 3–4 contain some of Paul's most concentrated uses of scripture, and yet in the first two chapters of the letter he makes use of no citations at all, and in the last two chapters only one.[7] Two of the six citations in Gal 3:1–14 are clearly introduced as scripture (Dt 27:26 in 3:10 and Dt 21:23 in 3:13, both introduced with γέγραπται), while at least two are seamlessly integrated into Paul's own diction (Gen 15:6 in 3:6; Hab 2:4 in

---

[4]It is not at all uncommon to see this issue discussed in terms of Paul's use of "the LXX" or "the Hebrew text," but such unqualified terms tend to obscure significant text-critical issues. Was there such a thing as *the* LXX available to Paul? To what extent had the text of the Jewish scriptures—in Greek or Hebrew—been standardized? Are the texts to which we now have access, which for the most part postdate Paul by several centuries, adequate representatives of the text(s) to which Paul may have had access? What part should Paul's citation of scripture play in the text-critical reconstruction of texts—should his citations be seen as independent witnesses, weighing in favor of certain readings, or should they rather weigh against certain readings, due to the likelihood of assimilation? Part of the discussion of Paul's use of scripture has, of course, been directed to precisely these sorts of text-critical questions. For a careful examination, see Stanley, *Paul and the Language of Scripture*, 37–51.

Fortunately, for the purposes of the current investigation, the question of the precise text(s) from which Paul quotes, while interesting, is of secondary importance. In the survey of scholarship below, therefore, the term LXX will be used rather loosely, often dependent on the usage of the scholar under examination, or to refer to the commonly available text found in Rahlf's *Septuaginta*.

[5]Cf. ibid., 69.

[6]For a convenient summary presentation of the data, see Smith, "The Pauline Literature," 267–76, especially the table on pp. 270–72.

[7]Even in chapters 3–4, there is a very long stretch devoid of citations or even much allusion to any particular passage of scripture (i.e., 3:17–4:20, in which Paul talks only about the law or scripture in general). By no means does this invalidate the common observation that Paul's use of scripture is concentrated in those places where he addresses the relationship of Jews and Gentiles in the church, but it does perhaps suggest the need to proceed cautiously in determining the full scope and significance of such an observation—a task which unfortunately cannot be pursued here. Cf. Hays, *Echoes*, 6–8.

3:11).[8] Though it is generally accepted that Paul's use of scripture depends on a Greek *Vorlage*, none of the citations in this passage precisely agrees with the LXX, and yet the disagreement occurs in different ways and to different degrees.[9]

It is this last point that has garnered the most attention. What is the significance of the fact that Paul's citation of scripture does not always agree with the texts we have? Many early investigations, particularly motivated by apologetic concerns, tended to approach the variance in Paul's citations as unconscious and/or non-deliberate in nature. They are evidence for Paul's use of an alternate text form, or for his tendency to quote from memory, or for his habit of making his own translations from a Hebrew *Vorlage*, or so on.[10] For the most part such explanations have largely been discredited or discarded by modern scholarship.[11]

Increasingly, scholars are seeing the divergences in Paul's citations as *deliberate* alterations made by Paul in order to convey or reinforce the point of his argument. This is the explicit conclusion of two recent major studies of Paul's citation technique, one by Dietrich-Alex Koch, and the other by Christopher D. Stanley. In particular, Koch concludes that Paul's use of scripture reflects and is dictated by his understanding of scripture as a witness of the eschatological age which has now come to fruition in Christ; Paul therefore cites scriptures in ways

---

[8]How seamlessly the citations are integrated is, of course, a somewhat subjective judgment on the part of each scholar; here I am following Stanley, *Paul and the Language of Scripture*, 37, 66. Stanley sees the citation of Lev 18:5 in Gal 3:12 as clearly indicated by its syntactic tension with its context; he is apparently following Koch, *Schrift*, 13–14—but note that Koch also sees the citation of Gen 15:6 in Gal 3:6 as clearly indicated for the same reason. I am not entirely persuaded that either citation stands in *syntactic* tension with its context; what is clear is that Paul incorporates these citations into his argument in quite a different and less obvious way than those introduced by γέγραπται.

[9]The claim that a given citation agrees or disagrees with the standard Greek or Hebrew texts varies from scholar to scholar, depending partly on what is used as "the standard text" (cf. n. 4 above) and partly on what counts as agreement and/or where the citation is considered to begin. Thus, for example, Smith, "The Pauline Literature," 271, lists the citation of Gen 15:6 in Gal 3:6 as the one instance in this passage fully in agreement with the LXX, while Stanley, *Paul and the Language of Scripture*, 234–35, identifies in the same citation two changes from the LXX.

[10]Cf. ibid., 8ff.

[11]Ibid. Of these now largely discarded explanations, the one most likely still to occur is that the variances in Paul's citations are evidence for Paul's use of an alternate textual tradition; see for example Max Wilcox, "'Upon the Tree'—Deut 21:22–23 in the New Testament," *JBL* 96 (1977): 85–99.

that help to draw out this witness.[12] Similarly, Stanley concludes that Paul deliberately alters citations of scripture as needed to suit his rhetorical and theological purposes.[13] Interestingly, a similar understanding appears to be assumed implicitly in a number of investigations which concern or touch on specific citations in Gal 3:1–14.[14]

The Hermeneutics of Citation: Paul as Interpreter of Scripture

When one begins to talk about *intentional* alterations, one begins to move beyond the issue of Paul as quoter of scripture to Paul as *interpreter* of scripture. The question of Paul's interpretation of texts goes well beyond his alteration of them, of course; quite apart from the way he *cites* a given text, Paul often seems to *use* scriptures in ways that are altogether out of keeping with their original context and intent. One need only mention one of the most obvious examples to see the problem. In Romans 10, Paul reworks Dt 30:12–14, a passage that in its own context clearly argues for obedience to the law as something that is well within human ability, into an argument *against* "the righteousness from the

---

[12] Koch, *Schrift*, 186–90; 322–53. Hays, *Echoes*, 105, makes a similar point: "If the ends of the ages have come upon Paul and his readers, then all God's dealing with Israel in the past—as recounted in Scripture—must have pointed toward the present apocalyptic moment. If God was authoring the sacred story, then all the story's narrative patterns must foreshadow the experience of the community that has now encountered the apocalypse of God's grace." See also Dietrich-Alex Koch, "Der Text von Hab 2 4b in der Septuaginta und im Neuen Testament," *ZNW* 76 (1985): 68–85, in which Koch concludes that Paul and the author of Hebrews deliberately altered the original LXX text of Hab 2:4b (ὁ δὲ δίκαιος ἐκ πίστεώς μου ζήσεται, preserved in B and various other mss.), to suit their own purposes; variants in other LXX mss. are to be explained by assimilation with the citations in Romans, Galatians, and Hebrews.

[13] Stanley, *Paul and the Language of Scripture*, 252–64, esp. 259ff.

[14] Whenever an author derives conclusions about Paul's intended meaning based, in part, on his *alteration* of his presumed *Vorlage*, it seems safe to say that the author assumes Paul is deliberately altering his text in order to suit the purposes of his argument. A common example of this sort of argument concerns Paul's alteration of the LXX text of Hab 2:4 to exclude the word μου; cf. H. D. Betz, *Galatians: A Commentary on Paul's Letter to the Churches in Galatia*, Hermeneia (Philadelphia: Fortress Press, 1979), 147; J. Louis Martyn, *Galatians*, AB 33A (New York: Doubleday, 1997), 314; D. Moody Smith, "Ο ΔΕ ΔΙΚΑΙΟΣ ΕΚ ΠΙΣΤΕΩΣ ΖΗΣΕΤΑΙ," in *Studies in the History and Text of the New Testament: In Honor of Kenneth Willis Clark*, ed. B. C. Daniels and M. J. Suggs, Studies and Documents 29 (Salt Lake City: University of Utah Press, 1967), 14–16. Discussions of Paul's citation of Dt 27:26 in Gal 3:10 often raise a similar idea, with the suggestion that Paul deliberately chose the LXX form over the Hebrew because the former emphasizes the word "all"; thus, as the argument generally goes, Paul indicates that the problem with the law is the impossibility of doing *all* (see below, 67).

law."¹⁵ Such a disregard for the original context would not be well received today, any more than would the alteration of a citation to suit one's argument. The question must be asked, "What hermeneutical principles guide—and perhaps even more important, legitimize—the way Paul both cites and interprets scripture?"

One way of addressing this question is to attempt to fit Paul's hermeneutical methodology into some sort of recognized category. At one extreme, such an effort might concede that Paul is merely using prooftexts—that he is in fact arbitrarily extracting scriptures and forcing them into a service for which they were never intended—but that in so doing, he is simply following the accepted conventions of his day.¹⁶ Much more common is the effort to describe Paul's methods in terms of "midrash" or "pesher" (or both), thereby not only relating Paul's practices to those of other Jewish interpreters (the rabbis; the community at Qumran), but also seeming to describe those practices in terms of a more acceptable and well-defined methodology.¹⁷ As Richard Hays has recently argued, however, such arguments have generally failed to show any consistent methodology at work, and ultimately amount to little more than an excusing of Paul's hermeneutical practice by way of an anachronistic historical precedent.¹⁸ We are

---

¹⁵Cf. Hays, *Echoes*, 1–5. A similar example from Gal 3:1–14 is found in Paul's citation of Dt 27:26, a passage which in its own context requires observance of the law, to support his argument *against* the law. As will be seen below, however, the citation itself, and not just its context, seems to be in tension with Paul's argument.

¹⁶So for example E. P. Sanders, *Paul, the Law, and the Jewish People* (Minneapolis: Fortress, 1983), 21–22, 53n25 (hereafter cited as *PLJP*); Betz, *Galatians*, 137–38. See below, 74–75.

¹⁷See for example E. E. Ellis, *Paul's Use of the Old Testament*, esp. 139–49; cf. Carol K. Stockhausen, "2 Corinthians and the Principles of Pauline Exegesis," in *Paul and the Scriptures of Israel*, ed. Craig A. Evans and James A. Sanders, JSNTSS 83 (Sheffield: JSOT Press, 1993); idem, *Moses' Veil and the Glory of the New Covenant: The Exegetical Substructure of II Cor 3:1–4, 6* (Rome: Pontificio Instituto Biblico, 1989). Philipp Vielhauer, "Paulus und das Alte Testament," in *Studien zur Geschichte und Theologie der Reformation*, FS Ernst Bizer, ed. Luise Abramowski and J. F. Gerhard Goeters ([Neukirchen-Vluyn]: Neukirchener Verlag, 1969), 51, as cited by Heikki Räisänen, "Paul's Theological Difficulties with the Law," in *Papers on Paul and Other New Testament Authors*, ed. E. A. Livingstone, Studia Biblica 3, JSNTSS 3 (Sheffield: JSOT Press, 1980), 316, rejects the view that Paul makes use of rabbinic methodology, but in so doing illustrates the assumption that the rabbis followed strict, if unhistorical, rules: "Paulus ... auch gemessen an der zeitgenössischen jüdischen Exegese den alttestamentlichen Texten Gewalt antut. Die rabbinische Exegese verfährt, wenn auch unhistorisch, so doch streng methodisch ... Die paulinische Exegese ist durch keine Methode reguliert, Paulus wechselt und mischt die Methoden nach Belieben."

¹⁸Hays, *Echoes*, 10–14. Particularly with respect to the rabbinic sources, the issue of dating any sayings to pre-Pauline practice is fraught with difficulty, so that "it is more

left still with the nagging suspicion that Paul uses scripture in ways that are either unacceptable or unconvincing to the modern mind.[19]

Hays himself offers a different approach. Rather than describing or justifying Paul's methodology in terms of practices contemporary with Paul, Hays applies insights drawn from the modern discipline of intertextuality.[20] Though at first glance this may seem like an even worse anachronism, the key to this approach is the recognition that intertextuality is not so much a modern methodology as it is an ongoing phenomenon: "Intertextuality" describes the way(s) that authors have *always* grappled with predecessor texts.[21] What is particularly of interest to Hays, therefore, is not to justify Paul's interpretation of scripture in terms of a particular rabbinic or Hellenistic methodology, but rather to explore the meaning which drives and shapes (and is shaped by) his "echoing" of scripture, to describe the hermeneutical lens which focuses and directs Paul's hermeneutical practice. Hays finds this focus to be Paul's ecclesiology.[22]

Hays' description of Paul's hermeneutic as ecclesiocentric is in part a conscious challenge to the common claim (or assumption) that Paul's use of scripture is christocentric:[23] Though Paul does at times apply scripture specifi-

---

valid methodologically to use Paul as a background source for the study of rabbinic traditions than vice versa" (ibid., 11). On the issue of midrash as a methodology, cf. Gerald L. Bruns, "The Hermeneutics of Midrash," in *The Book and the Text: The Bible and Literary Theory*, ed. Regina M. Schwartz (Cambridge, MA: Basil Blackwell, 1990), 189–213.

[19]Cf. Richard N. Longenecker, *Galatians*, WBC 41 (Dallas: Word Books, 1990), 110: "Before we comment directly on vv 6–14, however, the obvious must be said: Paul's exegesis of Scripture in these verses (and throughout the rest of chaps. 3 and 4) goes far beyond the rules of historico-grammatical exegesis as followed by biblical scholars today." Cf. Hays, *Echoes*, 9.

[20]See chap. 4 below for a more extensive discussion of intertextuality.

[21]Hays, *Echoes*, 14–21. Daniel Boyarin has argued that rabbinic midrash in particular is essentially an intertextual activity; see Daniel Boyarin, *Intertextuality and the Reading of Midrash* (Bloomington: Indiana University Press, 1990); idem, "The Song of Songs: Lock or Key? Intertextuality, Allegory, and Midrash," in *The Book and the Text: The Bible and Literary Theory*, ed. Regina M. Schwartz (Cambridge, MA: Basil Blackwell, 1990), 214–30; cf. also Gerald L. Bruns, "Midrash and Allegory: The Beginnings of Scriptural Interpretation," in *The Literary Guide to the Bible*, ed. Robert Alter and Frank Kermode (Cambridge, MA: Harvard University Press, 1987), 625–46.

[22]Hays, *Echoes*, 84ff.

[23]Hays identifies, as some of those who have made arguments in support of the claim that Paul's interpretation of scripture is christocentric, Ellis, *Paul's Use of the Old Testament*, 115–16; Richard N. Longenecker, *Biblical Exegesis in the Apostolic Period* (Grand Rapids: Eerdmans, 1975), 104–105, 205–209; and C. E. B. Cranfield, *A Critical and Exegetical Commentary on the Epistle to the Romans*, 6th ed. (Edinburgh: T & T Clark, 1975–1979), 2:867. A. T. Hanson, *Studies*, 262, takes it for granted that Paul interprets christocentrically: "Christ discovered [Paul], and he used the tradition of exegesis in which he had been educated to interpret the scriptures christocentrically." Similar as-

cally to Christ (e.g., the "seed" in Gal 3:16), he more often sees scripture functioning to instruct the church or to portray its situation. Certainly this is the case in Gal 3:1–14, where Paul rereads the promised blessing to the Gentiles through Abraham in light of his Gentile churches' experience of the Spirit.[24]

While Hays' ecclesiological understanding of Paul's use of scripture has generated a good deal of interest and debate, it is by no means the first time that someone has challenged the common understanding of a christocentric emphasis or hermeneutic in Paul. Barnabas Lindars, for example, had already noted the absence in Paul's writings of the great christological texts found elsewhere in the New Testament (especially in the gospels), as well as the absence of arguments in proof of Jesus as Messiah.[25] Similarly, Philipp Vielhauer has argued that Paul's use of scripture is more *soteriological* than christological, that is, it is primarily focused on salvation through faith in Christ rather than through the Law.[26]

The difference between these various proposals for understanding Paul's use of scripture—soteriological, christological, ecclesiological—is not as great as it might first appear. Those who have argued for a christocentric hermeneutic in Paul, for example, have not necessarily thought that Paul uses scripture only or primarily to establish Jesus as the Messiah, but rather that Paul understands scripture in light of what God has accomplished in Christ, the transformation that he has wrought in the world—a transformation that includes not only salvation through faith, but also God's establishing of a people of faith, the church.[27] What is important to note in all of these proposals is a common perspective. Rather than primarily using scripture casuistically, to define and enjoin moral behavior, Paul tends to see scripture as the prefiguration of that which is now

---

sumptions and arguments routinely occur also in investigations of Paul not specifically concerned with his use of scripture; see for example J. Christiaan Beker, *Paul the Apostle: The Triumph of God in Life and Thought* (Philadelphia: Fortress, 1980), 109–31, esp. 120–21; Sanders, *PLJP*, 5, 41.

[24]Hays, *Echoes,* 105–11.

[25]Barnabas Lindars, *New Testament Apologetic: The Doctrinal Significance of the Old Testament Quotations* (Philadelphia: Westminster, 1961), 247.

[26]Vielhauer, "Paulus und das Alte Testament," 43.

[27]Certainly for Beker, in spite of his christocentric understanding of Paul's hermeneutic (*Paul*, 120–21), the key concept, and indeed the coherent center of Paul's thought, is found in "the imminent cosmic triumph of God. Indeed, after the Christ-event, the imminent apocalyptic triumph of God already discloses its proleptic presence in history to the eyes of faith in the power of the Spirit and so foreshadows its public manifestation in glory, when 'God will be everything to all things'" (ibid., 19). Similarly, Sanders, though he speaks of Paul's christological reading of scripture (Sanders, *PLJP*, 5, 41), denies that Jesus as Messiah is central or even very evident in Paul's thinking (ibid., 25–26); rather, Paul's central concern, at least in Galatians, is the relationship between Jews and Gentiles in the church.

coming to fulfillment through Christ in the church.²⁸ In a sense, for Paul, scripture contains or describes the *shape* of God's saving activity through history, which prefigures the shape of the church.

EFFORTS TO DEAL WITH TENSIONS:
PAUL'S USE OF SCRIPTURE IN GALATIANS 3:1–14

All of the issues and approaches sketched out above have in common their attention on resolving *external* tensions in Paul's use of scripture; that is to say, they address the tension between Paul's citations and his *Vorlage*, or between Paul's interpretation of scripture and our own hermeneutical conventions, or so on. One must wonder, however, whether such tensions would have existed for Paul's intended audience. Would the Galatians, for example, even have recognized—or cared—that Paul had altered the wording of the citations? Likewise, would they have noticed anything peculiar or questionable in Paul's hermeneutical tendencies? Whether or not his readers would or could have discerned these external tensions does not, of course, reduce our need to address them.²⁹ But it does raise a question: are there any *internal* tensions in Paul's use of scripture that *would* have been obvious even to someone who might come to the letter with a minimal background of scriptural expertise?³⁰

At least with respect to Galatians 3:1–14, there is in fact a more basic level of tension in Paul's use of scripture, a series of "internal" tensions that is evident apart from anything external to the letter itself. Immediately obvious to any reader of the letter is, first, tension between certain citations and the arguments

---

²⁸Smith, "The Pauline Literature," 275, 277.

²⁹Indeed, much of what follows below can been seen as an effort not only to reduce "internal" tensions, but also to reduce or remove some of the "external" tensions as well by showing that Paul's use of scripture is not quite as capricious or ill-considered as it may otherwise appear.

³⁰This might seem to raise the question of whether, without some prior knowledge of the scriptures Paul cites, the Galatians would even have recognized the citations *as* citations. We cannot, of course, go very far in commenting on the literary perspicuity or scriptural expertise of Paul's readers, but certainly with respect to Gal 3:1–14, they could not miss the overt indications that at least some scripture is being cited ("as it is written . . ."). Furthermore, Stanley, *Paul and the Language of Scripture*, 37, 65–66, has argued that, of the four citations in this passage not overtly introduced by γέγραπται, three can be distinguished as citations on other grounds. The one exception is the citation in Gal 3:11 of Hab 2:4—a passage which, one could certainly argue, would be as likely to be known to a Pauline congregation as any text; cf. W. M. Ramsay, *A Historical Commentary on St. Paul's Epistle to the Galatians*, 2ⁿᵈ ed. (London: Hodder and Stoughton, 1900), 346: "It is noteworthy that he gives [Hab 2:4] as a formal quotation, when writing to those who had not heard his teaching [i.e., to the Romans]; but to the Galatians he uses [it] as a familiar axiom."

to which Paul applies them, and second, tension between the claims advanced by at least two of the citations. Nearly every investigation of Galatians 3, on the way to an exegesis or interpretation or application of the passage, has noted and attempted to resolve or explain some point or another of such internal tension. We therefore turn to a summary and analysis of such attempts below.

Tension Between Paul's Argument and the Citations

The structure of Galatians 3:10 seems very clear. Paul first advances a thesis ("All who are of works of law are under a curse") and then cites Dt 27:26 in support ("for it is written, 'Cursed is everyone who does not abide by all things written in the book of the law, to do them'").[31] There is only one problem: rather than supporting Paul's thesis, the citation appears to say the very opposite.[32] According to Dt 27:26, there is indeed a curse, but it falls precisely on those who do *not* remain in and do the law, not on those who do. If the structure of Paul's argument is obvious, so also is the internal tension generated by the way Paul has used scripture within that structure.

The tension between Paul's argument and the citation of Dt 27:26 is intensified by his use of Lev 18:5 two verses later. As he continues his argument *against* observance of the law, Paul cites a scripture that apparently promises life to those who *do* the law: "The one who does these things will live by them." Indeed, the combination of Dt 27:26 and Lev 18:5 seems to make an unassailable case for observing the law. One is cursed if one does *not* do the law, but receives life if one *does* do it. Furthermore, it must be noted that it is the citations *as Paul cites them*—even apart from their original context or intent—that are at odds with his own argument. How can this tension be resolved?

---

[31]Cf. Longenecker, *Galatians*, 108: "Structurally, . . . the movement of the argument in vv 10–12 rests on three sets of particles, each of which introduces a statement and then a biblical text in support." See further discussion of the function of this and other citations in chap. 5 below.

[32]This tension is explicitly recognized by Betz, *Galatians*, 145: "On the surface, Deut 27:26 says the opposite of what he claims it says." The explicit recognition of this tension is nothing new; see for example Ernest De Witt Burton, *A Critical and Exegetical Commentary on the Epistle to the Galatians*, ICC (Edinburgh: T & T Clark, 1921), 164–65. Quite often, however, commentators have masked any awareness of the tension by their immediate introduction of one of the solutions outlined below (most often the "missing premise").

Two "Standard" Solutions

The "Missing Premise"

By far the most common solution to the problem is to understand the tension as both requiring, and supplying the primary evidence for, a "missing premise," a premise so obvious to Paul that he simply failed to mention it: "No one can actually do all the law."[33] With this missing premise supplied, the logic of Paul's argument becomes perfectly clear. Anyone who does *not* do *all* the law is under a curse (premise supplied by Dt 27:26); no one can do all the law (missing, but assumed, premise); therefore anyone under the law is under a curse (stated conclusion).[34] Given the simplicity of this solution, it is not surprising that it has garnered the support of scholars from Luther to the present.[35]

What is particularly interesting about this approach is that it advances the missing premise not simply as a way to resolve the tension in Paul's argument, but as one of the major points of that argument. What Paul is really getting at, the point he really wants to drive home, is the very thing he does not say, namely, that no one can perfectly fulfill the law.[36] There is a certain "intertextual" quality to this approach, in that it finds the meaning of the text, or at least the essential clue to its meaning, in the unstated but yet resonant intertextual

---

[33] Indeed, the missing premise appears to be so self-evident to many commentators that the tension is scarcely seen; cf. J. B. Lightfoot, *Saint Paul's Epistle to the Galatians* (London and New York: MacMillan, 1896), 137; Longenecker, *Galatians*, 117–18; Ronald Y. K. Fung, *The Epistle to the Galatians*, NICNT (Grand Rapids: Eerdmans, 1988), 142; etc.

[34] The logical form as expressed above is that of syllogism, though it can be expressed in other ways; see further discussion in chap. 5 below. The logic can be described similarly in the case of Lev 18:5: one who does the law thereby receives life (Lev 18:5); no one can do all the law (assumed); therefore, the law cannot give life.

[35] The summary of this approach given above largely follows Thomas Schreiner, "Is Perfect Obedience to the Law Possible? A Re-Examination of Galatians 3:10," *JETS* 27 (1984): 151. As noted above, 18, Schreiner is the most vigorous proponent of this approach in recent years. For a response to Schreiner's position, see Michael Cranford, "The Possibility of Perfect Obedience: Paul and an Implied Premise in Galatians 3:10 and 5:3," *NovT* 36 (1994): 242–58.

[36] Cf. H. J. Schoeps, *Paul: The Theology of the Apostle in the Light of Jewish Religious History*, trans. H. Knight (Philadelphia: Westminster, 1961), 175: "Paul's intention is to demonstrate the 'unfulfillability' of the law as its intrinsic meaning"; F. F. Bruce, *The Epistle to the Galatians*, NIGTC (Grand Rapids: Eerdmans, 1982), 159: "Here, however, he is concerned to stress the unfulfillable character of the law: by the standard of the law every one is 'under a curse' because no one is able to keep it in its entirety"; Robert H. Gundry, "Grace, Works, and Staying Saved in Paul," *Biblica* 66 (1985): 25: "Thus non-performance [of the law] lies on the main track, not on a spur, of his argument."

"space" between Paul's citation and his argument.[37] Whether this is the only or the best way to approach the problem from an intertextual perspective remains to be seen below.[38] In any case, the point of this approach is clear: Paul says that because humans cannot keep the law, they must therefore be saved by faith.

Unfortunately, in spite of the logical clarity that it brings to Paul's argument, and in spite of its venerable history and widespread support, this solution creates as many problems as it solves, if not more. E. P. Sanders, for example, has vigorously argued against the "missing premise" on two fronts. First, Jewish understanding of the law never supposed that perfect obedience to the law was either possible or necessary, either for maintaining the blessing or avoiding the curse; second, Paul himself actually claimed to be blameless in the law—presumably not because he had never committed a transgression, but because he had made use of the law's own provisions for repentance, atonement, and forgiveness.[39] To adopt the missing premise is therefore to make Paul either ignorant of his own religious heritage, or willing to caricature it almost beyond recognition. Though these arguments are in a sense "external" to the letter itself—they depend on a knowledge of Judaism and of Paul's other writings that may well have been unavailable to the Galatians—they have been enormously influential in recent years, and rightfully so.

Quite apart from such "external" issues, however, the "missing premise" solution suffers from *internal* problems as well. It solves one internal tension only

---

[37]Cf. Schreiner, "Is Perfect Obedience to the Law Possible?" 156: "Fuller's objection here is that such a view adds the implied proposition to the verse that no one can keep the law entirely, and he thinks this is indefensible. However, the presence of an implied proposition should not be excluded out of hand. Implied propositions are, after all, a common feature of human language." There is also a sort of intertextual flavor to the view that sees, in Paul's use of the LXX rather than the Hebrew text of Dt 27:26, a deliberate emphasis on the word "all," which is not present in the Hebrew; cf. e.g. Schoeps, *Paul*, 176; Hans Hübner, *Law in Paul's Thought: A Contribution to the Development of Pauline Theology*, trans. J. C. G. Greig, Studies of the New Testament and Its World (Edinburgh: T & T Clark, 1984), 19.

[38]See below, chap. 5. Cranford, "The Possibility of Perfect Obedience," 248, rejects Schreiner's reasoning concerning the common use of implied propositions: "Schreiner's argument is as follows. 'All bachelors are men. Tom is a man.' What should be obvious is that it is *not* logical to accept the implied proposition, 'Tom is a bachelor.'" Cranford's critique suffers from one major flaw: he argues as if Schreiner is treating the implied proposition as a *conclusion*: "In fact, to *derive* that from the previous two statements is a formal fallacy" (ibid.; emphasis added). If, on the other hand, one asks of Cranford's example, "What premise is needed to arrive at the conclusion, 'Tom is a man'?" then certainly one can make a very good case that "Tom is a bachelor" completes a logically valid argument.

[39]See above, 28; cf. George Howard, *Paul: Crisis in Galatia. A Study in Early Christian Theology*, SNTSMS 35 (Cambridge: Cambridge University Press, 1979), 49–54.

to create a quagmire of other internal tensions, all revolving around the application of the law and its curse to Paul's Gentile readers. On the one hand, if in 3:13 Paul is including the Gentiles in the "us" whom Christ has redeemed from the curse of the law[40]—if the curse of the law has *already* applied to his Galatian readers—then why is performance of the law even in dispute? If the Galatians are already cursed for non-performance of the law, already in need of redemption from that curse, how could they be any more cursed—or any less redeemed—if they, like Jewish Christians, take on the law?[41] They are no worse off if they attempt to keep the law, even knowing that they cannot keep it perfectly, and indeed they may find it helpful for moral guidance.[42]

If, on the other hand, it is only the Jews whom Paul sees as redeemed from the curse of the law in 3:13,[43] then the "missing premise" leads to two equally unsatisfactory options. Either one should avoid the law altogether in order to avoid its curse—and thereby also to have no need to be redeemed—or else one could or even should join with the Jews in being under the law, in order to experience with them the redemption from it. In other words, either Gentiles do not need to be redeemed (not being under the law), or they need to be under the law in order to experience the redemption which Christ has accomplished (since he redeems from the curse of the law).[44] Needless to say, neither of these options seems compatible with Paul's thinking.[45]

---

[40]So Bruce, *Galatians*, 166–67; Charles B. Cousar, *Galatians*, Interpretation (Atlanta: John Knox, 1982), 77; Martyn, *Galatians*, 317; Lloyd Gaston, "Paul and the Law in Galatians 2 and 3," in *Paul and the Torah* (Vancouver: University of British Columbia Press, 1987), 74; G. Walter Hansen, *Abraham in Galatians*, JSNTSS 29 (Sheffield: JSOT Press, 1989), 96; Howard, *Crisis in Galatia*, 58–62.

[41]Note that, in Jewish understanding, Gentiles would by definition fall under the law's curse, since they are outside the law and thus do not keep it; hence the designation of Gentiles as "sinners" (cf. Gal 2:15).

[42]Howard, *Crisis in Galatia*, 52–53, poses a similar objection to the missing premise approach. Howard, however, bases his argument on the assumption that, for Paul and for all early Christians, Jewish Christians *were* expected to *continue* in the law; it is only Gentiles for whom Paul is so adamant that they not take up the law. This raises questions that cannot be satisfactorily explored here, but given Paul's vehement confrontation with Peter over *Peter's* law-observance (Gal 2:11ff), it seems difficult to assume that Paul completely agreed that Jewish Christians should continue to practice the law.

[43]So Betz, *Galatians*, 148; Burton, *Galatians*, 169; Lightfoot, *Galatians*, 139; Longenecker, *Galatians*, 121; Richard B. Hays, *The Faith of Jesus Christ: An Investigation of the Narrative Substructure of Galatians 3:1–4:11*, SBLDS 56 (Chico, Calif.: Scholars Press, 1983), 113.

[44]Betz, *Galatians*, 145–46, rejects the missing premise on grounds which are somewhat similar to the above, though his argument is a bit too abbreviated to be entirely clear. Noting that Paul never actually states the missing premise in the letter, but rather says the opposite, Betz goes on to observe that "the Law was given to generate sin; sin is

The point at which the "missing premise" runs into difficulty, with each of the above objections, is in the assumption that the real issue has to do with *performance* (or rather, non-performance) of the law. Not only does this assumption run contrary to the expectations expressed in Jewish writings (including Paul's own testimony) about the possibility of keeping the law, but also it runs into

---

not the result of man's inability to keep it but the necessary presupposition for salvation" (ibid.). If I understand Betz correctly, he is pointing to the dissonance between sin as defined by the missing premise (i.e., as failure to keep the law perfectly) and sin as Paul actually presents it (as something to which all are subject, regardless of their affiliation with the law).

⁴⁵There is a third option, along the lines proposed by Martin Noth, "'For All Who Rely on Works of the Law Are Under a Curse,'" in *The Laws in the Pentateuch and Other Studies*, trans. D. R. Ap-Thomas (Edinburgh: Oliver & Boyd, 1966), 118–31; N. T. Wright, *The Climax of the Covenant: Christ and the Law in Pauline Theology* (Minneapolis: Fortress, 1992), 137–56; James M. Scott, "'For As Many As Are of Works of the Law Are Under a Curse' (Galatians 3.10)," in *Paul and the Scriptures of Israel*, ed, C. A. Evans and J. A. Sanders, JSNTS 83 (Sheffield: JSOT Press, 1993); and Frank Thielman, *From Plight to Solution*, 67–68. Though there are significant differences among these scholars, they share in common an understanding of the curse in terms of the history of Israel. The issue is not whether one *can* keep the law, but rather is that Israel, in its history, *has not* kept the law, as evidenced by having already experienced the curse (in particular, the curse of exile). Christ's redemption from the curse of the law is therefore a redemption of the people of Israel, not so much from an ongoing inability to keep the law, but rather from the curse which has already been experienced; this redemption for Israel then opens the way for blessings to the Gentiles. One could thus understand Paul's arguments against the law as arguments against attempting to enter into an already completed historical sequence.

On the one hand, this approach may avoid some of the problems associated with the "missing premise," since it makes moot the question of *whether* one can keep the law by way of the historical appraisal that Israel apparently has not done so. On the other hand, it does run into a number of difficulties. First, it is not clear how Israel's history of failure speaks against the Galatians' desire to take up the law, unless the point is that the Galatians will likewise fail—but that then amounts to simply a variation on the "missing premise," and brings us back to the problems of the "missing premise" approach. Second, even if the curse has fallen on Israel for non-performance of the law, it does not seem to be the case that Judaism therefore looked for release from the law; on the contrary, the history of failure is presented more as encouragement to be faithful to the law than as a discouragement about the possibility of keeping it. Third, this approach does not account for the way Paul uses the citations in his argument. Rather than presenting Dt 27:26 as evidence for a historical curse, Paul presents it as an argument against *current* attempts to keep the law. Likewise, he does not draw the contrast between Hab 2:4 and Lev 18:5 in historical terms, e.g., between a "present-tense" means of life via faith and the "past-tense" failure of the promise of the law. In short, unlike Gal 3:1–5, where Paul does seem to be arguing on the basis of historical experience, Gal 3:6–14 seems rather to be discussing alternative existential choices.

problems explaining just exactly how the Gentiles fall under the curse by attempting to perform the law while avoiding the curse by failing even to make the attempt. If the real issue is *performance* of the law, if the curse from which humanity needs to be redeemed comes from failure to keep the law perfectly, then whether one attempts to keep the law and fails, or whether one ignores the law (and thus fails to keep it) is irrelevant. There seems to be no escaping the conclusion that performance of the law, adequately or inadequately, is not the issue Paul is addressing. Human inability to keep the law perfectly is therefore *irrelevant to Paul's argument.*[46]

Qualified Meaning of ἐξ ἔργων νόμου

The second common solution to the problem posed by Dt 27:26 is in some sense a response to the problems posed by the "missing premise." If inadequate performance of the law is not the issue Paul is addressing, perhaps the curse of which he speaks derives instead from misunderstanding or misuse of the law.[47] Rather than looking for a missing premise to complete the logic of Paul's argument, therefore, one can reconsider and redirect the thrust of that argument. This is, in effect, to resolve the problem by redefining the terms, in particular by seeing ἐξ ἔργων νόμου as a reference not so much to the law or its perfect performance, but rather to a particular attitude towards the law.

There are many variations on this theme. Perhaps the most extreme comes from Heinrich Schlier, who understands the significance of ὅσοι ἐξ ἔργων νόμου in terms of *doing* rather than *believing*. Those who are cursed are not just those who fail to keep the law perfectly, but rather those who even attempt to *do* the law, and thereby rely on doing, rather than having faith.[48] More common is the view of C. E. B. Cranfield, Daniel P. Fuller, and others, that Paul's emphasis on "works of law" refers to the Jewish distortion of the law into legalism. Those who are cursed, ὅσοι ἐξ ἔργων νόμου, are those who rely on legalism; Christ redeems us from the curse of legalism, freeing us to embrace the true purpose of the law.[49] More recently, J. D. G. Dunn has offered a "new perspective" on Paul,

---

[46] A further problem created by the missing premise has to do with the ethical instructions and positive remarks about the law later in the letter. Many of those who argue for the missing premise turn around and argue that the law should still be kept in some sense—"in Christ"—but that is precisely the condition the Galatians already find themselves in. They are in Christ, so why not do the law? Cf. Howard, *Crisis in Galatia*, 52–53; see above, n. 42.

[47] The contrast here is analogous to Hübner's distinction between the quantitative and qualitative; cf. Sanders, *PLJP*, 17.

[48] Heinrich Schlier, *Der Briefe an die Galater*, 10th ed., Kritisch-exegetischer Kommentar über das Neue Testament 7 (Göttingen: Vandenhoek & Ruprecht, 1949), 89ff.

[49] C. E. B. Cranfield, *Romans*, 2:848; Daniel P. Fuller, "Paul and 'The Works of the Law,'" *Westminster Theological Journal* 38 (1975): 28–42. Cf. Burton, *Galatians*, 163–

understanding ἔργα νόμου in terms of those specific "boundary markers" by which Judaism had excluded Gentiles; ὅσοι ἐξ ἔργων νόμου are those who misuse the law to serve a narrow, arrogant nationalism.⁵⁰

Whatever the individual strengths or weaknesses of each of these variations, they all share two problems.⁵¹ First, none of them directly resolves the problem of the tension between Paul's citation and his argument; indeed, they seem rather to exacerbate the tension. Whether Paul wants to say that the real problem with the law is reliance on "doing" (vs. "believing"), or that it is a legalistic or nationalistic distortion or attitude, Dt 27:26 does not help him, because it does *not* pronounce a curse on those who do the law, or who legalistically misunderstand it, or who nationalistically misuse it, but rather on those who *fail to do* the law.⁵² What this approach, in any of its variations, must therefore assume is that,

---

64: "The word νόμου is, as always in the phrase ἔργα νόμου, used in its legalistic sense ... and ὅσοι ἐξ ἔργων νόμου are not οἱ ποιηταὶ νόμου, of whom Paul says in Rom. 2¹³ that they will be justified, but men whose standing and character proceed from (ἐκ) works of legalistic obedience to statutes." Rudolf Bultmann, *Theology of the New Testament*, trans. K. Grobel (New York: Charles Scribner's Sons, 1951, 1955), 1:264–67, certainly embraces the view that the ultimate problem with the law is legalism, or more specifically, self-righteousness rather than dependence on God. However, he does not deal with this topic as a way to address the tensions in Gal 3:10. Gerhard Ebeling, *The Truth of the Gospel: An Exposition of Galatians*, trans. David Green (Philadelphia: Fortress, 1985), 178, does not use the word "legalism," but does resolve the problem with the citation in a similar way: "Everything depends on our interpretation of ἔργα νόμου .... Works of the law are works devoid of faith. As such they lead to the false faith of self-justification." Some have seen Ragnar Bring, *Commentary On Galatians*, trans. Eric Wahlstrom (Philadelphia: Muhlenberg Press, 1961), as one who understands the problem in terms of legalism; cf. Bruce, *Galatians*, 158. Bring's position is actually a bit more subtle. The problem with the law is not exactly legalism in the usual sense, but rather is a misunderstanding about the availability of righteousness through the law. Paul now understands that the law never actually claimed to produce righteousness; those who are cursed, ὅσοι ἐξ ἔργων νόμου, are those who still mistakenly suppose that they can obtain righteousness through observance of the law (Bring, *Galatians*, 115–25).

⁵⁰See above, 30–31. Cranford, "The Possibility of Perfect Obedience," takes a position substantially similar to Dunn's.

⁵¹See above, 31–33, for an evaluation of Dunn's approach; cf. also 40–42. The approach which focuses on legalism (Cranfield, Fuller, and others) has come under severe critique from E. P. Sanders; see especially *PLJP*, 23–24, 154ff. The most significant point of Sanders' critique is the refutation of the common assumption that Judaism was a legalistic religion.

⁵²Schlier's position, in particular, takes Paul to be saying the exact opposite of what Dt 27:26 says, since Dt 27:26 pronounces the curse on those who do *not* do the law, not those who do or attempt to do it; cf. Thomas R. Schreiner, *The Law and Its Fulfillment: A Pauline Theology of Law* (Grand Rapids: Baker Books, 1993), 50; idem, "Is Perfect Obedience to the Law Possible?" 159; Cranford, "The Possibility of Perfect Obedience," 245.

once again, something is missing from Paul's argument—not so much a missing premise, but rather a "missing qualifier" that transforms, for example, "anyone who does not do the law" into "anyone who attempts to do the law" (or "anyone who legalistically relies on the law," or "anyone who nationalistically misuses the law").[53]

Certainly one could argue that Paul's use of the citations, in the context of his argument properly understood, implies just such a "missing qualifier."[54] But this leads to the second problem common to this sort of approach: the "missing qualifier" has to be imported, not only into the citations, but practically everywhere else as well. Paul *never* actually argues about qualifiers, but only about the law. He does not urge the Galatians to grasp a correct understanding of the law; he threatens them with excommunication if they so much as take up its most basic requirement (Gal 5:2, 4). Paul's point is not, "Correctly use (or correctly understand) circumcision"; rather he says, "Do not be circumcised."

If one takes any of the approaches sketched out above, it is hard to see why circumcision (or any other practice of the law) should be such a problem, so long as one does not rely on it for salvation (or approach it legalistically or nationalistically)—precisely because Paul provides us with no such argument.[55] We might have expected Paul to admonish the Galatians to come to the correct understanding of circumcision, or to adopt the proper attitude towards it. Since instead he rules it out altogether, we should certainly expect him to explain why circumcision is intrinsically incompatible with the proper understanding or use of the law, why other commandments of the law can be "properly understood," but this one cannot. Nowhere does Paul do any such thing.

On the other hand, a similar point could be made about Lev 18:5. It does not associate life with those who *correctly understand* the law, but rather with those who "*do* these things."

[53]It is worth noting that the phrase ὅσοι ἐξ ἔργων νόμου does not occur within any of the citations. The more that one's understanding of Paul's argument depends on a particular definition of ὅσοι ἐξ ἔργων νόμου, therefore, the more that one is in danger of distancing Paul's argument from the citations that supposedly support that argument; one must either qualify what the citations "really" refer to—i.e., not to the law or its performance, as they seem to say, but rather to the improper understanding of the law—or assume that Paul is simply twisting the scripture to suit his own ends.

[54]In other words, one could argue that, given the way Paul uses the citations, he must have understood (or we must understand) Dt 27:26 to say, "Cursed be anyone who does not do the law *in the right way* [or *with the right attitude*]," Lev 18:5 to say, "The one who does these things *in the right way* [or *with the right attitude*] will live by them."

[55]Someone like Dunn might argue that circumcision is inevitably nationalistic, i.e., that one cannot ever take up circumcision without invoking its role as a boundary marker. This argument has some merit, but it does not answer the objections raised against Dunn's position above (see above, 40–42). Why *not* ask the Gentiles to become Jews, especially since Paul *does* describe them as children of Abraham?

It might, of course, be argued that verses such as Gal 5:6, 14; 6:2, 15 indicate some qualification of how one should use or understand the law in general, and circumcision in particular. Indeed, it is precisely these verses that give the most support to the various approaches sketched out above. Closer examination of these verses, however, shows that such an argument suffers from a number of problems. First, the extent to which these verses qualify the law and/or circumcision depends primarily on the exegetical construction of the interpreter, and not on what Paul directly says. While Paul does note in passing that life in the spirit *will fulfill* the law (whatever exactly "fulfill" means), that is far different from saying that he wants the Galatians to take up the law with a properly qualified understanding or attitude. Second, Paul's explicit instruction to the Galatians is *not* to take up the law at all (5:3–4), but *instead* to walk by the spirit (5:16)—in which case *they will not be under the law* (5:18). Third, Paul's twice-repeated statement that circumcision is a matter of indifference in Christ (5:6; 6:15) hardly offers a clear qualification of how one might take up the proper practice of circumcision, particularly in light of the harshness of 5:2–4. It must be said again: when Paul speaks about doing the law, taking up the law, being under the law, he *never* qualifies it—he only rejects it.

Other Solutions

The Citations as Incidental to Paul's Thought

The effort to reconcile the tension between Paul's argument and the citations contains its own hidden assumption, namely the assumption that what is said in and by the citations must be factored in as a constitutive part of the meaning of the passage—that the citations add their own meaning to what Paul is saying, and that their meaning is partly determinative of the meaning of Paul's argument. It is precisely this assumption that E. P. Sanders has challenged when he describes the citations as nothing more than proof-texts. Rather than helping to determine the meaning of what Paul is saying, Sanders argues, it is the other way around. The proof-texts should be understood to mean (at least for Paul) only what Paul says they mean.[56] Thus, for example, Paul uses Dt 27:26 simply because it is the only verse in the Old Testament which combines the words *law* and *curse*; whatever else the verse might say is irrelevant, so long as it provides a sort of scriptural precedent for his own assertion combining law and curse:[57] When Paul says that "those who are of works of law are cursed," that is all that Dt 27:26 means for Paul in this argument.[58]

---

[56] Sanders, *PLJP*, 21–22
[57] Ibid., 21.
[58] Sanders argues the same way concerning Lev 18:5: all that citation means is that faith and law have nothing to do with one another (ibid., 22).

Sanders is not alone in taking this sort of approach. H. D. Betz, in his influential commentary, comes to much the same conclusion:

> We cannot expect more from Paul's method than what was expected in his own time. It was expected that a proof could demonstrate by some agreed method that one's ideas and notions were attested by or contained in the passage referred to as evidence. The basic skill, therefore, was to find passages in the Scriptures which had the same terminology one was using in the argument.[59]

For both Betz and Sanders, then, the tension between the citation and Paul's argument is to be resolved in favor of what Paul says.[60]

Recently, Christopher Stanley has offered what at first glance appears to be a critique of this approach, but which in the final analysis amounts to a variation of it.[61] On the one hand, he explicitly rejects Sanders' terminological approach:

> The fundamental problem with this [i.e., Sanders'] explanation is that it fails to take account of the seriousness of the 'curse' envisioned by Paul in the present passage—so serious in fact that it required the crucifixion of Jesus Christ to annul it (v. 13) before God's 'blessing' could come upon the Gentiles (v. 14). However it is to be understood, the 'curse' of Deut 27:26 is clearly regarded by Paul as a genuine ontological possibility for at least a portion of humanity, and not as a mere verbal stepping-stone in a fundamentally terminological argument designed to show that righteousness is not by the law.[62]

On the other hand, Stanley's own solution, based on rhetorical analysis and reader response criticism, focuses not on the "theological content" of the citations in the passage, but rather on "their *function*, i.e., the specific role played by each element with a carefully constructed argument aimed at producing a particular persuasive effect upon a specific audience within a concrete historical situation."[63] The function of Dt 27:26 in Gal 3:10 is not to describe an actualized curse, but rather to threaten the Galatians with the *potential* curse inherent in the

---

[59] Betz, *Galatians*, 137–38.

[60] Cf. ibid., 146.

[61] Christopher D. Stanley, "'Under a Curse': A Fresh Reading of Galatians 3:10–14," *NTS* 36 (1990): 482–511.

[62] Ibid., 485.

[63] Ibid., 486; cf. ibid., 491–92: "It becomes all the more vital that the modern interpreter keep one question in mind at every point in attempting to analyze Paul's letter to the Galatians: how does this fit into Paul's strategy to persuade his Galatian readers? Too often a single-minded focus on Paul's 'theology' or his 'opponents' has been allowed to obscure this fundamental question . . . . This attempt at persuasion will of course require him to confront opposing points of view, which may in turn lead him to introduce explicit theological formulations into his argument where it appears to suit his purpose. But it is Paul's persuasive intent that remains primary at every point, and the modern interpreter must read all that he says in the light of this concern or else risk misunderstanding."

law.⁶⁴ In effect, according to Stanley, Paul tells the Galatians not only that they can experience the promised blessing of Abraham apart from Torah observance, but also that those who take up Torah observance "have much to lose, since the threat of God's 'curse' continues to hang over all who fall short in any respect."⁶⁵

Stanley's argument is attractive in many respects, the most important of which is his distinction between an actualized curse and a potential curse, based in part on his distinction between Paul's use of ὑπὸ κατάρας and the citation's use of ἐπικατάρατος.⁶⁶ Unfortunately, Stanley's argument suffers from two major weaknesses. First, Stanley seems both to deny and to affirm the "missing premise." On the one hand, Stanley agrees that the classic "missing premise" understanding of these verses falters not only because Paul feels confident in his own ability to keep the law, but also because the idea that no one can perfectly keep the law is not actually relevant to the argument.⁶⁷ On the other hand, in order for this potential curse to function effectively as a threat with which to deter the Galatians from taking up Torah observance, Stanley continually suggests that Paul highlights the idea that Torah observance is precariously difficult, if not completely impossible.⁶⁸ Second, Stanley argues that Paul tries to shut the door on any potentially positive outcome of Law observance (such as the possibility that one might succeed in gaining life by doing the law) by denying the

---

⁶⁴Ibid., 495, 500–501

⁶⁵Ibid., 495.

⁶⁶Ibid., 499–500. Stanley argues that Paul uses ὑπὸ κατάρας in Gal 3:10a (instead of the ἐπικατάρατος that might have been expected both as a parallel with the citation in Gal 3:10b and as a contrast with the εὐλογοῦνται of Gal 3:9) to express the potential or threat of curse, rather than actualized curse, precisely because the curse in Dt 27:26 is pronounced on those who *fail* to do the law, and because in the citation itself the curse is not "an event that has already occurred," but rather is a threat to deter certain behavior.

⁶⁷Ibid., 482–83.

⁶⁸Stanley suggests that Paul's wording of the citation makes "the 'conditions' more stringent: (a) the *manner* of 'continuing' is specified as 'doing them' (i.e., good intentions are not enough), and (b) the *degree* of the required 'continuing' is qualified by reference to '*all* that is written' (i.e., not just obedience to the majority or 'most important' of the provisions of Torah)" (ibid., 500); he also emphasizes that the curse awaits "all who fall short *in any respect*" (ibid., 495; emphasis added), and that "the law itself pronounces a curse on anyone who fails to live up to *every single one of its requirements*" (ibid., 500; emphasis added). To be sure, in the citation of Dt 27:26, "the door remains open . . . for any who *do* fully obey the law to avoid the reality of this 'curse'"—but Stanley adds the qualification, "at least in theory" (ibid., 500). Stanley sums up his reading of the passage in this way: "The result is to leave the Galatian Gentile reader who wants to abide by the Torah in a no-win situation: observing Torah can add nothing to what faith promises in regard to 'life', but it can still place anyone who falls short of *perfect* fulfilment under God's 'curse'" (ibid., 505; emphasis added).

law's claim to provide life in Lev 18:5.⁶⁹ Thus, in effect, Stanley's attempt to resolve the tension inherent in the citation of Dt 27:26 only reinforces the tension between the citations of Hab 2:4 and Lev 18:5.⁷⁰

In the final analysis, then, Stanley has not actually advanced very far beyond the arguments of Betz and Sanders. Stanley argues that the tension between Paul's argument and the citation of Dt 27:26 arises only when we think of an actualized curse, since the actual curse would fall not on those who do but on those who do not do the law. But as a *potential* curse, the citation serves as a threat to the readers, thus supporting Paul's rhetorical purpose, to persuade them away from the law. In effect, this threat functions only if the readers disregard what the citation actually says (unless, as Stanley seems to suggest, Paul slips in the "missing premise" that no one can perfectly do the law) and instead attend to Paul's effort to draw a connection between law and curse.

In essence, what Sanders, Betz, and Stanley all propose, though in different ways, is that the function of the citations in Paul's argument is based not on what a citation itself *says*, but only on what it *does*. What a citation says is important only to the extent that it contains a few crucial words that link it into Paul's argument; what the citation does is to act as a sort of authoritative, rhetorical bludgeon with which to threaten or persuade his readers—so long, perhaps, as they do not look too closely at what the citation actually says!⁷¹ But Sanders, Betz, and Stanley go a step further: not only is this Paul's practice, but it is also the common practice of his time, both in rabbinic circles and in Hellenistic rhetoric. We need not be embarrassed by his exegetical irresponsibility, but rather, with a proper appreciation of the historical precedents, we should admire his skillful use of accepted rhetorical and/or rabbinical practice.

What Sanders, Betz, and Stanley have thus conceded is that there *is* a perceptible tension between what the citations say and what Paul says, at least for us; they simply deny that such tension was a problem—or even evident—to Paul and/or his contemporaries. In some sense, therefore, this approach simultaneously elevates the authority of Paul's intentions (we have to understand the citations based on what Paul meant them to say), even while it undermines the authority of his method (by *his* standards this was an acceptable use of scripture,

---

⁶⁹Ibid., 501–504.

⁷⁰Stanley points out that the citations would not have constituted a contradiction in Jewish thinking, but suggests that the way Paul places them in combination *forces* a sharp and direct contrast: "By placing ὁ νόμος in direct contrast to the ἐκ πίστεως picked up from the Habakkuk citation, v. 12a declares the law to be absolutely disqualified as a channel leading to 'life', despite its promises, for the simple reason that 'doing the law' is not 'faith'" (ibid., 504).

⁷¹Cf. Sanders, *PLJP*, 53n25: "Paul's argument proves the case to those who are convinced by proof-texts."

but of course we know better).[72] In any case, the question that must be explored further below is whether it is even possible (much less permissible) to ignore the content of a citation, even if we can apprehend its intended function. Once Paul has invoked a citation, is it possible for it *not* to contribute to the meaning of the passage, not just by its presence, but also by what it says?[73]

The Citations as Arguments from Paul's Opponents

C. K. Barrett, J. Louis Martyn, and others offer yet another approach to the problem of the tension between Paul's citations and his argument. If some of the citations seem to say the opposite of what Paul is trying to say, it is because they were chosen, not by Paul, but by his opponents.[74] The logic of this approach is quite simple. Surely Paul would not himself choose such unsuitable citations; therefore those citations must already have been brought to the table by others. Paul had to include them in his own discussion only because he must, somehow, overcome the weight of his opponents' scriptural exegesis: "Paul's words can be best explained if we may suppose that he is taking up passages that had been used by his opponents, correcting their exegesis, and showing that their Old Testament prooftexts were on his side rather than on theirs."[75]

This approach, like the previous one, essentially concedes the tension between Paul's citations and his argument. Indeed, according to Martyn, it is precisely because of the tension that we can be confident that the "Teachers" were responsible for introducing Dt 27:26 into the debate:

> In the present verse Paul interprets Deut 27:26 in a way that is the precise opposite of its literal meaning . . . . He might have selected this text in order to

---

[72]Even in Stanley's "reader-response" approach to the passage, the focus seems to be more on the rhetorical effect Paul intended to achieve than on the effect any actual readers may or may not have experienced. One might say that this is a reader-response method that is focused on the "implied reader," but Stanley seems more often to look to Paul, and not just to the text or to the "implied author," for the rhetorical intentions that shape his understanding of the passage.

[73]This question is relevant not just for modern readers of Paul's letter, but also for his original readers/hearers. Even if they, too, held it to be acceptable to use scriptures as proof-texts in the sense argued by Sanders, et al., is it possible for the content of the citations *not* to play some part in how the letter was understood? One certainly can imagine, at the very least, that some of the agitators would be more than ready to point out the discrepancy between Paul's arguments and the scripture he cites!

[74]C. K. Barrett, "The Allegory of Abraham, Sarah, and Hagar," in *Essays on Paul* (Philadelphia: Westminster Press, 1982), 158–59; Martyn, *Galatians*, 294ff, 328–34.

[75]Barrett, "Allegory," 158.

stand it on its head, but it seems probable that his concern is to turn one of the Teachers' texts against them.[76]

Whereas proponents of the previous approach generally point to historical precedent (rabbinic and rhetorical practice in the use of prooftexts) in an attempt to ameliorate the tension, this approach uses a historical reconstruction (the opponents' introduction of various scriptures into the debate) to explain only how the tension arose. Unfortunately, knowing how the tension came about does nothing to relieve that tension, no matter how plausible the historical reconstruction. Indeed, one is left with one of two impressions: either Paul lost the argument—because his own argument remains so obviously at odds with the citations which, even if they first came from the opponents, he finds himself bound to repeat—or he cites the opponents' scriptures only to deny their validity by countering them with a different set of scriptures of his own (for example, Lev 18:5 countered by Hab 2:4). The latter impression brings us to the second type of tension found in Paul's use of citations in Gal 3:1–14: Paul uses citations in a way that seems to pit one scripture against another.

Tension Between Citations

The Problem: Contradictory Citations

Just as the tension between Paul's citations and his argument should be obvious even to someone lacking in scriptural expertise, so also should the tension between two of the scriptures Paul cites. In Galatians 3:11–12, Paul quotes two scriptures of which each seems to advance a claim about the true path to life, one from Habakuk 2:4 ("The righteous shall live by faith"),[77] and the other from Leviticus 18:5 ("Those who do these things shall live by them"). In Jewish

---

[76]Martyn, *Galatians*, 309.

[77]There has been a long-running argument over the exact translation of this verse, in particular with respect to how ἐκ πίστεως functions in the sentence (as a modifier of ὁ δίκαιος or of ζήσεται); for a discussion of the issues, see Smith, "Ο ΔΕ ΔΙΚΑΙΟΣ ΕΚ ΠΙΣΤΕΩΣ ΖΗΣΕΤΑΙ"; H. C. C. Cavallin, "'The Righteous Shall Live by Faith': A Decisive Argument for the Traditional Interpretation," *Studia Theologia* 32 (1978): 33–43. Richard B. Hays, "The Righteous One as Eschatological Deliverer," in *Apocalyptic and the New Testament: Essays in Honor of J. Louis Martyn*, JSNTSS 24, ed. J. Marcus and M. L. Soards (Sheffield: JSOT Press, 1989), 191–215, has recently proposed a "Messianic" reading of the verse, understanding ὁ δίκαιος as a reference to Christ. For our present purposes, however, the choice of one (or none) of these readings over another makes little difference. In each case, the primary contrast interpreters have drawn has to do with how life is *gained*. Hab 2:4 indicates that life is gained by faith—whether by the Messiah's faith, or by the faith of the one who is righteous, or the faith that makes one righteous—while Lev 18:5 promises life to those who "do these things." See below, 169–73.

thought, of course, these two claims are not incompatible; doing of the law is how one demonstrates and enacts one's faith, and faithful obedience results in (or continues one in) life.[78] Paul, however, seems deliberately intent on forcing a contradiction:[79] He first declares that justification by law *is not possible*, and clearly so, since "the righteous will live *by faith*"; he then drives home the point by declaring that law and faith have nothing in common, since the law's own claim to life is based, not on faith, but on "doing these things." It would appear, in short, that Paul presents the two citations as competing claims for how one gains life.[80] How can these claims, both contained in scripture, be reconciled?[81]

Two "Standard" Solutions

No Contradiction, No Problem

The most common solution to the problem is to show, in some way, that there is no actual contradiction between the citations. Most often, such an argument depends, once more, on the "missing premise":[82] There is no actual contradiction involved between these two verses of scripture, as long as one keeps in mind the unstated but extremely important premise, "No one can actually keep all the law." What Lev 18:5 offers is a *theoretically* true promise of life: in *theory*, anyone who actually does keep the law will live. In fact, however, no one can keep the law; in practice it is therefore only by faith that one

---

[78]Cf. Nils A. Dahl, "Contradictions in Scripture," in *Studies in Paul: Theology of the Early Christian Mission* (Minneapolis: Augsburg, 1977), 170: "A pious Jew would see no contradiction here: for him, keeping the commandments is part of genuine faith." Cf. Howard, *Crisis in Galatia*, 63: "The whole law and the Prophets were fundamentally and primarily concerned with faith in God with all that that implied .... Paul would have been laughed off the scene even to have suggested a contrary notion."

[79]Cf. Stanley, "'Under a Curse,'" 504; J. S. Vos, "Die Hermeneutische Antinomie bei Paulus (Galater 3:11–12; Römer 10:5–10)," *NTS* 38 (1992): 257; Martyn, *Galatians*, 328–34.

[80]While these verses have normally been understood in terms of *gaining* life, we will argue below against this common understanding; see below, 169–73.

[81]The question assumes, of course, that they must be reconciled. This assumption is not shared by all scholars; see below, 82–84.

[82]See above, 67; cf. Hübner, *Law*, 19ff; idem, "Pauli Theologiae Proprium," *NTS* 26 (1980): 461ff. Note that Hübner further qualifies Paul's use of scripture in this passage by his understanding of several different intentions involved in the law. The intention of the law itself was not deceptive, since its promise (Lev 18:5) was theoretically true; the intention of the angels who gave the law, however, was to provoke sin and thus defeat humanity, while the intention of God was to use it in bringing all humanity to salvation (*Law*, 24–30).

can receive justification and life. Thus both citations are true—one in theory, and the other in practice.[83]

Certainly one of the strengths of the "missing premise" approach is that it thus offers an answer not only to the tension between Paul's argument and the citations, but also to the tension between citations. We have already seen, however, that the "missing premise" is not without serious problems with respect to the former, and many of those same problems would apply equally to the latter.[84] There is, however, an even more serious difficulty with the missing premise, a theological difficulty in terms of its understanding of God and his promises. According to this view, God essentially holds out what amounts to a false promise.[85] Even if Lev 18:5 is true in theory, it *is* false in practice—and worse yet, that precise combination, the fact that God offers a promise which he must certainly know can never be actualized, makes the promise seem not just false, but deceptive, the perpetration of a divine fraud.

It could, of course, be argued that this promise *was* actualized, by Jesus.[86] But the same exception would then apply also to the "missing premise". It is not that *no one* can keep the law perfectly, but rather *no one but Jesus*. These exceptions leave us with the same problems as before. On the one hand, Paul never actually says what he supposedly really meant; nowhere does he argue that Jesus is the lone exception to the premise that no one can perfectly keep the law. On the other hand, even if this is what Paul meant, it still leaves the promise of Lev 18:5 as a false promise—for everyone except Jesus. In effect, it would seem as though God were offering to *everyone* a promise which really belongs only to *Jesus*. Alternately, one could argue that Israel had misunderstood a promise meant only for the Messiah as though it applied generally,[87] but if this is what Paul has in mind, he certainly has hidden it well. Nowhere does he urge the Ga-

---

[83]Thus Schreiner, *Law*, 60–61; Gundry, "Grace," 24–25; Hübner, *Law*, 19. As demonstrated by Ebeling, *The Truth of the Gospel*, 177, one can use essentially the same distinction between theory and practicality to resolve the tension between Hab 2:4 and Lev 18:5 without necessarily embracing the missing premise: "Another possibility is to interpret the statement [of Lev 18:5] as a hypothetical contrary-to-fact condition: someone who really did what the law requires, someone whose works truly fulfilled the law, would have life thereby—but where is such a person to be found?" For Ebeling, no such person can be found because reliance on works ("the one who *does* these things," as Lev 18:5 says) inevitably leads to self-righteousness rather than faith in God.

[84]See above, 68–71.

[85]Alternately, one can argue that it is not God, but rather the law which offers a false promise—thus divorcing the law from God's intentions. This approach essentially concedes that the scriptures are in contradiction; see further below, 82–89.

[86]This argument has been made, though not necessarily as a corollary to the "missing premise" approach; see, e.g., R. Bring, *Galatians*, 128–42; C. E. B. Cranfield, *Romans*, 522n2.

[87]Cf. Gal 3:16.

latians to avoid the law because its promise of life only really applied to Jesus. Indeed, to take the promise of Lev 18:5 as meant only for Jesus ruins Paul's use of the citation. He *cannot* show that law and faith are incompatible by appealing to a promise which applies only to the one person who *did* perfectly combine law and faith.

If we take the missing premise approach, therefore, we are left with a promise in Lev 18:5 that must be seen as misleading at best, if not absolutely false.[88] It may be possible to accommodate the resulting picture of God,[89] but even so, a further issue remains. When all is said and done, one still has, if not an outright contradiction, at least an enormous tension between the citations. Paul holds up Hab 2:4 as the *right* way to gain life, and Lev 18:5—whether or not it is true or feasible in practice—as the *wrong* way. Even if both promises are true, in other words, they are not true in the same way, and only one is valid for the Galatians. In effect, in the effort to safeguard the consistency of scripture in the sense of *truth*, the missing premise approach has overlooked the consistency of scripture in the sense of *application*. One might be comforted to know that every promise she encounters in scripture is true in theory, until she realizes that she has no way of knowing whether a particular promise has any validity for her in practice.

Contradiction Is No Problem

The effort to eliminate the contradiction between Lev 18:5 and Hab 2:4 rests on the assumption that Paul would not intentionally (or even unintention-

---

[88]In general, *any* approach to resolving the tension between Hab 2:4 and Lev 18:5 by seeing the latter as only a theoretical possibility that cannot in practice be actualized will lead to the same problem, whether one arrives at that view by way of the missing premise or by some other avenue (see, e.g., n. 83 on Ebeling's view).

[89]It must be admitted that Paul does not feel obligated to hold God to our sense of "fairness," as Romans 9–11 amply demonstrates. Moreover, the missing premise approach can claim further strength to the extent that it anticipates (indeed, necessitates) Paul's own question: why would God *offer* such a promise, knowing as he did that it could never be actualized—or in other words, "Why then the Law?" The standard answer is that God gave the law to expose or increase sin, but this is an answer that comes more from Romans than Galatians (cf. Betz, *Galatians*, 161n1). What Paul says in response to his own question in Gal 3:19 is that the law "was added on account of transgressions" (τῶν παραβάσεων χάριν προσετέθη). The most natural reading of this phrase would seem to be that the law was added to restrain or control or otherwise respond to transgressions, rather than to increase or expose them. (For a more thorough treatment of this issue, see Betz, *Galatians*, 164–67; while Betz concludes that the law was given to *produce* sin, it is clear that he arrives at this conclusion primarily on the basis of Romans.) It should be noted, in any case, that the standard answer—the law given to provoke sin or to expose sin as sin—does not really ameliorate the problem of a God who holds out a false promise, even with the best of intentions.

ally) contradict one portion of scripture with another.[90] As we have just seen, however, even if we can somehow resolve the citations with each other, we still are left with the sense that Paul is, in effect, urging the Galatians to choose one scripture, and reject the other.[91] It may be, therefore, that we need to reassess that initial assumption. Is it possible that Paul would intentionally set up or point out a contradiction between two citations of scripture in order to prove his point? Is it possible that Paul might consider one portion of scripture to be valid, while another is not?

Ernest deWitt Burton takes a step in this direction in his discussion of Paul's use of Dt 27:26 and Lev 18:5:

> It is of capital importance for the understanding of the apostle's argument to observe that the sentence which he here quotes [Dt 27:26] does not at all express *his own* conception of the basis of God's judgment, but a verdict of law. This sentence, though stated negatively, implies the corresponding affirmative, viz., that he who faithfully performs all the things written in the book of the law lives thereby, and this is actually so stated as the principle of law in v.[12]: "He that doeth them shall live in them." That this is the principle of *God's* action towards men, *Paul expressly denies both directly and indirectly*.[92]

What Burton thus seems to imply is that, while Hab 2:4 correctly expresses "the principle of God's action towards men," Dt 27:26 and Lev 18:5 express something quite to the contrary of God's principle. But Burton is apparently unwilling to see an actual contradiction here;[93] it is not so much these scriptures which in and of themselves stand in contradiction to God's principle expressed in Hab 2:4, but rather the legalistic misunderstanding of the law, in its appeal to

---

[90]This assumption rests on at least two additional assumptions. First, the meaning of the text must be located in Paul's intentions, and second, scripture cannot contradict itself. We will not pursue the first of these for the moment (cf. below, 103–106). Note that the second of these assumptions need not necessarily be held as a matter of faith and conviction by the interpreter of Paul, so long as it is understood to be held by Paul himself (and so long as the meaning of the text is seen in terms of Paul's intentions). In essence, when one assumes that Paul would not intentionally contradict one scripture with another, one is assuming that, for Paul, all of scripture monolithically reflects God's own voice, God's own intentions and promises.

[91]Sanders, *PLJP*, 22, argues that, rather than setting the two citations up as alternatives, Paul uses Lev 18:5 only to prove his point that law and faith have nothing to do with each other. Even if that is all Paul intended to do, however, his juxtaposition of citations has left us with the strong impression of a contradiction.

[92]Burton, *Galatians*, 164–65.

[93]Burton does not use the word "contradiction" in his discussion, but it seems fairly clear that he would not be comfortable with an understanding that the scriptures were in actual contradiction; cf., e.g., his concern to preserve the "harmony of this position with the apostle's belief that the law is of God" (ibid., 165).

and incorrect interpretation of scriptures such as Lev 18:5, which forms the contradiction.[94]

What Burton has thus implied, but with qualifications, other scholars have made explicit. J. Christiaan Beker, for example, sees the contradiction between the citations as a deliberate and "daring" strategy on Paul's part:

> In a daring move, Paul opposes Scripture to Scripture (cf. Rom. 10:5–9) and thus splits Scripture apart, because Lev. 18:5 is antithetical to God's will in Christ. The law then seems indeed an antidivine agency.[95]

Similarly, Alain Gignac argues that Paul deliberately sets out to accentuate and exploit a tension that was only marginally present in the original contexts of the citations;[96] only by forcing the citations into contradiction can Paul support his argument, which presupposes the antithesis between Christ and the law.[97]

In many ways, the solution offered by Gignac and Beker (and in a limited way, by Burton) is rather elegant. Rather than making any attempt to resolve the contradiction, they celebrate it. In effect, they argue that, rather than being an embarrassing defect, the scriptural contradiction is part of the way Paul advances his argument. If Paul's point is that faith and law are incompatible, one should not be surprised to find him drawing a sharp contrast between those scriptures which illustrate faith and law.

---

[94]Ibid, 165; 169; 443ff, esp. 451–52. Other scholars would take a more-or-less similar view, that Paul cites Lev 18:5 to illustrate a misunderstanding of law, or at least a misunderstanding of God's intended principle of justification by faith; e.g., Fuller, "Paul and 'The Works of the Law,'" 30, 40–42; James D. G. Dunn, "Works of Law and the Curse of the Law (Galatians 3.10–14)," *NTS* 31 (1985): 227–28. This position suffers from some problems already discussed above (71–74); moreover, it, like the "missing premise" approach, does not really relieve the tension between the citations. According to this view, when Paul says that "law and faith have nothing in common," he is really speaking of the legalistic misunderstanding of law, not law itself—but then Paul must be citing Lev 18:5 *as an illustration of legalism*. Thus, Paul still cites one scripture which the Galatians are to follow, and one which, since it illustrates legalistic misunderstanding of the law, they should reject.

[95]Beker, *Paul the Apostle*, 54.

[96]Alain Gignac, "Citation de Lévitique 18,5 en Romains 10,5 et Galates 3,12," *Église et Théologie* 25 (1994): 367–403, esp. 370–75. Gignac supports his thesis largely by an examination of the textual changes Paul makes to the citations, changes that emphasize the tension between Lev 18:5 and Hab 2:4. In Paul's use of Lev 18:5 in Romans 10, incidentally, Gignac sees a very different strategy at work; there Paul does not push the citation into tension with Dt 30:12ff, but rather seeks to make it complementary.

[97]Cf. Dahl, "Contradictions," 170: "The whole train of thought in Gal. 3:1–12 rests on the presupposition that Hab. 2:4 and Lev. 18:5 contradict one another, and that the two corresponding principles 'by faith' and 'by (works of) the law' mutually exclude one another as qualifications for justification and life."

Elegant as it is, however, this solution is not without at least three interrelated problems. First, Lev 18:5 and Hab 2:4, as they are usually understood, do more than simply *illustrate* faith and law; they make competing claims about the basis for justification and life—and only one of these claims can be valid. Therefore, according to this approach, Paul is saying that *only one of these scriptures is valid*.[98] But this leads directly to the other two problems. On the one hand, how can Paul credibly appeal to one scripture to support his own arguments if, at the same time, he is willing to deny the validity and authority of another?[99] Has he not "shot himself in the foot" by thus indicating that scripture is not universally authoritative? On the other, how is it that Paul has come to such an understanding of scripture, or how can he justify such an understanding? Where does Paul provide the rationale for determining which scriptures are valid and which are not?

J. Louis Martyn's apocalyptic approach supplies a possible answer to at least some of these problems. As Martyn understands it, the whole point of Paul's argument, the basis for his gospel, is that the old world—including that aspect of the world in which scripture was a unified authority—has come to an end in Christ:

> [Paul] takes his bearings from the good news that in Christ—and thus in the act of *new* creation—God has invaded the cosmos. Paul does not argue, then, on the basis of a cosmos that remains undisturbed, a cosmos that he shares with the Teachers. A basic part of his message, in fact, is the announcement of the death of that shared cosmos with its legal elements, and the emergence of the new cosmos with its new elements ... [Gal 3:11–12] suffices to show that Paul cannot and does not argue on the basis of the assumed integrity of the cosmos to which the Teachers point when they speak of "the Law."[100]

Nevertheless, Paul does appeal to scripture in his argument against the Teachers. Indeed, according to Martyn, it is precisely because the Teachers have mounted an exegetical argument in favor of the law that Paul must take up their own scriptures and turn them against the Teachers' position.[101] Paul accomplishes this by showing that the scriptures cited by the Teachers, as well as other scriptures that they might later cite (e.g., Lev 18:5), do not speak with the blessing voice of God—represented by certain scriptures such as Hab 2:4—but rather

---

[98]For Burton (and generally for those who approach the passage from the perspective of a legalistic misunderstanding of the law), both scriptures are valid, but Lev 18:5 must be carefully qualified to show how it is compatible with faith (i.e., to show how to understand it apart from legalism, which is what it apparently illustrates in Paul's argument). In effect, we have to introduce yet again a "missing qualifier"; see above, 73.

[99]See below, 147–53.

[100]Martyn, *Galatians*, 22.

[101]Ibid., 294ff.

with the cursing voice of the law. He thus defeats the Teachers' exegetical argument by denying their fundamental assumption, that the law represents the voice and will of God.[102]

One of the most innovative features of Martyn's argument is his understanding of Paul's use—or rather, radical alteration—of a standard five-step model for dealing with contradictory texts, current in both Hellenistic and Jewish circles, which Martyn calls the Textual Contradiction.[103] The standard, "relatively fixed" form of the Textual Contradiction, as Martyn presents it, is as follows:

1. An assertion, or halakah, by party A
2. Citation of an authoritative text supporting party A's position
3. A contradictory assertion, or halakah, by party B
4. Citation of an authoritative text supporting party B's position (thus a text contradictory to that cited in step 2)
5. "One of the parties wins the debate by giving a new interpretation to his opponent's text, being thereby able not only to honor both texts as aspects of the indivisible law but also to show that, correctly read, both texts support his own assertion."[104]

According to Martyn's reconstruction, Paul *anticipated* that the Teachers would make use of the Textual Contradiction, and that they would argue in the following way:

1. Paul asserts that no one is justified before God by the Law.
2. Paul cites Hab 2:4 in support: "The one who is rectified by faith will live."
3. We assert that one *is* rectified by observing the law
4. Our assertion is supported by Lev 18:5: "The one who does the commandments will live by them."
5. "We can say in conclusion, then, that, being the word of the one God, the Law does not really contradict itself. At the level of intention the text quoted by Paul and the text quoted by us actually say the same thing. Habakkuk's reference to life by faith is God's assurance of life to the

---

[102]Ibid., 324–28.

[103]See Comment #35 in Martyn, *Galatians*, 328–34, or the slightly more comprehensive discussion in idem, "The Textual Contradiction Between Habakkuk 2:4 and Leviticus 18:5," in *Theological Issues in the Letters of Paul* (Edinburgh: T&T Clark, 1997), 183–90. Martyn draws heavily on the work of Vos, "Die Hermeneutische Antinomie bei Paulus," which is further described below, 91–93.

[104]Martyn, *Galatians*, 329. Except where indicated by quotation marks, I have paraphrased Martyn's descriptions of the form for the sake of conciseness.

one who faithfully observes God's commandments, as stated in Leviticus."[105]

Rather than allowing the Teachers to establish such an argument first, therefore, Paul cuts them off at the pass by giving his own version of the argument, based on a *modified* form of the Textual Contradiction:

1. I assert that no one is justified before God by the Law.
2. I cite Hab 2:4 in support: "The one who is rectified by faith will live."
3. "In light of the way in which the Teachers quote—and will continue to quote—from the Law, I must add a second assertion: The Law does not have its origin in faith."
4. In support of my second assertion, I will cite one of the Teachers' favorite texts, Lev 18:5: "The one who does the commandments will live by them."[106]

Obviously, according to Martyn's reconstruction, Paul makes some key changes to the form of the Textual Contradiction. First, he has not advanced the competing halakah in step 3, but rather advanced his own, second assertion, an assertion that undercuts the Teachers' basic presupposition that the Law is indivisible and cannot contradict itself. He then usurps the text they would have quoted in step 4; he still cites it, but he makes it serve his purpose of *reinforcing* the contradiction. There is therefore neither need or room for the interpretation in step 5 that would resolve the contradiction; Paul leaves the two texts in tension. Paul thus makes his point that the old world inhabited by the Teachers, in which the Law is indivisible, is not the new cosmos of the gospel.[107]

Martyn's argument is fascinating and skillful, but it has at least two major flaws. First, it is not at all clear that Paul is, in fact, working with or altering the form of the Textual Contradiction. At first glance it might seem that he is, since one could say that he reproduces three of the five steps of the Textual Contradiction (steps 1, 2, and 4). On closer examination, however, it appears that the two missing steps, steps 3 and 5, are actually the *crucial* elements of the pattern—crucial not only for the presupposition that Paul allegedly wants to overthrow (the indivisibility of scripture), but crucial also for establishing the form in the first place. Without the statement of a competing halakah (step 3), and even more so without the interpretation which resolves the contradiction (step 5), one does not have a recognizable Textual Contradiction. All that is left is a pair of assertions and scriptural proofs—the same sort of pattern (assertion with proof)

---

[105]Ibid., 330–31.
[106]Ibid., 331.
[107]Ibid., 331–32.

that has already occurred in 3:10, and will occur again in 3:13.[108] Unless we are prepared to see modified Textual Contradictions lurking in every corner of Paul's argument, therefore, it would seem better not to look for one here.[109]

Second, in spite of straining everything in Galatians through his apocalyptic sieve,[110] Martyn still has not described how Paul can use scripture against scripture without undercutting his own exegetical argument. In some ways, Martyn's approach sounds only a little different from that of other scholars—in setting the cursing voice of the law against the blessing voice of God, Paul indeed "splits Scripture apart" and makes of the law "an antidivine agency."[111] What should promise to keep Martyn from falling under the same critique as Beker and others is the apocalyptic understanding that in the new creation, the unity of scripture is no more. But it is precisely this latter point that *Paul does not argue*. Nowhere does Paul give the Galatians an explanation of how scripture is now to be divided, some of it indeed speaking with God's voice and some of it not.[112] On the contrary, he engages, as Martyn describes it, in an exegetical argument, an argument, in other words, which appeals to scripture for support.[113] It is hard to imagine that the Galatians would *not* have come away thinking that Paul had

---

[108] See below, 151–69, for a detailed exploration of how and whether these citations are actually functioning as proof. In particular, I will argue that the citation of Hab 2:4 in Gal 3:11 does *not* function as proof. If this argument is accepted, then even less is left of the form of the Textual Contradiction.

[109] It could be argued that there is a bit more of the form present, in that the two citations (steps 2 and 4) are, in fact, contradictory—it is not *simply* a pair of assertions with scriptural proofs, but a pair of assertions with *contradictory* scriptural proofs. It must be noted, however, that the form of the Textual Contradiction is really misnamed. As Vos develops it, and as Martyn acknowledges, the key to this form is not competing *texts* but rather competing *assertions*; cf. ibid., 329: "The parties' citation of contradictory texts is secondary to their voicing of contradictory assertions." Moreover, one could very nearly as easily construct a "modified Textual Contradiction" with 3:10–11, using citations that are, if not directly contradictory, at least in a certain degree of tension.

[110] See above, 55.

[111] Beker, *Paul the Apostle*, 54.

[112] It might be suggested that Paul upholds the words of *prophecy* but not the words of the *law*—but this does not account for Paul's apparently favorable use of scriptures such as Gen 15:6, also from the Pentateuch, and in any case Paul never suggests such a basis for distinction; cf. Sanders, *PLJP*, 96ff. Martyn's reference to the *law's* cursing voice should not be mistaken for a distinction between law and prophecy; rather, Martyn's thesis is that wherever blessing is promised, scripture speaks with God's voice; wherever cursing is threatened, it speaks with the voice of the law (Martyn, *Galatians*, 324–28). Once again, however, this is not a point that *Paul* ever advances. Nowhere does Paul suggest that, when scripture mentions a curse, it does not represent God's voice. On the contrary, Paul uses scriptures that speak of both blessing and cursing in ways that equally suggest his assumption of their authority; see below, 147–53.

[113] Martyn, *Galatians*, 25–26.

"shot himself in the foot" when he thus appealed to some scriptures for support, but denied others, without giving any indication of how the two were to be distinguished.[114] In effect, Paul would seem to be saying little more than, "My scriptures are better than theirs are."

Solutions from Historical/Cultural Antecedents

Rabbinic Antecedents

In an oft-cited article, Nils Dahl suggests an alternative way to approach the problem of resolving the tension between Lev 18:5 and Hab 2:4.[115] His alternative is in many ways a happy medium between the two previous approaches sketched out above. On the one hand, he suggests that Paul did indeed see a tension, even a contradiction between the two citations. On the other hand, he does not suggest that Paul celebrated the contradiction; quite to the contrary, he argues that Paul shared the conviction, common to Judaism and Christianity alike, that scripture could not contradict itself.[116] What Paul did, therefore, was to make use of a standard rabbinic practice for resolving contradictions in scripture.

As Dahl acknowledges, he is following the suggestion already made by H. J. Schoeps, that Paul's discussion of Lev 18:5 and Hab 2:4 in Gal 3 "must be understood against the background of the treatment of contradictory scriptural passages in contemporary Jewish hermeneutics."[117] But Schoeps, according to

---

[114]It might be argued that Paul does provide the basis for distinguishing the various scriptures, namely by the criteria of the Spirit. There is some truth to this; Paul's appeal to the experience of the Spirit in 3:1–5, for example, may suggest "the hermeneutical priority of Spirit-experience" (Hays, *Echoes*, 108). What Hays suggests, however, is not that the Spirit guides Paul to reject some scriptures in favor of others, but rather that, based on the experience of the Spirit in the church, Paul is led to a "charismatic rereading" of scripture (ibid.). If one tries to extend Hays' point to explain how Paul can use one scripture to *contradict* another, one is left once again with a Paul who is less than convincing. While Paul may appeal to Spirit-experience in 3:1–5, in 3:6–14 he is making an *exegetical* argument and thus is appealing to *scripture* to support his arguments. If Paul thinks that some scripture is valid and some is not, and only by the Spirit can we distinguish between them, why would he appeal to scripture at all? Why support his argument with an appeal to something that has no actual authority of its own, but which alternately, even unpredictably, speaks truth or falsehood?

[115]Dahl, "Contradictions in Scripture."

[116]Ibid., 160–61: "The discussions about the extent of the canon show that both Jews and Christians thought that the Holy Scriptures could contain no irreconcilable contradictions. But the discussions also reveal that there was an awareness of contradictions and that attempts were made to deal with them."

[117]Ibid., 161; cf. Schoeps, *Paul*, 177ff. Schoeps himself is following Gottlieb Klein, *Studien über Paulus* (Stockholm: Bonniers, 1918), 67ff.

Dahl, misunderstands the contemporary hermeneutical practice and thus misconstrues Paul's argument; Schoeps understands R. Ishmael's thirteenth middah to say that when two passages are in contradiction, one should search for a third passage to resolve the contradiction.[118] Accordingly, he sees Paul holding up Gen 15:6 (in Gal 3:6) as the third passage which decides between the contradictory Lev 18:5 (in Gal 3:12) and Hab 2:4 (in Gal 3:11).[119]

Drawing on an earlier version of the rabbinic principle, Dahl offers a corrected understanding of R. Ishmael's thirteenth middah: "Two scriptural passages which correspond to one another yet conflict with one another, should be upheld in their place until a third passage comes and decides between them."[120] The basic strategy, not only as expressed in this rule but as practiced numerous times by the rabbis, was not to search for a third passage to decide *between* two conflicting passages, but rather that two conflicting passages must *both* be upheld, each in "its place," until and unless a third passage should be introduced which requires a new interpretation. For each passage to be upheld in place, one determines the manner and extent to which each passage can apply without contradiction; more specifically, one determines which passage is primary, and then shows how to interpret the other passage so as to avoid contradiction.[121]

Dahl sees Paul following precisely this procedure. In 3:13–18, Paul shows that Hab 2:4 is the primary passage, while in 3:19–25 he resolves the apparent contradiction by his interpretation of Lev 18:5. When it is understood that the law had only a subordinate role, not to lead to life, but rather to consign all things to sin, then there is no contradiction between Lev 18:5 and Hab 2:4; there would only be a contradiction if the law had ever, even if only temporarily, offered a valid path to life.[122] Thus, both citations are upheld, "each in its place."

---

[118] Ibid.

[119] As pointed out by Hays, *Faith*, 219, Schoeps' argument suffers not only because of his misunderstanding of the thirteenth middah, but also because the sequence is backwards—he appeals to a verse that occurs well before the contradiction is presented.

[120] Dahl, "Contradictions," 162.

[121] In addition to rabbinic examples, Dahl offers examples from Hellenistic Judaism, particularly Philo (ibid., 162ff).

[122] Ibid., 171ff. Both Hays' and Martyn's depictions of Dahl require correction at this point. Both understand Dahl to say that the key to resolving the contradiction is the *temporary* nature of the law (Hays, *Faith*, 220–21; Martyn, *Galatians*, 331n139). To be sure, Dahl does note that the law, as Paul describes it, was a temporary provision, but he goes on to say that "neither can it [the Law] be understood as a provisional arrangement so that 'by faith' would be valid for Abraham and for the time of the Messiah, while 'by the Law' and therefore 'by works of the law' would be valid for the time between Moses and Christ. The unity of the will and purpose of the one God excludes such a duality" (Dahl, "Contradictions," 173). Rather, "Paul asserts that it was unable to do this [to lead to justification and life] and that this was never even God's intention for it. The Law served another purpose: 'Scripture consigned all things to sin, that what was promised to faith in

One of the strengths of Dahl's approach is that it thus suggests that Paul himself recognized and addressed the tension between the citations—but this is, ironically, also the point on which Dahl has been most severely criticized.[123] In effect, Dahl portrays the whole point and structure of Paul's argument as the resolution of a scriptural contradiction, as though "the contradiction between Hab 2:4 and Lev 18:5 may have kept a lonely Paul awake at night until he 'solved' it."[124] That Paul did not write his letter to the Galatians simply to share with them the resolution to a puzzling scriptural tension goes without saying.

Hellenistic Antecedents

Like many others, J. S. Vos critiques Dahl for setting the issue of Gal 3 in terms of an abstract rabbinic effort to resolve contradictory citations.[125] But Vos' critique of Dahl is more of a correction than a rejection. On the one hand, Vos agrees that the primary question for Paul is not how to resolve competing scriptures, but rather how to resolve the law and the promises to Abraham (the gospel). On the other hand, Vos argues that since the law and the gospel are each supported with explanatory and authoritative scriptures, Paul cannot avoid taking up the issue of the contradictory scriptures.[126]

Like Dahl, Vos looks to contemporary practices to find a historical antecedent for Paul's treatment of these scriptures; unlike Dahl, Vos finds that antecedent not in the writings of the rabbis, but rather in the *legum contrarium* described in the handbook of Hellenistic rhetoric.[127] Several elements of the *legum contrarium* are relevant to Paul's situation.[128] For example, the *legum contrarium* is framed in terms of a juridical context, with two opposing parties each bringing a competing point of law as support for their position; at the same

---

Jesus Christ might be given to those who believe' (v. 22). Thus Paul finds no contradiction here. Rightly understood, the Law is in harmony with the promises. It had a subordinate function which contributed to the realization of the promises" (ibid., 173–74).

[123]Hays, *Faith*, 218–22, offers a thorough examination and critique. Hays points out, in addition to the problem described above, a number of additional problems, including the fact that Paul never indicates in 3:19–25 that he is "interpreting" Lev. 18:5.

[124]Martyn, *Galatians*, 329n133; cf. Betz, *Galatians*, 138n8; Hays, *Faith*, 220: "Paul does not introduce the two passages as conflicting texts which pose an interpretive dilemma. Rather, they are introduced into the midst of a discussion in progress . . . ."

[125]Vos, "Die Hermeneutische Antinomie bei Paulus," 256.

[126]Ibid., 257–58; 260. Vos also sees a similar pattern at work in Romans 10.

[127]Ibid, 260. Vos does note that there are numerous rabbinic parallels to the type of argument he finds in the rhetorical handbook (ibid., 262), but he gives precedence to the Hellenistic antecedent, seeing the Jewish hermeneutical parallels only as variations (ibid, 260).

[128]Ibid., 263–64.

time, however, the law cannot be allowed to contradict itself.[129] The *legum contrarium* therefore describes several tests or questions to determine which point of law applies in the given argument: which law is older? Which law has more weight or power? Which law is more clear and direct? Which position better expresses what the law-giver intended? Which position can best incorporate within itself the opponents' point of law?[130]

Vos sees Paul working out just such a juridical argument in Galatians 3.[131] Interestingly, for Vos, the first of the competing positions and supporting scriptures—Paul's position—is found not in 3:11, but rather in 3:6–9, with the promise to Abraham; the position of Paul's opponents is then set out in 3:10–12.[132] In 3:15–4:7, Paul then works through the tests to see which scripture applies and therefore which position prevails. In 3:15–16, Paul asks about the intentions of the law-giver (what does σπέρμα mean?), and in 3:17–18 he asks which law is older; in 3:19–20 Paul again asks about the intentions of the law-giver (why then the Law?), and in 3:21–22 he asks which law has more power (the Law has no power to give life).[133] In the end, Paul "wins" the argument by incorporating his opponents' scripture: the intention of the law-giver is to use the Law only indirectly in the giving of life.[134]

There are at least two problems with Vos's approach. First, it is hard to avoid the impression that he is forcing Paul's argument to fit the model. For example, it is rather less than clear that Gal 3:6–9 and 3:10–12 represent oppos-

---

[129]Ibid., 265.

[130]Ibid., 260–61.

[131]Ibid., 265–66. Vos points to Gal 3:15 to establish the juridical context of Paul's discussion, and to Gal 3:21 to establish that Paul could not accept any unresolved contradiction in the law.

[132]This is both a strength and a weakness in Vos' discussion. On the one hand, he does not ignore the citations that precede 3:11; on the other hand, 3:10–12 hardly seems to be a clear-cut presentation of a position supported by scripture(s) competing with 3:6–9. Not only is the citation of Hab 2:4 in Gal 3:11 obviously not in accord with the citation of Dt 27:26 and Lev 18:5 in Gal 3:10 and 3:12, but also it is not at all clear that Gen 15:6 and 12:3 (in Gal 3:6–9) are contradictory with Dt 27:26 or Lev 18:5. Note that Martyn, who commends Vos's model, nevertheless limits his discussion of the "Textual Contradiction" to 3:11–12; see above, 86–87.

[133]Vos's discussion, following the *legum contrarium*, uses the terminology of competing *laws* rather than competing *citations*. This makes the discussion confusing, given that one of the positions is that of the Law. In the sentences above, I have capitalized Law when it refers to the position, and left it in lowercase when it refers to the supporting citation.

[134]Ibid., 266. In essence, even though his understanding of the argumentative model is quite different, the position at which Vos arrives is little different from that of Dahl. Paul reconciles the competing scriptures by saying that the law had only a provisional and indirect role to play in bringing life.

ing positions, especially since the two scriptures which seem most obviously to contradict one another—Hab 2:4 in Gal 3:11 and Lev 18:5 in Gal 3:12—are thus lumped together under the position of Paul's opponents. Furthermore, whichever positions or scriptures are seen to be contradictory, nowhere in Gal 3:15–4:7 does Paul suggest that he is offering a reinterpretation in order to ease the contradiction.[135] At most, therefore, one should perhaps note some interesting parallels in the way Paul argues, without claiming that Paul is actually carrying out this specific form of argument.[136]

Second, even if we are convinced that Paul is following Vos's model—or Dahl's, for that matter—it is not at all clear that the model has provided a satisfactory solution to the apparent contradiction in scripture. When Hab 2:4 and Lev 18:5 are understood as two competing claims for how one gains life, it is only with the most extreme qualification of Lev 18:5 that one can avoid an obvious contradiction, and nowhere does Paul apply that qualification to Lev 18:5. In other words, though it is clear that Paul wants to address the question of how law and gospel relate ("Why then the law?"), he never actually helps us to "reread" Lev 18:5 accordingly—he never says, as we might expect him to say, "Now when it says 'will live,' it means . . . ." If Paul is following Vos's model, the model has let Paul down. We are left with the nagging sense that all of his arguments are but a stop-gap effort to try to cover up an obviously false promise in scripture itself.

THE CITATIONS AS EVIDENCE FOR PAULINE INCONSISTENCY?

There is one further option for dealing with the tensions in Paul's use of citations that should be mentioned: perhaps Paul is simply inconsistent. This is the thesis vigorously defended by Heikki Räisänen.[137] To be sure, Räisänen argues his thesis with respect to Paul and the law in general; the citations Paul uses in Galatians 3 play only a very small part in his overall argument. In particular, Räisänen argues that the logic of Galatians 3:10–12 requires the assumption that

---

[135]Vos rightly points to ζωοποιέω in Gal 3:21 as a link back to the citations in Gal 3:11–12 (ibid., 258)—but this only suggests, at most, that Paul is continuing to explore the issues he had raised with the citations; it offers no indication that he is addressing the contradiction between them. Cf. Hays's critique of Schoeps and Dahl (see above, nn. 119, 123–124).

[136]Much less should one go so far as to say that Paul had read the handbook of Hellenistic rhetoric (cf. Vos, "Die Hermeneutische Antinomie bei Paulus," 270). The kinds of arguments Paul employs—asking which law is older, what the intention of the law was, etc.—could as easily have come from a rabbinic influence, or from Paul's own common sense.

[137]See especially Heikki Räisänen, "Paul's Theological Difficulties with the Law"; idem, *Paul and the Law*, Wissenschaftliche Untersuchungen zum Neuen Testament 29 (Tübingen: J.C.B. Mohr, 1983).

no one can do all the law, but Romans 2:14–15, 26–27 and Philippians 3:6 show that Paul can admit that both Gentiles and Jews can fulfill the law.[138] On the basis of this and many other such problems, Räisänen concludes that Paul was too caught up in polemical exchanges with his opponents (and also in cognitive dissonance) to be able to work out a carefully consistent theological understanding of the law.[139]

It must be admitted from the start that Räisänen *might* be right, but it must equally be admitted that he might be wrong. The difficulty in critiquing Räisänen's position is that it has, quite simply, "solved" all inconsistencies in Paul's argument by making Paul himself inconsistent.[140] In effect, then, the only question one might ask of Räisänen is whether he has given up too easily. Where problems with the "missing premise" have caused us to seek for other solutions—of which, as we have seen, there are many, but each of which, as we have also seen, has its own problems—such problems have convinced Räisänen that no solution is ultimately possible. In some sense, it comes down to an aesthetic question: is Räisänen's explanation satisfying, or should we continue to search for another?

Conclusions

In the previous chapter, we concluded that the various answers that have been offered for why and to what extent Paul rejects the law have proved to be less than satisfactory. In this chapter, we must draw a parallel conclusion, that the various attempts to explain how Paul uses citations to support or develop his argument for rejecting the law have failed to resolve the tensions inherent in his use of scripture in the context of Gal 3:1–14. Is there any way to move forward in understanding Paul, his use of citations, and his view of the law, or must we resign ourselves to the conclusion that Paul is simply inconsistent?

One possible way of moving forward would be to ask different questions of the text, or rather to ask whether we have correctly identified the questions the text is asking or answering. This is hardly a new idea, of course; it is something of a standard technique of scholarship to suggest the need for new questions or

---

[138]Räisänen, "Paul's Theological Difficulties with the Law," 308–309. In the same article, Räisänen also suggests that "Paul's interpretation of the Old Testament in support of his position is arbitrary" (ibid., 305), but he does not argue this point.

[139]Ibid., 313–14.

[140]There is a certain ironic inconsistency in Räisänen's own position. He claims that Gal 3:10–12 *must* require the assumption that no one can do all the law, and that *therefore* Paul is inconsistent. But Räisänen has apparently not stopped to consider the basis on which the assumption is required: the "missing premise" is required only to prevent Paul from being inconsistent, or rather to prevent an inconsistency between his argument and the scripture he cites in support.

to point out the failure of old ones.[141] Unfortunately, all too often the new questions that are asked differ from the old ones more in surface detail than in substance. For example, Michael Cranford typifies many recent scholars when he suggests that "the question giving rise to the discussion here [in Gal 3] is not, 'How do I, as an individual, became [sic] saved?' but rather, 'What is the basis for Gentiles to be considered sons of Abraham?'"[142] Unfortunately, Cranford's new question deals with essentially the same issue as the old one, namely, soteriology (in the sense of defining membership in the group that is saved): "The issue of sonship is a question regarding group membership, and what the identifying characteristic is of the group to be identified with Abraham."[143] In effect, Cranford has shifted the question from *how* one is saved, to *who* is saved—but still the focus is soteriological.

We saw in the previous chapter that understanding Paul's argument in Gal 3 in terms of soteriology—whether in terms of how one is saved, or who is saved, or what it takes to remain among the saved—may be problematic. In this chapter, in the discussion of the tension between citations, a soteriological focus has again contributed to some of the problems that have emerged. So long as Lev 18:5 and Hab 2:4 are understood in terms of *gaining* life, it is difficult to avoid the impression that Paul has contradicted one soteriological claim from scripture with another.[144] At the very least, therefore, we need carefully to examine whether soteriological questions offer the best approach to understanding Paul's argument in Gal 3.

---

[141]Cf. e.g., Cranford, "The Possibility of Perfect Obedience," 247, 250; Gundry, "Grace," 8; Hays, *Echoes*, 9–10; Martyn, *Galatians*, 23; idem, "Apocalyptic Antinomies in Paul's Letter to the Galatians," *NTS* 31 (1985): 416; Vos, "Die Hermeneutische Antinomie bei Paulus," 257–58.

[142]Cranford, "The possibility of Perfect Obedience," 250. Cranford earlier gives an expanded version of the question he rejects: ". . . how an individual procures salvation, with the possible alternatives being mere human effort (i.e., obeying the law) and faith (i.e., believing, understood as something other than obedience)" (ibid., 247).

[143]Ibid., 250.

[144]Cf. Ebeling, *The Truth of the Gospel*, 177, concerning ways to resolve the tensions that arise from Paul's citation of Lev 18:5: "One possibility is to strip the verb ζήσεται . . . of its soteriological overtones (which is also a possible reading of Hab. 2:4). Then the passage would be speaking only of the different principles on which life can be based: in the case of someone who is (truly) righteous it is faith, in the case of someone who does what the law requires it is these very requirements." Cf. Dieter Lührmann, *Galatians: A Continental Commentary*, trans. O. C. Dean (Minneapolis: Fortress, 1992), 61: "This [combination of citations] can have the power of proof only if *live* in the two texts is understood without any emphasis and not taken in the sense of the full promise of life, which would then be given also to the law in Lev. 18:5." Unfortunately, neither Ebeling nor Lührmann follow up on this possibility.

As noted in the previous chapter, the apocalyptic perspective of Martyn offers an example of a different sort of question with which to approach the text. Rather than the typical question, "How to be saved?" Martyn suggests that the two fundamental questions asked and addressed by Paul are "What time is it?" and "In what cosmos do we actually live?"[145] While we have found reasons to fault the details of Martyn's arguments at various points, it is clear that with these questions he has offered a strikingly different approach to Paul's argument in Galatians 3. It may be that these questions, or one(s) like these, will prove helpful in overcoming the difficulties associated with the usual varieties of soteriologically focused questions.[146]

Before we can begin to search for or evaluate questions such as those posed by Martyn, however, our survey above of approaches to the citations suggests the need to address an even more basic, foundational question: how can we best understand the way(s) the citations interrelate, both with each other and with Paul's argument? In part, this question speaks to the issue of function: how do the citations function within Paul's argument? Terms such as "proof" and "proof-text" are used with great frequency, but rarely with any clear definition. It would be well to explore, not only what sort of proof the citations might offer, but also whether proof is even the best way to understand their function. Beyond simply asking about function, however, this question points to the need to examine Paul's use of scripture, not on a piecemeal basis—treating each citation independently of all the others[147]—but in a holistic fashion, allowing the citations to reveal an interconnected and dynamic interaction and dialogue between Paul and scripture.

In short, given the problems posed by the citations, it would seem that we need to take them seriously as a major factor in, contributor to, and influencer of meaning. We need to ask how the presence of citations shapes the meaning of what Paul says. How important are the citations—and how are they important—for understanding what Paul says? To answer this sort of question, we need to explore the issue of how texts interact, both in an author's use and in a reader's experience. In other words, we need to explore an approach that has developed in recent years, first in literary studies, and lately in biblical studies, known as intertextuality. To this task we now turn.

---

[145]Martyn, *Galatians*, 23

[146]In chap. 5 we will further explore the issue of the question addressed by Paul's argument; there we will suggest that, with respect to Gal 3:1–14, the best way to formulate the question is not "how to live," but rather is *"where* to live."

[147]Cf. Betz, *Galatians*, 138n8: "For Paul, Hab 2:4 and Lev 18:5 do not contradict each other, but prove *separate* points in a *consecutive* argument" (emphasis added). In other words, Betz assumes without argument that the citations do not interact with one another in Paul's thinking; instead, he treats the citations in Gal 3:6–14 as a *series* of scriptural proofs, rather than as an integrated argument from scripture.

Chapter 4
INTERTEXTUALITY

In the last decade, biblical scholars have begun to show increasing interest in the literary critical approach known as intertextuality. No small part of that interest, particularly among New Testament scholars, is directly attributable to Richard Hays' book, *Echoes of Scripture in the Letters of Paul*.[1] Though Hays' *Echoes* has been the first introduction to intertextuality for many, however, it certainly does not stand alone. Already before *Echoes*, interest had been developing along lines that, if not strictly to be described as intertextuality, nevertheless share many of its concerns, particularly in terms of the way biblical authors make use of earlier biblical texts—not only the way the New Testament makes use of the Old Testament, but also the way that later Old Testament texts adapt and shape and reshape earlier Old Testament texts.[2]

---

[1]Richard B. Hays, *Echoes of Scripture in the Letters of Paul* (New Haven: Yale University Press, 1989). Many scholars who have undertaken intertextual investigations of a New Testament passage acknowledge dependence on, or at least the influence of, Hays' book; see for example Karen H. Jobes, "Jerusalem, Our Mother: Metalepsis and Intertextuality in Galatians 4:21–31," *WTJ* 55 (1993): 299–320; L. Ann Jervis, "'But I Want You to Know . . .': Paul's Midrashic Intertextual Response to the Corinthian Worshipers (1 Cor 11:2–16)," *JBL* 112 (1993): 231–46; Robert L. Brawley, "An Absent Complement and Intertextuality in John 19:28–29," *JBL* 112 (1993): 427–43; Peter Tschuggnall, "'Das Wort ist kein Ding': Eine theologische Einübung in den literaturwissenschaftlichen Begriff der Intertextualität," *ZKTh* 116 (1994): 160–78; Sylvia C. Keesmat, "Exodus and the Intertextual Transformation of Tradition in Romans 8.14–30," *JSNT* 54 (1994): 29–56; Timothy W. Berkley, *From a Broken Covenant to Circumcision of the Heart: Pauline Intertextual Exegesis in Romans 2:17-29*, SBLDS 175 (Atlanta: Society of Biblical Literature, 2000). See also Craig A. Evans and James A. Sanders, eds., *Paul and the Scriptures of Israel*, JSNTSS 83 (Sheffield: JSOT Press, 1993).

[2]See for example Michael A. Fishbane, *Biblical Exegesis in Ancient Israel* (Oxford: Clarendon Press, 1985); idem, "Inner Biblical Exegesis: Types and Strategies of Interpretation in Ancient Israel," in *Midrash and Literature*, ed. Geoffrey H. Hartman and Sanford Budick (New Haven: Yale, 1986), 19–37; Jacob Neusner and William Scott

With the advent of Hays' book and others like it, however, interest in intertextuality itself has burgeoned.[3] Numerous studies have appeared which attempt to apply intertextuality to the study of the New Testament, the Old Testament, and even rabbinic writings.[4] In all of these studies, however, one encounters a bewildering diversity of methods and claims about methods, all of them purporting to represent intertextuality. Indeed, studies that claim to be intertextual range from not much more than traditional historical-critical investigations of sources used and shaped—a sort of redaction-critical approach—to rather unstructured assemblings of texts which only superficially and arbitrarily seem to be related.[5] Clearly, for all its growing popularity in biblical scholarship, intertextuality is a term in need of some clarification and definition.[6]

A BRIEF SYNOPSIS OF INTERTEXTUALITY

THEORY

What exactly is intertextuality? In terms of its *practice*, this question is rather difficult to answer with any precision, due to the "bewildering diversity" encountered not only in biblical scholarship, but even among those literary critics most closely associated with the concept.[7] Indeed, those who have attempted to summarize and describe intertextuality do not even entirely agree on whether

---

Green, *Writing With Scripture: The Authority and Uses of the Hebrew Bible in the Torah of Formative Judaism* (Minneapolis: Fortress, 1989); J. A. Sanders, *From Sacred Story to Sacred Text: Canon as Paradigm* (Philadelphia: Fortress, 1987).

[3] We will address below the question of just what "intertextuality itself" is, and how it is to be related to and/or distinguished from traditional historical criticism.

[4] The major impetus to apply intertextuality to the study of rabbinic writings, and to some extent to the study of the Old Testament and even the New Testament as well, has come from the work of Daniel Boyarin; see below, 115–19.

[5] For examples of studies which represent only an incremental movement beyond traditional historical-critical methodologies and concerns, see Beat Weber, "Philipper 2,12–13: Text–Kontext–Intertext," *Biblische Notizen* 85 (1996): 31–37; Gail R. O'Day, "Jeremiah 9:22–23 and 1 Corinthians 1:26–31: A Study in Intertextuality," *JBL* 109 (1990): 259–67; see also below, 110–14 and nn. 49, 79, 83–84. For an example of a study that assembles texts which only superficially and arbitrarily seem to be related, see Susan Lochrie Graham, "Intertextual Trekking: Visiting the Iniquity of the Fathers Upon 'The Next Generation,'" *Semeia* 69/70 (1995): 195–219.

[6] For reasons that will emerge below, it is not my purpose to make claims about what truly counts as intertextuality in any given study; rather, my goal is to clarify what will be meant by intertextuality in the current investigation.

[7] Contrast, for example, the very different approaches of Julia Kristeva, Roland Barthes, and Michael Riffaterre. At the risk of oversimplifying, one could describe Kristeva as author-centric, Barthes as reader-centric, and Riffaterre as text-centric. See further below, 105, 127.

certain major figures of literary criticism qualify as representatives of the approach.[8] In terms of the *theory* of intertextuality, however, the question can be answered relatively simply. Intertextuality is semiotics applied to texts. Just as semiotics understands signs as having meaning only in relation to other signs, so too intertextuality understands *texts* to have meaning only in relationship with other texts.[9]

This definition requires two points of clarification. First, the interrelationship of texts with other texts is not optional. It is not that intertextuality comes into play only when an author has deliberately and demonstrably cited or alluded to another text, but rather that texts are constantly and inevitably in dialogue with other texts. Indeed, a text has meaning only in terms of that dialogue. Only by differentiating what is said in the text from everything else that has

---

[8]Several articles provide an excellent introduction to intertextuality: Jay Clayton and Eric Rothstein, "Figures in the Corpus: Theories of Influence and Intertextuality," in *Influence and Intertextuality in Literary History*, ed. Jay Clayton and Eric Rothstein (Madison: University of Wisconsin, 1991), 3–36; Jonathan Culler, "Presupposition and Intertextuality," in *The Pursuit of Signs: Semiotics, Literature, Deconstruction* (Ithaca: Cornell University, 1981), 100–118; Thaïs E. Morgan, "Is There an Intertext in This Text?: Literary and Interdisciplinary Approaches to Intertextuality," *American Journal of Semiotics* 3 no. 4 (1985): 1–40. Each of these presents intertextuality from a slightly different angle and, as noted, each differs somewhat on whether certain literary critics use an intertextual approach. Culler, for example, implies that Harold Bloom represents intertextuality, at least to some degree ("Presupposition," 107–108); Clayton and Rothstein, on the other hand, present Bloom as a paramount example of influence rather than intertextuality ("Figures in the Corpus," 8–10); Morgan, meanwhile, takes something of a middle road as far as Bloom is concerned ("Is There an Intertext," 7–8), but also implies that T. S. Elliot is, if not quite in the circle of intertextuality, at least on its edge (ibid., 4–5).

[9]Though the general principles are the same, actual definitions of intertextuality have been expressed in a wide variety of ways. The definition offered here does not, as far as I am aware, coincide exactly with anyone else's; it takes its cue from the origins of the term itself in the work of French semioticist Julia Kristeva, Σημειωτική: *Recherches pour une sémanalyse* (Paris: Du Seuil, 1969). Although Kristeva coined the term "intertextuality," she drew upon the work of others, including especially Mikhail Bakhtin and Jacques Derrida; see the excellent summary and analysis in Clayton and Rothstein, "Figures in the Corpus," 18–21.

For other definitions and useful discussions of intertextuality, see Culler, "Presupposition"; Morgan, "Is There an Intertext"; Judith Still and Michael Worton, "Introduction," in *Intertextuality: Theories and Practice*, ed. Michael Worton and Judith Still (Manchester: Manchester University Press, 1990), 1–44; John Frow, "Intertextuality and Ontology," in *Intertextuality: Theories and Practice*, 45–55; Owen Miller, "Intertextual Identity," in *Identity of the Literary Text*, ed. Mario J. Valdés and Owen Miller (Toronto: University of Toronto Press, 1985), 19–40; Manfred Pfister, "Konzepte der Intertextualität," in *Intertextualität: Formen, Functionen, anglistische Fallstudien*, ed. Ulrich Broich and Manfred Pfister (Tübingen: Niemeyer, 1985), 1–30.

been said or might be said in other texts can the meaning of a text emerge. This point can perhaps best be seen by way of a spatial analogy in which texts rise from the depths of a pond onto a surface already crowded with a multitude of other texts. The "space" which any given text occupies has to be created by pushing aside all the other texts which already fill the discursive space; its "shape" is therefore determined through the process of pushing aside those other texts to make room for itself.[10]

The second point of clarification has to do with exactly what is meant by the term "text." The fact that a text takes shape only in relationship to other texts means that it is not so much an independent, self-contained object as it is a network of intertextual traces, a mosaic of textual interaction.[11] In a sense, just as in semiotics the basic building blocks of language are signs, so in intertextuality *texts* are the building blocks of texts. This is true not just with respect to direct citation and obvious allusion, but also with respect to countless traces and fragments of *anonymous* texts—texts which cannot necessarily be identified, and yet which leave behind their mark, their trace in the text's struggle to emerge into the crowded pool of textuality:

> L'intertextuel dans lequel est pris tout texte, puisqu'il est lui-même l'entre-texte d'un autre texte, ne peut se confondre avec quelque origine du texte: rechercher les "sources", les "influences" d'un oeuvre, c'est satisfaire au mythe de la filiation: les citations dont est fait un texte sont anonymes, irrépérables et cependant *déjà lues*: ce sont des citations sans guillemets.[12]

To speak of anonymous texts and fragments and traces of texts is to suggest another way in which intertextuality redefines the traditional understanding of a text. In the same way that semiotics takes the concept of *sign* well beyond a simple equation between signs and words, so also intertextuality extends the concept of *text* well beyond the understanding of text as a written object:

> The distinguishing mark of a semiotic is perhaps less the concept of the "sign"—the principle that every unit of meaning can be analyzed into a signifier and a signified—than the systematicity of signs. Thus, "signification" depends upon the positioning of signs within rule-governed or "coded" structures. The product of encoding signs or *semiosis* can be termed a "text," so that

---

[10] Cf. Morgan, "Is There an Intertext," 12: ". . . language can never communicate just one denotative meaning or even the sole viewpoint of the speaker, for each utterance is always caught up in *the crowded space of interdiscursivity*" (emphasis added).

[11] Cf. Julia Kristeva, *Desire in Language: A Semiotic Approach to Literature and Art*, ed. Leon S. Roudiez, trans. Thomas Gora, Alice Jardine, and Leon S. Roudiez (New York: Columbia University, 1980), 66: ". . . any text is constructed as a mosaic of quotations; any text is the absorption and transformation of another."

[12] Roland Barthes, "De l'oeuvre au texte," *Revue d'Esthétique* 24 (1971): 229; cf. idem, *S/Z*, trans. Richard Miller (New York: Hill and Wang, 1974), 10.

the text may be as small as a phrase or gesture, or as large as a novel or football game.[13]

A text understood in semiotic or intertextual terms is therefore not limited to what is written. Every "product of encoding signs," everything that conveys meaning within a society or culture, is part of the intertextual space within which every other text participates. This extension of the concept of text reinforces the point made above. Texts necessarily take on meaning only in interaction with all the other texts of a particular society or culture—not just the written texts, but the "texts" of customs, ideologies, political agendas, sporting events, films, art, and on and on.

We can further clarify the theory of intertextuality by comparing it with the traditional model of literary criticism that it attempts to displace, a model characterized by a concern with *influence*.[14] From roughly the eighteenth century on, the task of literary criticism was defined by the tracing of the sources which influenced an author, in order to distinguish what, if anything, was truly new in the literary composition. Inherent in this approach is a set of value judgments which emphasize the value of a source over later works which cite or allude to it—the later works being devalued as mere copies—and which, conversely, find the literary value of a work in its originality, its freedom from any dependence on prior sources.[15]

In contrast, intertextuality insists that no work is ever truly free from dependence on other texts, both written and unwritten. Every text engages in dialogue with every other text within the discursive space, every text is in some sense woven together out of every other text, because every author and every reader, whether consciously or unconsciously, participates in (and in some sense is defined by) that intertextual space. A text is not a static, independent entity with inherent meaning, but rather is a dynamic *process*—a process of differentiation from (or from another perspective, integration within) the intertextual

---

[13]Morgan, "Is There an Intertext," 8.

[14]One should not overlook the point that this way of describing intertextuality is especially appropriate: one can only fully understand intertextuality in relationship to the "texts" which it displaces.

[15]Morgan, "Is There an Intertext," 2–3; Clayton and Rothstein, "Figures in the Corpus," 4–5. The valuing of the new (i.e., inspiration rather than imitation) represents a paradigm shift dating from the nineteenth century. Prior to that time, value was placed on *imitation* of the great classics rather than on innovation and creativity; cf. Ellen van Wolde, "Trendy Intertextuality?" in *Intertextuality in Biblical Writings: Essays in Honour of Bas van Iersel*, ed. Sipke Draisma (Kampen: J. H. Kok, 1989), 43–44. The valuing of imitation represents just as much a concern with influence as does the valuing of inspiration; in either case, the crucial step in literary evaluation is to determine the author's sources and influences.

space of countless other texts.[16] Intertextuality finds meaning in the intersection of texts—in the struggle of one text to displace or assimilate or overshadow or be submerged in or even attempt to ignore an infinite set of other texts.[17]

To sum up, one might say that at the heart of intertextuality is a profound consciousness of the hermeneutical circle. Meaning always requires a context. In the case of texts, that context is every other meaningful "text," written or unwritten, of the culture and experience of the author and/or reader. Quite aside from any deliberate use or recognition of sources, authors and readers cannot help but encounter a text only in the context of countless other texts which have defined and expressed their experience and understanding.

PRACTICE: PROBLEMS AND LIMITATIONS

Limiting the Scope

Given the theoretical description sketched out above, it is not surprising that the *practice* of intertextuality is so diverse.[18] The scope of intertextuality is, by definition, boundless. It seeks to study the relationships of a text with the whole range of culture and society, not only as expressed in written texts but also as incorporated in unwritten texts, such as cultural, political, and sexual assumptions, attitudes, feelings, and so on. Clearly, no practical application of intertextuality can fully encompass this unlimited scope; one can proceed only by setting limits on the range of texts that will be considered.[19]

---

[16] Cf. Kristeva, Σημειωτική, 219.

[17] On the potentially infinite scope of intertextuality, cf. Morgan, "Is There an Intertext," 8: "... the signs and codes in a text are presumed to be capable of interrelating in an unforeseeable number of ways, so that semiosis is always open, actually infinite." Cf. likewise Miller, "Intertextual Identity," 24–25: "... the intertextual relationships of any work of literature are theoretically infinite, since potentially any sentence of a text (or fragment thereof) may engender a series of presuppositional statements."

[18] Cf. Willem S. Vorster, "Intertextuality and Redaktionsgeschichte," in *Intertextuality in Biblical Writings*, 18. Following his definition of intertextuality as a concern "with the relationship between texts," he notes that his definition is "a minimum definition because of the many ways in which intertextuality is conceived and the many relationships which are involved."

[19] Cf. Culler, "Presuppostion," 104–111; Ellen van Wolde, "Texts in Dialogue with Texts: Intertextuality in the Ruth and Tamar Narratives," *Biblical Interpretation* 5 (1997): 1–28, esp. 3–4. As noted by Culler, the setting of such limits inevitably results in a failure to live up to the unlimited scope of the theory: "Theories of intertextuality set before us perspectives of unmasterable series, lost origins, endless horizons; and, as I have been suggesting, in order to work with the concept we focus it—but that focusing may always, to some degree, undermine the general concept of intertextuality in whose name we are working" (Culler, "Presupposition," 111). In a sense, then, there are no truly or fully

The "bewildering diversity" in the practice of intertextuality is a function of the different ways that scholars set these limits. The principles and assumptions which guide one's choice to include or exclude a certain text or set of texts as potential candidates for intertextual investigation largely determine the "flavor" of intertextuality that one practices. Of particular importance are two sets of options which largely determine the character of an intertextual investigation: *text production* vs. *text reception*, and *diachronic* vs. *synchronic textual relationships*.[20]

Text Production or Text Reception

One of the parameters which significantly determines the nature and focus of an intertextual investigation is the degree to which it is directed towards text production or text reception. Are the intertextual relationships of interest understood to be the product of the author's intertextual matrix, or rather the product of the reader's? In other words, does one focus one's investigation on the texts of our world—the intertextual relationships we create and apprehend as we read—or on the texts of the world of the author—the intertextual relationships operative in the author as he or she wrote?[21]

It has been suggested that true intertextuality almost inevitably incorporates a reader-response approach to the text, so that intertextuality lies strictly on the side of text reception, not text production.[22] This suggestion is, of course, in step

---

intertextual investigations, but only partial approximations that channel the theoretical intertextual insight within boundaries dictated by pragmatic necessity.

[20]These options are often folded in as assumptions about the theory of intertextuality; I would argue that they should be distinguished as secondary to the "core" theory. Beyond these basic parameters, scholars use a variety of tests or paradigms to limit the selection of texts, most of which are based on some type of observed similarity between the texts or the contexts in which they function. Vorster, "Intertextuality and Redaktionsgeschichte," 21, for example, suggests that "the texts that really matter are those intertexts which have been used in comparable contexts"; James W. Voelz, "Multiple Signs and Double Texts: Elements of Intertextuality," in *Intertextuality in Biblical Writings*, 30, suggests that "textual events or ideas are matrixed with other textual events or ideas which are in proximity, alike or contrasting in content or portrayed by the same vocables as signs" (emphasis removed).

[21]Note that the theoretical definition sketched out above carefully leaves this choice open. In saying that "meaning emerges only in dialogue with other texts," we have not specified *where* that meaning is understood to emerge, whether from the intentions of the author, in the mind of the reader, or somewhere in between.

[22]See, e.g., George Aichele and Gary A. Phillips, "Introduction: Exegesis, Eisegesis, Intergesis," *Semeia* 69/70 (1995): 7–18, esp. 11; van Wolde, "Texts in Dialogue with Texts," 4–5; Benjamin D. Sommer, "Exegesis, Allusion, and Intertextuality in the Hebrew Bible: A Response to Lyle Eslinger," *VT* 46 (1996): 487.

with the prevailing trend in hermeneutical theory which rejects the traditional effort to locate the meaning of a text in the intentions of its author. Whatever an author may or may not have intended to mean, it is the *reader* who must perceive meaning. According to intertextuality, that process of perception is unavoidably intertextual, shaped by all the written and unwritten texts that define the world and experience of the reader. An intertextual analysis focused on text reception, therefore, seeks to reveal the ways that we as readers interact with a given text to promote or resist the written and unwritten texts of our ideological, political, sexual, and moral agendas:

> [Intertextuality] means nothing less than a deconstructive search for the inherent conflicts, tensions, and aporias in the transposition of systems and subjectivities, in the violent juxtaposing, to borrow the Gospel of Matthew's words, what is new and what is old from the treasure room (13:52). It also means a close scrutiny of the roles readers—especially critical readers—play in perpetuating these systems, as subjective agents engaged in the violent acts of neutralization.[23]

To insist that a truly intertextual investigation can *only* focus on text reception, however, is to fail to consider the full implications of the theory. Just as a reader can only discern meaning by intertextual differentiation, so too must there be an intertextual differentiation on the part of any author who wishes to create a meaningful text. Whether or not the meaning the author intends to convey can actually be apprehended by a reader in a different historical and cultural context is almost beside the point. According to the theory of intertextuality, text production *must* be just as intertextual a process as is text reception.[24]

In moving from theory to practice, the key point is that one *must* set limits on a potentially unlimited scope of investigation. To focus on the intertextual relationships operative within the reader's reception of a given text is therefore not a purer application of intertextuality; *it is simply* one *way of setting limits on the scope of one's investigation.* Likewise, to focus on intertextual relationships operative in the process of text production is no less and no more valid a way of

---

[23] Aichele and Phillips, "Introduction," 11; cf. ibid., 13: "Theoretical reflection upon intertextuality is demanded to help explain and to engage the complexities and power of biblical texts within culture, both past and present, and to expose the narrative unconscious that shapes a West in which the Bible functions as a primary sub-text that legitimizes hatred not only of Jews but of women, gays and lesbians, the poor, and any marginalized other."

[24] Perhaps intertextuality as a theory should be distinguished from hermeneutics. The latter asks *where* the meaning of a text lies—in the mind of the author or reader, or in the text itself, or so on—while the former offers insights about the *process* out of which meaning emerges, *wherever that may happen.* See further below, 110–14.

setting limits.[25] As far as the theory of intertextuality is concerned, each approach is equally valid—and, perhaps one should say, equally invalid. To focus on text production or on text reception is simply to make different choices about how to set those limits which any practical investigation *must* impose, even though imposing any limits is in some sense a violation of a theory which insists on a potentially unlimited range of intertextual relationships.[26]

Two of the leading figures in the history of development of intertextuality, Julia Kristeva and Roland Barthes, illustrate these different choices. Kristeva, who coined the term "intertextuality," operates primarily in the region of text production. She is concerned to show how a particular author's work emerges as the trace of the process of producing the text, a process that is as much psychological as it is literary.[27] Barthes, on the other hand, focuses on the reader who processes the text—the reader who is him/herself a construct of countless "anonymous but already read" texts:[28]

> A text is made of multiple writings, drawn from many cultures and entering into mutual relations of dialogue, parody, contestation, but there is one place where this multiplicity is focused and that place is the reader, not, as was hitherto said, the author. The reader is the space on which all the quotations that make up a writing are inscribed without any of them being lost; a text's unity lies not in its origin but in its destination. Yet this destination cannot any longer be personal: the reader is without history, biography, psychology; he is simply

---

[25] Again, whether or not a reader can actually apprehend the intertextual process operative in the author's production of the text is a separate issue from whether or not the latter is a truly intertextual process—and even less whether an investigation based on text production can be truly intertextual. Even one convinced that meaning lies solely in the mind of the reader (or in the process of reading) could choose to examine those texts which he or she suspects, for whatever reason, may have played a role in the production of the text, with the understanding that by so choosing, he/she has incorporated those texts into his/her own intertextual context. From that point on, he/she cannot avoid reading the text in light of these chosen texts.

[26] Cf. n. 19 above.

[27] See for example Kristeva, Σημειωτικὴ, 219: the task of the literary critic is not simply to explore the *phenotext*—the written text—but rather to explore the *genotext*—the intertextual, psychological process which culminated in the written text. As noted by Morgan, "Is There an Intertext," 23–24, and Culler, "Presupposition," 106, Kristeva's practice is, in many ways, not too different from traditional studies which focus on the intentions of and influence on the author; cf. Clayton and Rothstein, "Figures in the Corpus," 21.

[28] The phrase is drawn from Barthes' oft-quoted statement, "The citations which go to make up a text are anonymous, untraceable, and yet *already read*" (Roland Barthes, "From Work to Text," in *Image-Music-Text*, trans. Stephen Heath [New York: Hill and Wang, 1977], 160; see above, 100, for the same quotation in the original French). Cf. Culler, "Presupposition," 102.

that *someone* who holds together in a single field all the traces by which the written text is constituted.[29]

Diachronicity or Synchronicity

The second set of options which significantly determines the nature and focus of an intertextual investigation is the degree to which it sets limits on its use of texts based on diachronic or synchronic textual relationships. Diachronicity refers to chronological relationships between texts. One determines whether text A preceded text B, and therefore whether text A could have had any influence on text B.[30] Synchronicity, on the other hand, ignores chronological sequence. One looks for and exploits points of contact between texts A and B without regard to which preceded which, or whether one can trace any history of influence from one to the other. In a sense, a focus on synchronicity replaces the traditional chronological order with a "spatial" one:

> Instead of the temporalization of authorial and literary relations in theories of influence and inspiration, semiotics proposes a spatialization of textual relations that subordinates diachronic developments to synchronic structuration of the field.[31]

On the surface, at least, this set of options seems to be very nearly synonymous with the previous one. Attention to diachronic relationships between texts seems both to require and to facilitate attention to text production, while attention to text reception seems both to require and to validate the freedom to look for synchronic relationships between texts. In an intertextual exploration focused on text reception, for example, it is not a question of whether or how a particular text historically preceded or influenced the text under investigation, but rather a question of whether or how it participates in any way in the reader's perception and appreciation of that text. Conversely, in an investigation focused on text

---

[29]Roland Barthes, "The Death of the Author," in *Image-Music-Text*, trans. Stephen Heath (New York: Hill and Wang, 1977), 148.

[30]van Wolde, "Trendy Intertextuality," 43, 46, suggests that the key element which defines diachronicity (and traditional historical or comparative studies) is not just chronology but rather *causality*. To the extent that one ignores whether text A played any part in causing text B, one is working synchronically. Cf. Frow, "Intertextuality and Ontology," 46.

[31]Morgan, "Is There an Intertext," 8. Cf. Miller, "Intertextual Identity," 24: "[A text is] a mosaic composed of many fragments of linguistic matter quoted from anonymous sources, a collage of pieces of language brought into *spatial* proximity and inviting the reader to create some sort of patterning by forcing them to discharge some of their interrelational energy" (emphasis added). Cf. Culler, "Presupposition," 103: "Intertextuality thus becomes less a name for a work's relation to particular prior texts than a designation of its participation in the discursive *space* of a culture" (emphasis added).

production, it would seem obvious that one must determine which texts were actually available to the author, which therefore could have played a role in the intertextual differentiation by which he or she produced the text.[32]

Given the apparent linkage between these sets of options, it is not surprising that certain intertextual practitioners have viewed any concern for establishing diachronic textual relationships with suspicion, just as they have any focus on text production.[33] Indeed, the combination of text production plus diachronicity may well seem to add up to nothing more than the traditional concern with influence which intertextuality seeks to escape.[34] Just as the rejection of text production represents a misunderstanding of the theory of intertextuality, however, so too does the rejection of diachronicity, especially when it is understood that the linkage between text production and diachronicity (and between text reception and synchronicity) is not as tight or necessary as it might seem.

Is it possible to carry out an intertextual investigation that focuses both on *diachronic* textual relationships and on text *reception*? Certainly! Since one must in any case set practical limits on the range of texts considered, one can do so by focusing on those texts which happened to precede and perhaps even contribute to the text under investigation—not, however, in order to investigate their effect on the author's production of the text, but rather on the reader's reception of it.[35] In effect, the set of texts that would be in a diachronic relationship with another text are a *subset* of those texts that could be in a synchronic relationship with that text, since the synchronic set of texts includes any text for which the reader perceives any relationship whatsoever, whether analogical *or* chronologi-

---

[32]Cf. the table constructed by van Wolde, "Texts in Dialogue with Texts," 4–5, in which she links text production with the writer, diachronic relationships, concern with sources, causality, "indexicality" (textual relationships treated as indexes to sources), and compulsory relations between texts, while with text reception she links the reader, synchronic relationships, functions (how texts interact to shape meaning rather than to indicate sources), analogy (relationships perceived on the basis of analogy rather than because one text influenced the other), iconicity (textual relationships which indicate an analogy of phenomena rather than an index to a source), and potential relations between texts. The column associated with text production describes, for van Wolde, traditional historical and comparative studies, while the column associated with text reception describes intertextuality.

[33]See, e.g., Aichele and Phillips, "Introduction," 7; van Wolde, "Trendy Intertextuality," 43–46.

[34]Cf. van Wolde, "Texts in Dialogue with Texts," 4–5.

[35]To some extent, this is what Hays does in *Echoes*. He focuses on texts which are certainly prior to Paul and which Paul certainly knew; he does not, however, limit himself to exploring only those "echoes" which Paul himself intended, but rather explores the echoes that we as readers perceive. See below, 113.

cal.[36] Since one must choose *some* subset of texts, there is no theoretical reason one cannot choose the diachronic subset rather than some other subset.[37]

It may seem more difficult to argue the reverse possibility, that one could carry out an intertextual investigation that is focused on text production and yet is not limited to diachronic textual relationships. After all, if one wishes to trace the *influence* of texts in the process of text production, one *must* limit one's attention to those texts which preceded the text under investigation.[38] Intertextuality, however, is not limited to the tracing of influence; rather, intertextuality insists that texts are interrelated even apart from any direct or conscious influence. Intertextuality therefore permits one to investigate texts which, though prior to or contemporary with the text under investigation, cannot be shown to have been known by the author. These texts, though not related by influence, were nevertheless part of the same "pool" of texts from which the author's text emerged.[39] But one can go a step further. Even texts which postdate

---

[36]In a traditional study of influence, potentially interesting intertextual relationships are discarded if they are not drawn from diachronically prior texts. Intertextuality insists that *any* potentially interesting intertextual relationships are relevant, without regard to chronological sequence. This means that, from an intertextual perspective, chronological sequence and causality can neither rule texts in nor rule them out. If one must set limits, however, and if *any* limits are—from the perspective of intertextuality—artificial and arbitrary, then one can just as (il)legitimately happen to choose a set of texts which *are* diachronically prior as any other set of texts.

One might argue that texts which have *only* a diachronic relationship with the text under investigation would not truly qualify under the heading of synchronic relationships—i.e., that synchronicity implies some sort of relationship between texts other than simply a chronological sequence or even simply a causative relationship. This argument is precarious for two reasons. First, it is directed at a "straw man." It is unlikely that even the most traditional study of historical influence would have an interest in a prior text *solely* because it preceded the text under investigation; the interest would lie in some apparent point of contact between the texts, some perceived similarity or interaction which could lead one to sense the possibility of causality—in short, some relationship that might be evident quite apart from any knowledge of their chronological sequence. Second, even if it were mere chronological sequence which created a connection between texts in the mind of a reader, once that connection is established, the reader cannot avoid reading one text in light of the other. However unlikely it is that mere chronological sequence would ever cause a reader to relate texts, in other words, the theory of intertextuality does not permit one to reject the possibility.

[37]As pointed out to me by Richard Hays, one's choice of subset thus depends on the questions one is asking, i.e., what one wants to know.

[38]Influence is, by definition, a historical category, i.e., it refers to causality; see nn. 30 and 32 above.

[39]Using the spatial metaphor of a pool of texts, one can argue that text A contributes to the shape of text B, not by direct contact, but rather through its pressure on any number of intervening texts.

the time of the author could be relevant to the intertextual investigation of text production, on the grounds that they too arose out of that same pool, even if at a later date; at the very least, they demonstrate something of the "shape" and intertextual "pressures" of that pool.[40] Indeed, in the broadest sense, one could argue for the intertextual relevance even of texts dated many centuries after the production of the text under investigation on the basis of a vast intertextual matrix, spanning all the centuries of human history, made up of countless written and unwritten texts of common human experience: pain, anger, fear, hunger, greed, temptation, and so on:

> 'Intertextuality,' as most literary critics use the term, focuses on manifold linkages among texts or on connections between a text and commonplace phrases from the cultural systems in which the text exists. These connections do not arise exclusively from an intentional and signalled use of an earlier text, such as citation (which might be studied under the rubric of influence or allusion). Rather, they also result from the way a text reflects its linguistic, aesthetic, or ideological contexts; other texts may share those contexts, and hence readers may notice links among many texts, whether the authors of the texts knew each other or not.[41]

Once again, the key point is that one *must* set practical limits on an intertextual investigation, even though all such limits by definition lie outside of the theory. To limit one's focus to a "strictly synchronic" scope, in the sense of rejecting any texts which have a diachronically prior relationship with the text under investigation, is no more and no less valid than to limit one's focus to a strictly diachronic scope.[42] If on the one hand intertextual theory denies that an influence-based relationship of texts is privileged with normative control of meaning, on the other hand it denies the same privilege to any other basis for

---

[40]Cf. Craig A. Evans, "Listening for Echoes of Interpreted Scripture," in *Paul and the Scriptures of Israel*, 47–51. Evans critiques Hays's *Echoes* for failing to pay sufficient attention to the role that the exegesis of scripture in late antiquity must have played in mediating scripture for Paul; this exegesis is reflected or revealed in various extrabiblical sources. Cf. Richard B. Hays, "On the Rebound: A Response to Critiques of *Echoes of Scripture in the Letters of Paul*," in *Paul and the Scriptures of Israel*, 70–96, for his response to this and other critiques.

[41]Sommer, "Exegesis, Allusion, and Intertextuality," 486–87. Though Sommer speaks in terms of the links which *readers* notice, one can focus on those links in terms of the process of text production, i.e., as intertextual traces of the author's struggle with the pool of texts of his own culture and human experience.

[42]Cf. Stuart Lasine, "The Ups and Downs of Monarchical Justice: Solomon and Jehoram in an Intertextual World," *JSOT* 59 (1993): 40: "... 'intertextuality' is just as crucial for diachronic studies of biblical texts as it is for 'literary' synchronic ones." As noted above, even though some practitioners seem to assume that they are mutually exclusive, the scope of synchronicity actually encompasses that of diachronicity.

relating texts—and conversely, it insists that every relationship of texts, whether synchronic or diachronic, has equal potential for participating in determining the meaning of the text.

This point is especially important in connection with a text like Galatians 3:1–14. Since Paul explicitly cites several Old Testament texts, there is no question about the diachronic relationship thus established. What is in question is whether these citations, and/or the texts from which they are drawn, are appropriate candidates for intertextual investigation.[43] What we have seen above is that these citations are viable but not necessarily privileged candidates. They are not the only intertexts that may be of interest, nor is the interest only in how these texts influenced Paul—one may wish to examine, for example, how Paul's use of these texts influences the reader's understanding of the passage—but the citations certainly offer a convenient, obvious, and justifiable way to limit the scope of the investigation.

Observations

Our discussion of intertextuality leads to two observations. First, it would seem that the theory of intertextuality simply does not address a number of key hermeneutical issues, including whether the locus of meaning lies in the intentions of the author, the response of the reader, or somewhere in between; whether texts have normative meanings; and whether and how one can judge the validity of an interpretation. If on the one hand intertextuality opens up the possibility of reading a text in conjunction with other texts the author never knew, of finding intertextual relationships that exist only in the perceptions of a given reader, on the other hand it also legitimates investigating the historical context of the author, seeking out his/her sources, and asking about the issues and influences that might have contributed to his/her production of the text.[44] The theory of intertextuality insists that *all* of these are potential intertexts, that *all* of these potentially play a role in the meaning of a text. If intertextuality thus includes

---

[43]Cf. Laurent Jenny, "La Stratégie de la forme," *Poétique* 27 (1976): 263, who argues that not even allusion should be considered in an intertextual investigation because in the mere repetition of an element from an earlier text no actual relationship is established between the texts—i.e., no relationship except the diachronic. Cf. Culler, "Presupposition," 105, for a critique of Jenny.

[44]Whether or not one can adequately identify all such sources and influences, or whether one can objectively remove oneself from one's own historical context in order to grasp the intertextual relationships operative in the author's context is once again beside the point. Every intertextual investigation must, in practice, limit the potentially unlimited range of intertextual relationships. How it does so is a matter which by definition lies *outside* of the theory, because any such limitation is in some sense a violation of that theory.

all, it provides no mechanism by which one can insist that only *some* intertexts are appropriate for investigation or normative for interpretation.

Second, given this hermeneutical flexibility, it would seem that intertextuality poses less of a break from traditional historical studies than some have insisted. One way to state this point is that, at least in the way that some are practicing it, intertextuality is more of an evolution than a revolution—more of an *extension* of traditional studies of influence than a *rejection*.[45] In particular, the most significant extension would be in the area of intentionality. Intertextuality permits one to investigate texts, even when the investigation is focused on text production and diachronicity, without any need to prove direct or conscious influence or authorial intention.[46]

There is, however, a much more profound way to understand the connection between intertextuality and traditional historical criticism. Intertextuality is neither an extension nor a rejection of traditional approaches, but rather it is a fundamental characteristic of *every* critical (and uncritical) investigation of texts. Whether in a simple, unsophisticated reading of a comic book, or a scholarly investigation of historical influence in the work of Shakespeare, or a whimsical comparison between Paul and *Star Trek*, or the difficult and tedious writing of a dissertation, intertextuality asserts that authors and readers are constantly and inevitably interacting with a plethora of texts, and that only in that dynamic interaction does meaning emerge. Intertextuality, in other words, describes what scholars *have already been doing*:[47] They have been understanding texts in rela-

---

[45]Clayton and Rothstein, "Figures in the Corpus," 3–4. Clayton and Rothstein point to American literary scholars in particular as those who tend towards extension rather than rejection; one might also point to biblical scholars in this category. Cf. Vorster, "Intertextuality and Redaktionsgeschichte," 19: "Traditional source-influence studies need not necessarily be regarded negatively . . . . The study of sources and influence of texts on other texts is the historical forerunner of intertextuality."

[46]It is worth noting, however, that even when interpreters disavow any interest in authorial intention, it may still creep in the back door. Vorster, "Intertextuality and Redaktionsgeschichte," 26, for example, sets limits on his intertextual reading of Mark 13 by noting that "one should keep in mind that he [Mark] absorbed many fragments of texts into his own speech by convention and not necessarily to get his reader to react to each little aspect of his text." In other words, Vorster suggests that one should only give attention to those intertexts which Mark *intended* to have a meaningful impact on the reader, disregarding those that Mark "absorbed . . . by convention." Cf. similarly Lasine, "The Ups and Downs of Monarchical Justice," 42.

[47]Cf. Vorster, "Intertextuality and Redaktionsgeschichte," 20: "It is, however, necessary to point out that the phenomenon of intertextuality is not at all new or modern. What is different is the way in which the phenomenon is perceived."

tionship to other texts, some written (e.g., sources) and some unwritten (e.g., historical context).[48]

Rather than evaluating *whether* any particular investigation is truly intertextual, therefore, it would seem better to ask in what *ways* it is intertextual:[49] How does this investigation specifically or consciously make use of intertextual insights? What sorts of limits guide the choice of texts to include in the investigation? As we turn now to a brief survey of some recent investigations in biblical studies which attempt to apply intertextuality, these are the kinds of questions that will guide us.

INTERTEXTUALITY IN BIBLICAL STUDIES

As noted above, intertextuality is rapidly becoming a hot topic in biblical studies. In what follows, we will briefly survey a few recent studies that have consciously adopted an intertextual approach. Our purpose here is two-fold. On the one hand, we need to see how the theoretical and practical issues sketched out above are worked out in actual investigations. On the other hand, we need to survey a representative (though not comprehensive) sample of intertextual investigations which may be relevant to the current investigation of Paul's use of citations in Galatians 3:1–14.

Echoes of Scripture: Richard Hays

As mentioned above, Richard Hays' book, *Echoes of Scripture in the Letters of Paul*, has been very successful in generating interest in intertextuality. Part of the reason for this success is the fact that Hays is much more evolutionary than revolutionary in his practice of intertextuality. On the one hand, he

---

[48] Intertextuality also, of course, calls into question the normative assumptions that have accompanied traditional historical scholarship, i.e. that *only* those particular intertexts which are diachronic and focused on text production are both relevant and sufficient for determining the meaning of the text. On the contrary, intertextuality insists that a potentially unlimited range of intertexts are relevant. As we have noted above, however, this insistence likewise invalidates any other normative assumptions about any particular set of limits one might impose; if historical criticism is defective, from the standpoint of intertextual theory, so is every other investigation which sets practical limits on the range of texts to consider.

[49] Cf. Sommer, "Exegesis, Allusion, and Intertextuality," 487n22, who critiques various scholars' claims to intertextuality; cf. likewise Aichele and Phillips, "Introduction," 7, who disparage the use of intertextuality by several biblical scholars including Hays, Buchanan, and Draisma "as a restrictive tool for nailing down authorial intent and literary influence.... Thinly veiled in such efforts are conservative ideological and theological interests in maintaining the primacy of certain (usually Christian) texts over against secondary (usually Jewish) precursors." As we have shown above, such claims to defend "true" intertextuality from its false pretenders are specious.

focuses the majority of his attention on texts which can be placed in diachronic priority to Paul's letters (specifically, of course, the texts of Paul's scripture).[50] On the other hand, Hays takes a somewhat intermediate position with respect to authorial intention and the question of text production versus text reception. He is willing to concede that the meaning he finds in the echoes he traces may never have consciously occurred to Paul, but at the same time he proposes the common-sense claim "that there is an authentic analogy—though not a simple identity—between what the text meant and what it means."[51] Furthermore, Hays locates the "hermeneutical event . . . in my *reading* of the text," but he seeks to make his readings convincing to an interpretive community which values historical investigation: "Claims about intertextual meaning effects are strongest where it can credibly be demonstrated that they occur within the literary structure of the text and that they can plausibly be ascribed to the intention of the author and the competence of the original readers."[52] In short, by speaking of *echo* rather than *allusion*, Hays sidesteps or "finesses" questions about authorial intention and the like, while at the same time he acknowledges and even preserves the traditional desire to locate normative meaning in what *Paul* says.

The evolutionary nature of Hays' approach is particularly evident in the seven tests which he develops to determine whether or not a given echo qualifies as convincing.[53] Six of these tests—availability of the echoed material (to Paul and to his audience), "volume" of echo (degree of correspondence or distinctiveness of echoed material), recurrence (Paul's use of the echoed material elsewhere), thematic coherence, historical plausibility, and history of interpretation—would easily find a home in any traditional historical investigation.[54] Only

---

[50]Cf. Hays, *Echoes*, 29–30: "echo is a diachronic trope;" cf. ibid., 20. Along similar lines, note Hays' reluctance to make use of rabbinic materials to inform the study of Paul, due to their late date—i.e., because they are *not* diachronically prior to Paul's letters (ibid., 11). As he has pointed out to me in response to a previous version of the current investigation, however, Hays does occasionally use later texts—even much later texts—"to shed light on Paul's reading practices"; cf. ibid., 102–104, 150.

[51]Ibid., 27; cf. ibid., 33: "To limit our interpretation of Paul's scriptural echoes to what he intended by them is to impose a severe and arbitrary hermeneutical restriction. In the first place, what he intended is a matter of historical speculation; in the second place, his intertextual echoes are acts of figuration. Consequently, later readers will rightly grasp meanings of the figures that may have been veiled from Paul himself."

[52]Ibid., 28.

[53]Ibid., 29–32. Several scholars have made use of some or all of these tests in subsequent investigations; cf. Brawley, "An Absent Complement," 436; Keesmat, "Exodus and the Intertextual Transformation of Tradition," 34–35.

[54]Indeed, the fact that tests are offered to "validate" an echo—to help to decide if an echo is "real"—speaks directly to traditional historical concerns. In effect, Hays is willing to be bound by authorial intention when it comes to determining *that* an echo is present,

in the seventh test does Hays move from a focus on text production and authorial intention to a concern with text reception. The seventh test is "satisfaction"—the degree to which the reading "produce[s] for the *reader* a satisfying account of the effect of the intertextual relation."[55]

Where Hays goes the farthest in his use of intertextual insights is in his adaptation and application of the "trope" which John Hollander calls *transumption* or *metalepsis*: "When a literary echo links the text in which it occurs to an earlier text, the figurative effect of the echo can lie in the *unstated* or *suppressed* (transumed) points of resonance between the two texts."[56] Throughout Hays' readings of Paul's letters, key points of meaning arise not only from what Paul says directly, but even more from the "cave of resonance" in which his intertextual echoes resonate.[57] In Paul's use of Dt 30:12–14 in Rom 10:5–10, for example, it is a number of suppressed echoes from Dt 8:17, Dt 9:4, and various Wisdom traditions—as well as "the hermeneutical framework developed through his interpretations of Hab. 2:4 ... and Gen. 15:6"—which reveal the coherence of Paul's thought:[58]

> Thus, Paul's interpretation presupposes what it argues and argues what it presupposes: that the real meaning of Deuteronomy 30 is disclosed not in lawkeeping but in Christian preaching. The argument, at its explicit level, rests on sheer force of assertion. Implicitly, however, the intertextual echoes created by Paul's evocation of Deut. 9:4 and of the Wisdom tradition suggest hauntingly that Paul's reading is less arbitrary than it sounds. From Deuteronomy, Paul echoes the idea that the covenant depends on grace from start to finish rather than on Israel's own righteousness. Echoing Job, Baruch, and Sirach, Paul hints at the notion that the word of God spoken in the Law is identical with the Wisdom of God, who "appeared on earth and lived among men" (Bar. 3:37)—not as Torah, as Israel's sages affirmed, but in the person of Jesus Messiah.[59]

Unfortunately, Hays makes the least use of intertextual insights precisely in the passage which is the focus of the current investigation, Galatians 3:1–14. There seem to be three reasons for this. First, by the time Hays reaches Galatians, his interest has shifted somewhat from hearing and exploring echoes to

---

even though he reserves the right to go beyond authorial intention when it comes to determining the meaning of that echo (see above, n. 51).

[55] Hays, *Echoes*, 31 (emphasis added).

[56] Ibid., 20 (emphasis added); Hays draws the ideas of echo, transumption, and metalepsis from John Hollander, *The Figure of Echo: A Mode of Allusion in Milton and After* (Berkeley: University of California Press, 1981).

[57] The "cave of resonance" also comes from Hollander; see Hays, *Echoes*, 21.

[58] Ibid., 77.

[59] Ibid., 82.

exploring and defending the thesis that Paul's exegesis is ecclesiological:[60] "Of special interest for our purposes are two passages (Gal. 3:1–14 and 4:21–31) at the beginning and end of the letter's central argumentative section, both discovering in the story of Abraham a prefiguration of the church."[61] Second, because his interest is in Abraham, Hays chooses to avoid getting entangled in the "quagmires of exegetical controversy" surrounding the heart of this passage (the "notoriously vexing" Gal 3:10–12); he skims over it only as it helps to establish his thesis.[62] Third, and perhaps most significant, in Galatians Hays no longer hears *echoes*, but rather direct broadsides: "[In Galatians] Paul employs biblical texts not allusively (the rhetorical strategy of this broadside does not permit such delicacy) but directly."[63] Thus deprived of his primary intertextual tool, metalepsis, Hays resorts to a more direct exegesis, finding the key to the passage in Paul's citation of scripture in Gal 3:8.[64]

Intertextuality and Midrash: Daniel Boyarin

Just as Richard Hays has generated a great deal of interest in intertextuality especially among New Testament scholars, so too has Daniel Boyarin generated a great deal of interest, particularly among scholars in Old Testament and/or rabbinic studies.[65] In a number of articles and in his book, *Intertextuality and the Reading of Midrash*, Boyarin has proposed that rabbinic midrash is a fundamentally hermeneutical and intertextual activity.[66] For Boyarin, the familiar pattern

---

[60]See above, 63.

[61]Hays, *Echoes*, 105.

[62]Ibid., 109.

[63]Ibid., 105.

[64]Ibid., 105–107. Though Gal 3:8 is a conflation of Gen 12:3 and 22:18, Paul does not have "to impose a labored christological exegesis on the Genesis texts. The LXX texts in fact say exactly what Paul wants them to." (ibid., 106). As we will see in chap. 5 below, however, even in the explicit citation of scripture there may be metaleptic silences.

[65]See, e.g., Lasine, "The Ups and Downs of Monarchical Justice," 38–39; Aryeh Cohen, *Rereading Talmud: Gender, Law, and the Poetics of Sugyot*, Brown Judaic Studies 318 (Atlanta: Scholars Press, 1998). Boyarin has also influenced many New Testament scholars; see, e.g., Steve Moyise, "Intertextuality and the Book of Revelation," *ET* 104 (1993): 295–98; Jervis, "'But I Want You to Know,'" 233.

[66]Daniel Boyarin, *Intertextuality and the Reading of Midrash* (Bloomington: Indiana University, 1990); idem, "The Song of Songs: Lock or Key? Intertextuality, Allegory and Midrash," in *The Book and the Text: The Bible and Literary Theory*, ed. Regina M. Schwartz (Cambridge, MA: Basil Blackwell, 1990), 214–30; idem, "Inner Biblical Ambiguity, Intertextuality, and the Dialectic of Midrash: The Waters of Marah," *Prooftexts* 10 (1990): 29–48. Cf. Martin S. Jaffee, "The Hermeneutical Model of Midrashic Studies: What It Reveals and What It Conceals," *Prooftexts* 11 (1991): 67–75.

of juxtaposed fragments of scripture and competing rabbinic interpretations is best explained not by assuming redaction of the text or by tracing the historical development or theological tendencies of individual rabbis, but rather by seeing the text holistically as "the establishment of an intertextual connection between two signifiers which mutually read each other."[67]

Boyarin's intertextual investigation of midrash is in some ways both diachronic and synchronic, focused both on text reception and on text production. To the extent that Boyarin himself is reading midrash, he focuses on diachronic text production. He investigates midrash as the result produced by rabbis bringing together texts which were clearly prior and available to them. For the most part, however, Boyarin's approach is less an intertextual reading of midrash than it is a description of the rabbis' intertextual reading of scripture; to the extent that he is describing *rabbinic* hermeneutics, he focuses on the rabbis' freedom to read the texts of scripture synchronically. Thus, for example, in the practice of *gezerah shewa*, the rabbis bring together texts without regard to historical relationships of influence or intention, but rather on the basis of a synchronic intertextual relationship perceived by way of a word or phrase in common.[68]

One model which Boyarin finds helpful in describing the intertextual hermeneutics of rabbinic midrash is Michael Riffaterre's "ungrammaticalities."[69] For Riffaterre, an inconsistency or difficulty in a text—an "ungrammaticality"—forces the reader to go beyond a surface reading to discover the underlying intertext in which the tension is resolved. This Boyarin compares to the rabbinic tendency to exploit the "bumps in the text" of scripture and to resolving those "bumps" by bringing in other texts.[70] With this model, Boyarin circumvents the charge that midrash reflects a purely arbitrary hermeneutic. The opposing points of view expressed by different rabbis, encoded in the form of snippets of other scriptures, reflect an actualization of the tensions and ambiguities already present in the text.[71] Furthermore, these snippets of scripture are more than just prooftexts meant to *support* a rabbi's interpretation of the text; rather the interpretation lies in the intertextual connection thus established:

> The Rabbis as assiduous readers of the Bible developed an acute awareness of these intertextual relations within the Holy Books, and consequently their own hermeneutic work consisted of a creative process of further combining and recombining biblical verses into new texts, exposing the interpretive relations already in the text, as it were, as well as creating new ones by revealing linguis-

---

[67]Boyarin, "Song of Songs," 219; cf. idem, "Inner Biblical Ambiguity," 30ff; Jaffee, "The Hermeneutical Model of Midrashic Studies," 68–69.

[68]Boyarin, "Inner Biblical Ambiguity," 29ff.

[69]See below, 123–30, for an overview of Riffaterre's thought.

[70]Boyarin, "Inner Biblical Ambiguity," 28–29.

[71]Ibid., 30, 41. Note the similarity to Riffaterre's insistence that the *text* controls the reading that is produced; see further below, 127.

tic connections hitherto unfelt. As we have seen in the above examples, what characterizes midrash is an understanding of interpretation not as the translating of a text to a higher or deeper level of signification, or, to use a different metaphor, the pairing of a signifier with a signified, but rather, as the laying bare of an intertextual connection between two signifiers which mutually read each other.[72]

Though Boyarin's work is not directly applicable to Galatians 3, it does raise some interesting issues. One issue which would be worth further investigation, though unfortunately not here, is whether or to what extent Paul's usual exegesis of scripture should be described as midrash when midrash is understood as Boyarin has defined it.[73] Another issue which our survey of Boyarin has indirectly raised is whether to describe Paul's intertextual interpretation of scripture, or whether to attempt an intertextual interpretation of Paul. (To the extent that one can make such a distinction, we will tend more towards the latter in the next chapter below.) Most of all, however, Boyarin has suggested one helpful model for understanding Paul's use of scripture in Galatians 3. Rather than simply piling up prooftexts, Paul is combining scriptures as a way of making sense of the "bumps" in his text—perhaps not so much bumps in his scriptural text, but rather bumps in the "text" of God's work of salvation through a crucified Messiah, proclaimed to the Gentiles.

Short Intertextual Studies on Paul: Keesmat, Jervis, Jobes

Three recent articles, by Sylivia C. Keesmat, L. Ann Jervis, and Karen H. Jobes, illustrate the variety of ways that the rising interest in intertextuality has been expressed in studies of particular passages in Paul's letters.[74] Despite some common roots—all three acknowledge their dependence on Hays, and Keesmat and Jervis also on Boyarin—each of these scholars applies intertextuality in different ways, particularly in terms of how and where they identify significant intertexts. In her study of Romans 8:14–30, for example, Keesmat makes explicit use of Hays' seven tests for echoes, but in fact she is less concerned with finding any specific text which Paul is echoing than with identifying the general intertextual matrix or resonant context in which this passage takes shape and has

---

[72]Boyarin, "Song of Songs," 223.

[73]Cf. Jervis, "'But I Want You to Know'"; see further below, 118. Before this question can adequately be addressed, one would need to deal with a major point of criticism which has been raised against Boyarin's work, namely that his conclusions, seemingly applicable to all rabbinic midrash, are actually based on only one, possibly not very representative, example (Mekhilta); cf. Jaffee, "The Hermeneutical Model of Midrashic Studies," 72–75.

[74]See n. 1 above for full citation of these articles.

meaning:[75] Understood within the pervasive intertextual matrix of the exodus, phrases such as "as many as are led by the Spirit" and "sons of God" and "spirit of freedom" have little to do with individuals and their status or their free will, but rather take shape in the context of the historic understanding of God as the one who leads His people out of slavery.[76]

In her study of 1 Corinthians 11:2–16, by contrast, Jervis identifies and/or reconstructs four specific subtexts which one must recognize in order properly to understand Paul's teaching. Two of these subtexts are the two Genesis creation accounts; one is Paul's original teaching to the Corinthians on the subject of men and women, which Jervis reconstructs along the lines of Gal 3:28 (which in turn she believes was based on Gen 1:27); and the last is the Corinthians' misunderstanding of Paul's original teaching, which Jervis reconstructs along the lines of Philo's idea of an original *genderless* image of God in creation.[77] According to Jervis, "Paul's corrective strategy is typically midrashic".[78] To correct the Corinthian misunderstanding, he reinterprets his original teaching by combining it with the second creation account.[79]

---

[75]Though Keesmat does point to some specific passages which help to describe the intertextual matrix of the exodus (e.g., Dt 32, Is 63, Tob 13:4–5, Bar 5:6), she insists that Paul is not so much echoing or alluding to these scriptures as he is appealing to an intertextual space common to Jewish thought and experience of which these scriptures are representative (Keesmat, "Exodus and the Intertextual Transformation of Tradition," 43). The intertextual matrix, in other words, "is informed by specific texts, but is not a text in itself" (ibid., 33). Here Keesmat notes the influence of Boyarin's idea of "cultural codes" and likewise Hayden White's description of the "story lines of a culture" (ibid., 33).

[76]Ibid., 37–43.

[77]Jervis, "'But I Want You to Know,'" 234–38. Jervis appears somewhat similar to Keesmat in her use of Philo less as a specific text to which either Paul or the Corinthians would have appealed than as a representative of a sort of cultural intertext which the Corinthians may have shared. Whereas Keesmat can point to innumerable examples showing the pervasiveness of the exodus as a cultural intertext, however, Philo is the *only* basis on which Jervis reconstructs the Corinthian misunderstanding.

[78]Ibid., 235. A major concern for Jervis is to establish that Hays is wrong in distancing Paul from rabbinic midrash, particularly in light of Boyarin's description of intertextuality in midrash (ibid., 231–34).

[79]There are a number of problems with Jervis' approach, starting with whether the strictly allusive use of scripture in 1 Cor 11:2–16 is truly comparable to the pattern of citation of snippets of scripture found in rabbinic midrash. One might also question whether the two creation accounts are the only or even the most obvious scriptural subtexts to which Paul alludes (especially in v. 10). Ultimately, it appears that Jervis' analysis is driven more by her reconstruction of the Corinthian misunderstanding, a la Philo, than by the intertextual or midrashic combination of creation accounts. In short, her study does not actually go very far beyond a fairly standard historical exegesis which gives particular attention to the insight which arises from a comparison of the passage with Philo. This is not to say that her study is not intertextual—see above, 110–14—but

The emphasis in Jobes' reading of Gal 4:21–31 lies in metalepsis, that is, in what Paul leaves unsaid. Part of what he leaves unsaid forms a puzzle which, Jobes contends, has too often been overlooked. Paul's citation of Is 54:1 appears to be given to explain that "(1) the Jerusalem above is free; (2) the Jerusalem above is our mother; (3) Christians are like Isaac, i.e., Sarah is our mother (and therefore Abraham is our father)"—but on the surface it explains none of these.[80] The key to resolving this puzzle lies in something else Paul leaves unsaid, namely Isaiah's transformation of the resonant theme of barrenness in the Old Testament:

> Isaiah's transformation of the story of Israel's childless matriarchs, beginning with Abraham and Sarah, provides a canonical basis for at least three points with which Paul later resonates. Isaiah's proclamation (1) provides an interpretation of Sarah's motherhood that can be taken to have wider reference than to the nation of Israel; (2) merges the concepts of matriarchal barrenness and the feminine personification of capital cities to produce female images of two Jerusalems, a barren, cursed Jerusalem and a rejoicing Jerusalem; and (3) introduces the concept of a miraculous birth to a barren woman as a demonstration of God's power to deliver a nation of people from death.[81]

One final thing that Paul leaves unsaid is the connection between the barren woman giving birth and the resurrection of Jesus:

> I believe Paul is arguing that the nation which God promised to bring from Sarah's dead womb and the population of the new Jerusalem prophesied by Isaiah are those people who are born through the resurrection of Jesus.... When Paul cites Isa 54:1, he is metaleptically announcing to the Galatians that when Jesus arose from death, all of the elect seed of Abraham were also born.[82]

Analysis

Despite their differences, each of these scholars exhibit certain common tendencies which are representative of the ways intertextuality is most often being used in biblical scholarship. For example, as the brief sketch above illustrates, a majority of scholars continue to operate primarily on the basis of text production and diachronicity, focusing on the ways that later writers have made use of earlier texts.[83] On the other hand, most scholars embrace a certain free-

---

rather that her use of intertextuality has not advanced much beyond the level already present in traditional historical exegesis.

[80] Jobes, "Jerusalem, Our Mother," 303.
[81] Ibid., 309.
[82] Ibid., 316.
[83] As an example of the pervasive tendency of biblical scholars to think in diachronic terms, cf. the dialogue between Stuart Lasine, "Jehoram and the Cannibal Mothers (2

dom from traditional concerns about historical reconstruction and authorial intention—at least in theory, if not always in practice.[84] That freedom raises what is perhaps the most significant common tendency among biblical scholars who embrace intertextuality, namely the way they deal with difficulties in the text. Rather than seeing such difficulties as evidence for and impetus towards some sort of historical reconstruction, they see them as *hermeneutical* opportunities. The most important issue is not the history of the text, nor the history of its author or original readers; the most important issue is finding meaning in the text, including (or even especially in light of) not only its difficulties but also all the other texts to which those difficulties might lead us.

INTERTEXTUALITY AND GALATIANS 3: SELECTED INSIGHTS AND METHODS

LIMITING THE SCOPE OF THE INVESTIGATION

As we have stressed above, any practical intertextual investigation must set some limits on the intertextual scope. It might seem obvious what those limits must be for the current investigation, given its focus on Paul's use of explicit citations. Surely the focus of the investigation will be on texts that are diachronically prior to Paul, namely the citations themselves, along with the contexts from which they are drawn and other scriptures with which they may resonate. Surely also, since no one would question that Paul has used these citations deliberately and consciously, this investigation must be primarily concerned with text production and even authorial intention.

In fact, however, the limits of the current investigation will not be framed exclusively in terms of either diachronic textual relationships or text production.

Kings 6.24–33): Solomon's Judgment in an Inverted World," *JSOT* 50 (1991): 27–53, and Hugh S. Pyper, "Judging the Wisdom of Solomon: The Two-Way Effect of Intertextuality," *JSOT* 59 (1993): 25–36; cf. also Lasine's rebuttal, "The Ups and Downs of Monarchical Justice." Pyper argues that Lasine fails to recognize that one should read not only 2 Kings 6 in light of 1 Kings 3 (the later text in light of the earlier), but also vice versa. Though this would seem to be a call for synchronicity, what Pyper is actually doing is suggesting a possible historical motivation for the writing of the later text: 2 Kings 6 was written as a parody of 1 Kings 3, in order to make us revise our understanding of it.

[84]From time to time scholars relapse (especially at the end of their investigations) into language more typical of a traditional historical critical investigation than the type of intertextual enterprise they have described and carried out; cf. for example Jobes, "Jerusalem, Our Mother," 318, where her "journey through the intertextual space defined by Galatians and Isaiah and Genesis" ends in historical speculation about the teaching Paul must have given to the Galatians on precisely those areas of resonance that are metaleptically hidden in his letter. Again, such a "relapse" does not mean that an investigation is any less intertextual; rather it points to the evolutionary nature of most intertextual investigations by biblical scholars.

Certainly the citations will provide both an obvious and a convenient way to limit the scope of the investigation, and to that extent the investigation will be diachronically focused on text production, since these citations are texts which chronologically precede Paul and which he used deliberately. As with other intertextual investigations, however, the emphasis of this investigation is hermeneutical rather than historical. The major concern is not to establish that Paul used these citations, nor to determine the historical circumstances in which he did so, but rather to explore the meaning(s) that are generated by these citations within Paul's argument. In other words, the question this investigation seeks to answer is how these citations function within Paul's argument, that is, how they contribute to the meaning of the passage.

To state the issue in this way is to raise at least three points that require investigation. First, the function of citations in general must be explored: how do citations work? The point here is not so much to ask what *Paul* has done with *these* citations, but rather to ask what the presence of any citation contributes to any text, and how. Second, in light of the significant problems posed by these specific citations, we need to explore the function of problematic features of a text: how do the problems of a text contribute to its meaning? Finally, we need to ask about the meaning that emerges from the functioning of these particular citations in this particular text: what does Galatians 3:1–14 say?

The exploration of each of these points will push the investigation beyond the boundaries of text production and diachronicity. For example, to ask how citations work in general is to explore what in effect is an intertext or set of intertexts. Whether the way citations work is a matter of assumptions or logical necessity or cultural expectations—a matter that will need to be explored below—it seems clear that this functioning can be described as one or more of those "unwritten, anonymous, and yet already read" intertexts that impact the way meaning emerges from texts.[85] Furthermore, if the function is a matter of logical or rhetorical necessity, these intertexts are essentially timeless—they are available to, though quite possibly not consciously apprehended by, any reader or any author at any time.[86] Ironically, therefore, even though its focus is on explicit citations from written, known, and diachronically prior sources, this investigation must give a significant amount of attention to implicit, anonymous, unwritten, and quite possibly timeless intertexts.

If some of the significant intertexts that contribute to the meaning of this passage are implicit, anonymous, unwritten, and timeless, it seems clear that we

---

[85] In a similar way, it seems likely that exploring how problems in a text are incorporated into or contribute to its meaning will lead to the discovery of unwritten intertexts; in effect, this is how the "missing premise" solution emerges in answer to the problems posed by Dt 27:26 in Gal 3:10 (see above, 67–68).

[86] One could accordingly describe these intertexts as diachronically prior to Paul, but it seems more appropriate to describe them as synchronically related to his argument.

cannot limit the meaning of the text only to that which we can demonstrate that Paul consciously intended to produce (assuming that such a demonstration would even be possible). On the contrary, to ask about how the citations function within the passage and contribute to its meaning is to leave open the question of where that meaning may lie, whether in the intentions of the author or in the perception of the reader—or both. Hays' common-sense approach may be helpful here, suggesting that in some sense meaning straddles both text reception and text production because there is an analogy between what something means to us as readers and what it meant to Paul. To the extent that we can generate a persuasive reading of the text (text reception), we might well assume that we have approximated something at least of what Paul was grappling with, consciously or unconsciously, as he produced the text. More specifically, to the extent that we can discover the ways that the citations shape our reading and understanding of the text, we may also have discovered something about the ways that the citations constrained and shaped Paul's thought.

SELECTED METHODS

What specific intertextual methods or approaches would be most useful for exploring how the citations function within and contribute to the meaning of Galatians 3:1–14? In light of the points discussed above, there are two approaches which seem particularly well suited. The first of these is Michael Riffaterre's notion of the role of "ungrammaticalities" in semiosis. As noted above, Boyarin compares Riffaterre's understanding of ungrammaticalities to the "bumps in the text" which generated so much rabbinic discussion. To be sure, we have already rejected the idea that in Gal 3:1–14 Paul is engaged in a rabbinic exercise to smooth out the bumps of scripture, at least in the sense in which Dahl, for example, might suggest.[87] On the other hand, Paul's use of citations has created a number of rather severe bumps for us; it may well be that Riffaterre's approach can give us insight, not so much into how to smooth out these bumps, but rather into how they generate or contribute to the meaning of the passage.

The second approach which seems particularly well suited for the current investigation is Jonathan Culler's discussion of "presuppositions." Presuppositions, as Culler describes them, are a way of getting at the anonymous and unwritten intertexts that play a vital role in how we understand a text—intertexts such as those that describe how citations function in a text. Furthermore, while Culler does not develop the idea of presuppositions with a specific concern for problems or difficulties in a text, this approach may be a complement to Riffaterre's notion of ungrammaticalities, offering another way for us to address

---

[87]See above, 91.

and explore how the difficulties posed by the citations contribute to the meaning of the passage.

Michael Riffaterre's "Ungrammaticalities"

Michael Riffaterre has been one of the leading figures in the development of intertextuality;[88] indeed, according to Clayton and Rothstein, he is "the writer who has used intertextuality most effectively in his practical criticism."[89] As we have seen with Boyarin, Riffaterre is also a writer whose ideas have already made inroads into biblical studies, particularly with respect to his notion of ungrammaticalities.[90] As Boyarin has used the idea, however, it has amounted to little more than using the difficulties or "bumps" of one scriptural text as an opportunity to insert some other text of scripture to help interpret it. This is only a partial understanding of what Riffaterre himself means by ungrammaticalities.[91]

Riffaterre's idea of ungrammaticalities arises out of his understanding of the differences between ordinary communication or texts and literary communication or texts.[92] He identifies a number of interrelated differences. First, literary communication consists only of a text and a reader, while ordinary communication includes also an author, a linguistic code, and most importantly, reality.[93] This last item points out another important difference. Ordinary communication is mimetic or referential—words and phrases refer to things, and the communication has a direct relationship with reality. Literary communication, however is characteristically *indirect*: "To put it simply, a poem says one thing and means

---

[88] Michael Riffaterre, *Semiotics of Poetry* (Bloomington: Indiana University, 1978); idem, *Text Production*, trans. Terese Lyons (New York: Columbia University, 1983). Jonathan Culler, "Riffaterre and the Semiotics of Poetry," in *The Pursuit of Signs*, 80–99, offers a useful summary of Riffaterre.

[89] Clayton and Rothstein, "Figures in the Corpus," 23.

[90] See above, 116; see also Brawley, "An Absent Complement," 429, 432–34, 440; van Wolde, "Texts in Dialogue with Text," 4.

[91] For an example of a study which follows Riffaterre's program much more closely than Boyarin's does, see Brawley, "An Absent Complement."

[92] Riffaterre, *Text Production*, 1–25; *Semiotics of Poetry*, 1ff. These differences are not only theoretical, but phenomenological. Throughout his works, Riffaterre appeals to the ways that readers actually experience literary texts. This is a deliberate strategy, for according to Riffaterre, "no theory is worth consideration unless it is solidly grounded upon the phenomena it claims to elucidate" (ibid., ix).

[93] Riffaterre, *Text Production*, 3–5; idem, *Semiotics of Poetry*, 1. Riffaterre is, in other words, very much a reader-response critic; he defines the literary phenomenon as "not only the text, but also its reader and all of the reader's possible reactions to the text" (idem, *Text Production*, 3)—but for Riffaterre, the text is firmly in control of the reader's responses (ibid., 6, 75, 98; cf. below, 127).

another."[94] Unlike ordinary texts, therefore, literary texts cannot properly be judged by comparing them to reality.[95] Such a comparison would be a judgment about *meaning* ("the information conveyed by the text at the mimetic level"), but to understand literary texts one must move beyond meaning to *significance*—that which gives a literary text its characteristic unity.[96]

Ungrammaticality is a phenomenon which not only guides the reader to recognize the indirection of the text, but also leads him or her to its essential unity, or significance.[97] A reader's first reading of a text, which Riffaterre calls the heuristic reading, operates at the mimetic level. The reader decodes the text from beginning to end, apprehending its meaning (what it appears to say about reality).[98] In that mimetic reading, however, the reader encounters ungrammaticalities—anomalies not only at the level of grammar and syntax, but also of form and structure, or of style, or of linguistic or cultural expectations.[99] These ungrammaticalities push the reader to a second reading, a retroactive and hermeneutical reading in which the reader begins to see how the different ungrammaticalities fit together:[100]

> As he moves through the text he comes to recognize, by dint of comparisons or simply because he is now able to put them together, that successive and differing statements, first noticed as mere ungrammaticalities, are in fact equivalent, for they now appear as variants of the same structural matrix. The text is in effect a variation or modulation of one structure—thematic, symbolic, or whatever—and this sustained relation to one structure constitutes the significance.[101]

This is the point at which ungrammaticality is linked to intertextuality. The single structural matrix from which the text and all its ungrammaticalities are

---

[94] Riffaterre, *Semiotics of Poetry*, 1. As the quotation suggests, poetry provides the primary model (and almost all the examples) for Riffaterre's understanding of literary phenomena. Riffaterre's use of the word "means" in this quotation is unfortunate, since he goes on to argue that the point of a literary text is not so much its meaning but rather its significance.

[95] Riffaterre, *Text Production*, 26ff.

[96] Riffaterre, *Semiotics of Poetry*, 2–3.

[97] Cf. ibid., 6: "I cannot emphasize strongly enough that the obstacle that threatens meaning when seen in isolation at first reading is also the guideline to semiosis, the key to significance in the higher system, where the reader perceives it as part of a complex network."

[98] Ibid., 4–5.

[99] Riffaterre initially speaks of ungrammaticality as one of three ways that the indirection of a literary text threatens its representation of reality (ibid., 2); in general, however, he tends to use it as the generic term for any anomaly in the literary text.

[100] Ibid., 5–6.

[101] Ibid., 6.

derived is, in effect, an intertext, or rather the crucial intertext, in light of which the text must be understood.[102] For Riffaterre, however, this crucial intertext is *not* some other specific, written text.[103] To be sure, some ungrammaticalities may refer to specific texts. A word or phrase that seems out of place may be recognized as an allusion to some other poem or text, for example.[104] But while such recognition will enrich the reader's experience of the text, it is not essential to finding its significance:

> What happens, one may well ask, when a literary tradition is forgotten and cultural changes wash away the paragram [i.e., intertext]? The efficacy of the text is in no way altered, because the text remains unchanged. The text is the starting point of the reader's reactions, not its paragrams. Obviously, the reader who shares the author's culture will have a richer intertext. But he will be able to draw on that wealth only when semantic anomalies in the text's linearity force him to look to nonlinearity for a solution. And the reader who is denied access to the intertextual paragram still sees the distortion, the imprint left upon the verbal sequence by the absent hypogrammatic referent.[105]

For Riffaterre, the matrix from which the entire text is derived, in light of which its ungrammaticalities are resolved and its unity and significance are found, is always based on a commonplace, a cliché, a "semantic given"[106]—not necessarily even a complete sentence; perhaps only a generative phrase or even

---

[102]It would be an oversimplification to suggest that the matrix is the *only* intertext. For Riffaterre, intertextuality enters in at every step of transformation from the matrix to the text; cf. ibid., 81ff, 115ff. Nevertheless, these other intertexts are significant only in connection with the matrix (idem, *Text Production*, 10, 77). (Note also that though the hypograms by which the matrix is transformed may depend on a specific text, they more often consist of clichés or descriptive systems, i.e., associated sets of words.)

[103]Actually, Riffaterre seems to reserve the term "intertext" for those points at which a *specific* text *is* in view. Based on our description of intertextuality, however, it seems clear that Riffaterre's "matrix" or "semantic given" is indeed an intertext, albeit an anonymous, non-specific, unwritten one. Cf. ibid., 115: "The semiosis-producing ungrammatical constants result from *intertextuality*"; cf. also his idea of the dual sign, ibid., 81ff.

[104]Thus, for example, Riffaterre traces Baudelaire's choice of the word *ingénu* in a line from his "Hymne à la Beauté" to Vergil's description of the Cyclops (ibid., 25).

[105]Riffaterre, *Text Production*, 87. This quote illustrates the extent to which Riffaterre is text-centric in his approach. Though he is concerned with the reader's response, it is the text which controls that response, regardless of the competence or experience of the reader.

[106]Riffaterre alternates somewhat confusingly between the terms "matrix" and "the given"; a possible solution to the confusion may be found in Riffaterre's definition of the matrix as the structure of the given (Riffaterre, *Semiotics of Poetry*, 13).

a single word. For example, the commonplace cliché of "life as a journey" is the given which unifies the following poem by Cocteau:

> Car votre auberge, ô mort, ne porte aucune enseigne.
> J'y voudrais voir, de loin, un beau cygne qui saigne
> Et chante, cependant que lui tordez le cou.
> Ainsi je connaîtrais ce don't je ne me doute:
> L'endroit où le sommeil interrompra ma route,
> Et s'il me faut marcher beaucoup.

> [For your inn, O Death, bears no signboard. I would like to see it from afar, showing a beautiful swan bleeding and singing, while you wring his neck. Thus I should know what I cannot even guess: the place where sleep will end my road and whether I have a long way to go.][107]

Cocteau expands and transforms the matrix of "life as a journey" to include death as an inn at the end of the road; a swan as a typical sign for an inn; the swan as the bird known for singing as it is killed; and so on.[108]

Two key points must be stressed. First, the matrix or given of the text is *not* its meaning, nor can the text be reduced to the given.[109] Though the text is derived from the given, that derivation is not simply a restatement, much less any sort of explication or defense, of the given. On the contrary, the derivation always involves some sort of transformation.[110] The goal in finding the significance (unity) of a text is not therefore to find its meaning per se, nor is it simply to resolve all the tensions and ambiguities; the goal is, rather, to *perform* the text—to encounter the ungrammaticalities, to trace the transformations, to play the "score" of the text, and perhaps in so doing to find oneself transformed

---

[107] As quoted and translated by Riffaterre, *Text Production*, 77–78.
[108] Ibid., 78–82.
[109] Cf. Culler, "Riffaterre and the Semiotics of Poetry," 90–91, who suggests that Riffaterre's approach tends to result in a certain reductionism, though he qualifies that critique by noting that for Riffaterre, "the meaning of the poem is not the matrix but the entire experience of moving from mimetic reading to the pursuit of hypograms to the discovery of semiotic unity" (ibid., 92). (Note that as Riffaterre defines it, however, the *meaning* of the text is the information it conveys at the mimetic level—which will be problematic or even nonsensical due to the presence of ungrammaticalities.)
[110] At the level of signs, Riffaterre describes derivation in terms of hypograms, in which "a word or phrase is poeticized when it refers to (and, if a phrase, patterns itself upon) a preexistent word group" (Riffaterre, *Semiotics of Poetry*, 23). This is another opportunity for intertextuality. The "preexistent word group" will be at the least a cultural or literary cliché, but may also be another specific written text. At the level of text, Riffaterre describes derivation in terms of conversion and/or expansion of signs (ibid., 47ff).

in the process.[111] Reading, as Riffaterre describes it, is something like a game or a calisthenics, something of which we do not ask a message, but rather an experience.[112]

The second key point is that the ungrammaticalities are not an invitation to free play. Though one "plays" the text, it is the text that dictates the score.[113] The ungrammaticalities of a text do not permit the reader to choose any intertexts, but rather constrain the reader to trace them through to arrive at the single given or matrix in which the significance of the text is found. This constraining is, in fact, a fundamental characteristic of literary texts: "No text is a work of art if it does not command the response of readers, if it does not provoke a reaction and, to a certain extent, control the behavior of those readers."[114]

For our purposes—the study of Paul's use of citations in Galatians 3:1–14—Riffaterre offers both some intriguing possibilities and some challenges. Foremost among the possibilities, of course, is the hope that approaching the text from the standpoint of ungrammaticalities will offer a solution to the vexing problems posed by the citations. Is there some sort of matrix, some intertext (whether anonymous or specific), to which the ungrammaticalities point and in light of which the text takes on new and deeper significance? Another attractive possibility is that Riffaterre's approach promises what amounts to a *normative*

---

[111]Ibid., 12. Riffaterre does not quite describe the experience as a transformation of the reader, but he certainly implies that the text pushes the reader to go in certain directions despite the reader's resistance: "It is a hierarchy of representations *imposed* upon the reader, despite his personal preferences, by the greater or lesser expansion of the matrix's components, an orientation *imposed* upon the reader despite his linguistic habits . . ." (ibid.; emphasis added).

[112]Ibid., 13–14; idem, *Text Production*, 4. Riffaterre goes so far as to compare poetry to a joke—the joke doesn't "go" anywhere or have any particular message as such; its significance lies in the experience of gratuitous transformation. At this point, of course, we may need to question whether poetry is an adequate model for the sort of literature with which we are concerned. It hardly seems responsible to suppose that Paul is putting together citations and arguments merely for the experience, with no message involved. Nevertheless, we need to be sensitive to the possible similarities between what Paul is doing and what Riffaterre is describing. Part of what Paul's message achieves may be achieved through our experiencing of the transformation of the text.

[113]Riffaterre makes this point again and again throughout his writings; see e.g. ibid., 4, 6, 75, 98; idem, *Semiotics of Poetry*, 12, 165: "Far from freeing the imagination, far from giving the reader greater leeway as it invites him to greater participation, reading is actually restrictive." Cf. idem, "The Making of the Text," in *Identity of the Literary Text*, 54–70; idem, "Compulsory Reader Response: The Intertextual Drive," in *Intertextuality: Theories and Practices*, 56–78.

[114]Riffaterre, *Text Production*, 98. For Riffaterre, literary texts are "monuments"—they endure, not only through history but also in spite of the desires and tendencies of its readers (ibid., 6, and frequently throughout).

reading of the text. There is only one matrix to which the text leads. This feature may help compensate for the major challenge of applying Riffaterre's approach, namely whether we can transfer his insights, based on poetry (in which the text is a sort of game), to letters now received as scripture. Certainly it will seem less than satisfactory to describe Paul's letter to the Galatians as having no message—and yet, if we understand scripture as that which constrains us and transforms us, if the message of scripture is as much or more a matter of its *effect* on us as it is the truths it conveys, then perhaps Riffaterre's model of a text which constrains its readers to undergo a particular (normative) experience will prove to be very useful indeed.

Jonathan Culler's "Presuppositions"

In a chapter describing the current state of intertextuality, Jonathan Culler points out that every practical attempt to implement intertextuality always threatens to subvert its ideals:

> [Intertextuality] is a difficult concept to use because of the vast and undefined discursive space it designates, but when one narrows it so as to make it more usable one either falls into source study of a traditional and positivistic kind (which is what the concept was designed to transcend) or else ends by naming particular texts as the pre-texts on grounds of interpretive convenience.[115]

> Theories of intertextuality set before us perspectives of unmasterable series, lost origins, endless horizons; and, as I have been suggesting, in order to work with the concept we focus it—but that focusing may always, to some degree, undermine the general concept of intertextuality in whose name we are working.[116]

Culler's response to the problem is not to abandon intertextuality, but rather to urge practitioners to seek out multiple strategies, multiple ways of focusing and limiting one's scope. To that end he offers an approach based on "the notion of presuppositions in linguistics and the literary analogues it suggests."[117]

Following "the notion of presuppositions in linguistics," Culler describes two different types of presuppositions at work in texts. The first, which he calls *logical presupposition*, Culler draws directly from its linguistic equivalent. A logical presupposition is anything implied to be true by a sentence, whether the sentence itself is affirmed or denied.[118] A classic example is found in the ques-

---

[115] Culler, "Presupposition," 109.
[116] Ibid., 111.
[117] Ibid.
[118] Ibid. The formal definition is as follows: "A sentence S logically presupposes a sentence S' just in case S logically implies S' and the negation of S, $\sim S$, also logically implies S'" (ibid.).

tion, "Have you stopped cheating on your spouse?" Whether answered "yes" or "no," this question presupposes that one has been in the habit of cheating on one's spouse.

In terms of literary texts, such presuppositions place assertions into an intertextual space, making them an implied prior discourse to which the text will relate—a prior discourse that is assumed as given or "already read," regardless of whether or not anyone has ever actually said any such thing.[119] Culler offers an example drawn from Baudelaire:

> Quand le ciel bas et lourd pèse comme un couvercle
> Sur l'esprit gémissant en proie aux longs ennuis
>
> [When the low and heavy sky weighs like a lid on the spirit groaning from the long anxieties that prey on it][120]

By placing this description of the sky in a temporal clause ("*When* the low and heavy sky weighs like a lid . . ."), Baudelaire does not need to defend or explain it, but rather can react to it as if it were an established figure in poetic tradition:[121] "Thus the problem of interpreting the poem becomes essentially that of deciding what attitude the poem takes to the prior discourse which it designates as presupposed."[122]

The second type of presupposition which Culler describes is analogous to, but not quite the same as, the linguistic notion of *pragmatic presupposition*. Essentially, pragmatic presupposition has to do with context:

> These presuppositions are defined not on the relations between sentences but on the relations between utterance and situation of utterance: 'An utterance of a sentence pragmatically presupposes that its context is appropriate.' That is, the context must be such as to allow one to interpret the utterance as the kind of speech act which it is. *Open the door* presupposes, pragmatically, the presence, in a room with a door that is not open, of another person who understands English and is in a relation to the speaker which enables him to interpret this as a request or command.[123]

Given the types of utterance for which linguistics has begun to explore the idea of pragmatic presupposition—commands, warnings, promises, etc.—Culler sees only a limited possibility for direct application to literary texts. There is an analogy, however, with the sort of literary or rhetorical presupposition that has

---

[119] Ibid., 112.
[120] As quoted and translated in ibid., 112.
[121] Ibid., 112–13.
[122] Ibid., 114.
[123] Ibid., 116.

to do with how a text or statement relates to the context which makes it intelligible, i.e., in particular, its genre:[124]

> *Once upon a time there lived a king who had a daughter.* Poor in logical presuppositions, this sentence is extremely rich in literary and pragmatic presuppositions. It relates the story to a series of other stories, identifies it with the conventions of a genre, asks us to take certain attitudes towards it (guaranteeing, or at least strongly implying, that the story will have a point to it, a moral which will govern the organization of detail and incident).[125]

Culler's approach to intertextuality by way of presuppositions is in many ways complementary to Riffaterre's ungrammaticalities. For one thing, both tend to use intertextuality less in terms of specific (written) intertexts than in terms of anonymous, already read but yet unwritten intertexts.[126] For another, presuppositions and ungrammaticalities may often be two sides of the same coin; part of what makes an ungrammaticality ungrammatical may be the presupposition(s) it violates.[127] Finally, just as with Riffaterre's ungrammaticalities, Culler's category of presuppositions offers an intertextual approach which respects the authority of the text. Presuppositions, as Culler has described them, are not so much that which a reader brings to the text, but rather that which the text itself forces the reader to bring.

What remains for us now is to see how these complementary approaches can illuminate the problem of Paul's use of citations in Galatians 3:1–14. Promising though they seem to be, they will prove to be little more than interesting intellectual exercises unless they lead us to new insights into a very difficult, and yet very important, passage of scripture.

---

[124]Ibid., 116–17.

[125]Ibid., 115. Culler offers another example, drawn from Baudelaire's 'Un Voyage à Cythère': "[It was not a temple with bosky shades/Where the young priestess, in love with flowers,/Passed, her body consumed by secret flames,/Her robe blowing open in the fleeting breezes.] Logically, *it was not a temple* presupposes only that there was something, but rhetorically it presupposes that someone would have expected it to be a temple or had claimed that it was"; the line thus becomes "a negation of the language which poetic tradition might have applied to Cythère" (ibid., 115–16).

[126]Culler alludes to their compatibility at this point when he singles out Riffaterre as offering one "valuable project" for addressing intertextuality using multiple strategies, alongside his own proposal for using presuppositions (ibid., 111).

[127]Cf. Riffaterre, *Semiotics of Poetry*, 25ff.

Chapter 5
UNGRAMMATICALITIES AND PRESUPPOSITIONS IN GALATIANS 3:1–14

The hardest part of reading scripture intertextually is knowing where to begin. As we have stressed repeatedly in the previous chapter, intertextuality draws on a potentially infinite number of connections that can arise between texts and intertexts, both written and unwritten. Even when one has, for practical purposes, set a limit on the intertexts to be considered, the multiplicity of synchronic interconnections that can arise presents one with the challenge of how to explore them, and how to present that exploration in a clear and compelling manner. There is no obvious starting point, nor is there any obvious sequence of steps which must be followed in tracing out the intertextual links. One faces something like the phenomenon of the Internet, a vast array of interconnected texts, any one of which can lead to any other.

Two observations emerge from the problem sketched out above. First, that which makes an intertextual reading convincing is not likely to be its logical sequence of deductions, but rather its density and quality of interconnections. Second, an intertextual reading is not easily captured in the form of a single written text. One can only build up the web of interconnections one at a time, perhaps leaving one or many points dangling until the next one is put into place. Somehow, one must invite or cajole the reader to move from the sequential text at hand to take the intertextual plunge, to begin to see and appreciate the whole web of interconnections that both give rise to and arise from the intertextual reading, rather than seeing merely a series of half-finished arguments.

Still, we must begin somewhere and proceed somehow to assemble a web of intertextual connections arising from Paul's citations of scripture in Gal 3:1–14. We will approach the problem from three angles. First, we will begin by examining the form and structure of the citations as a group, following the lead of Michael Riffaterre. Second, drawing on the insights of Jonathan Culler, we will explore some of the presuppositions implicit within the passage. Third, again following Riffaterre, we will examine the ungrammaticalities that arise from the preceding steps (including the preceding chapters), seeking a "matrix" by which they are brought into unity and significance. Finally, we will attempt to weave all of these threads together into a fresh reading of the passage.

STRUCTURE AND FORM

According to Michael Riffaterre, intertextual investigation (or, to use a word that perhaps better suits Riffaterre's approach, *performance*) of a text begins with what he calls the heuristic reading, or the reading of the text at the mimetic level.[1] This reading seeks to make sense of the text at face value, attempting to relate its signs in sequence to the reality to which they appear to refer. It is in this process that ungrammaticalities come to light. One begins to be aware of anomalies not only in *what* the text appears to say about reality, but also in *how* it says what it says, i.e., in its grammar, syntax, form, structure, and style. These ungrammaticalities push one to explore the underlying intertextual transformations that give the text its true unity and significance.

To a large extent, we have already carried out the heuristic reading of Galatians 3:1–14—or rather, we have closely examined the readings of others—and as a result we have already noticed a number of ungrammaticalities arising from Paul's use of citations.[2] These heuristic readings have included some concern not only with *what* the citations say, but also with *how* they say what they say, particularly with respect to the form in which individual citations occur. As we pointed out above, however, investigations concerned with the form of citation have tended to deal with one citation at a time, often with the rather limited purpose of determining which text Paul may have used or how he may have modified the texts from which he quotes scripture.[3] Only rarely have they looked at the form of the citations *as a group*, in order to see if any anomalies or intertextual clues may lurk in the overall structure and arrangement of the citations within Paul's argument. It is to this task that we must turn first in order to complete the heuristic phase and move fully into the hermeneutical and intertextual phase of our reading of the text.

THE CHIASTIC STRUCTURE OF THE CITATIONS

The starting point for our examination of the overall structure and arrangement of the citations in Galatians 3:1–14 is the last group of four citations, found in verses 10–14. In part, our attention is already drawn to these four citations because they are the ones that have proved especially troublesome, for reasons

---

[1] See above, 124.
[2] See chap. 3 above.
[3] See above, 58–61.

that we have explored above.⁴ The first two citations, Gen 15:6 in Gal 3:6 and Gen 12:3 in Gal 3:8, have generated relatively little debate among scholars, no doubt because these both seem to be entirely appropriate to Paul's purposes:⁵ Gen 15:6 ("Abraham believed in God and it was reckoned to him as righteousness") seems to establish the connection between righteousness and faith, with Abraham as the paradigm of faith; Gen 12:3 ("Through you shall all Gentiles be blessed") seems to establish the connection between Abraham and the Gentiles.⁶

The four citations in Gal 3:10–14, on the other hand, stand out not only because they have proved especially troublesome for interpreters, but also because they form a chiastic pattern:⁷

Curse: "Cursed be anyone . . ." (Dt 27:26)
　Life: "The righteous will live by faith" (Hab 2:4)
　Life: "The one who does these things will live in them" (Lev 18:5)
Curse: "Cursed be anyone . . ." (Dt 21:23)⁸

---

⁴See chap. 3 above.

⁵The citation in Gal 3:8 appears to be a conflation of more than one text in Genesis; for example, it may be drawn not only from Gen 12:3 ("in you all the families of earth shall be blessed," NRSV) but also Gen 18:18 ("all the nations of the earth shall be blessed in him," NRSV). For our purposes, however, the exact source(s) of the citation is not important. For convenience, we will refer to the source of the citation in Gal 3:8 as Gen 12:3.

⁶See for example the treatment of these verses by any of the major commentaries, including H. D. Betz, *Galatians: A Commentary on Paul's Letter to the Churches in Galatia*, Hermeneia (Philadelphia: Fortress Press, 1979), 140–43; Richard N. Longenecker, *Galatians*, WBC 41 (Dallas: Word Books, 1990), 113–15; and J. Louis Martyn, *Galatians*, AB 33A (New York: Doubleday, 1997), 296–302. It should be noted that Paul's reading of Gen 15:6 (and to some extent Gen 12:3 as well) is revisionary in relation to Jewish interpretation of his day; cf. Betz, *Galatians*, 141; Martyn, *Galatians*, 299–300, 302–306. Nevertheless, it is relatively easy to see how he can co-opt these verses to his purposes, while it is much harder to understand how a verse like Dt 27:26, for example, supports his argument.

⁷Cf. Alain Gignac, "Citation de Lévitique 18,5 en Romains 10,5 et Galates 3,12," *Église et Théologie* 25 (1994): 381; Dietrich-Alex Koch, *Die Schrift als Zeuge des Evangeliums: Untersuchungen zure Verwendung und zum Verständnis der Schrift bei Paulus*, BHT 69 (Tübingen: J. C. B. Mohr; Paul Siebeck, 1986), 120; Christopher D. Stanley, *Paul and the Language of Scripture: Citation Technique in the Pauline Epistles and Contemporary Literature*, SNTS 74 (Cambridge: Cambridge University Press, 1992), 239.

⁸Paul's citation of Dt 21:23 in Gal 3:13 (ἐπικατάρατος πᾶς ὁ κρεμάμενος ἐπὶ ξύλου) is in a substantially different form than that found in the LXX (κεκατηραμένος ὑπὸ θεοῦ πᾶς κρεμάμενος ἐπὶ ξύλου). Gignac, "Citation," 382, argues that Paul makes the change from the perfect participle κεκατηραμένος to the adjective ἐπικατάρατος in order to lessen the sense of a permanent curse. Perhaps a more significant effect, however, is to strengthen the correspondence with the citation of Dt 27:26 in Gal 3:10, which

This chiastic structure becomes even more striking if one "backs up" one citation, to include verse 8:[9]

Blessing: "Through you the nations will be blessed" (Gen 12:3)
    Curse: "Cursed be anyone . . ." (Dt 27:26)
        Life: "The righteous will live by faith" (Hab 2:4)
        Life: "The one who does these things will live in them" (Lev 18:5)
    Curse: "Cursed be anyone . . ." (Dt 21:23)
[**Blessing:** ". . . in order that the blessing of Abraham . . ." (allusion to Gen 12:3)][10]

What is especially striking about this chiastic structure is that its terms are not simply random catchwords. On the contrary, blessing, curse, and life are three of the four terms with which the Deuteronomist sums up the giving of the Law: [11]

> I call heaven and earth to witness against you today that I have set before you life and death, blessings and curses. Choose life that you and your descendants may live, loving the Lord your God, obeying him, and holding fast to him; for that means life to you and length of days, so that you may live in the land that

---

occurs in substantially (though not exactly) the same form as the LXX (ἐπικατάρατος πᾶς ὅς . . .). Cf. Stanley, *Paul and the Language of Scripture*, 245–46; Koch, *Die Schrift*, 120; Martyn, *Galatians*, 321.

[9]Gignac, "Citation," 381, similarly expands the chiasm to include 3:8 and 3:14. However, Gignac makes the connection using more than just the word "blessing"; he ties the chiasm even more firmly together using three terms: the **blessing** of **Abraham** to the **Gentiles**. Gignac thus sharpens the point that Paul's argument has to do with how the blessing of Abraham comes to the Gentile Galatians. While I in no way disagree with Gignac on this point, I have chosen to focus specifically on the word "blessing" because of the intertextual links thus established with the giving of the law; see below.

[10]The last term of this enlarged chiasm (blessing in 3:14) does not occur within an explicit citation, but it does seem evident that in verse 14 Paul is alluding back to the citation of Gen 12:3 in Gal 3:8.

[11]Many commentators note the obvious connection between the blessing/curse or blessing/curse/life/death motif and the giving of the Law; cf. e.g., Martyn, *Galatians*, 324–25; Richard B. Hays, *Echoes of Scripture in the Letters of Paul* (New Haven: Yale University Press, 1989), 109; Gignac, "Citation," 384–85; Stephen Westerholm, *Israel's Law and the Church's Faith: Paul and His Recent Interpreters* (Grand Rapids: Eerdmans, 1988), 198; Vincent M. Smiles, "The Gospel and the Law in Galatia: Paul's Response to Christian Separatism and the Threat of Galatian Apostasy," (Ph.D. diss., Fordham University, 1988), 243; James M. Scott, "'For as Many as are of Works of the Law are under a Curse' (Galatians 3.10)," in *Paul and the Scriptures of Israel*, ed. Craig A. Evans and James A. Sanders, JSNTSS 83 (Sheffield: JSOT Press, 1993), 195; Dieter Lührmann, *Galatians: A Continental Commentary*, trans. O. C. Dean (Minneapolis: Fortress, 1992), 62–64.

the Lord swore to give to your ancestors, to Abraham, to Isaac, and to Jacob (Dt 30:19–20, NRSV).[12]

Thus, the chiastic structure of the citations contributes to an intertextual web, resonating with a key motif in scripture, and pointing to the questions that Paul—and we—will ultimately have to address: why then was the Law given? What is the place of the Law in the life of the Christian believer?

There is, of course, one more citation that we have not yet incorporated into the chiastic structure. At first glance, it may seem that the first citation in this section of the letter, the citation of Gen 15:6 in Gal 3:6 ("Abraham believed in God and it was reckoned to him as righteousness"), cannot be incorporated. After all, if we are going to build the chiasm out of citations, we seem to be out of them; within this section of Paul's argument, there is no other citation or even any clear allusion to scripture following the probable allusion to Gen 12:3 in Gal 3:14a.[13] On the other hand, if one were to try to match the citation of Gen 15:6 with one of the other citations Paul has used in this section, there is at least one potential candidate. Paul's citation of Hab 2:4 matches two of the key terms from Gen 15:6, namely faith and righteous(ness).[14] Unfortunately, a match between the citations of Gen 15:6 in 3:6 and Hab 2:4 in 3:11 would threaten the tightly coupled structure of the chiasm as developed thus far—not only because it would disrupt the sequence, but also because it would introduce some key terms, faith and righteousness, that do not fit so neatly into the motif of blessing, curse, and life and its intertextual resonance with the giving of the law.

One obvious alternative is simply to leave the first citation out—to treat it as an introductory citation, one that perhaps expresses Paul's true thoughts be-

---

[12]Cf. similarly Dt 11:26 and 30:1 (blessings and curses) and 30:15 (life and death), as well as the extended catalog of blessings and curses in Dt 28.

[13]There is, of course, another citation available in Gal 3:16, but 3:15ff, though certainly related to the theme of the blessing of Abraham, seems to take the argument in a new direction. Most commentators agree that 3:14 is the end of this section of Paul's argument; so, for example, Betz, *Galatians*, 154. From the standpoint of intertextuality, of course, this poses no barrier to the interrelation of texts; from the standpoint of form and structure, however, it seems best not to attempt to span the chiasm across an obvious boundary. In any case, there is no term in common between Gen 15:6 and the citation in Gal 3:16 ("and to your seed," drawn from any one of several passages in Genesis).

[14]Martyn, *Galatians*, 312, considers Gen 15:6 and Hab 2:4 to be Paul's own scriptural texts, cited as brackets around the Teachers' two texts of Gen 12:3 and Dt 27:26. In so doing he is following the suggestion of E. P. Sanders, *Paul, the Law, and the Jewish People* (Minneapolis: Fortress, 1983), 21 (hereafter cited as *PLJP*); Sanders observes that Gen 15:6 and Hab 2:4 are the only two verses in the Old Testament which refer both to faith and to righteous(ness).

fore he turns to the difficult exegetical argument that follows.[15] On the other hand, it may be better to press on a bit further, to see if one can overcome the difficulties of incorporating this citation into the chiasm. Though there is the danger of forcing something to fit, there is also a certain intertextual necessity of seeing how far a pattern plays out once it has been established. In other words, from the standpoint of text reception, once the reader has perceived a clear chiastic structure established by the other citations, he or she can hardly avoid looking for ways to carry it through.

As it turns out, there is at least one term that could tie the citation of Gen 15:6 to Gal 3:14b, the last remaining clause in this section of Paul's argument:

Faith: "Abraham had faith . . . it was reckoned to him as righteousness" (Gen 15:6)
    Blessing: "Through you the nations will be blessed" (Gen 12:3)
        Curse: "Cursed be anyone . . ." (Dt 27:26)
            Life: "The righteous will live by faith" (Hab 2:4)
            Life: "The one who does these things will live in them" (Lev 18:5)
        Curse: "Cursed be anyone . . ." (Dt 21:23)
    [**Blessing:** ". . . the blessing of Abraham . . ." (allusion to Gen 12:3)]
[**Faith:** ". . . in order that we might receive the promise of the Spirit through faith"]

As we have already noted, the final element in this expanded chiasm, Gal 3:14b, is neither a citation from nor an obvious allusion to scripture; on the surface, the only connection between Gal 3:14b and Gen 15:6 is the Greek root πιστ-. On closer examination, however, there is more to recommend the connection. The citation of Gen 15:6 in Gal 3:6 comes as the culmination of the argument by experience that Paul advances in Gal 3:2–5; the heart of that argument is the connection between faith and the receiving of the Spirit.[16] This is

---

[15]Cf. Betz, *Galatians*, 140–42; Betz treats Gal 3:7 as the "exegetical 'thesis,'" based on the citation of Gen 15:6 in the previous verse, which will then be supported with "five proofs from Scripture" (ibid., 141–42). Cf. G. Walter Hansen, *Abraham in Galatians: Epistolary and Rhetorical Contexts*, JSNTSS 29 (Sheffield: JSOT Press, 1989), 69, 104ff; Hansen sees the citation of Gen 15:6 in Gal 3:6 as the "biblical restatement of this point of agreement" (the point of agreement being the doctrine of justification by faith) as well as the introduction of an argument directed at the point of disagreement concerning the distinction between Jews and Gentiles (ibid., 69).

[16]Contra most major commentators, I see 3:6 as belonging with 3:1–5, or at least as a bridge between 3:1–5 and 3:7ff, rather than as the beginning of a new section. In particular, I would see the καθώς of 3:6 as expressing a concluding summation of the preceding verses, while the ἄρα of 3:7 indicates the development of the implications of all of these verses (3:1–6), not just of the citation in 3:6. Cf. Longenecker, *Galatians*, 109; while Longenecker also sees 3:6 as the beginning of a new section in Paul's argument, he argues for a close connection between 3:1–5 and 3:6–14, and especially between 3:2–5 and 3:14b; cf. Christopher D. Stanley, "'Under a Curse': A Fresh Reading of Galatians 3:10–14," *NTS* 36 (1990): 493. The only major commentator who groups 3:6 with

precisely the point that is made in Gal 3:14b, so that 3:14b works very well as the chiastic counterbalance to the thoughts expressed in 3:1–6.

SIGNIFICANCE OF THE CHIASTIC STRUCTURE

The Citations as the Framework of Paul's Argument

To the extent that the reader finds this chiastic structure plausible, he or she is faced with an important question: what is its significance?[17] At the very least, such a structure calls into question certain assumptions that some scholars have brought to the discussion of these verses. Are these citations *merely* proof-texts, as H. D. Betz and E. P. Sanders claim?[18] Does Paul use several of these particular verses *only* because they have been used or are likely to be used by his opponents, as C. K. Barrett and J. Louis Martyn assert?[19] The presence of a striking chiasm does not completely rule out either possibility, but it does suggest at a minimum that Paul has not used these citations idly, carelessly, or even reluctantly. The careful structure of these citations, which highlights the very point under discussion—the place of the Law in the life of the people of God—suggests that these citations play a major role in Paul's thought and argument.

3:1–5 is F. F. Bruce, *The Epistle to the Galatians*, NIGTC (Grand Rapids: Eerdmans, 1982), 147, 152–53. Bruce also understands 3:6 as a bridge: "V 6 both concludes one section of his argument and begins a new one: it is connected with what goes before it by καθώς and with what follows by the ἄρα of v 7" (ibid., 153).

[17]Both Koch, *Die Schrift*, 120 and Stanley, *Paul and the Language of Scripture*, 239, 245, affirm the significance of chiasm in general, and the significance of this chiasm in particular. According to Stanley, the reinforcement of the chiastic structure that results from Paul's alteration of wording "is surely no accident, though the value of such constructions in leading the hearer through a complex and closely reasoned argument is often underappreciated by modern readers." Unfortunately, neither Koch nor Stanley explores the details of *how* the chiasm is significant in Paul's argument in Gal 3.

[18]See above, 74–78.

[19]See above, 78–79. Martyn specifically argues that Gen 12:3, Dt 27:26, and Lev 18:5 are texts which have been (or, in the case of Lev 18:5, will be) used by the Teachers in their exegetical argument against Paul. Note especially his comment on Paul's citation of Gen 12:3: "As Paul's prefixed exegesis makes clear, his attention is focused on God's present deed of *rectifying* the Gentiles. The text, however, speaks of *blessing*. If Paul were freely selecting a text, it is likely that he would have chosen one that refers literally to God's act of rectification" (Martyn, *Galatians*, 301). Given that Gen 12:3 fits so neatly into the chiastic structure and contributes to a significant intertextual resonance with the law, however, it seems equally if not more likely that this text is perfectly suited to Paul's purposes.

Indeed, it may not be too much to suggest that they act as the framework of his argument in this section of his letter.[20]

To say that the citations act as the framework for Paul's argument (or, from the perspective of text reception, to say that they act as the framework for the reader's understanding of Paul's argument) is to say more than simply that the citations play an important or even crucial role. Rather, it is to suggest that the citations give *shape* to the argument—specifically, a chiastic shape. How then does that chiastic shape affect our understanding of the argument? Two possibilities come to mind. First, a chiasm has the obvious rhetorical result of linking ideas together in the minds of the readers or hearers.[21] To say it another way, chiasm creates an intertextual connection, regardless of whether such a connection would have been perceived apart from the chiasm; once linked by the perceived chiastic structure, the linked pairs can no longer be understood apart from one another. Second, it seems likely that a chiasm may focus particular attention on certain sets of linked pairs, namely its innermost and outermost pairs (perhaps most of all the innermost).[22]

The Crux of the Chiasm: The Crux of the Argument?

In the case of the innermost pair of citations, the net effect of the chiastic structure in Gal 3:1–14 is to force into relationship two citations that seem decidedly at odds with one another, Hab 2:4 and Lev 18:5.[23] The full significance of this contrasting relationship will be further explored below;[24] the task we need to undertake for the moment, however, is to examine, from a formal or structural perspective, precisely how the relationship is constituted. In particular,

---

[20]These statements (and the preceding footnote) have been framed in terms of text production, i.e., in terms of Paul's intentions, but the point need not rest on whether or not we can ascertain anything about Paul's actual intentions. Essentially the same point can be made in terms of text reception: once we as readers have perceived this chiastic structure, we cannot easily dismiss these citations as incidental to the text; the structure becomes for the reader a framework for understanding this section of Paul's letter, regardless of whether this was Paul's intention.

[21]Cf. Stanley, *Paul and the Language of Scripture*, 239.

[22]Unfortunately, at this time I have no evidence to offer in support of this suggestion other than intuition—but it is a strong intuition. Just as the emphasis in a Greek sentence falls on the endpoints, that is to say, at the beginning and end rather than in the middle, so also with a chiastic structure—but with the difference that the "endpoints" of a chiasm occur in pairs, namely, the innermost and outermost pairs of terms. Of these two, it would seem self-evident that the innermost pair serves as a hinge-point, a "crux" for the chiasm—and perhaps therefore a crux for the argument.

[23]See above, 79.

[24]See below, 167–73.

we need to see how the terms of each citation match up. There are two main possibilities:

ὁ δίκαιος   ἐκ πίστεως   ζήσεται
ὁ ποιήσας   αὐτὰ   ζήσεται ἐν αὐτοῖς

or

ὁ δίκαιος   ἐκ πίστεως   ζήσεται
ὁ ποιήσας αὐτὰ ἐν αὐτοῖς   ζήσεται[25]

While the first of these has the advantage of following the word order of the Greek as cited by Paul, the second seems much more likely: "The natural parallelism is to be found between the two prepositional expressions, ἐκ πίστεως and ἐν αὐτοῖς on the one hand and the adjective ὁ δίκαιος and the participle with its object ὁ ποιήσας αὐτά on the other."[26] While scholars have vigorously debated the advantages or disadvantages of linking the prepositional phrase ἐκ πίστεως to the verb (ζήσεται) or to the substantival adjective (ὁ δίκαιος), the more significant point for our purposes is to note the middle term:[27] The center of the two citations, the point around which the contrast is drawn—and therefore, the center of the whole chiastic structure of this section of Paul's letter—is

---

[25]The majority of discussion about how to align these two citations in Galatians arises out of a concern for how to understand the citation of Hab 2:4 in Rom 1:17; for an overview, see D. Moody Smith, Jr., "Ο ΔΕ ΔΙΚΑΙΟΣ ΕΚ ΠΙΣΤΕΩΣ ΖΗΣΕΤΑΙ," in *Studies in the History and Text of the New Testament in Honor of Kenneth Willis Clark*, ed. Boyd L. Daniels and M. Jack Suggs, Studies and Documents 29 (Salt Lake City: University of Utah Press, 1967), 13–25, and H. C. C. Cavallin, "'The Righteous Shall Live by Faith': A Decisive Argument for the Traditional Interpretation," *Studia Theologia* 32 (1978): 33–43. The debate centers on whether ἐκ πίστεως modifies ὁ δίκαιος or ζήσεται; the latter, supported by Smith and Cavallin, is represented by the KJV, "The just shall live by faith," and the former, supported by various scholars, including E. P. Sanders, *PLJP*, 53n23, is represented by the RSV, "He who through faith is righteous shall live."

[26]Cavallin, "Decisive Argument," 38. He goes on to suggest that, since ἐν αὐτοῖς clearly modifies the verb ζήσεται in the citation of Lev 18:5, the parallelism demands that ἐκ πίστεως must do the same in the citation from Hab 2:4; cf. Smith, "Ο ΔΕ ΔΙΚΑΙΟΣ," 19. Stanley, "'Under a Curse,'" 504n60, argues that the parallelism between Hab 2:4 and Lev 18:5 favors the reading which takes ἐκ πίστεως with ὁ δίκαιος, but his argument depends largely on supplying the phrase ἐν αὐτῷ to the citation of Hab 2:4.

[27]Cf. Martyn, *Galatians*, 314, who argues that either option would ultimately have the same meaning for Paul, because, in Martyn's reading of Gal 3:21, Paul "equates rectification with making alive." See below, 170n122.

ζήσεται. Oddly, this is precisely the term that has received the least attention from scholars, an omission that we will attempt to rectify below.[28]

Righteousness, Faith, and the Spirit

The case of the outermost pair of elements in the chiasm is rather different from that of the innermost pair. Instead of an unmistakably parallel structure that almost forces us to find a relationship between the citations, here we have no obviously parallel structure; it is only the presence of chiasm elsewhere in the passage that invites the attempt to find an intratextual correlation. We did find it possible to extend the chiasm by way of the common term "faith" in Gal 3:14b and the citation of Gen 15:6 in Gal 3:6, as well as a more general correlation between Gal 3:2–5 and Gal 3:14b. Since our focus has been on the structure of the *citations*, however, the question that remains is how tightly the chiastic parallel can be drawn just using the citation of Gen 15:6. In particular, other than the Greek root πιστ-, is there any structural parallelism between Gal 3:14b and the citation of Gen 15:6 in Gal 3:6? Can we match up the terms of each as we did with the terms of the innermost pair of citations?

As it turns out, even though there is no grammatical or syntactical parallelism between the citation of Gen 15:6 and Gal 3:14b, there is a certain structural parallelism at a deeper level. In both cases, we have a subject who receives something of infinite value by way of faith. Abraham is granted righteousness because he has faith in God; we receive the promise of the Spirit through faith.

What is particularly intriguing about this structural parallelism is the connections it suggests between matching sets of terms. One of the links comes as no surprise: "We" are matched up with "Abraham"—and of course, Paul makes it clear that we who are of faith are the heirs ("sons") of Abraham, in some way following in Abraham's footsteps. The other link, however, is not so obvious, but perhaps equally or even more significant: the Spirit that we have received is linked with the righteousness that Abraham received. The relationship established by this link could of course be one of comparison, contrast, equivalence, or something else. Given the position of the citation from Gen 15:6 as a sort of summary of the reminder to the Galatians about how they received the Spirit by faith, and especially in light of the use of καθώς to connect this citation with

---

[28] See below, 167–73. It is not that scholars give no attention at all to this term, but rather that there is little debate over its significance. Instead there is a widely shared assumption that the term is used not only eschatologically but soteriologically in both citations, so that they offer competing claims for how one gains life. Smith, "Ο ΔΕ ΔΙΚΑΙΟΣ," 19–20, voices a decidedly minority viewpoint when he suggests that the term lacks eschatological significance in the citation of Lev 18:5, and therefore must be understood similarly in the citation of Hab 2:4; unfortunately, however, he does not defend or pursue this point.

what precedes, it would seem that the link implies some sort of equivalence: you received the Spirit by faith, just as Abraham was reckoned as righteous by faith.

A key question that arises at this point is what Paul understands (or what we should understand) *righteousness* to mean. E. P. Sanders is well known for his demonstration that in Palestinian Judaism, righteousness does not refer to an accumulation of merit by way of legalistic good works, but rather it refers to belonging to and being faithful to the covenant.[29] He is equally well known for his claim that in Paul, on the other hand, righteousness functions only as a "transfer term," and is never used to describe "continuing correct behavior":[30]

> The important thing to note is that 'righteousness' is primarily a *transfer term* in Paul. One who becomes a Christian is 'justified' from sins (1 Cor 6:9–11) or from the power of sin (Rom 6:7). Paul hardly if ever applies it to the continuing life of the Christian; nor, as we have said repeatedly, does he derive ethics from it.[31]

If we are right in seeing a connection between righteousness and the gift of the Spirit, however, we must question whether Sanders is correct in limiting righteousness to a transfer term, at least in Galatians 3:1–14. According to Sanders, "life in the Spirit" is *not* transfer terminology, but rather describes Paul's view of how the Christian is to live while awaiting the final redemption of God; more importantly, it describes the way Christians are to live *ethically*: "One dies with Christ to the power of sin and lives in the Spirit which also concretely means that one stops (and is acquitted of) sinning and produces the fruit of the spirit."[32] Furthermore, while Sanders has provided voluminous evidence for his description of the Jewish understanding of righteousness, he provides little argument to support his assertion that righteousness functions strictly as a transfer term in Paul.[33]

We must at least raise the question, therefore, whether Sanders has perhaps incorrectly understood Paul's use of the term righteousness, at least within Gal

---

[29] E. P. Sanders, *Paul and Palestinian Judaism* (Philadelphia: Fortress Press, 1977), 205, 518n5, 544 (hereafter cited as *PPJ*).

[30] ibid., 470–71, 501, 544; idem, *PLJP*, 45.

[31] Sanders, *PPJ*, 501.

[32] ibid., 507; cf. 440, 507ff.

[33] The closest he comes to arguing the point, rather than simply asserting it, is when he notes that Paul tends to use the verb (δικαιόω) more than the adjective (δίκαιος, which is more common in Jewish usage): "The adjective, which more readily implies the *status* of being among the righteous, tends to give way to the verb, which Paul can stretch to mean *being changed*" (ibid., 545). Note, however, that in the citation of Gen 15:6 in Gal 3:6, it is not the verb but rather the noun that appears; similarly, in the citation of Hab 2:4 in Gal 3:11, it is not the verb but rather the adjective that appears; cf. Rom 2:13; 5:19; Phil 4:8.

3:1–14. Must we understand Paul to have rejected the sense that the word had for him as a Jew, imposing instead a new sense that would presumably have been unknown to his Judaizing opponents? Or could it be that Paul continues to use the word to describe, not just how one gets in, but what it means to stay in? In short, is Paul's argument only about soteriology, or is he equally or even more concerned with how one lives a righteous life as a Christian? Is such a dichotomy between "soteriology" and "how one lives a righteous life" even appropriate for Paul's thinking?[34] As we continue to build up the web of intertextual connections, these are questions to which we will return.

Metaleptic Ungrammaticality: Blessing, Curse, Life, and . . . ?

Though to this point we have not specifically identified them as ungrammaticalities, several anomalies have already emerged as we have explored the chiastic structure of the text; this is in keeping with the pattern of reading suggested by Riffaterre. So far, these anomalies or ungrammaticalities have been essentially similar. The perception of a chiastic structure has encouraged us to forge an intertextual link between citations or statements, but the resulting intertextual relationship remains somewhat puzzling. In the case of the citations in Gal 3:11 and 3:12, the obviously parallel grammatical structure forces together what seem to be competing claims for gaining life; in the case of Gal 3:14b and the citation in 3:6, we have an intriguing parallel at the level of a deeper structure, which suggests a relationship between righteousness, the Spirit, and faith.

Further reflection on the chiastic structure of the passage leads us to consider another ungrammaticality, but of a different sort. Rather than an ungrammaticality arising from an unexpected joining of terms, this one arises from the absence of an expected term.[35] In the inner elements of this chiasm, we noted a matrix of terms that resonate with the theme of the giving of the Law: blessing and curse, life and . . . but where is the term needed to complete the matrix? The term death—and in particular, the idea of a *threat* of death, to go along with the threat of curse vs. the promise of blessing and life—is nowhere to

---

[34] As pointed out by Richard Hays in response to an earlier draft of this investigation, this dichotomy may be "purely the legacy of Luther." As we saw above, Sanders is regularly critiqued for making too sharp a distinction between getting in and staying in, but those critiques are not without problems; see above, 30–32, 35, 42–45.

[35] This is the phenomenon of metalepsis, which figures prominently in Richard Hays' intertextual readings (see above, 112–17); in effect, metalepsis is a type of ungrammaticality. As we pointed out above, Hays abandons his metaleptic procedure when it comes to Gal 3, since Paul's use of scripture here is no longer in the form of subtle echoes but rather direct "broadsides." Perhaps the noise of broadsides can just as effectively hide transumed points of resonance as the whisper of echoes!

be found in this section of Paul's argument.³⁶ This omission particularly stands out in comparison to Paul's treatment of similar topics in his letter to the Romans; there, he freely makes use of the motif of threatened death vs. promised life.³⁷

There are two places where we might particularly expect a threat of death to appear in order to complete the matrix. On the one hand, in lieu of the existing chiastic structure, we might have expected a threat of death to balance the promise of life offered by the citation of Hab 2:4. In other words, rather than citing Lev 18:5, a scripture that appears to offer a competing or contradictory promise of life (and thus to undercut his own argument), we might have expected Paul to offer a citation that links the Law and death.³⁸ On the other hand, given the chiastic structure extending from Gal 3:8 through 3:14a, we might expect that the outermost elements of the chiasm would include some mention of death—but instead we have a citation in 3:6 and a summary in 3:14b that speak about faith, righteousness, and the Spirit.

The only mention of death (though not the word itself) that does occur in this section of Paul's letter is the reference to the crucifixion of Christ in 3:1 and the corresponding allusion to his crucifixion in the citation of Dt 21:23 in Gal 3:13. Could the crucifixion supply the missing element in the blessing and curse, life and death motif? If so, it is heavily "transumed":³⁹ Whereas we might expect a threat of death for those who fail to heed Paul's words (in keeping with the pattern established in the giving of the law), the death of Christ is neither threatened nor is it a threat; is an already accomplished death with entirely positive consequences. To be sure, one might understand these consequences in terms of a substitutionary atonement by which the threat of death is averted, so that Paul

---

³⁶There are only three explicit references to death in all of Galatians: 1:1 (God raised Christ from the dead), 2:19 (through the law I died to law), and 2:21 (if righteousness comes through law, then Christ died in vain). There are also a number of allusions to death in the form of references to the crucifixion of Christ: 2:19, 3:1, 13; 5:24; 6:14 (cf. also 1:4 and 6:12). It should be noted that *all* of these references and allusions to death are tied directly to the death *of Christ*, even those that also refer to the "death" of believers (2:19, 5:24, 6:14). Nowhere is there any hint of a *threatened* death, to complete the matrix that offers a threat of curse vs. the promise of blessing and life.

³⁷Cf. especially Rom 8:1–13.

³⁸Though I suspect Paul could quickly find even better possibilities, one could imagine that it would require very little editing to turn Dt 30:17–18 into a suitable candidate: καὶ ἐὰν μεταστῇ ἡ καρδία σου καὶ μὴ εἰσακούσῃς . . . ἀναγγέλλω σοι σήμερον ὅτι ἀπωλείᾳ ἀπολεῖσθε (LXX). With a little exposition to link εἰσακούσῃς to the ἀκοῆς πίστεως of Gal 3:4, the point would seem to be clear: choose life by way of faith, or risk death (destruction). Of course, this would be an egregious example of taking scripture out of context—but no worse than what Paul does with some of the preceding verses from Deuteronomy (Dt 30:12–14) in Romans 10.

³⁹See above, 114–17, for a description of transumption in Hays' methodology.

is putting, in place of the death that might otherwise threaten us, the substitutionary death of Christ. However, as Paul makes clear throughout the letter, Christ's death is not one that believers avoid, but rather one that they are expected to share (Gal 2:19; 5:24; 6:14).[40] Ultimately, then, this mention of Christ's crucifixion does less to supply the missing element in the blessing and curse, life and death motif—except perhaps as a distant, dissonant, transumed echo—than it does to highlight the absence of the expected threat of death.

Summary

Although we have explored only a few of the threads that make up our intertextual reading of Gal 3:1–14, it may be helpful to pause at this point and offer a summary and tentative conclusion about the intertextual web that is developing. So far, the issues seem to revolve around *life*. What seems to be developing is not, as we might have expected, a choice between life and death, but rather a choice between life and life—between a life of blessing, characterized by the Spirit and righteousness and faith, and a life under curse, characterized by the law. In short, Paul has reworked the traditional equations in which law = blessing = life and disobedience = curse = death, so that now the equations are faith = blessing = righteousness = Spirit and law = curse = flesh.[41]

At first glance, it may not seem that we have made any real advance over previous efforts to understand this passage. Numerous commentators have noted that Paul takes over the blessing-curse motif and reworks it so that blessing now is associated with faith, while curse is associated with law.[42] There is, however, a crucial difference. Most commentators understand this passage in terms of soteriology, in the sense that the focus is on how one *gains* life—they assume, in other words, that Paul presents a contrast between a choice that leads to life (faith) and one that leads to death (law).[43] What we have tentatively suggested above, however, is that Paul is *not* talking about a life vs. death choice, but rather a life vs. life choice. In other words, Paul is *not* focusing on soteriology in this passage; he is not telling those who already have life how to gain it, nor is he describing what happens to those who fail to gain life.[44]

---

[40]Gal 3:27 may also be an indirect reference to sharing in Christ's death; cf. Rom 6:3. One would not go too far to say that for Paul, being crucified with Christ is synonymous with being a Christian.

[41]Paul has already laid the groundwork for equating life under the Law with the flesh, not only in this passage (Gal 3:3), but even earlier in the letter (Gal 2:16); he will further develop this theme in Gal 4–5.

[42]Cf., e.g., J. Christiaan Beker, *Paul the Apostle: The Triumph of God in Life and Thought* (Philadelphia: Fortress Press, 1980), 48–52; Lührmann, *Galatians*, 59, 62–65.

[43]See chaps. 2 and 3 above.

[44]To say that Paul is not focusing on soteriology in this passage is not to suggest that his argument has no relationship to soteriological issues; rather it is to suggest that Paul is

If this is so, then the questions we raised earlier about the meaning of ζήσεται and δικαιοσύνη become all the more urgent. What does Paul understand "will live" to mean in the citations from Hab 2:4 and Lev 18:5? Is he using "righteousness" and related forms strictly as transfer terminology, or could he perhaps have something to say about righteousness in a more Jewish sense? These are questions that we will pursue in the next two sections below. For now, it appears that the matrix which best brings coherence and significance to the ungrammaticalities we have encountered so far is not "how to gain life," or still less "how to be righteous enough to live," but rather is something like "how to carry out life" or even "how to live righteously." Before we can test and refine that matrix, however, we need to uncover more of the anonymous intertexts that help to shape our understanding of this passage.

Presupposed Intertexts

In addition to seeking out the matrix that provides coherence and significance for a text's ungrammaticalities, another way to uncover some of the significant but anonymous intertexts in a text is to follow Jonathan Culler's proposal concerning logical and pragmatic (or rhetorical) presuppositions.[45] As Culler uses the term, presupposition does not refer to an assumption or preconception that an author or a reader may bring to a text, but rather to something which the text itself requires in order to make sense of its syntactical and/or rhetorical structure.[46] Indeed, the author or the reader or even the text may not necessarily affirm a presupposition as true, but by its structure the text forces its

---

not primarily dealing with questions about whether or how one is saved. He is dealing with questions concerning how those who are saved should carry out their lives.

[45] See above, 128–32.

[46] Culler uses *presupposition* as a technical term, whereas general usage more or less equates it with *assumption* or *preconception*. There is, of course, a relationship between these terms. The presuppositions required by the text may well overlap with and even give rise to the assumptions which a reader brings to the text or which the reader identifies as Paul's own assumptions. Nevertheless, it is important to distinguish the technical use of *presupposition* from these other terms, for at least two reasons. First, as suggested above, a presupposition may *not* be held to be true by any of the participants in the production and reception of the text; it may be an intertext *against* which the text or its author or readers strive, rather than one that they affirm. Second, we are not, in this investigation, attempting to read the mind or gauge the intentions of Paul or anyone else, but rather are attempting to read the text, noticing the presuppositions that it requires and with which it intertextually relates. For the purposes of this investigation, therefore, we will reserve the term *presupposition* for those intertexts which we can demonstrate to be logically or pragmatically required by the text; we will use the terms *assumption* and *preconception* to refer to a conviction that the reader or author or others may bring to the text.

readers (and in some sense also its author) to interact with the presupposition as an intertext, whether by accepting, rejecting, revising, or otherwise responding to it, though not necessarily at a conscious level.

Following Culler's approach, one could identify a number of presuppositions in Gal 3:1–14. To take only one example out of many, consider Gal 3:12, "Now the Law is not of faith, but rather . . . ."[47] Logically, this is a simple denial; rhetorically, however, it presupposes that someone has or might have claimed that Law *is* of faith—a claim that is nowhere made explicit. Quite apart from any knowledge that we may or may not possess about the Jewish background concerning the relationship between the Law and faith(fulness), the text presupposes a claim about such a relationship as one of the unwritten and anonymous intertexts to which it (and we) must respond.

The problem for the current investigation is the relative ease with which one can identify such presuppositions.[48] How can we limit the number of presuppositions, both for the practical purpose of not having too many to handle, and for the purpose of narrowing our focus to those that are most significant for the task at hand? The latter qualification already gives some hint for how to proceed: we need to focus on presuppositions that have specifically to do with Paul's use of citations. Furthermore, it may be profitable to begin with some of the *assumptions* that scholars have brought to the discussion of the citations and their function, already identified in our survey above, since those assumptions may unconsciously reflect the perception of a presupposition required by the text.[49]

THE ROLE OF SCRIPTURE IN PAUL'S ARGUMENT

What is presupposed by Paul's citation of scripture in his argument with his opponents? As discussed in chapter 3 above, there has been a long-standing debate between those who insist that Paul must assume all scripture to be authoritative (so that, therefore, he would never willingly set two citations in contradiction, as he appears to do in Gal 3:11–12), and those who insist that Paul *is* deliberately setting up one scripture over another (e.g., choosing Hab 2:4 as the valid promise of life over the invalid promise offered by Lev 18:5).[50] J. Louis Martyn has recently added a new twist to the debate with his argument

---

[47]This verse begins much like one of the illustrations used by Culler; see above, 130n125: "It was not a temple with bosky shades . . . ."

[48]In particular, the questions in Gal 3:1–5 give rise to a series of rhetorical presuppositions: "Who has bewitched you?" presupposes that someone has, in fact, bewitched the Galatians; "Did you receive the Spirit through works of law, or through the hearing of faith?" presupposes that they have, in fact, received the Spirit; "Having started with the Spirit, are you now ending with the flesh?" presupposes that they did, in fact, start with the Spirit; and so on.

[49]See above, n. 46.

[50]See above, 80–89.

that Paul is not simply setting one scripture against another, but rather is challenging his opponents' (the Teachers') preconceptions about the nature and authority of scripture.[51] As indicated above, however, *presuppositions* are not the same as *assumptions* or *preconceptions*; we need therefore to determine what is presupposed by the use of citation in Gal 3:1–14, and to distinguish this presupposition from some of the assumptions that have been brought to or discussed in connection with this passage.

Authority and Applicability

Pragmatic (or rhetorical) presuppositions, as described by Culler, have to do with the way that a sentence relates to its context, particularly how it invokes certain expectations and conventions of genre.[52] Given the genre of argument—which surely is the genre of Gal 3:1–14—what expectations or conventions does the use of citation invoke? Note that the question, for the moment, does not concern how these particular citations relate to the specific context of Gal 3:1–14, but rather concerns what is pragmatically presupposed by the use of *any* citation in *any* argument. It may be easier to approach this question, therefore, by stepping back for a moment from the specific citations found in Gal 3:1–14 to examine an obviously artificial example.

Consider an argument in which the participants exchange the following statements: "I know that ice cream is bad for you, because I read in the newspaper that 'the sky is blue.'" "Ah, yes, but since the sky is blue, then, just as it says in the cookbook, 'Eggplant tastes bitter.'" Why do these two statements sound more than a little ridiculous? If the obvious answer is that the "citations" that are offered seem to have nothing whatsoever to do with the argument at hand and do nothing to carry the argument forward, then one has just identified what is pragmatically presupposed by the presence of a citation within an argument. The use of a citation in the course of an argument invokes the expectation that what is cited will be relevant to one's argument and will carry a certain weight of evidence in support of that argument. In short, a citation within an argument pragmatically presupposes that the citation is both applicable and authoritative.[53]

---

[51] See above, 86.
[52] See above, 129–32.
[53] Cf. Stanley, "'Under a Curse,'" 499: "With the appearance of γέγραπται γάρ [in Gal 3:10], the reader is led to expect two things: an explanation/clarification of the preceding statement . . ., and an authoritative word from Scripture, possibly one that would offer a definitive clarification of the issue at hand." Though Stanley's remarks are specific to the citation of Dt 27:26 in Gal 3:10 and are constructed in terms of reader response/rhetorical criticism, he seems to be identifying precisely the same presupposition of authority and applicability.

There are three important observations that need to be made concerning this thesis. First, as the example above illustrates, the *source* of the citation (that is, whether or not it is scripture) is not what presupposes applicability and authority; it is the mere use of *citation* that generates the presupposition. In the patently ridiculous example given above, one might claim that newspapers and cookbooks carry a certain authority, at least in certain contexts. However, even if the sources that were cited had been, for example, Dr. Seuss and the *Daily Liar*, that would merely intensify the dissonance that one feels between the ridiculous citation of ridiculous sources, and the expectation that the citations *should* have been relevant to, and *should* have offered some weight of evidence for, the argument. In other words, the citation of *any* source invokes the *presupposition* of applicability and authority, even when the citation does not seem to live up to that presupposition.[54]

Second, to say that the presence of citation in an argument pragmatically presupposes that the citation is applicable and authoritative is *not* to say that either the author or the audience shares that assumption.[55] On the contrary, not only may the audience reject the relevance or authority of a citation, but also the author may use a citation in a way that deliberately violates the presupposition, for example, humorously, with tongue firmly in cheek, or sarcastically, or with the intention of setting up a straw man to be knocked down, or so on. The important point, from an intertextual perspective, is that in each of these cases the audience and the author, even if they reject or qualify the presupposition, must nevertheless interact with it. In fact, the expected authority and applicability of a citation is the unwritten, anonymous intertext that makes *possible* the sarcasm, or the parody, or the irony, or so on.

Third, if the author and/or audience may or may not assume what the presence of citation pragmatically presupposes, then the use of citation in unexpected ways offers an opportunity for dissonance—or, in other words, for ungrammaticality. Riffaterre's description of reading seems to capture precisely the process one follows when one encounters a citation that does not seem, at face value, to be applicable to or authoritative for the argument in which it occurs. The experience of ungrammaticality forces one to search for some sort of deeper significance that resolves the dissonance. If one sees the wink or the smile that indicates a joke, or notes a sarcastic tone to the context, or sees evidence of parody, one knows how to respond. One understands that the text is in some way relating to the presupposition negatively, calling into question the anonymous intertext that claims authority and applicability for the citation, in

---

[54]Indeed, as the example above illustrates, it may be *especially* when the use of citation does not seem to live up to the presupposition that one is most aware of the presupposition, precisely because of the dissonance generated by the failure of one's expectations.

[55]Cf. above, n. 46.

order to create a joke or a parody or a sarcastic critique. On the other hand, if one *does not* see any evidence of parody or joke or sarcasm—if the argument and its citation is presented with a "perfectly straight face"—then one either believes that the person making the citation is crazy or foolish, or one wonders if, perhaps, one has just not yet "gotten it."[56]

This brings us to the case of Paul's citations in Gal 3:1–14. As we have seen, his use of citations in this argument leads to a number of ungrammaticalities. In no small degree, these ungrammaticalities arise from the dissonance between the presupposition of authority and applicability on the one hand, and what Paul actually seems to do with the citations on the other. If Paul cites Dt 27:26, one should expect the citation to *support* his argument, rather than seeming to undercut it; if he cites Lev 18:5 and Hab 2:4 together, one would expect them *both* to be authoritative and applicable, rather than one seeming to be used to deny the other. The expectation of authority and applicability is the pragmatic presupposition, the unwritten intertext, with which the text interacts to create the dissonance arising from these citations.

The particular question interpreters face is *how* the text relates to the presupposition of applicability and authority. Is there any evidence that the text deliberately calls the presupposition into question? Is there any wink or smile, or sarcasm, or parody? One might argue that the presence of ungrammaticality provides all the evidence needed. Paul does not use citations of scripture in expected ways; therefore Paul must reject the presupposition of authority and applicability. Such an argument, however, ignores the nature of ungrammaticality; the presence of ungrammaticality does not by itself indicate how the ungrammaticality is to be resolved.[57] Certainly there is no consensus among scholars. While some argue that the resolution lies in Paul's rejection of the authority of scripture, others suggest that these ungrammaticalities are to be resolved by way of hidden assumptions, while still others conclude that Paul is simply inconsistent, if not downright foolish.[58] The problem with all of these, however, is that they offer no particular *textual* evidence, *other than the ungrammaticality itself,* for how the text relates to the presupposition of authority and applicability.[59]

---

[56]Cf. Michael Riffaterre, *Semiotics of Poetry* (Bloomington: Indiana University, 1978), 14–15. Unless one gets its point, the details of a joke seem pointless, just as the message of a poem, understood only at the mimetic level, may say nothing at all.

[57]In effect, such an argument fails to move very far from the heuristic to the hermeneutical level of reading; it sees that the signs of the text do not match up with reality, and so rejects the signs, without seriously undertaking a search for a matrix in which the ungrammaticalities find significance.

[58]See chap. 3 above.

[59]Many of these arguments depend, at least to some degree, on a reconstruction of Paul's understanding of scripture, based on his culture or the historical situation at hand.

J. Louis Martyn is perhaps the only scholar to identify what could be textual evidence of a deliberate challenge to the presupposition of authority and applicability. He argues that in Gal 3:11–12, Paul has altered the standard form of the "Textual Contradiction," as typically used by his opponents, the Teachers. In so doing, Paul is not only challenging their exegesis of scripture, but more importantly he is challenging the assumption of the authority and indivisibility of scripture on which the Textual Contradiction depends.[60] Unfortunately, as discussed above, there is little if any real evidence that Paul is reworking the form of the Textual Contradiction.[61] Martyn's argument therefore rests primarily (if not entirely) on the presence of the ungrammaticality. Once again, however, the mere presence of ungrammaticality does not provide conclusive evidence that Paul is seeking to reject the presupposition of authority and applicability.

It would seem, in fact, that there is no evidence within this text that encourages the reader to resolve the ungrammaticalities by way of humor, or sarcasm, or parody, or any other sort of rejection or qualification of the presupposition of authority and applicability invoked by a citation.[62] Nowhere, for example, does the text call into question the authority of a citation in the way that it calls into question the authority of certain "pillars" of the church (Gal 2:1–10). Nowhere does it qualify a citation with words such as, "As it is written, for what that is worth" or "If you believe what is written." Nowhere does it offer an antithesis between a citation and the words of God or Christ or the Spirit.[63] It would seem, in other words, that the text cites scripture with a "perfectly straight face." One

---

Rather than attempting to read the mind of Paul, however, it seems better to focus on the text itself. Does the text provide any evidence that suggests a qualification or rejection of the presupposition invoked by the use of citation?

[60]See above, 86–87. Martyn calls this a "presupposition" of the Teachers, which Paul rejects; using the terminological distinction drawn above, this is better described as an assumption or preconception or conviction. For our purposes, it does not matter whether one can actually reconstruct the *Teachers' assumptions* about scripture; the point remains that the use of citation in this text invokes the *pragmatic presupposition* of authority and applicability. Likewise, one need not attempt to know whether Paul held different assumptions about scripture; the issue is whether *this text* gives any evidence that the presupposition of authority and applicability is rejected or qualified.

[61]See above, 87.

[62]Note once again that the presupposition is invoked simply by *citation*, regardless of what is actually cited. Regardless of the extent to which Paul's challenge of the Law may or may not have implications for his understanding of scripture, he nevertheless *cites* scripture *without qualification*—and therefore invokes the presupposition that what he cites, *whatever it is*, is authoritative and applicable to the argument at hand.

[63]Cf. for example Matt 5:21ff. Without in any way attempting to resolve the infamous difficulties of interpreting the Antitheses, one can nevertheless see a marked contrast between Jesus' citation of scripture in this section of the Sermon on the Mount and Paul's citation of scripture in Gal 3:1–14.

is left, then, with two options. One can conclude, along with Räisänen, that Paul is simply inconsistent (if not foolish), or one can suspect that one still has not yet "gotten it," and search for the deeper significance that has so far been elusive.[64] As indicated above, this investigation opts for the latter.

Citation as Proof, Premise, or Conclusion

To aid in the search for deeper significance, it will be helpful to observe one further point concerning the presupposition invoked by the use of citation within an argument: to say that the use of citation presupposes authority and applicability is not to describe the exact function of a citation within its argument, nor is it to suggest that there is only one way a citation can function. Consider again the artificial example used above: "I know that ice cream is bad for you, because I read in the newspaper that 'the sky is blue.'" "Ah, yes, but since the sky is blue, then, just as it says in the cookbook, 'Eggplant tastes bitter.'" In each statement, the use of citation invokes the same expectation that what is cited will be applicable to and authoritative for the argument at hand. Note, however, that the precise manner in which each citation functions differs significantly. In the first of these statements, the citation functions in effect as the premise of a deductive proof, with the accompanying assertion as the conclusion; in the second, if the form is to be understood as a logical argument, the citation appears not as the premise, but as the conclusion.

Unfortunately, scholars routinely use terms such as premise, proof, and conclusion—terms drawn from the elements of formal, deductive logic—without closely examining exactly what such terms mean. Even more unfortunately, by using such terms, scholars adopt the assumption, again without careful consideration, that logical argument is the proper context in which to look for the function of a citation. At the very least, such an assumption needs to be examined, as does the precise meaning of these terms; therefore, a brief discussion of the nature and forms of logical argument is in order.

---

[64]In effect, both Räisänen's conclusion that Paul is inconsistent (see above, 93) and Sanders' and Betz's assertion that Paul is merely offering proof-texts (see above, 74–75) amount to the charge that Paul is foolish—at least a little, at least from our perspective. He does not recognize, or does not care, that his citations do not quite add up (see critique of Sanders and Betz on this point, above, 77–78). There is no easy way to refute such a charge; after all, one may only be indulging in wishful thinking to suppose that there is some deeper significance that resolves the ungrammaticalities. On the other hand, as argued above, the tightly coupled structure of the citations suggests that Paul's use of citations was not as careless or thoughtless as Räisänen or Sanders or Betz imply.

Logical Argument

According to a standard textbook on logic, a logical argument requires "two essential features":[65]

> In the first place, the person who presents the argument must be claiming that if certain things (the premises) are true, then something else (the conclusion) should be true also. That is, he is claiming that the premises would support the conclusion, would make it reasonable to believe. In the second place, he must be claiming that the premises are indeed true. In making both these claims together, he aims to give a reason for accepting the conclusion as true. We shall say that there is an actual argument ... when and only when both these claims are present.[66]

Strictly speaking, the preceding quotation describes only an argument that claims to be logical, rather than an actual logical proof.[67] In order for the argument to constitute a proof, not only must the premise(s) actually be true (not just claimed to be true), but also they must actually lead to the stated conclusion; that is, there must be a valid deduction from premise to conclusion.[68]

There are many ways to construct a valid deduction, and from that deduction to construct a proof. One of the simplest of these, and the one which most clearly reflects the "essential features" of logical argument, is the form known as *modus ponens*.[69] *Modus ponens*, along with the closely related form *modus tollens*, is a type of argument based on a conditional sentence, typically expressed as, "if p then q." In *modus ponens*, the antecedent (p) of the conditional is affirmed, whereupon the consequent (q) can validly be concluded:

---

[65] Stephen F. Barker, *The Elements of Logic*, 3rd ed. (New York: McGraw-Hill, 1980), 7.

[66] Ibid.

[67] Ibid., 11.

[68] Ibid., 11, 18–22. Note that, while a discussion about logical argument can theoretically include both deductive and inductive arguments, the use of the term proof suggests that the discussion is more narrowly focused on deductive argument; this is the primary area of study in the field of logic (ibid., 16–18).

[69] Ibid., 92. In effect, the basic structure of any logical argument can be expressed in the form of *modus ponens*. One or more premises are asserted as leading to a conclusion, i.e., "if premise(s), then conclusion"; the premises are affirmed as true; therefore the conclusion can be drawn.

Modus ponens
If p then q	e.g.,	If you won the jackpot, then you are rich.
p		You won the jackpot.
∴ q		Therefore you are rich.[70]

In a *modus tollens* argument, the consequent is denied, whereupon one can validly conclude that the antecedent is false:[71]

Modus tollens
If p then q	e.g.,	If you won the jackpot, then you are rich.
Not q		You are not rich
∴ not p		Therefore you did not win the jackpot.

It may also be helpful to note two common logical fallacies related to these forms. The first is known as *affirming the consequent*, while the second is known as *denying the antecedent*:[72]

Fallacy of affirming the consequent
If p then q	e.g.,	If you won the jackpot, then you are rich.
q		You are rich.
∴ p		Therefore you won the jackpot.

Fallacy of denying the antecedent
If p then q	e.g.,	If you won the jackpot, then you are rich.
Not p		You did not win the jackpot.
∴ not q		Therefore you are not rich.

In both of these fallacies, the problem is that, while p implies q, q does not necessarily imply p. While winning the jackpot will make you rich, you can also be rich for other reasons; being rich does not necessarily depend on winning the jackpot, nor does failing to win the jackpot keep you from being rich through other means.

Just as was true with logical arguments in general, so also is true with deductions in the form of *modus ponens* or *modus tollens*. Simply to state an argument in one of these *forms* does not guarantee that the argument provides an actual proof of its conclusion. To constitute a proof, in the case of *modus ponens*, the antecedent must really be true, and not just claimed to be true (or, in the case of *modus tollens*, the consequent must really be false, and not just denied), and in either case the antecedent must also really lead to the consequent (that is, the conditional must be true). There are various ways to ensure the lat-

---

[70]The form of this and the following examples, though not the precise wording, is taken directly from ibid., 92–93.

[71]Ibid., 93.

[72]Ibid.

ter. The conditional may be true based on empirical experience (e.g., winning the jackpot generally makes one rich), or it may be *necessarily* true, either because of the definition of terms (e.g., "if Joe is a man, then Joe is male"), or because the conditional is based on some other valid logical deduction. An example of the latter would be a valid syllogism expressed in the form of a conditional statement: "If all dogs are animals and if my pet is a dog, then my pet is an animal."[73]

Citation as Premise: Deductive Proof

With this brief discussion of logical arguments, we are ready to examine the claim advanced above concerning the function of the citation in the statement, "I know that ice cream is bad for you, because I read in the newspaper that 'the sky is blue.'" Here, the word "because" signals the possibility of a logical argument, and furthermore identifies its clause (the citation from the newspaper) as the premise advanced in support of the conclusion given in the first clause (the claim that ice cream is bad for you).[74] The essence of this logical argument can be expressed in the form of *modus ponens*, starting with the following conditional: "If 'the sky is blue,' then ice cream is bad for you."

In order to complete the logical proof, not only must the premise be affirmed as true, but also the inference from premise to conclusion must be validated. It is at this point that the presupposition of authority and applicability is especially important for the function of the citation. Because the use of citation presupposes that what is cited is relevant to the argument at hand and helps to move it forward, the use of a citation tends to suggest that what is cited will, in fact, lead to the stated conclusion; thus, the use of citation suggests that if the sky really is blue, then ice cream must necessarily be bad for you. At the same time, because the use of citation presupposes that what is cited is authoritative for the issue at hand, the citation in effect is self-affirming: the sky must really

---

[73] A discussion of syllogisms and other logical deductions would go beyond the space and needs of the current investigation; for a complete discussion, see ibid., 35ff. As the example above suggests, whenever syllogisms and other logical deductive forms are used in an actual proof, that proof essentially takes the form of *modus ponens*. The logical deduction assures that the premises lead to the conclusion, or in other words, "if premises, then conclusion"; the premises—the antecedent of the conditional—are affirmed (e.g., my pet really is a dog); therefore the conclusion is proved to be true (cf. ibid., 27).

[74] For a discussion of how ordinary discourse can be translated into logical form, cf. ibid., 8. Note that the order in which propositions are given is irrelevant for determining which is the conclusion and which is the premise. What is determinative is the function of each proposition, as signalled by words or phrases such as "because," "since," and "for" (which identify premises), or "therefore" and "it follows that" (which identify conclusions).

be blue. Therefore, the conclusion is inescapable: ice cream must be bad for you.[75]

In general, then, the use of any citation in the form "A (assertion) is true, because it is written, C (citation)" sets up the following deductive argument:

> **If C, then A** (that C leads to A is "asserted" by the presupposition of applicability)
> C ("asserted" by the presupposition of authority)
> ∴ A

Citation as Conclusion: Extension and Evidence

In contrast to the previous discussion, it is not at all clear that the following statement is best understood as a deductive argument: "Ah, yes, but since the sky is blue, then, just as it says in the cookbook, 'Eggplant tastes bitter.'" To be sure, this statement is already in the form of a conditional sentence; here, however, the citation functions not as the antecedent but rather as the consequent: "If the sky is blue, then 'eggplant tastes bitter.'"[76] The presupposition that the citation is applicable once again appears to affirm that the antecedent leads to the consequent, that if the sky really is blue, eggplant must really taste bitter. Likewise, the presupposition that the citation is authoritative once again appears to affirm the truth of what is cited; since the cookbook says so, eggplant must really be bitter. What is different, in this case, is that rather than affirming the antecedent, so that one can then conclude the consequent, this form affirms the consequent, leaving the antecedent in doubt. In short, one is left either with an invalid deduction, or no deduction at all:[77]

---

[75]It must be remembered that the presupposition enters in only as an anonymous, unwritten intertext. The author, the readers, or even the text itself may call this presupposition into question. Certainly most readers will call into question at least part of what is presupposed in the example above: it is not at all evident that what is cited in this case really leads to the given conclusion. Nevertheless, to the extent that this example creates dissonance for the reader, that dissonance arises precisely from the violation of the presupposition invoked by citation. The citation "should" be applicable; it "should" lead to the given conclusion. When it does not, the reader encounters ungrammaticality. Cf. ibid., 17: "Here the wording indicates that the speaker is claiming that his premises are strictly sufficient to yield the conclusion, so that we shall classify his argument as deductive, although it is a bad deductive argument (the truth of the premises would not in this case guarantee the truth of the conclusion)."

[76]Note that the word "since" signals that "the sky is blue" again serves as the premise. Note also that, even though "the sky is blue" was introduced as a citation in the previous sentence, in this sentence it is the statement, "eggplant tastes bitter," which is identified as a citation; therefore it is this statement to which we must look for the purpose of analyzing the function of citation in the second sentence.

[77]Note that if the citation could be used to *deny* the consequent, rather than affirming it, then one could validly conclude the denial of the assertion, using the form *modus tol-*

> **If A, then C** (that A leads to C is "asserted" by the presupposition of applicability)
> C ("asserted" by the presupposition of authority)
> ∴ ???[78]

As deductive proof of its accompanying assertion, then, the use of a citation positioned as a conclusion is either futile or fallacious; the citation can only either "prove" itself (by way of the presupposition of authority) or be proven (by an external affirmation of the premise, thus completing a valid *modus ponens*). But must a citation function only as deductive proof?[79] Can a citation, together with the presupposition it invokes, serve any other rhetorical function in an argument?

There are at least two other important rhetorical functions that a citation, used as the consequent of an assertion, can potentially serve.[80] First, a citation, together with the presupposition invoked by its use, can serve to extend a point already made by showing further consequences or drawing additional conclusions. Given point A, which has already been established or conceded or agreed upon, C then follows. In the artificial example above, the use of citation suggests that if one concedes that the sky is blue, then one must also concede that eggplant tastes bitter. Here, the presupposition of applicability is particularly important, as it appears to affirm that what is cited really does follow from the points already established.[81] The presupposition of authority and applicability thus presents the citation as both a true and a necessary consequence. The rhetorical point is not to *prove* either the citation or the assertion that accompanies it, but rather to show further implications of the argument.

---

lens. In this example, however, the citation is given *as* the consequent, not as its opposite. That is, the conditional is, "If A, then C"; what would be needed for *modus tollens* would be the conditional, "If A, then *not* C," which could then be countered with the citation C, to result in the conclusion "not A." Cf. the discussion of the form of citation in Gal 3:12 below, 159.

[78]To conclude A, in this case, would be to commit the fallacy of affirming the consequent. It might be argued that in the full example given above, the previous deduction has supplied a term that asserts A. In that case, the conditional "if A, then C" could be used to conclude C—but it is already possible to conclude C, since it is given as one of the asserted terms (asserted by way of citation). In effect, if treated as nothing more than a logical deduction, this argument simply reduces to a mere tautology: C, ∴ C.

[79]There is a certain tendency, at least among biblical scholars, to assume that citations must function as proof.

[80]This discussion is not intended to represent a complete list of possible functions of citations; as will be seen below, there are other possible functions and variations of functions.

[81]Once again, it must be recognized that this is the pragmatic presupposition invoked by the use of citation; the participants in the argument may or may not agree.

Second, a citation used as the consequent of an assertion can serve the rhetorical function of offering inductive evidence.[82] Though affirming the consequent cannot offer a valid deductive proof of the antecedent, denying the consequent *would* deductively require the *denial* of the antecedent, by way of *modus tollens*. Affirming the consequent, then, offers in place of deductive proof, a certain amount of inductive confirmation: if A, then one should expect C—and C is, in fact, the case.[83] Once again, the presupposition of applicability affirms that A really does lead to C, that if the sky really is blue, eggplant really must taste bitter. Also, the presupposition of authority affirms that eggplant really does taste bitter. Here, however, the rhetorical point is not to extend the implications of the argument thus far, but to offer evidence (not proof) in support of the assertion. When the audience recognizes the truth of the citation, they will be more inclined to believe the assertion.

There could, of course, be any number of other rhetorical functions that the use of a citation can serve, including variations on or combinations of the two described above. For example, a citation may serve the rhetorical function of "narrating or elaborating a symbolic world,"[84] or it might simultaneously extend the implications of a preceding argument while at the same time offering additional inductive evidence. While the two rhetorical functions sketched out above may be combined, however, it should not be overlooked that there is a key difference between them, a difference that has to do with whether or not the accompanying assertion is a point that has been established in the argument. To the extent that the assertion is in doubt, it may be in need of confirming inductive evidence, even if no logical proof is available; to the extent that the assertion has already been proven or conceded, additional evidence is redundant, but new implications can help to move the argument further along.

---

[82]Cf. ibid., 93: "We say that these arguments [the fallacy of affirming the consequent and the fallacy of denying the antecedent] are invalid because, for the present, we are considering only *deductive* reasoning However, such arguments are not always fallacious when they are intended as *inductive* arguments. In inductive reasoning the speaker claims only that his premises help to make his conclusion reasonable to believe . . . ."

[83]It might be worth exploring how often the fallacy of affirming the consequent occurs in scholarly discussion. It is a common fallacy in part because it is closely related to a basic tenet of the scientific method. In science, one cannot actually *prove* a hypothesis; one can only attempt to *disprove* it by showing that its predictions (i.e., its consequents) do not hold up. Confidence in a theory increases as experiments repeatedly fail to disprove the theory. While these experiments can be seen as evidence in favor of the theory, it is a mistake, though a common one, to regard them as *proof* of the theory. Cf. Carl G. Hempel, *Philosophy of Natural Science* (Englewood Cliffs, NJ: Prentice Hall, 1966), 3–18.

[84]As pointed out by Richard Hays in response to an earlier draft of this investigation.

The Functions of the Citations in Gal 3:1–14

How does all of this apply to Gal 3:1–14? Given what has been discussed above, the first and obvious point that must be made is that the six citations in Gal 3:1–14 need not all function in the same way.[85] Although one could possibly construe the function of all six citations in terms of deductive proof (though not all in precisely the same way), at least one citation cannot very directly or easily be understood to function in this way. Furthermore, two other citations are better understood in terms of the rhetorical functions of evidence and extension. The functions of each of the six citations are examined below.

Gal 3:10 and Gal 3:13. The citations in Gal 3:10 and 3:13, citing Dt 27:26 and Dt 21:23 respectively, are each introduced using an explicit citation formula including a causal conjunction (γάρ or ὅτι). In other words, each of these citations is part of a construction that fits the model described above: "A is true, because (for) it is written, C." Both of these uses of citation, therefore, would seem to be ideal candidates for functioning as *modus ponens* deductive arguments; in each case one expects the citation to lead directly and deductively to the assertion ("if C, then A").[86] The fact that in each case the citation does *not* quite seem to lead to the assertion is, as noted above, what gives rise to un-

---

[85] Cf. Ardel Caneday, "'Redeemed from the Curse of the Law': The Use of Deut 21:22–23 in Gal 3:13," *Trinity Journal* 10 n.s. (1989): 193; Gerhard Ebeling, *The Truth of the Gospel: An Exposition of Galatians*, trans. David Green (Philadelphia: Fortress, 1985), 167–69. Caneday, following Ebeling, suggests that in Gal 3:6–9 the citations are given as "premises leading to conclusions" while in 3:10–12 the citations "support assertions." Caneday's and Ebeling's point seems mainly to have to do with the order in which the citation is given (before or after the assertion or conclusion which it supports), rather than with the actual logical or rhetorical function of the citations. As will be shown below, however, neither of the citations in Gal 3:6–9 seem to fit the model of "premises leading to conclusions," while two of the citations in Gal 3:10–12 *do* seem to fit that model, at least in terms of their function, if not in terms of the order in which they are given.

[86] More precisely, these uses of citation can be and often are described in terms of *syllogism* (with a missing premise; cf. above, 67). As noted above, a syllogism can establish the validity of the conditional in a *modus ponens* argument, e.g., "If all S are M, and all M are P, then all S are P." In the case of the syllogism as it might be constructed for Gal 3:13, the assumed premise is that Christ hung on a tree, and the syllogistic conditional that is formed is as follows: "If all who hang on a tree are cursed, and Christ hung on a tree, then Christ was cursed." In the case of the syllogism as it is usually constructed for Gal 3:10, the missing premise is that all fall short of the law, and the conditional would read as follows: "If all people who do not do the law are cursed, and all people do not do the law, then all people are cursed." Note, however, that in each case the conclusion to which the syllogism leads is not quite the conclusion Paul advances. Furthermore, it is not strictly necessary, nor may it be helpful, to describe either of these in terms of syllogism; see further discussion below.

grammaticality, by way of the violated expectation of the presupposition of applicability invoked by the use of citation.

Gal 3:12. It is not immediately obvious that the citation of Lev 18:5 in Gal 3:12 functions to form a deductive proof. Rather than an assertion followed by a citation introduced with the formula, *"because* it is written," we have an assertion followed by a citation introduced with the disjunctive ἀλλά. Potentially, a citation introduced by ἀλλά could function rhetorically to extend some point already made by adding contrast: "Roses are red, but 'the sky is blue.'" In this example, using a citation suggests that the contrast of a blue sky to red roses is both relevant to and authoritative for the argument at hand, but there is nothing to suggest that this use of citation in any way proves that roses are red, nor for that matter is there anything to suggest that the assertion that roses are red is in need of proof.

There is, however, a subtle but crucial difference between the form of the example given above and that of Gal 3:12. In the example, "Roses are red, but 'the sky is blue,'" there is no indication that anything is being denied by the introduction of the citation; in effect the "but" in this case means "but also." In the case of Gal 3:12, however, the assertion is given in negative form, so that instead of "but also," the ἀλλά seems most naturally to mean "but instead" or "but rather." Instead of "A, but also C," the form is *"not* A, *but rather* C." In this case, the citation *does* seem to deny something that is said or implied in the accompanying assertion. In other words, the citation introduced by ἀλλά does not so much assert that something is true, but rather that something is false, or that what is true is something other than what might have been suggested.

In Gal 3:12, Lev 18:5 appears to be cited in order to counter any suggestion that law could be of faith. The citation functions as a negative proof, a proof that can be stated in the form either of *modus ponens* or *modus tollens.*[87] The *modus tollens* form more readily captures the sense of denial implied by the ἀλλά: "If the law were of faith, then living by the law would mean living by faith; but instead of living by faith, 'the one who does these things will live by them'; therefore, the law is not of faith." The *modus ponens* form, on the other hand, can be drawn more directly from the wording of the text: "If living by the law does not mean living by faith, then the law is not of faith; 'the one who does these things will live by them' (rather than living by faith); therefore the law is not of faith." In either case, the use of the citation in Gal 3:12 offers deductive proof that "the law is not of faith."[88]

---

[87]Given a conditional, "if p then q," its contrapositive is "if not q then not p"; "the contrapositive always is equivalent to the original sentence" (Barker, *Elements of Logic,* 98). One can therefore convert a *modus tollens* argument (if p then q; not q; ∴ not p) into an equivalent *modus ponens* argument (if not q then not p; not q; ∴ not p).

[88]Cf. Sanders, *PLJP,* 22: "... 'the law is not of faith,' a statement which he proves by citing Lev. 18:18 [sic] ...." Sanders does not precisely trace the logic by which Lev

Gal 3:6. Potentially, the citation of Gen 15:6 in Gal 3:6 could function either deductively or rhetorically, due to the flexibility of the introductory conjunction καθώς.[89] On the one hand, using καθώς to introduce the premise of a deductive argument would suggest that the logic of the argument is based on analogy or comparison, such as an *a fortiori* argument, or an argument from the general to the specific, or so on. Stated as a conditional for use in a *modus ponens* argument, the general form implied by the καθώς would be as follows: if C, then, by analogy, A. On the other hand, καθώς could just as easily introduce a clause which functions, not as the premise of an argument, but as its summary, or as an extension by way of analogy, or as inductive evidence to support the argument.[90]

Further complicating the issue is the uncertainty over whether the καθώς in Gal 3:6 ties the citation to what has already been said (3:1–5), or to what follows (3:7ff. The choice between these options is neither obvious nor easy, as is evidenced by the differences in punctuation in major editions and translations.[91] One might argue that 3:6 belongs with 3:7ff on the basis of the inferential particle ἄρα in 3:7; this particle might suggest that 3:7 functions as the conclusion of the premise given by the citation in 3:6.[92] On the other hand, the ἄρα may be functioning more broadly to indicate that 3:7ff is drawing conclusions from all

---

18:5 proves that the law is not of faith, but the context of his discussion makes clear that his focus is on righteousness as a transfer term. Note, however that either form of the proof as analyzed above puts the emphasis not on how one achieves life, but rather on how one carries out life.

[89]Cf. Longenecker, *Galatians*, 112. While Longenecker distinguishes at least three possible functions for καθώς (comparative, as part of an introductory formula for citation, or as an *exemplum* reference), all three of these are variations on the idea of comparison. According to H. E. Dana and Julius R. Mantey, *A Manual Grammar of the Greek New Testament* (New York: MacMillan, 1927), 275–77, comparative clauses, such as those introduced by καθώς, generally function to offer description or emphasis; these categories are rather broad, as their examples illustrate.

[90]The first two of these, summary or extension, fall within the "descriptive" function illustrated by Dana and Mantey. The latter, inductive evidence, is essentially a variation on the use of a comparative clause as the premise of a deductive argument. The difference has to do with whether the analogy has deductive force. For example, an argument from the general to the specific (e.g., "Just as all humans have sinned, I have sinned") would have the force of deductive proof, but an argument from the specific to the general (e.g., "Just as I have sinned, all have sinned") can only be inductive.

[91]The 4th edition of the UBS *Greek New Testament*, Westcott and Hort, Goodspeed, and the NEB insert a paragraph break between 3:6 and 3:7, while the 26th edition of the Nestle-Aland *Novum Testamentum Graece*, RSV, NRSV, NIV, and TEV insert a paragraph break between 3:5 and 3:6. The RV, ASV, and NAS insert no paragraph break until after 3:14.

[92]So Longenecker, *Galatians*, 114.

of 3:1–6, not just from the citation in 3:6.⁹³ Furthermore, even if 3:7 is drawing a conclusion on the basis of 3:6 alone, 3:6 may still be functioning partially or even primarily as the concluding word of 3:1–5.⁹⁴

While there is no way to rule out the possibility of taking the citation in 3:6 together with the inference in 3:7 to form a deductive proof, therefore, neither is there any way to rule out the possibility that the citation in 3:6 primarily summarizes, extends, and/or provides inductive evidence for the argument by experience in 3:2–5. Of these, the latter function seems most pertinent to the argument Paul is making. While it is not entirely clear how the citation of Gen 15:6 in Gal 3:6 might logically lead to the conclusion expressed in Gal 3:7, it is clear how it provides inductive evidence for the argument by experience in Gal 3:2–5. Although the Galatians certainly cannot deny their own experience— presumably, they would have to answer ἐξ ἀκοῆς πίστεως in response to Paul's questions in 3:2–5—they might question whether their experience is normative. The comparison of their experience with the experience of Abraham, while not at this point providing them with deductive proof, certainly offers strong inductive evidence that their experience *is* normative.

Gal 3:8. Of all the citations in this section of Galatians, the citation in Gal 3:8, a conflation of Gen 12:3 with Gen 18:18, 22:18, or 26:4, is least possible to understand in terms of deductive proof. To be sure, Gal 3:9 draws a conclusion (ὥστε), for which one might argue that the citation forms the premise. In terms of syntax, however, the citation in 3:8 cannot stand alone; it supplies the content of the direct discourse "pre-proclaimed" to Abraham by scripture. Therefore, the conclusion in 3:9 must be drawn not so much from the citation alone, but rather from the whole sentence in 3:8. Indeed, one key point in 3:9 is that οἱ ἐκ πίστεως are the ones who will be blessed with faithful Abraham; while the citation speaks of blessings to the nations via Abraham, it is the rest of the sentence in 3:8 that makes the connection to faith.

What is particularly important to note is that the use of citation in 3:8 does *not* advance the argument from blessing to faith, so that one can draw a conclusion about who is blessed in Abraham (οἱ ἐκ πίστεως, as opposed to someone else); rather it moves from faith to blessing. Indeed, this is where the theme of

---

⁹³Dana and Mantey, *A Manual Grammar*, 241–42, suggest that while ἄρα is normally inferential, it is "more subjective and indirect than οὖν or διό"; they specifically cite Gal 3:7 as an example of this broader sense, translating the ἄρα as "therefore" rather than "then."

⁹⁴Cf. Longenecker, *Galatians*, 112. Longenecker argues that καθώς in 3:6 functions in a "bridging fashion, signaling directly an *exemplum* argument but also setting up arguments from Scripture." Hays, *Echoes*, 108, similarly suggests that the καθώς "posits a direct analogy between the story of Abraham and the Galatians' experience" outlined in 3:2–5, even though he treats 3:1–5 and 3:6–9 as separate units; cf. Martyn, *Galatians*, 296n3.

blessing is first introduced. The citation adds the new implication of blessing to the discussion of faith already in progress. This becomes even more clear if the participle προι+δοῦσα is understood as a causal participle, resulting in the following translation:[95] "Because the scripture foresaw that God justifies the Gentiles by faith [as the Galatians' own experience indicates], it pre-proclaimed the good news to Abraham that 'All the nations will be blessed in you.'" Translated this way, the citation is in effect functioning as a key part of a *conclusion* drawn from the premise of scripture's foresight, rather than functioning as a premise from which a conclusion is to be drawn. In other words, as discussed above, this citation is functioning not as a deductive proof, but rather as a rhetorical extension of the argument, and Gal 3:9 is offering a conclusion or summary, not to a premise advanced in the citation alone, but rather to the argument as a whole.

Gal 3:11. At first glance, there would seem to be no question that the citation of Hab 2:4 in Gal 3:11 functions in terms of deductive proof. As it is typically translated, the form clearly follows the pattern established above for a *modus ponens* argument ("A, because [it is written] C"): "Now it is evident that no one is justified before God by the law; for 'The one who is righteous will live by faith'" (NRSV).[96] The δῆλον seems to add additional emphasis to the deductive force of this use of citation; not only does this citation offer proof, it offers *clear* proof.

The function of this citation as proof, however, is crucially dependent on the placement of the comma after the δῆλον. If the comma is placed *before* the δῆλον, the reading changes significantly: "*Because* no one is justified before God by the law, *it is clear that* 'The righteous will live by faith.'" In this reading, all that has changed grammatically is that the δῆλον now goes with the ὅτι that immediately follows, rather than with the ὅτι that begins the preceding clause; the first clause is now subordinate to the second, rather than the reverse. In terms of the function of the citation, however, the change is profound. In this alternate reading, the citation no longer functions as the premise, but rather as the conclusion. According to the discussion above, therefore, the citation in this reading cannot offer deductive proof, but rather must serve some other rhetorical function, such as extension or evidence.

---

[95]Ernest De Witt Burton, *A Critical and Exegetical Commentary on the Epistle to the Galatians*, ICC (Edinburgh: T & T Clark, 1921), 160, asserts that the participle is causal; Longenecker, *Galatians*, 115, suggests that it is "probably circumstantial"; neither offers any support for his position. The most natural reading of the participle seems to be causal, particularly in light of the apparent function of the citation.

[96]Cf. the RSV: "Now it is evident that no man is justified before God by the law; for 'He who through faith is righteous shall live.'" In terms of how it is functioning, it does not matter which way the citation itself is translated.

Scholarship of the last half of the twentieth century has been virtually unanimous, not so much in rejecting the alternate reading suggested above, but in totally ignoring even the possibility of such a reading.[97] Even before that time, only a few commentaries and articles discuss the issue, with most of the discussion occurring in German scholarship.[98] When the issue is discussed, the major argument against the reading suggested above seems to be based on the assumption that scripture would naturally be cited as proof rather than as conclusion in Paul's argument. Burton's brief discussion is illustrative:

> That the clause preceding δῆλον is the subject of the proposition δῆλον ἐστι, and the following clause the proof of it, rather than the reverse, which is grammatically possible, is proved by the fact that the following clause is a quotation from the O. T., and, therefore, valuable for proof of the apostle's assertion while not itself requiring to be proved.[99]

There are, however, three important reasons to recommend the reading suggested above, placing the comma before the δῆλον. First, in typical Greek usage,

---

[97] I am aware of only two exceptions currently in publication. First, N. T. Wright, *The Climax of the Covenant* (Minneapolis: Fortress, 1991), 149n42, indicates that the possibility of this alternate reading was suggested to him by his student Christopher Palmer; Wright, however, does not explore the issue further. Second, Richard B. Hays, "The Letter to the Galatians," in *2 Corinthians, Galatians, Ephesians, Philippians, Colossians, 1 & 2 Thessalonians, 1 & 2 Timothy, Titus, Philemon*, vol. 11 in *The New Interpreter's Bible* (Nashville: Abingdon, 2000), 259 has adopted this reading based on an earlier draft of the current investigation.

[98] In the twentieth century, see Burton, *Galatians*, 166; Hermann Hanse, "ΔΗΛΟΝ (Zu Gal 3:11)," *ZNW* 34 (1935): 299–303; Theodor Zahn, *Der Brief des Paulus an die Galater* (Leipzig: Deichert, 1922), 153–54. In the nineteenth century, see Heinrich August Wilhelm Meyer, *Critical and Exegetical Handbook to the Epistle to the Galatians*, trans. G. H. Venables (New York: Funk & Wagnalls, 1884), 113; in the eighteenth century, see J. A. Bengel, *Gnomon Novi Testamenti* (Tübingen: Philipp Schramm, 1742), ET *Gnomon of the New Testament* (Edinburgh: T & T Clark, 1860), 4:22. Of these, only Bengel suggests that δῆλον should be read with the following ὅτι, but his discussion nevertheless treats the citation more as the proof than as the conclusion: "The former [that no one is justified before God by works of the law] is alleged ... as if still open to doubt, but the latter is τὸ δῆλον, a thing quite *manifest*, by which even the former ought to be placed beyond a doubt." Hanse and Meyer also note that δῆλον is taken with the following ὅτι by J. F. von Flatt, *Vorlesungen über den Brief an die Galater und Epheser* (Tübingen: L. F. Fues, 1828) and J. C. K. von Hofmann, *Die Heilige Schrift des neuen Testaments zusammenhängend untersucht* (Nördlingen: C. H. Beck, 1863); unfortunately, I have not been able to obtain these works for verification.

[99] Burton, *Galatians*, 166.

ὅτι follows δῆλον about twice as often as it precedes δῆλον.[100] Of course, that means that ὅτι can and often does precede δῆλον.[101] The question in the case of Gal 3:11, however, is whether, presented with a ὅτι both before and immediately after a δῆλον, one would most naturally take the δῆλον with the ὅτι that precedes or the one that follows. The evidence from Greek literature and other writings suggests the latter, not only because δῆλον ὅτι is more common than ὅτι ... δῆλον, but even more because, in those cases when ὅτι both precedes *and* immediately follows δῆλον, Greek usage hardly ever matches the δῆλον with the ὅτι that precedes.[102]

---

[100] Based on a search of all Greek writings up through the first century C.E. contained in the Thesaurus Linguae Graecae (TLG version D CD-ROM, searched with Silver Mountain Software TLG Workplace™ 8.0), ὅτι follows δῆλον approximately twice as often as it precedes (1613 vs. 790). The ratio was almost identical (303 vs. 152) when the search was limited to the Hellenistic period (third century B.C.E. through first century C.E.). These results are only approximate; because there were too many matches to examine each one individually, false results (i.e., results in which the ὅτι and the δῆλον found in the computerized search do not actually go together) have not been ruled out, nor is it certain that all possible combinations of ὅτι and δῆλον were found, due to the need to set limits on the search interval. In the case of ὅτι preceding δῆλον, the search interval was set to allow up to twenty-five intervening words; in the case of δῆλον followed by ὅτι, the search interval was set to allow no more than one intervening word (allowing for a single postpositive particle such as δέ, οὖν, or γάρ, but potentially overlooking examples in which a longer phrase intervenes, e.g., δῆλον ἐκ τούτων ὅτι). These limits were selected so that the results, if skewed, would tend to be skewed against the argument made above.

[101] As Hanse, "ΔΗΛΟΝ," points out, challenging a claim to the contrary made by Zahn. Hanse assembles several examples from Greek literature; the most important of these are those in which ὅτι both follows and precedes δῆλον; see further below.

[102] In a search of Greek writings from the third century B.C.E. through the first century C.E. contained in the TLG database, using a search interval of up to twenty-five intervening words, only thirty-two instances of ὅτι ... δῆλον ... ὅτι were found, not counting Gal 3:11; see the appendix for a chart of the data. (To be precise, the search returned fifty-four matches, not counting Gal 3:11; on closer examination, however, twenty-two of these turned out to be false matches, in some cases because the second ὅτι was far distant from the δῆλον and obviously used in some other way, and more often because *both* occurrences of ὅτι were matched with δῆλον, either in the form οτι ... δῆλον, δῆλον ὅτι or, more commonly, δῆλον ὅτι ... δῆλον ὅτι.) In only three of these thirty-two instances does the δῆλον go with the preceding rather than the following ὅτι—and one of those (Philo, *Arithmetica* 23b) is a verbatim copy of another (Philo, *De Plantatione* 123).

In most of the examples in which ὅτι both precedes and follows δῆλον, there are two main patterns which clearly indicate that the δῆλον goes with the following ὅτι. Either the first ὅτι is recitative, following a verb such as λεγεῖν, ἰδεῖν, γινωσκεῖν, etc., or there is a conjunction (εἰ, ἐάν, ἤ, γάρ, οὖν, etc.) which clearly marks the boundary of the sec-

To be sure, the evidence for the case where ὅτι both precedes and follows δῆλον is relatively scarce; this is not a particularly common pattern. It is even less common if one looks for an example that exactly parallels the structure of Gal 3:11 (two clauses, the first of which is introduced with ὅτι, the second by ὅτι or δῆλον ὅτι, depending on where the comma is placed). In fact, there is only *one* example from Greek literature of the third century B.C.E. through the first century C.E.[103] That one example, however, is more than a little intriguing, because it also makes use of citation from scripture: ὅτι δὲ ὁ θερισμὸς πολὺς καὶ οἱ ἐργάται ὀλίγοι, δῆλον ὅτι ἐν τοῖς καιροῖς ἡμῶν λιμός ἐστιν τοῦ ἀκοῦσαι λόγον κυρίου.[104] The first clause contains a citation from Mt 9:37 (par. Lk 10:2); the second clause contains a citation from Amos 8:11 (LXX).[105] Not only does this example provide a nearly exact parallel to the structure of Gal 3:11, and not only does it seem most likely to take the δῆλον with the ὅτι that follows rather than the one that precedes, but also in any case it places a citation from scripture in the conclusion:[106] "Now because 'the harvest is great, but the

---

ond clause. Hanse offers a two examples which he feels demonstrate a pattern similar to that found in Gal 3:11. One of these, Philo *De Plantatione* 123, also emerged in the TLG database search as one of the few cases in which the δῆλον goes with the preceding ὅτι: ὅτι μὲν οὖν τοὺς πρὸ αὐτῆς, παντί τῳ δῆλον· ὅτι δὲ καὶ τοὺς μετ' αὐτήν, ἐξ ἐπιλογισμοῦ ῥᾴδιον ἰδεῖν. In fact, however, this example is *not* strictly parallel to Gal 3:11. Not only does the μὲν ... δὲ strongly suggest a parallel structure in which each clause begins with ὅτι, but the ῥᾴδιον ἰδεῖν at the end of the second clause is essentially synonymous with δῆλον. In effect, this example is little different from the other offered by Hanse (*Corpus Hermeticum* XI 11), in which each ὅτι has a matching δῆλον: καὶ ὅτι μὲν ἐστί τις ὁ ποιῶν ταῦτα, δῆλον· ὅτι δὲ καὶ εἷς, φανερώτατον δῆλον. In effect, both of these are not so much examples of a ὅτι both preceding and following δῆλον as they are back-to-back examples of ὅτι preceding δῆλον.

[103]Based on a search of the TLG D CD-ROM. This example should almost certainly be dated later, but it shows up in the TLG database search because of its attribution to Clement of Rome.

[104]*Epistulae de Virginitate* 1.13. This work, spuriously attributed to Clement of Rome, is extant in Greek only in fragments. Here, the Greek text does not exactly match the Syriac text, which was used for the translation contained in *Ante-Nicene Fathers*, ed. Alexander Roberts and James Donaldson (Peabody, MA: Hendrickson, 1994), 8:60: "That 'the harvest is great, but the workmen are few,' this also is well-known and manifest." In addition to the TLG D CD-ROM, the Greek text can be found in F. X. Funk and F. Diekamp, eds., *Patres Apostolici*, vol. 2, 3rd ed. (Tübingen: Laupp, 1913), 1–45.

[105]In the lines that follow, in both the Greek and Syriac texts, the author continues the quotation from Mt / Lk, and then goes on to describe the sort of workers who should be sent: διὸ δεηθῶμεν τοῦ κυρίου τοῦ θερισμοῦ, ὅπως ἐκβάλῃ ἐργάτας εἰς τὸν θερισμὸν αὐτοῦ, ἀλλ' ἐργάτας τοιούτους ...

[106]Since this example places a citation from scripture in each clause, one of the citations must wind up in the conclusion, even if the δῆλον were taken with the ὅτι that

workers are few,' it is clear that in our time 'There is a famine to hear the word of the Lord.'"[107]

The second reason to recommend the reading suggested above, placing the comma before the δῆλον in Gal 3:11, is that the point stated in the first clause ("in the law, no one is justified before God") has already been established in Paul's letter:

> We ourselves are Jews by birth and not Gentile sinners; yet we know that a person is justified not by the works of the law but through faith in Jesus Christ. And we have come to believe in Christ Jesus, so that we might be justified by faith in Christ, and not by doing the works of the law, because no one will be justified by the works of the law. (Gal 2:15–16, NSRV)

Although Gal 2:15–16 raises a number of questions and issues of its own,[108] it seems clear, at the very least, that Paul is stating a point of agreement between himself and his opponents.[109] Gal 3:11a is essentially a restatement of this point of agreement: no one is justified before God by works of the law. If the first clause in Gal 3:11 is therefore a point that has already been established in the course of the argument, then it is not in need of further proof. It can serve rather as the basis from which to draw further conclusions.

The third reason to recommend the reading suggested above is that elsewhere in Paul's letters, he can and does use citations in ways other than deductive proof, including as a conclusion.[110] In 1 Cor 1:31, for example, Paul

---

precedes. Note that in Gal 3:11, the first clause could be taken as an allusion to Ps 142:2 (LXX; 143:2 MT), in which case the parallel with this example becomes even stronger.

[107] Note that the Syriac version takes the δῆλον with the ὅτι that precedes; see above, n. 104. The Syriac text, however, apparently lacks the second clause altogether, so there is no ὅτι following the δῆλον.

[108] Two of the most significant issues raised by Gal 2:15–16 have to do with the exact meaning of ἐὰν μή, and the type of genitive represented by the phrase πίστεως ['Ιησοῦ] Χριστοῦ. Note that the essential point for the current investigation does not rest on one's solution to these problems; the essential point is that Paul is advancing a position which, he seems to expect, represents a point of agreement between himself and his opponents, and that this position includes the understanding that no one is justified by [works of] law.

[109] Cf. Martyn, *Galatians*, 246–47: "When one notes in v 16 the content of the knowledge that is shared by Paul, Peter, and the Teachers (shared indeed by all Jewish Christians), and when one takes account of the way in which Paul makes use of that knowledge in formulating his argument, one sees his strategy." Cf. ibid., 249, 263–68. Cf. James D. G. Dunn, "The New Perspective on Paul," in *Jesus, Paul, and the Law: Studies in Mark and Galatians* (Louisville: John Knox, 1990), 189: "The format of his words shows that he is appealing to an accepted view of Jewish Christians."

[110] We have established above that it is theoretically possible to use citations in these other ways, and we have argued that Paul does in fact do so in Gal 3:6 and 3:8. Here the

uses a citation from Jer 9:24 which appears as the content of a ἵνα clause; clearly, it supplies, not the proof, but rather the result or purpose of the preceding verse: ἐξ αὐτοῦ δὲ ὑμεῖς ἐστε ἐν Χριστῷ Ἰησοῦ, ὃς ἐγενήθη σοφία ἡμῖν ἀπὸ θεοῦ, δικαιοσύνη τε καὶ ἁγιασμὸς καὶ ἀπολύτρωσις, ἵνα καθὼς γέγραπται, Ὁ καυχώμενος ἐν κυρίῳ καυχάσθω.[111] Even more striking is his use of the same citation in 2 Cor 10:17; here the syntax suggests that the citation supplies the conclusion for which (γάρ) the following verse supplies the premise: Ὁ δὲ καυχώμενος ἐν κυρίῳ καυχάσθω· οὐ γὰρ ὁ ἑαυτὸν συνιστάνων, ἐκεῖνός ἐστιν δόκιμος, ἀλλὰ ὃν ὁ κύριος συνίστησιν.[112]

It would seem, therefore, that not only is there no compelling reason not to read Gal 3:11 with the comma before the δῆλον, but there is in fact a good bit of evidence in favor of that reading. When read in this way, the citation does not offer deductive proof of the point already established in the argument, that no one is justified before God by the law; rather it builds on and rhetorically extends that point: "Because no one is justified before God by the law, it is clear that 'The righteous will live by faith.'" Not only does the function of the citation change when read this way, therefore, but also the point of the argument changes. Rather than an argument over how one is to be justified, complete with scriptural proof, this verse moves from an *agreement* on how one is justified to an argument about how one who is justified should live, or perhaps, how one should live righteously. To put it in the terms that Paul uses in Gal 3:3, this discussion is not about how one begins, but how one continues and completes what was begun through faith.

Presuppositions of Contrast: Ζήσεται as the "Hinge-Point" of the Argument

As noted above, Gal 3:11–12 poses difficulties for interpretation because it seems to place two citations of scripture, Hab 2:4 and Lev 18:5, into sharp contrast with one another. Some scholars, assuming that Paul could not hold scripture to be self-contradictory, have denied that any real contradiction is implied by this contrast.[113] Other scholars have implied that Paul, in the course of proof-texting, simply overlooked the potential contradiction between the cita-

---

point is that he clearly does so elsewhere in his letters as well. Space does not permit a full survey and analysis of all of Paul's uses of citation, though such a project would be worthwhile. For now, a few brief examples will illustrate the point.

[111] The translation of the RSV suggests that the citation serves not just as purpose or result, but even as conclusion: "He is the source of your life in Christ Jesus, whom God made our wisdom, our righteousness and sanctification and redemption; therefore, as it is written, 'Let him who boasts, boast in the Lord.'"

[112] "'Let the one who boasts, boast in the Lord.' For it is not those who commend themselves that are approved, but those whom the Lord commends" (NRSV).

[113] See above, 80–82.

tions.[114] Others have argued that Paul recognized a real contrast between the verses, but that he sought to resolve the tension according to recognized rabbinic or rhetorical principles.[115] Yet others have suggested that Paul deliberately intensified a minor contrast between Hab 2:4 and Lev 18:5 into a full-blown contradiction.[116] In any of these cases, whatever means have been used to try to resolve or explain away the potential contradiction, it is evident that the sharp contrast between the citations gives rise to ungrammaticality.

As suggested above, this ungrammaticality arises from, and is evidence for, a pragmatic presupposition concerning the use of citation in an argument: the use of citation presupposes that what is cited is both authoritative and applicable to the argument at hand. How can *both* citations be authoritative when they appear to be in conflict with one another? In effect, the arguments briefly sketched out above seek to show either that, at some level, the citations really do not contradict one another, or that Paul is deliberately challenging or rejecting the presupposition of authority and applicability.

There is, however, another presupposition that plays an important role in this particular ungrammaticality. This presupposition has to do with the use of contrast. What is pragmatically presupposed when one item is contrasted with another? Once again, it may be helpful to take an obviously artificial (and obviously dissonant) example. Consider the following contrast: "The sky is blue, but eggplant tastes bitter." Once again, something seems odd about this contrast, and once again that dissonance points to the expectations that have been violated. What makes this contrast so odd is that the two items being contrasted seem to have absolutely nothing in common, so that the contrast seems to make no sense.[117] What is presupposed by the use of contrast, therefore, is that there is at least one point in common between the items being contrasted, from which the contrast can be drawn. To put it another way, the differences described in a contrast must be measured from a common point in order to be meaningful.

---

[114]See above, 74–78; though this point is made with regard to the tension between the citations and the argument in support of which Paul uses them, the same point is made also with respect to the potential contradiction between the citations.

[115]See above, 89–93.

[116]See above, 82–89

[117]The dissonance in this artificial example is far greater than in the common expression, "comparing apples to oranges." Apples and oranges have several things in common: they are both fruit; they are both edible; they are both somewhat round in shape; they weigh a similar amount; and so on. Any of these points of contact offer various opportunities for drawing a meaningful contrast, e.g., "Apples are crunchy when you bite into them, but oranges are juicy." About the only thing eggplant and the sky have in common is that both have color, but though the color of the sky is involved in the contrast, it has been compared, not to the color of the eggplant, but rather to its taste—hence the dissonance.

In the case of the citations of Hab 2:4 and Lev 18:5, the point in common, the point from which the contrast is drawn, is obvious: ζήσεται.[118] Certainly this is the point in common that is assumed in the many discussions of these verses in scholarly debate; unfortunately, the attention of these debates has been almost entirely focused on the *differences* that the contrast draws—doing vs. "faithing," being righteous vs. being self-righteous, and so on—with virtually no attention given to defining the precise point of similarity from which those differences have been drawn. What has almost always been *assumed*—with little in the way of debate or defense—is that the specific point in common between these verses, the point of similarity implicit in the verb ζήσεται, is the claim for how to *gain* life (that is, in the final judgment).[119] In other words, according to the traditional assumption, these citations describe different means to obtain salvation.

There are, however, two major problems with this traditional assumption. The first problem has to do with Jewish understanding of the law. As E. P. Sanders has so ably demonstrated, Judaism never claimed that observance of the law was a means of obtaining salvation. One "gets in," or in other words is counted among those who will be saved, by being part of the covenant; observance of the law is merely how one "stays in," or in other words is what is expected of those who are "saved."[120] Even if one argues that Paul is contrasting a *misunderstanding* of how one gains life with a true understanding, the problem remains that he apparently cites a verse in support of or to illustrate a position that neither he nor his opponents hold—a position that, according to Gal 2:15–16, they *agree* is false. In effect, even those who decry the caricature of Judaism as a legalistic, merit-based religion continue to smuggle in that view as the essence of Lev 18:5, against which Paul contrasts the citation of Hab 2:4.

The second major problem with the traditional assumption has to do with the context, or rather contexts, in which ζήσεται appears. Either in the context of Galatians, or in the original context of the citations, does the verb ζάω typically refer to the *gaining* of life, or to the living or carrying out of life? There is at least some evidence in Galatians in favor of the former. In Gal 5:25, for example, it appears that ζάω must mean something like "gain life": "If we live (ζῶμεν; i.e., have gained life) by the spirit, let us also conduct ourselves (στοιχῶμεν; i.e., carry out life) by the spirit." One might also point to Gal 6:8,

---

[118]That this is the point in common becomes even more obvious in light of the discussion above concerning the structure of the citations; see above, 132–42.

[119]See above, 79ff.

[120]See above, 24–25. This is one of the weakest points in Sanders' argument. According to Sanders' understanding of these citations, in order to prove that law has nothing to do with faith, Paul has to treat a citation as though it says something that neither he nor his opponents believe to be true. Thus, Sanders can only describe Paul's strategy at this point as "proof-texting."

where Paul uses the noun ζωή in a reference to eternal life:[121] "The one who sows in his own flesh will reap corruption from the flesh, but the one who sows in the spirit will reap eternal life (ζωὴν αἰώνιον) from the spirit."[122]

On the other hand, however, there is also quite a bit of evidence in Galatians that favors reading ζάω as "living life" or "carrying out life." Clearly in Gal 2:14, the first use of the word in the letter, ζάω refers to the way Peter is living life, not how he gains it: "If you, being a Jew, are living (ζῇς) like a Gentile and not like a Jew, how can you compel the Gentiles to Judaize?" Likewise, in 2:19–20, at least part of what Paul describes is "the life I live *in the flesh*." To be sure, this passage is full of eschatological overtones; clearly the life Paul is describing is in some sense that eschatological life which he has gained, paradoxically, by dying with Christ. *This eschatological life, however, is a life that Paul carries out in the flesh.*[123] When ζάω next occurs in the letter, in the paired citations from Hab 2:4 and Lev 18:5, it should therefore come as no surprise if ζήσεται, with or without eschatological overtones, refers primarily to carrying out life rather than gaining it.

---

[121]It is not entirely clear that this reference to eternal life should necessarily be understood soteriologically, at least in the narrow sense of focusing primarily on the issue of whether and/or how one is saved. Certainly Paul is speaking here of an *eschatological* life, but as we will see below, a focus on eschatological life is not necessarily identical with a soteriological focus (in this narrow sense).

[122]Cf. also the use of the verb ζῳοποιέω in 3:21: "For if a law had been given that was able to make alive (ζῳοποιῆσαι), then righteousness would have been from the law." Note, however, that ζῳοποιέω may function in the New Testament in general and Paul in particular as a technical term for resurrection, with particular reference to the resurrection of Christ. Five of the six other occurrences of this word in the undisputed letters of Paul are explicitly linked with resurrection: Rom 4:17, 8:11; 1 Cor 15:22, 36, 45. Elsewhere in the New Testament, the word is also explicitly linked with resurrection in John 5:21 (twice) and 1 Pet 3:18. The remaining four uses of this word (Jn 6:63, 2 Cor 3:6, Eph 2:5, Col 2:13) do not make an explicit link to resurrection, but such a connotation would certainly not be out of place; for example, Eph 2:5, which is virtually synonymous with Col 2:13, speaks of being made alive together with Christ (συνεζωοποίησεν τῷ Χριστῷ). In Gal 3:21, therefore, ζῳοποιέω may refer not so much to the law's inability to grant life to us (i.e., salvation), but rather its inability to effect resurrection (i.e., of Christ in particular) and thus to inaugurate the new age.

[123]For this reason, the distinction between an eschatological and non-eschatological use of ζήσεται in Lev 18:5 and Hab 2:4 (cf. Smith, "Ο ΔΕ ΔΙΚΑΙΟΣ," 19–20) is not as helpful as the distinction between soteriological and non-soteriological uses, even though the term soteriological is thus used in a narrow sense to refer primarily to the issue of whether or not one is saved. As Gal 2:19–20 suggests, the life that Paul has in mind for the Christian both to gain and to live is an eschatological life; the question is whether he is focusing more on gaining it or living it.

The major objection that might be raised to the preceding point concerns the tense of the verb in these two citations. Since ζήσεται is future in these verses—the only occurrences of the verb in the future in the letter—might it not refer to future life, that is, to the life to be gained in the final day of judgment? Certainly this is how the future tense has traditionally been understood in the context of Gal 3:11–12.[124] In the original context from which these citations were drawn, however, such a reading seems clearly out of place. In the context of the giving of the law, including not only the citation from Lev 18:5 but also the citations from Dt 27:26 and 21:23, life and death are clearly not eschatological or soteriological categories, but rather are much more prosaic; the life that is promised is long life in the land.[125] In the case of Hab 2:4, the interpretation is famously difficult, and those difficulties are compounded by the differences between the Hebrew text, the Greek text, and Paul's citation.[126] Nevertheless, the context seems once again to point to how the righteous person carries out life *while waiting for God's justice* (Hab 2:1–3), rather than how one gains life.

SUMMARY

Once again, it will be helpful briefly to summarize the results of the preceding section. First, we have established that, regardless of whatever Paul or his opponents or even his original audience may have assumed about scripture, Paul's use of citations invokes the pragmatic presupposition of authority and applicability. Furthermore, we have argued that the text offers no indication that that presupposition is being challenged or modified in any way, other than the

---

[124] Cf. Martyn, *Galatians*, 314; idem, "The Textual Contradiction Between Habakkuk 2:4 and Leviticus 18:5," in *Theological Issues in the Letters of Paul* (Edinburgh: T&T Clark, 1997), 183.

[125] Note, for example, the threat that is given in Lev 18:26–29: "But you shall keep my statutes and my ordinances and commit none of these abominations, either the citizen or the alien who resides among you (for the inhabitants of the land, who were before you, committed all of these abominations, and the land became defiled); otherwise the land will vomit you out for defiling it, as it vomited out the nation that was before you. For whoever commits any of these abominations shall be cut off from their people." Cf. Dt 30:15–16: "See, I have set before you today life and prosperity, death and adversity. If you obey the commandments of the LORD your God that I am commanding you today, by loving the LORD your God, walking in his ways , and observing his commandments, decrees, and ordinances, then you shall live and become numerous, and the LORD your God will bless you in the land that you are entering to possess."

[126] Cf. Cavallin, "'The Righteous Shall Live by Faith'"; Smith, "Ο ΔΕ ΔΙΚΑΙΟΣ"; J. A. Emerton, "The Textual and Linguistic Problems of Habakkuk ii 4–5," *JTS* ns 29 (1977): 1–18; James M. Scott, "A New Approach to Habakkuk II 4–5A," *VT* 35 (1985): 330–40; Dietrich-Alex Koch, "Der Text von Hab 2 4b in der Septuaginta und im Neuen Testament," *ZNW* 76 (1985): 68–85.

dissonance created by the use of the citations themselves; we must therefore either consider this use of citations to be inconsistent or foolish, or we must conclude that there remains some deeper significance, some matrix that resolves the ungrammaticality. Second, we have argued that, while the use of citation invokes the presupposition of authority and applicability, the actual *function* of citations within an argument can vary. In particular, we concluded that some of the citations in Gal 3:1–14 do *not* function as proof, but rather as rhetorical extension of a point already made (Gen 12:3 in Gal 3:8; Hab 2:4 in Gal 3:11), or inductive evidence to offer further support (but not proof) of some point (Gen 15:6 in Gal 3:6). Finally, we have established that the use of contrast invokes an additional pragmatic presupposition, namely that in any contrast there is some point of similarity from which the differences can be drawn. In the case of the contrast between the citations in Gal 3:11–12, we have argued that the point of similarity cannot be, as has usually been assumed, competing claims for how to gain life. The task that now remains is to see how these insights, together with those developed in the first section above, lead to a matrix of meaning which resolves and provides significance to the ungrammaticalities of the passage.

"Ungrammaticalities" and the Matrix of Meaning

That the citations in Gal 3:1–14 pose problems for interpretation—or in other words, give rise to ungrammaticalities—has been obvious long before the current investigation began. In chapter 3 above, we identified two key problems arising from the citations that have occupied scholarly debate for decades: 1) The citation of Dt 27:26 in Gal 3:10 seems to say precisely the opposite of what Paul uses it to argue; 2) the citations of Hab 2:4 and Lev 18:5 seem to contradict one another. We argued above that the various attempts to resolve these tensions have been less than satisfactory, and suggested that at least part of problem lies in the fact that no investigation prior to the current one has focused on the citations as a group, especially with sensitivity to their intertextual interactions. The question that now faces us is whether the results of the current investigation have paid off, not only in terms of tracing intertextual interactions, but also in terms of resolving those tensions. In other words, to use Riffaterre's mode of speaking, we are ready to ask how the intertextual insights developed above lead to a "matrix" by which the ungrammaticalities of this passage are resolved and in which they find significance.

At least one result of the current investigation up to this point has been to chart the dimensions of the problem by identifying the issues that both contribute to and constrain the resolution of the ungrammaticalities. Two key issues in particular have emerged from this investigation. First, one significant factor which gives rise to the ungrammaticalities is that, while the use of citation in the argument invokes the presupposition of authority and applicability, there is nothing in this text that in any way challenges or qualifies that presupposition. In other words, whatever attitude or understanding Paul or his opponents or the Galatians may or may not have had towards scripture is irrelevant to the ungrammaticalities posed by the text, because the text itself, as we have it, offers no indication that these citations are offered with anything other than a "perfectly straight face." Accordingly, any solution that is offered for resolving the ungrammaticalities must be constrained by that presupposition.[127] The text itself, in other words, seems to rule out those solutions that see Paul advocating one scripture over another or calling the authority of scripture itself into question.

The second key issue that has emerged from our investigation is the failure of the soteriological understanding of this passage in general, and of ζήσεται in particular.[128] It is clear, based on the examination of both structure and presuppositions, that ζήσεται is the key term in the pair of citations that form the chiastic crux—and perhaps also the *crux interpretatum* for the whole passage.[129] It has become clear also that the soteriological understanding of ζήσεται (how one *gains* life) is untenable for a variety of reasons. The omission of death from the curse-blessing-life motif suggests a choice of life vs. life, not life vs. death; the use of Hab 2:4 not as proof, but as conclusion, suggests that it extends and develops the implications of the already agreed-upon point about how one gains life (is justified); the contexts in which the citations containing ζήσεται occur, in Galatians and in their original settings in scripture, all operate against the understanding that the discussion is soteriological. When these points are added together with the questions that emerged above concerning Sanders' soteriological understanding of δικαιόω/δικαιοσύνη, it seems clear that we must therefore also rule out those solutions for resolving the ungrammaticalities that, even though they respect the presupposition of authority and applicability, nevertheless continue to assume that the primary focus of this passage is on the issue of whether and how one is saved.[130]

---

[127] Again, it is possible to seek no solution at all, that is, to agree with Räisänen that Paul is simply inconsistent. From an intertextual perspective, however, such a position is particularly unsatisfying. Whatever the "bumps" in the text may or may not tell us about Paul's internal consistency (assuming we can even hope to access such a thing), they become, from an intertextual perspective, opportunities to generate meaning.

[128] Again, it should be stressed that "soteriological" is being used here in the sense of focusing primarily on the issue of whether or how one is saved. Certainly the passage has soteriological significance even in this sense, but it seems problematic to understand questions about whether and how one is saved as the primary focus.

[129] Ζήσεται is by no means the only important term, of course, but as has been pointed out above, it is a term that has received only a fraction of the attention given to such terms as πίστις or δικαιοσύνη.

[130] As discussed in Chapter 3 above, essentially all of the approaches to Gal 3:1–14 suffer from the assumption of a soteriological focus in the passage as a whole and for many of these citations in particular.

While we have ruled out a solution that assumes a soteriological focus, however, we have not yet established that any sort of non-soteriological understanding is viable, either for the passage as a whole or for the citations within the passage; neither have we yet demonstrated that such an understanding goes any way towards resolving the ungrammaticalities posed by these citations. We need, therefore, to answer three questions. First, do these citations, particularly those which give rise to the tensions identified in chapter 3 above, make sense in the context of Gal 3 when read without a strictly soteriological focus? Second, does such a reading go any way towards resolving the tensions arising from these citations? Finally, what intertext emerges as the underlying "matrix" which resolves these ungrammaticalities and gives significance to the passage as a whole? These are the questions that will guide the discussion below, as we examine each of the tensions (or ungrammaticalities) identified in chapter 3, as well as those that have come to light in the first two sections above.

LEVITICUS 18:5 AND HABAKKUK 2:4: SCRIPTURE AGAINST SCRIPTURE

Do Hab 2:4 and Lev 18:5 make sense in the context of Gal 3 when read non-soteriologically?[131] In other words, can ζήσεται in these verses be understood to mean something like "carry out life"? In the case of the citation of Hab 2:4 in Gal 3:11, a non-soteriological understanding of ζήσεται certainly works rather well. As noted above, this citation should almost certainly be understood as a further conclusion drawn from the already agreed-upon point that no one is justified by way of the law, but only by faith. Read non-soteriologically, the citation of Hab 2:4 extends this point in a way that echoes the pattern of questions Paul asks in Gal 3:2–5: having begun with the hearing of faith, should they now complete (or perhaps, carry on) by the law? His answer, plainly, is "No." Having been made righteous by faith, not law, the righteous person should also live (carry out life) by faith, not law. It is almost certain that the life that is in view is, in some sense, an eschatological life, as we noted with regard to Gal 2:19–20. Nevertheless, the focus in this verse is not on how one *gains* that eschatological life, or even on whether or not one truly *has* that eschatological life, but rather how one carries out the life one already has.

In the case of the citation of Lev 18:5 in Gal 3:12, it may at first glance seem that a non-soteriological reading does not work so well. Indeed, it might seem that to read ζήσεται as "carry out life" renders the citation of Lev 18:5 as a mere tautology: "The one who does these things will carry out life by these things." There are, however, two slight but important nuances that suggest a

---

[131] For lack of a better term, we will continue to use "soteriological" to refer to a focus primarily on the issue of whether (or how) one is saved, and "non-soteriological" to refer to a focus that assumes one is saved, and thus asks how one who is saved should live.

meaning that goes beyond mere tautology. First, the contrast of the aorist tense of ποιήσας with the future tense of ζήσεται once again echoes the pattern developed in Gal 3:2–5 and renewed in Gal 3:11, the pattern of how one begins and how one continues (or completes). One might therefore render the verse as follows: "The one *having done* these things *will continue to live* this way." Second, if ζήσεται is not understood soteriologically, then it may well be that the ἐν should not be understood instrumentally, but rather locatively. Rather than the means by which one gains life, in other words, the phrase ἐν αὐτοῖς may instead express more the (figurative) location in which one carries out life.[132] Together, these two slight nuances suggest that the citation of Lev 18:5 can be understood non-soteriologically, saying in effect, "the one who buys into the law has to continue to live in it."[133]

J. Louis Martyn's apocalyptic approach to Galatians is especially relevant at this point.[134] According to Martyn, the two questions that Paul's letter answers are "What time is it?" and "In what cosmos do we actually live?"[135] In effect, both of these questions have the same answer: the time is the new age, and it is in the new age, the new cosmos brought about by God's action in Christ, that we are to live. To live under the law—whether by observing or breaking it—is to live within the old cosmos, which God has destroyed in Christ.[136] Paul is not calling the Galatians to a different or even superior way to gain entry into the covenant, therefore, but rather is urging them to recognize and live in the new creation that God has brought about.[137]

---

[132]Cf. Martyn, *Galatians*, 258–59, where Martyn discusses the phrases "in me," "in the flesh," and "in faith" in Gal 2:20 as "a valuable index to Paul's varied uses of the preposition 'in.'" Each of these uses form "spatial metaphors" in which "the accent lies on an orb of power." Unfortunately, Martyn does not explore the possibility that "in them" in Gal 3:12 could form a similar spatial metaphor, though he certainly does refer to the law as a power, particularly in connection with the preposition ὑπό; cf. ibid., 23, 272–73.

[133]Cf. Gal 5:3.

[134]See above, 49–56.

[135]Martyn, *Galatians*, 23.

[136]Cf. J. Louis Martyn, "Apocalyptic Antinomies in Paul's Letter to the Galatians," *NTS* 31 (1985): 413; idem, "Events in Galatia: Modified Covenantal Nomism versus God's Invasion of the Cosmos in the Singular Gospel: A Response to J. D. G. Dunn and B. R. Gaventa," in *Pauline Theology*, vol. 1, ed. J. M. Bassler (Minneapolis: Fortress, 1991), 165; idem, *Galatians*, 256–57: "It is crucial to note that Paul speaks about separation from the Law [in 2:19], not about commencing a life that is characterized by violation of the Law."

[137]Ibid., 23: ". . . in writing this letter Paul is not at all formulating an argument designed to persuade the Galatians that faith is better than observance of the Law. He is constructing an announcement designed to wake the Galatians up to the real cosmos, made what it is by the fact that faith has now *arrived* with the advent of Christ (3:23–25)." Cf. idem, "Events," 167–68.

Martyn's approach would seem to mesh perfectly with a non-soteriological (but yet thoroughly eschatological) understanding of ζήσεται: the point of the citations is not how one *gains* life, but rather where one lives—in the old cosmos, characterized by law, or in the new creation, characterized by faith. Unfortunately, this is not the way Martyn understands these citations; on the contrary, he continues to understand them in terms of competing soteriological claims.[138] For this reason he not only argues that these citations are contradictory, but also that Paul deliberately sets them into contradiction in order to undercut the Teachers' claim for the monolithic authority and applicability of the law.[139]

If one modifies Martyn's apocalyptic approach so as to include a non-soteriological reading of these citations, however, Hab 2:4 and Lev 18:5 become complementary rather than contradictory. Rather than competing claims for how one gains life, *only one of which can be valid*, Paul is presenting two systems of life (or two spheres in which to live), *both of which are available to the Galatians*. The Galatians *can* choose to carry out life as they have begun, in faith, but they can also choose—and some apparently have so chosen—to live under the law, and in so doing, they have returned to the old cosmos from which Christ set them free.[140] Lev 18:5 therefore does not offer a false claim about how to gain life, but rather describes the trap into which one enters when he or she attempts to carry out life by the law. The law offers no way out of the old cosmos, no way out from under the curse; "the one who has done these things will continue to live in them."[141]

---

[138]Martyn, "Textual Contradiction," 183. In effect, Martyn echoes the views of Sanders in seeing Paul's problem with the law or rejection of the law only in terms of salvific claims. Cf. idem, *Galatians*, 261n150: "When considered *salvific*, observance of the Law belongs on the human side of the divine/human antinomy" (emphasis added); ibid., 251: "On the contrary, *as regards salvation*, observance of the Law and the faith of Jesus Christ constitute a genuine antinomy" (emphasis added).

[139]See above, 86–88; cf. Martyn, *Galatians*, 506–14. The net effect is an oddly fractured view of the law and of scripture. Sometimes it applies, and sometimes it does not; sometimes it speaks with authority, and at other times has no authority; sometimes it represents the intention of God, and at other times it is inimical to God. This is, of course, precisely the point at which Martyn's argument runs afoul of the presupposition invoked by the use of citation within the argument. As noted above, Martyn fails to show any indication in the text, other than the tensions created by these citations in Gal 3, that the presupposition of authority and applicability is being challenged or modified.

[140]This has much of the same already-and-not-yet character as Paul's imperative-and-indicative teachings in Rom 6–8. Although we have already died to sin, it is clearly still possible for us to return to it.

[141]To be sure, this description of Lev 18:5 potentially has profound soteriological implications, in particular if one asks what happens to someone who remains caught in the trap, i.e., in the old cosmos. The point is, however, that Paul is *not* primarily focused

It would seem, therefore, that a non-soteriological reading of these citations is not only viable, but also crucial for resolving the ungrammaticality that arises from the use of these citations in Galatians 3. When these verses are read soteriologically, as competing claims for how to gain life, there appears no way to avoid a sense of dissonance between the presupposition of authority and applicability on the one hand, and the apparent contradiction between the citations of Hab 2:4 and Lev 18:5 on the other. When these verses are read non-soteriologically, that dissonance is resolved.

At the end of the first section of this chapter, we had already tentatively suggested that the matrix by which the ungrammaticalities of this passage could be resolved, and in which they would find significance, could not be a soteriological formula such as "how to gain life" or "how to be righteous enough to live," but rather must be something like, "how to carry out life" or even "how to live righteously." Based on the discussion above, however, we need to go a step further. The matrix is not just "how to carry out life," but "*where* to carry out life," or perhaps better, simply, "where to live." In other words, it is not so much *how* one lives but *where* one lives that identifies one as righteous.[142] It remains to be seen, in the case of the ungrammaticality arising from the tension between Paul's argument and the citation of Dt 27:26, whether this matrix continues to work, or how it might need to be refined.

Deuteronomy 27:26: The Threat of the Curse

As it is typically understood, the curse which is featured in the citations of Dt 27:26 and 21:23 in Gal 3:10 and 3:13, respectively, is in effect the soteriological counterpart to the life which is promised in the citations of Hab 2:4 and Lev 18:5 in Gal 3:11–12. The curse defines or identifies those who are excluded from salvation. To be "under the curse" is to be outside of the boundaries of those who are or will be saved; to be redeemed from the curse by Christ is to be saved (to gain life).

In and of itself, it would seem that the curse need not be understood soteriologically. James D. G. Dunn's approach to this passage, for example, could

---

on such implications. He is talking to those who have already truly experienced life in Christ. That life in Christ, however, is not yet totally effected; rather, Christians live "between the ages." To the extent that they live in Christ (or in the Spirit), they are already a part of the new age, but still they have not fully escaped the old. Thus, Paul's concern is to instruct them on where to live, to show them that taking up the law is to carry out life in the old age; his concern is not to tell them how to gain life nor to question whether they truly are saved.

[142]As we will see below, where one lives has both soteriological and ethical implications. One gains life by entering the new creation in Christ, thus leaving behind the old age and with it the law; one carries out life by living in the new creation in Christ (in the Spirit), not by returning to the old age (which is what one does in returning to the law).

be used to suggest a sociological understanding of the curse: to be under the curse is to be separated from one another by nationalistic barriers.[143] Alternately, one could go back to the original context of the citations and argue that the curse that is in view is the curse of exile, the loss of land, the loss of life—serious consequences for failure to obey the law, but not necessarily soteriological consequences.[144] Why then has the soteriological understanding of the curse prevailed, even for someone like Dunn?

The key point that drives the soteriological understanding of the curse is the assumption that Galatians 3 discusses the law as a possible (or even actual) means by which one can gain (or maintain) salvation. To be sure, that assumption can take different forms. According to Schreiner, for example, the law really could grant life, if only someone could live up to it. Because no one can live up to it, all fall under its curse, and therefore the conclusion is clear: no one can be saved by (works of) the law.[145] According to Sanders, Paul is calling on the curse of the law merely as a proof-text, but the proof-text is intended to drive home the point that Christ is the only entrance requirement, that is, the only way to "get in."[146] According to Dunn, ὅσοι ἐξ ἔργων νόμου believe that they live within the law, and thus remain in the covenant (and thus maintain their soteriological status), by doing those "works" by which Gentiles are excluded[147]—but Paul charges that they themselves fall under the curse of the law because, in their emphasis on the nationalistic and exclusivistic "works," they inevitably fall short of what the law really requires.[148]

---

[143]See above, 31; cf. James D. G. Dunn, "Works of Law and the Curse of the Law (Galatians 3.10–14)," *NTS* 31 (1985): 536; idem, "The Theology of Galatians: The Issue of Covenantal Nomism," in *Pauline Theology*, vol. 1, ed. J. M. Bassler (Minneapolis: Fortress, 1991), 132, 137; cf. also George Howard, *Paul: Crisis in Galatia. A Study in Early Christian Theology*, SNTSMS 35 (Cambridge: Cambridge University Press, 1979), 64. Even though Dunn identifies a sociological perspective to the curse, he nevertheless discusses the passage as a whole soteriologically; see above, 32.

[144]See above, 171; cf. above, 38n128.

[145]See above, 18, 67.

[146]See above, 74.

[147]As noted above, 32, though Dunn describes his argument in terms of "staying in," his focus is nevertheless soteriological. The point is not how one who is in behaves, but rather how one makes sure one is really in.

[148]Dunn, "Works of Law," 534: "To be of the works of the law is *not* the same as fulfilling the law, is *less* than what the law requires and so falls under the law's own curse.... To thus misunderstand the law by giving primacy to matters of at best secondary importance [i.e., nationalistic works of law] was to fall short of what the law required and thus to fall under the law's own curse." Note that Dunn's formulation seems to suggest that ὅσοι ἐξ ἔργων νόμου are right in thinking that the curse of the law excludes one from membership in the covenant; they are wrong in thinking that they themselves escape that curse by focusing on the nationalistic and exclusivistic "works."

So long as one understands the point of the discussion of the law in Galatians 3 to be soteriological, therefore, one must also understand the point of the curse to be soteriological.[149] Given a soteriological understanding of the law and of the curse, however, it is difficult to escape the tension between Paul's argument and the citation of Dt 27:26 in Gal 3:10. The difficulty arises in part because the soteriological understanding leads to an equation between "under a curse," "accursed," and "not saved." If ὅσοι ἐξ ἔργων νόμου are relying on a false means for gaining life, then they must not have gained life (they are not saved); therefore they are not just "under a curse," but accursed, since the curse is equivalent to being excluded from salvation. The soteriological understanding of the passage, in other words, leads to the understanding that "under a curse" necessarily means having *activated* the curse pronounced by the law, with soteriological consequences. Thus, ὅσοι ἐξ ἔργων νόμου are cursed—but again, this is just what the citation does not say; it pronounces a curse, not on those who do or attempt to do the law, but on those who fail to do it.[150]

On the other hand, what if one does not begin with a soteriological understanding of this passage? What if, as was suggested above, one understands the point of the discussion to be, not "how to gain (or maintain) life," but rather "how to carry out life," or better yet, "where to live"? Does such a reading of Dt 27:6 in the context of Gal 3:10 make sense? Does such a reading go any way towards resolving the tension between the citation and the argument in which Paul uses it?

As it turns out, to read Dt 27:26 in the context of Gal 3:10 in terms of "where to live" makes a great deal of sense. Read this way, the issue that is dealt with in Gal 3:10 is not whether or how ὅσοι ἐξ ἔργων νόμου have failed to gain life, but rather where they must carry out life:[151] Paul does not say that they are accursed, but rather that they are *under* a curse.[152] Neither does Paul say that they are dead, nor does he threaten them with death per se; rather, he cites Lev

---

[149]In effect, the tendency of many scholars has been to see the law's claim to give life as a false promise (false because one cannot do the law, or because law leads to self-righteousness, or so on; see above, 81–82), but yet to see the law's threatened curse as a true curse—and to see both as having essentially soteriological consequences.

[150]See above, 72–73. Note also that, as discussed above, 171, the original context of the citation does not suggest a soteriological or eschatological curse.

[151]It is worth noting that not only is ὑπὸ κατάραν in Gal 3:10 a spatial metaphor, but also the redemption effected by Christ can be understood in spatial terms, both in Gal 3:13 (ἡμᾶς ἐξηγόρασεν ἐκ τῆς κατάρας), and also (and especially) in Gal 1:4 (ἐξέληται ἡμᾶς ἐκ τοῦ αἰῶνος τοῦ ἐνεστῶτος πονηροῦ).

[152]Cf. Stanley, "'Under a Curse,'" 499, who argues that Paul deliberately avoids using ἐπικατάρατος in Gal 3:10a, which would have been more natural as a parallel or contrast to the εὐλογοῦνται of 3:9, "because it does not express what he actually wants to say." Cf. above, 76n66.

18:5 to show where they must carry out life.[153] Whether those who are thus under a curse are necessarily to be counted among those who are lost is beside the point.[154] The point is not how one gains or loses life, but rather that the system of life defined by the law is a life lived under a curse.

This reading not only makes sense, but also it resolves the tension between the citation of Dt 27:26 and the argument in which Paul uses it. The crucial point in this non-soteriological reading is that to live *under* a curse in no way implies that one has *activated* the curse. What the citation of Dt 27:26 shows is that the law pronounces a curse; curse is therefore integral to law. To live under the law, therefore, is to live under a curse, regardless of whether or not one fulfills the conditions of that curse.[155] The key issue, once again, is *where* to live. The point of the passage is not how one avoids or whether one can avoid activating the curse of the law, but rather is whether one will live under the law at all. Once again, Martyn's apocalyptic approach is extremely helpful at this point. Paul is urging the Galatians, not to keep *or* break the law, not even to avoid the curse per se, but rather to live in the new creation instead of in the old age of which both the law and its curse are a part.

Loose Ends and Implications: Redemption and Righteousness

Once again, the matrix that has emerged from our discussion is not a soteriological formula, such as "how to gain life," but rather is the eschatological question, "where to live"—will we live under the law and its curse, in the old age, or will we live in the Spirit, in the new creation? While we have shown how this matrix resolves the ungrammaticalities identified above in chapter 3, however, there remain at least two issues that need to be addressed. First, how does

---

[153] In it original context, as we noted above, 171, the curse *is* a threat of death—but not of soteriological death.

[154] In one sense, as we will see below, to be living under the curse of the law *is* to be lost rather than saved. In another sense, however, it is conceivable that a Christian could enter again into the law and thus find him/herself under its curse. The paradox is essentially the same as is found in Paul's already-not-yet, indicative-and-imperative instructions in Romans 6–7. Christians have died to sin and to the law—but they still may struggle with both. Cf. above, n. 141.

[155] This is the point that, at first glance, Stanley seems to be making with regard to his distinction between ὑπὸ κατάραν and ἐπικατάρατος; see above, n. 152. In the course of Stanley's argument, however, it becomes clear that the real force of the threat of potential curse, as he describes it, lies in the great likelihood that anyone who takes up the law will fail to do it perfectly, and thus will, in fact, suffer the actual curse. In other words, for Stanley the curse is potential precisely because it is so likely to occur, even though it is theoretically possible for someone to avoid it. Paul encourages the Galatians not to take up the law because in so doing they risk the very real danger of falling under its curse (see above, 76).

this matrix fit into and make sense of the redemption from the curse effected by Christ (Gal 3:13–14)? Second, how does the issue of righteousness fit into this matrix (Gal 3:6, 8, 11)?

While the non-soteriological reading of the curse, built around the matrix "where to live," resolves the ungrammaticality arising from the citation of Dt 27:26 in Gal 3:10, it may at first glance seem not to work in connection with the other citation concerning the curse, Dt 21:23 in Gal 3:13. Here, surely, the context *is* soteriological: "Christ redeemed us from the curse of the law." While 3:13 by itself may have a soteriological focus, however, it is not clear that the thrust of the whole sentence is soteriological. If one examines the whole sentence that extends, not just through 3:13 but also through 3:14, one sees that the ultimate focus is not on the redemption from curse, but rather on the receiving of the blessing in Christ, which is the promise of the spirit. Especially in light of the structural pattern identified in the first section of this chapter, it seems as though we are once again hearing a reiteration of the pattern first developed in Gal 3:2–5. How one begins is how one continues; the redemption begun in Christ results in the ongoing experience of the blessing in Christ, the blessing of life in the Spirit.[156]

Likewise, while redemption has a soteriological focus, it is not clear that the curse itself should be understood primarily in soteriological terms, in the sense that escaping from the curse is the key to salvation. On the one hand, the curse can be understood as a symptom of our need for redemption, rather than its cause. The old age from which Christ has rescued us includes the law and its curse, but is not solely defined in those terms; that old age also includes sin, death, and the flesh.[157] We are not saved *because* we have been freed from the curse of the law, but rather salvation *includes* freedom from the curse.[158] On the other hand, the curse in Gal 3:13 is contrasted with the blessing and the Spirit in Gal 3:14. To the extent that the blessing of the Spirit has more to do with how one carries out life than how one gains it, then the point of Gal 3:13–14 may be less how we are saved (by being freed from the curse), and more how we are now able to carry out life in the Spirit, because in redeeming us from the old age, Christ has also freed us from living under the curse of the law.

---

[156]Note that the word order in 3:14a puts emphasis on ἐν Χριστῷ Ἰησοῦ. The purpose is not just that the blessing might come to the Gentiles, but that it might come *in Christ*. Again, the issue is where to live, not how to gain the blessing.

[157]Note the key terms in the first reference to redemption in this letter, in Gal 1:4: "... who gave himself for our *sins*, so that he might rescue us *out of the present evil age* ..."

[158]Read this way, Gal 3:13 has more to do with the implications of redemption (i.e., implications for how we carry out life) than with the means and mechanisms of redemption itself (i.e., how we gain life).

Although the focus of Gal 3:13–14 as a whole may not be soteriological, however, understanding the curse in light of the matrix, "where to live," does have important implications for how Christ effects our redemption from the curse of the law. Many scholars have rightly objected to the traditional understanding of these verses in terms of substitutionary atonement[159]—and yet, so long as the curse itself is seen as soteriologically instrumental (as that which blocks salvation), it is difficult to avoid such a reading.[160] The logic of such a reading, however, is problematic. How is it that Christ redeems us from the curse if he himself becomes accursed? How can someone save us if he himself has joined us in our accursed condition?

The key, I would suggest, is not so much the death of Jesus—that is, that Jesus paid off the debt or satisfied the curse by dying in our place—but rather is the resurrection.[161] In the resurrection, Christ has left the law and its curse behind.[162] Indeed, in being raised from a death cursed by the law, he has shattered the curse, the law, and death. Becoming for us a curse is therefore not the final step of the process of redemption, but rather is an intermediate step; Christ became a curse for us only so that in the resurrection he might shatter the curse and with it the old age.[163] The resurrection thus not only signals the advent of the new age, but also the shattering of the power of the old age. How then are we redeemed? We are redeemed (and we also live out our lives) by being "in Christ," because those who are in Christ have died together with him to the old age, and live now in the new creation.[164]

---

[159] E.g., Sanders, *PLJP*, 25.

[160] Cf. Thomas R. Schreiner, *The Law and Its Fulfillment: A Pauline Theology of Law* (Grand Rapids: Baker Books, 1993), 66, 168.

[161] This distinction is potentially misleading, in that I take it that for Paul, the death of Jesus is virtually synonymous with his resurrection as an announcement of the new age; cf. Martyn's argument concerning the significance of Gal 6:14 as the death of the cosmos (see above, 50). The point is that what is effected in Jesus' death is not so much a substitutionary atonement as it is the shattering of the old age and the inauguration of the new. For believers, Christ's death has more to do with making it possible for us to live in the Spirit than it does paying off the curse of the law; cf. Gal 5:24–25. To say it another way, the curse is not satisfied in Christ's death; it is left behind. Cf. also below, 193n12.

[162] Note also the implications for understanding Gal 3:21. If ζωοποιῆσαι is understood as a reference to resurrection (see n. 122 above), then Paul's point is that the law fails to lead to righteousness because it provides no way into the new age. If a law *could* lead to *resurrection*, then righteouness—that is to say, life in the new age—would indeed be available through the law.

[163] If becoming a curse is the final or effective step in redemption—if Christ "paid off the debt" or satisfied the curse by dying in our place—then, at least as far as effecting atonement is concerned, the resurrection is unnecessary.

[164] Cf. Gal 2:19–20; 5:24–25; 6:14. This understanding of redemption strongly supports the reading of πίστις Χριστοῦ advanced and defended by Richard B. Hays, *The*

The matrix, "where to live," also has important implications for how righteousness is to be understood. As E. P. Sanders has demonstrated, righteousness in Jewish understanding is not something that is earned by deeds, but rather describes the state of being included in the covenant.[165] Given the matrix that has developed in our discussion above, there seems no reason whatsoever to change righteousness into a transfer term. Righteousness continues to be understood as a matter of where one lives. The difference is that, instead of living in the covenant defined by the law, Paul now understands righteousness to be found in the new age in Christ. Even the righteousness "reckoned" to Abraham (Gal 3:6) seems to be this righteousness of the new age—thus the scripture *pre*-proclaimed the gospel to Abraham (Gal 3:8); thus the true covenant with Abraham lay dormant until the coming of the faithful Christ (Gal 3:15–18, 23). When Paul cites Hab 2:4 in Gal 3:10, therefore, he is in fact describing "the *righteous* one"—the one who is truly righteous, because he is living by faith, that is, he is living in the new age, in Christ.

There is one further implication that emerges from this discussion. If redemption and righteousness are both understood in terms of where one lives, then in some sense there is no distinction between "getting in" and "staying in." What it means to "get in," to be saved, is to live in Christ—and thus to live in the new age. What it means to "stay in," to be righteous, is to live in Christ—and thus to live in the new age. Nevertheless, the *primary* focus of this matrix continues to be non-soteriological, in the sense that it does not focus on *whether* one has life, but rather on where one who has life lives. Thus Paul berates the Galatians for their foolishness: having entered into the life of the Spirit, into the new age, how is it that you seek to live righteously by re-entering the old age, the age of the law, the age of the flesh? *To attempt to live righteously anywhere except in Christ (in faith, in the Spirit, in the new age) is to re-enter the old age.*

J. M. G. Barclay's approach to Galatians is especially relevant at this point.[166] Two important and helpful features of Barclay's argument are his insistence that identity and behavior are two sides of the same coin, and his contention that the motivation for Paul's letter to the Galatians arose primarily out of their concern for some way to deal with inappropriate behavior. As noted above, however, Barclay's approach also suffers from two key weaknesses. On the one hand, though he helpfully explains why the Galatians might want to embrace the law as an antidote to immorality, he never adequately explains why Paul so vehemently rejects it. On the other hand, in spite of his insistence that

---

Faith of Jesus Christ: An Investigation of the Narrative Substructure of Galatians 3:1–4:11, SBLDS 56 (Chico, CA: Scholars Press, 1983), 157–76. The emphasis in this reading is not on what we do—our faith in Christ, our believing vs. our doing—but rather is on what Christ has done, i.e., the faith[fulness] of Christ.

[165] See above, 24–25.
[166] See above, 46–49.

identity and behavior are inextricably intertwined, he nevertheless treats Paul's argument in Gal 2–4 as primarily about identity rather than behavior, with the result that Barclay, like the majority of scholars, frames Paul's explicit rejection of the law in soteriological terms.

The results of our investigation have tended to coincide with Barclay's key points. As we have seen, the matrix which seems to provide the resolution to the ungrammaticalities posed by the citations in this passage also seems to lead to the conclusion that getting in and staying in, identity and behavior, are all ultimately the same for Paul. Where one lives defines not only one's soteriological status, but also one's righteousness. Nevertheless, as we have repeatedly seen, Paul's primary focus does not seem to be soteriological; he is not so much concerned with how one moves into the new creation, but rather with whether one can live in the new creation and at the same time live by the law. Paul's non-soteriological focus seems perfectly reasonable if, in fact, the reason the Galatians have taken up the law is not to try to gain life, but rather to find an antidote to immoral behavior.

At the same time, the results of our investigation suggest a way to overcome the weaknesses of Barclay's approach. According to our investigation, Paul rejects the law so vehemently, not because it perpetuates a sociological barrier between Jews and Gentiles, but rather because it is part of the old age:[167] One cannot live by the law, even in the sense—or perhaps, especially in the sense—of using it to regulate behavior, because to do so is to return to the old age. This old age is the age of the flesh, the age of sin (and therefore the age into which God gave the law as a response to sin), the age of the elemental powers, the age under a curse—in short, it is the present evil age from which Christ has rescued us.

SUMMARY: A READING OF GAL 3:1–14

All the pieces are in now place for our intertextual reading of Gal 3:1–14. Because the details have been worked out at some length above, this reading will provide only a summary and overview of Gal 3:1–14, plus a paraphrase of the passage, informed by the insights developed above. The key insight is the intertext or matrix, "where to live," that provides both coherence and significance to the difficulties of the passage. This intertext is fundamentally eschatological in its implications, but primarily non-soteriological in its applica-

---

[167] As pointed out by Richard Hays in response to an earlier draft of this investigation, the sociological barrier, set up by the law, is also a feature of the old age; therefore, Paul's reason for rejecting the law may be both/and, i.e., both because of the law's sociological barriers and because of its link with the old age. See however the critique of the sociological approach above, 40–42. While Hays' point is well taken, it seems best to keep the primary emphasis on Paul's rejection of the law as a feature of the old age.

tion in this passage. On the one hand, this intertext speaks not of different physical locales, but of different aeons; Paul is reminding the Galatians that they live, not in the old age, but in the new creation inaugurated by Christ's death and resurrection. On the other hand, at least in this passage, this intertext does not primarily speak about whether one lives, or how one gains life, but rather about where one who lives will carry out life.

Paul begins this passage by reminding the Galatians of their own experience of the turning of the ages. It began as he re-created for them, before their very eyes, the death of the Messiah; it unfolded with their experience of the Spirit, the sign and promise of the new creation inaugurated with the death and resurrection of Christ.[168] All of this began with "the hearing of faith" (ἐξ ἀκοῆς πίστεως)— a phrase which, I would suggest, points less to their response of belief as they heard of the gospel, but rather to their hearing the proclamation of the faith of Christ. In other words, as Martyn, Hays, and others have argued, the focus not only here but throughout the letter is not on what the Galatians have done, but on the action of God, who has invaded the cosmos to bring in the age of the Spirit.[169] All of this took place—God's action, their reception of the Spirit, and perhaps most of all the death of Christ—not within the law, but apart from the law.[170]

Though Paul reminds the Galatians of how their experience began, however, his primary focus is not on the beginning but on the continuation and completion of their experience. If the new creation in which they live was inaugurated, not by their observance of the law (nor by anything else that they have done), but solely by the power of God, how is it possible that they should try to carry out their lives in this new creation by returning to the law? Do they suppose that God—the one who is supplying the Spirit and demonstrating his power in their midst—must depend on the law to effect the new creation? Paul's goal is not to tell them how to gain life, but rather to remind them of where they live, in

---

[168]This is also where Paul begins the letter, with a reference to the death and resurrection of Christ (Gal 1:1) and to his rescuing us from the present evil age (Gal 1:4).

[169]See above, 52. Again, note that Paul has emphasized the power of God (rather than the actions of humanity) from the very beginning, starting with the defense of his apostleship as commissioned solely by God (Gal 1:1; 1:11ff).

[170]Indeed, as Paul points out in Gal 3:13, Christ's death was not in accordance with the law, but rather was cursed by it. Again, Paul has set the stage with his autobiographical remarks in chapter 2. Not only did the "pillars" not require law observance (circumcision) of Titus (2:1–10), but also Paul confronted Peter himself when he, under the influence of "certain people from James," began to withdraw from fellowship with Gentiles, presumably due to a concern with food laws (2:11–14). In other words, the history of Paul's apostleship shows in a very practical way that observance of the law has never been a part of what it means to carry out the Christian life.

the new creation which was not only brought about by God's power through the faith of Christ, but which is completely defined by that power and faith.

The Galatians, in fact, have experienced the same thing that Abraham experienced. Abraham, too, experienced the power of God to effect righteousness (Gal 3:6); Abraham, too, participated—though only proleptically—in the blessing of the Spirit which has come to the Galatians (Gal 3:8). All of this has come about by way of faith—which is to say, as the preceding section has already made clear, not by the law. Later, Paul will make this point even more clear: the promise to Abraham pre-dates the law (Gal 3:15–18); the covenant with Abraham was a covenant of *promise*, unlike the covenant of the law, which was based on fleshly inheritance (Gal 3:18; 4:21–31). Thus those who, like Abraham, live by faith (that is, by the power of God's promise) are the true heirs of Abraham (Gal 3:7, 29; 4:26–31).

There is a more subtle similarity between the Galatians' experience and Abraham's. Just as Abraham's experience was a proleptic experience, so also, to some degree, is that of the Galatians. Abraham heard the gospel *pre*-proclaimed; he received the *promise*; he was *reckoned* as righteous—but not until the coming of Christ ("the seed") was that promise, that gospel, that righteousness fulfilled. For the Galatians, the coming of Christ signals that the new creation, the age of promise, the fulfillment of righteousness, has already begun—but for the Galatians, also, that new creation is only proleptically present. More precisely, it is present only in Christ, and only those who are in Christ, who have been crucified with him to the world and live now in Him, can experience it (Gal 2:19–20; cf. 3:3:26–27; 6:14–15).[171]

Thus Paul challenges the Galatians with the question, "Where will you live?" Will they go back to the old age, back under the law and its curse (Gal 3:10) from which Christ has redeemed them (Gal 3:13)? Do they not realize that those who live by the law are trapped within its system (Gal 3:12)? Furthermore, do they not realize that it is those who live in the new age (that is, by faith), who are righteous (Gal 3:11)? They are righteous because they have died with Christ, not only to the law, but also to sin; they have experienced, in Christ, the shattering of the old age; in Christ they live now by the Spirit (Gal 3:13–14).

As Paul makes clear a little later in the letter, the law was indeed given in response to sin, but it had no power to break us out of the age of sin (Gal 3:21); it merely guarded us while we were locked up under sin (Gal 3:22–23). The place where the law functions, in other words, is in the old age. To try to live righteously by the law, therefore, is to return to the old age, and thus to return to

---

[171]Paul expresses the already-not yet character of the new creation much more clearly in Romans, especially Rom 6–8. Nevertheless, the same sort of already-not yet tension is present in Galatians. On the one hand they have died with Christ (Gal 2:19–20), put on Christ (Gal 3:26), crucified the flesh (Gal 5:24), and so on, but on the other hand they still struggle with the real possibility of living by the flesh (Gal 5:16–21; 6:8).

sin, to the curse of the law, to the powers of the cosmos (Gal 4:1–11), and so on. Not only is it not possible to gain life by the law, but more to the point, it is not possible to live righteously by the law, because the law is a feature of the old age. The ultimate question, again, is where to live—in Christ, in the Spirit, by faith (all synonyms for "in the new creation"), or in the law, in the flesh, under the curse, under the elemental spirits (all of which represent the present evil age).

A Paraphrase of Gal 3:1–14[172]

O foolish Galatians, who has bewitched you? Didn't you experience the crucifixion of Jesus, right before your eyes? And what was the result of the crucifixion, but the gift of the Spirit, the sign of the new age inaugurated by Christ's death and resurrection. Did you receive the Spirit by way of the law, or was it by the power of the message of faith? Thus you are foolish: having experienced the new age of the Spirit, you are trying to live righteously in the old age of the flesh! Did you experience the death and resurrection in vain? Or was it in vain? When you therefore experienced the overflowing of the Spirit and the power of the new age working among you, was it by way of the law? No, it was by the power of the message of faith—in the same way that Abraham experienced the righteousness of God by the power of faith: "He lived in the faith of God, and therefore he was promised righteousness."

Here's what you need to know: the ones who carry out their lives by faith are the ones who really participate in the new age that Abraham glimpsed. Scripture gave him a glimpse of how God was going to bring righteousness to the Gentiles—by faith. In fact, it promised a blessing to the Gentiles: "In you all the nations will be blessed." So then, those who carry out their lives by faith are now experiencing the blessing together with faithful Abraham.

On the other hand, those who live within the law are not experiencing the blessing of the new age, but rather they live under a curse, for the law itself pronounces curses: "Cursed is everyone who does not remain in everything written in the book of the law, to do it." In the old age, you're cursed if you don't do the law, but even if you do it you still live under the threat and power of curse. That's how the law works.

Look, we all know that no one can truly live righteously under the law; instead, if you want to live righteously—well, listen to what scripture says; it's clear enough: "The one who is righteous lives by faith."

---

[172] The following paraphrase is not intended to be "what Paul really meant to say"; rather, it is an attempt to capture, in a form that bears some faint resemblance to Paul's own words, some of the insights of the preceding investigation. To put it another way, it is an attempt to put into words some of what we have read between the lines by way of anonymous intertexts.

Why can't you use the law to help you live righteously in the new age? Does the law extend into the new age of faith? No, because scripture makes clear that the law is a closed system: "If you practice the law, you are stuck living in it." Basically, you have two choices of where to live—in the law, which is a feature of the old age, or in faith, that is, in the new age. Guess where righteousness is!

What was the cross and resurrection really all about? Was it so you could live righteously in the old age of sin and death and law? No, it was so that you could escape the old age, along with the law and its curse. Christ took on himself the law, dying under its curse—remember, the law itself pronounces "a curse on those who die on a cross"—and thus he experienced all that the old age represents ... so that he could shatter the old age with his resurrection. How can we escape this old age? By living in Christ, who has already inaugurated the new age.

When Christ inaugurated the new age, the promises that Abraham glimpsed were fulfilled. Gentiles can now experience the blessing of living in Christ; through his faithfulness, we can all receive and thus live within the Spirit, the sign and blessing of the new age.

Chapter 6
CONCLUSION: IMPLICATIONS FOR ISSUES IN PAULINE THEOLOGY

The current investigation began with the observation that Gal 3:1–14 is a passage which is not only exceedingly important for a number of areas of discussion in Pauline theology, but also exceedingly difficult. In the chapters above, we charted the difficulties of the passage, centered primarily on its citations from scripture, and explored a way to resolve those difficulties by way of an intertextual investigation of those same citations. The key insight that has emerged from this investigation is that the "matrix" which resolves the difficulties and provides significance to the passage as a whole is the phrase, "where to live." Rather than dealing with what might be described as primarily soteriological issues—whether or not one is saved, or how—this passage revolves around the eschatological issue of *where* one lives, in the old age which includes the law, or in the new age in Christ. Based on this insight, the preceding chapter culminated with a fresh reading of the passage.

What remains to be done is briefly to explore the implications this reading may have for some of the larger issues in the study of Pauline theology. Given the importance of this passage in the discussions of Paul's view of the law, for example, we need to see how this reading can contribute to those discussions, particularly with respect to the issues that we explored in chapter 2 above.[1] In addition, if the focus on "where to live" does not primarily concern questions of soteriology or identity—who is to be counted among the saved, and how—but rather speaks more to the issue of behavior, it would be useful to explore the practical implications of this reading for how Christians should conduct their lives. Finally, while we have given close attention to intertextual insights arising from the citations in Galatians 3, we have not yet investigated how these insights

---

[1] Once again the caveat needs to be offered, that this investigation (much less this conclusion) cannot hope to cover the whole topic of Paul and the law, especially with respect to writings other than Galatians. Nevertheless, we need to explore at least briefly what implications this reading of a key passage in Galatians might have for this topic.

might be extended beyond the boundaries set in this investigation. To these tasks we now turn.

PAUL AND THE LAW

In our survey of scholarship on Paul and the law in chapter 2 above, the overall question that guided our analysis was the following: from Paul's perspective, particularly as it pertained to the Galatian situation, what, if anything, is wrong with the law? Armed with a fresh reading of Gal 3:1–14, one of the key passages in the discussion of Paul and the law, we are ready to take up this question once again. As we do so, we will need to consider two additional questions that arose in our survey and analysis above. First, what is the place of the law in the ongoing life of the believer? Second, is Paul's problem with the law a problem specifically with the Jewish Torah, or is it a problem with law as law, that is, with any law that might be given?

WHAT IS WRONG WITH THE LAW?

What is wrong with the law? The preceding chapter has already sketched out an answer to this question, at least with respect to Gal 3:1–14. The problem with the law is that it is bound to or is a feature of the old age. If Paul's discussion is focused on "*where* to live," then Paul is *not* rejecting the law as an invalid means to *gain* life (invalid because no one can keep it, or because it inevitably leads to self-righteousness, or so on).[2] Rather he refers to the law, especially by way of the citations, as a *system* of life, a system in which one *can* live—but a system that is apocalyptically severed from the new age in Christ. One *can* take up the law, one *can* live under the law, but in so doing one is living in the old age.[3]

---

[2] Although these comments are phrased in terms of what *Paul* is doing, or what Paul means, etc., it is not my intention to suggest that we should entirely revert to a traditional historical critical stance in which the author's intentions define the meaning. To be sure, I would hope, following the suggestion of Richard Hays (see above, 113), that there is some correspondence between the meaning that we discover in the text and the meaning that Paul intended. Nevertheless, my use of "Paul" throughout this chapter should be seen as a convenient way to refer to something like the implied author or that which the text itself necessitates, rather than as a claim about the intentions of the historical figure of Paul.

[3] Cf. George Howard, *Paul: Crisis in Galatia: A Study in Early Christian Theology*, SNTSMS 35 (Cambridge: Cambridge University Press, 1979), 13–14: "[This is] Paul's underlying thought ... which permeates his theology at its very core, namely, the law places one under sin. To attempt to keep the law ends in one's being sold under sin and doing the desires of the flesh." Howard does not develop this idea in terms of apocalyptic

Although this understanding of the problem of the law has grown out of our reading of one particular passage in Galatians (Gal 3:1–14), it is very much in keeping with the rest of Galatians as well. In general terms, the apocalyptic motif of the old age vs. the new age, implied by the matrix "where to live," runs all the way through Galatians, from 1:4 through 6:14.[4] More specifically, this motif provides helpful insight into the way Paul develops his understanding of the law in at least two other significant passages in Galatians, Gal 3:19–4:7 and Gal 4:21–5:1.[5]

For our purposes, the significance of Gal 3:19–4:7 lies in the fact that in it Paul explicitly takes up the issue of the place and purpose of the law: "Why then the law?" (Gal 3:19). Paul's answer to that question is not without notorious problems of its own, not the least of which is how to understand his passing reference to the angels and the mediator. Whatever he means by this description of the giving of the law, however, it is clear, in light of our reading of Gal 3:1–14, that Paul is not identifying any particular defect within the law itself, nor is he calling into question its divine origin.[6] Instead, he is pointing to the law's placement and function within the old age.

Paul forcefully denies that the law is contrary to the promises of God (Gal 3:21); presumably, these promises specifically include the promised blessing of Abraham to the Gentiles, that is, the promise of the Spirit. We can go a step further by noting that, when Paul asks why the law was given, he gives what could well be a very positive answer: it was given in response to transgression (Gal 3:19).[7] One the one hand, therefore, the law is neither defective nor bad; it was

---

categories; ultimately he sees the problem with the law in terms of its sociological function, much like Dunn; see above, 31.

[4]J. Louis Martyn is the most vocal supporter of an apocalyptic understanding of Galatians; see above, 49–54. Martyn sees Gal 6:14 as a particularly significant verse, in that it announces not only Paul's death with Christ, but also the death of the cosmos.

[5]The reverse is also true: these passages also help to refine our understanding of Paul's problem with the law in light of the matrix, "where to live."

[6]As noted above, the view that Paul is calling into question the divine origin of the law, promoted in various ways by Martyn, Hübner, and others, is difficult to maintain, not only because such a view would be an astonishing violation of the understanding of the law which Paul would have held as a Jew (and which he seems to maintain in other letters, such as Romans), but even more because of the way the citations are used in Gal 3:1–14 (and indeed, throughout the letter). Even when citing from the law, the text never seems to call into question the presupposition of authority and applicability that is invoked by the use of citations; see above, 149–53.

[7]Unfortunately, Paul's answer, τῶν παραβάσεων χάριν προσετέθη, is rather cryptic concerning the exact relationship between the law and transgressions. Many of the recent major commentaries understand χάριν in terms of purpose, with the idea that the law was added to *provoke* transgression; cf. H. D. Betz, *Galatians: A Commentary on Paul's Letter to the Churches in Galatia*, Hermeneia (Philadelphia: Fortress Press, 1979),

given by God to meet our needs when we were locked up under sin. On the other hand, that is precisely why the law is not appropriate for the Galatian believers. Because the law exists or is defined in relationship with transgression, it is bound to the old age; its sphere of operation, in other words, is the same as that of sin.[8] Therefore, as Paul goes on to say, the law is locked up together with sin, or in some sense is that which locks us up under sin—it is, in other words, the prison guard and/or pedagogue of the old age (3:22–23).

In using the image of a pedagogue, Paul stresses the temporary function of the law; indeed, throughout this section he repeatedly calls attention to the fact that the law functions only until the coming of faith, that is, the coming of Christ. Obviously, however, Paul is not referring to a strictly temporal sequence, in which the law ceases to exist with the coming of faith; if that were the case, there would be no need to warn the Galatians against taking up the law now that faith has come.[9] Once again, the apocalyptic motif of the two ages is helpful at

---

165; J. Louis Martyn, *Galatians*, AB 33A (New York: Doubleday, 1997), 352–55; F. F. Bruce, *The Epistle to the Galatians*, NIGTC (Grand Rapids: Eerdmans, 1982), 175. Many other commentaries, and some English versions, suggest that the meaning is something like, "to make transgressions known"; cf. Ernest De Witt Burton, *A Critical and Exegetical Commentary on the Epistle to the Galatians*, ICC (Edinburgh: T & T Clark, 1921), 188; Richard N. Longenecker, *Galatians*, WBC 41 (Dallas: Word Books, 1990), 138–39; NEB; Phillips; NAS mg. Interestingly, many English versions opt for what may be the most neutral reading, "it was added *because of* transgressions"; cf. NAS, RSV, NRSV, NIV. While we cannot sort through all the pros and cons of these various interpretations, it may be helpful to note two points. First, as the discussion in the commentaries makes clear, both of the standard readings, "to provoke transgression" and "to reveal sin," reflect a significant dependence on Romans—it is in Romans (but *not* in Galatians) that Paul says explicitly that law makes sin known (Rom 3:20; 5:13) and that the law provokes sin (Rom 7:7–11). Second, Betz suggests that the most typical Hellenistic and Jewish understanding of the relationship between law and transgression is that the law is a response to transgressions, not only to define them but also to help hold them in check (Betz, *Galatians*, 164–65). Taking these two points together, one must wonder whether either of these standard readings is truly appropriate in the context of Galatians. Particularly in light of the law's role as a παιδαγωγός, it seems more likely that in Galatians Paul sees the law as a response to transgression, perhaps even as that which restrains sin. (Note that it is again in the context of Romans, not Galatians, that Paul makes a clear distinction between sin and transgression.)

[8]This point seems secure even if the argument of the preceding footnote does not stand. Even in the most negative interpretation, that the law was given to provoke transgression, it is clear that τῶν παραβάσεων χάριν προσετέθη makes a direct connection between the purpose of the law and transgression. Whether the law was added in reponse to transgression, or to reveal transgression, or to provoke transgression, its purpose is defined in relationship with transgression; it therefore assumes the existence of sin.

[9]Although it seems most likely that "the coming of faith" is a way of talking about the apocalyptic age inaugurated by the faith of Christ, a similar point could be made even

this point. Although the new age has been inaugurated at a specific point in time, i.e., with the coming of Christ, it is not simply the next epoch in the temporal sequence of the world; on the contrary, this new age is a wholly *other* world, an aeon that has intersected the present evil age. While these ages intersect—while we experience the meeting of the ends of the ages (1 Cor 10:11)—both remain possibilities for us; we can live under the law, the guardian of the old age, or we can live in Christ, the one who has already entered the new age. What we cannot do is live in both at the same time; we must choose where to live.

Just as Gal 3:19–4:7 is a passage which poses numerous difficulties for interpretation, so also is Gal 4:21–5:1, Paul's allegory of Sarah and Hagar. Though we cannot resolve or even address most of these difficulties here, we can note at least one difficulty on which the apocalyptic motif of the old age vs. the new age, implied by the matrix "where to live," may shed light. In this allegory, Paul describes *two* covenants, where earlier he seemed to suggest that only one, irrevocable covenant was in place (3:15–18). This passage therefore raises questions about Paul's understanding of the continuity or discontinuity of his Christian faith with his Jewish heritage. Does the coming of Christ represent a break from Judaism, a new covenant which replaces the old, or does it represent rather the culmination of the one and only covenant that God made with Abraham?

What may be particularly helpful at this point is to understand the two covenants in terms of the two ages.[10] The two ages signify both continuity and discontinuity. The discontinuity between the ages is obvious: the new age is a wholly new creation, inaugurated by the "triple death" of Christ, the believer, and the old age.[11] At the same, however, there are several elements of continuity between the ages. For one thing, the setting in which the new age has been inaugurated is the old age. The deaths which bring about the new age occur in the old age; indeed, they *must* occur in the old age, since presumably death is not a feature of the new age.[12] Likewise, as noted above, there is an overlap between

---

if "the coming of faith" is understood in existential terms. Paul cannot mean that once persons experience faith, law ceases to exist as a possibility for them, because otherwise he would have no need to warn the Galatians, who *have* already experienced faith (Gal 3:1–5).

[10] This understanding is already suggested by the way the two covenants are described, in terms of the child each covenant produced, in 4:29: one covenant is κατὰ σάρκα; the other is κατὰ πνεῦμα.

[11] Cf. Martyn's understanding of Gal 6:13–15; see above, 50.

[12] This connection between the old age and the new perhaps helps to explain the logic of Gal 3:13: Christ had to experience the curse which characterizes the old age in order to bring about the new age by way of his death and resurrection; cf. similarly Gal 4:4–5. Note also that, although we earlier described the inauguration of the new age pri-

the ages; both ages are possible options for the believer, as the matrix "where to live" suggests.

One of the most significant ways in which both continuity and discontinuity between the ages can be seen is by way of the theme of promise and fulfillment, a theme which is prominent not only in the allegory of Sarah and Hagar, but also in much of the rest of the letter to the Galatians. Obviously there is continuity between a promise and its fulfillment. At the same time, however, there is a significant sense of discontinuity between promise and fulfillment. Once a promise is fulfilled, it ceases to be promise, in the same way that hope that is seen ceases to be hope (Rom 8:24–25). In Galatians, the promise of the Spirit, the promised blessing of Abraham, is on the one hand that which points towards and describes the new age; yet as long as it remains *promise* (rather than fulfillment), it must remain a feature of the old age. This promise existed from the time of Abraham (Gal 3:8), but it was not fulfilled until the coming of faith, that is, the coming of Christ (Gal 3:22); its fulfillment marks the continuity of God's covenant with Abraham, and yet also its fulfillment marks the discontinuity of the inauguration of a new age.

WHAT IS THE PLACE OF THE LAW IN THE ONGOING LIFE OF THE CHRISTIAN?

It is worth stating yet again that the primary focus of Paul's discussion of the law in Galatians is not directed to soteriological issues, that is, whether or how one is saved. To be sure, the fact that the law is bound up with the old age certainly means that it cannot be used to achieve salvation; Paul says as much when he notes that the law has no power to effect resurrection, which means that it has no power to break out of the old age and inaugurate the new. This is not a defect of the law precisely because the law was never intended to offer such power. The law's place and function is in the *old* age, in which it serves as a guardian.

That the law has no power to bring about salvation is, however, the point on which Paul and his opponents agree (Gal 2:16). The issue on which they disagree, and the issue that has diverted the Galatians from the gospel of faith, is whether the law has the power to effect righteousness in the daily life of the believer. Can or should the believer make use of the law in order to behave righteously?[13] Quite a number of scholars would say "yes." Once one has avoided the pitfalls of attempting to use the law to achieve salvation, one is enabled by the Spirit to carry out the law as it was meant to be used.[14] Based on what we have said above, however, it is clear that the better answer is an em-

---

marily in terms of resurrection, resurrection likewise presupposes the context of death, and therefore the old age. Cf. above, 182–85

[13] See above, 46.

[14] See below, 199.

phatic "no." To attempt to live by the law, *even as a believer*, is to step back into the old age.

Of course, the reality for believers who live at the turning of the ages is that they do continue to deal with the old age; those who have died with Christ and in whom Christ lives continue to "live in the flesh" (Gal 2:20).[15] Could it not be, therefore, that the law continues to be of value?[16] At the very least, it is clear that the law continues to have value in pointing to Christ and the new age he has inaugurated,[17] but might it not have value also for directing one's behavior? At this point the reading of Gal 3:12 developed in the previous chapter is crucial. The problem with using the law to direct one's behavior is that "those who do these things will live in them"—to live by the law is to live in the system of law, or in other words to be imprisoned once again in the old age.

Why then does Paul talk about fulfilling the law (Gal 5:14)?[18] For that matter, why does Paul give instructions to the Galatians—is he not merely substituting one "law" for another?[19] There are, I believe, two key points to be made in answer to these questions. First, to the extent that believers continue to live in the old age, they do in fact live under the law, and the law continues to respond to sin. This response to sin, however, must not be misunderstood as a means for overcoming sin, i.e., so as to live righteously in the new age; as we have seen above, living under the law means living in the old age, and therefore

---

[15] This idea is even more evident in Romans. Even though we have died to sin, it is possible to let sin reign in our mortal bodies (Rom 6); we along with all of creation long for the redemption of our mortal bodies (Rom 8). I take the significance of "mortal" in these passages not in terms of a desire to escape death per se, but rather in terms of the connection between sin and death (Rom 5)—as long as we live in mortal bodies, we have not yet experienced the fullness of the new age. Though we who have been baptized into Christ walk in newness of life (Rom 6:4), we have not yet experienced resurrection for ourselves.

[16] Cf. Martin Luther, *A Commentary on St. Paul's Epistle to the Galatians: Based on Lectures Delivered by Martin Luther at the University of Wittenberg in the year 1531 and First Published in 1535* (London: James Clarke & Co., 1953), 24–25. In responding to the "Papists" who accuse him of rejecting good works, Luther notes that "the righteousness of the law is earthly and hath to do with earthly things, and by it we do good works"—though this is only true for those who have first received the "heavenly and passive" righteousness apart from works.

[17] As evidenced by Paul's use of citations from the law. In effect, the law is like the promise: it remains locked in the old age precisely because it *points to* the new age in Christ, rather than being the fulfillment of that new age.

[18] Cf. also Gal 6:2; what exactly Paul means by "the law of Christ," and whether it has any sort of relationship with the Torah, is of course a matter of considerable debate, which unfortunately we cannot explore here.

[19] This issue is closely related to the question of whether Paul's concern is with the Torah in particular, or with law in general; see below, 197–199.

being imprisoned in the realm of sin. The law therefore cannot function as a means to righteous living—but it *can* function in effect as a measure of sin:[20] Ironically, one can measure the extent to which one is living under sin by measuring the extent to which one is living under the law. To the extent that law is relevant, to the extent that it speaks to one's behavior, one is living under sin.[21]

Even though it is given in the form of *prescription*, therefore, the law functions in effect as *description* for Christians:[22] Keeping these prescriptions does not effect righteousness, but the extent to which one finds it necessary to keep them becomes a description of the extent to which one still lives in the old age.[23] Even Paul's own instructions may be understood in this way:[24] If one is truly living in the new age, one should need no instruction because sin has been left

---

[20] Cf. Rom 3:20: "Therefore no flesh will be made righteous before him by works of law, for through the law comes the knowledge of sin."

[21] Since, in Christ, neither law-keeping nor law-breaking has any relevance (Gal 3:15; cf. above, 50), it is not just the *breaking* of the law that reveals sin; rather it is the extent to which the law is relevant, i.e., the extent to which one finds oneself under the law. Thus, for example, it is not the failure to be circumcised that shows that one is living under sin, but rather it is the fact that circumcision is an issue. (For an analogy illustrating the way both law-keeping and law-breaking are irrelevant for the Christian, see below, 203–204.)

[22] Cf. Martyn, *Galatians*, 27: "There is indeed a positive relationship between the Law and daily life in the church. Even here, however, Paul places the major accent not on exhortation, but rather on an indicative portrait of the effects of two powers: the Impulsive Desire of the Flesh and the Spirit of Christ."

[23] When the issue is described in this way, one need not make a distinction between moral and ritual aspects of the law. Whether one finds it necessary to keep the commandment "You shall not kill," or the commandment "You shall be circumcised," the necessity of *keeping* the commandment reveals that one is operating in the old age, in which sin is a possibility. Put in converse terms, if one must be concerned about *breaking* the commandment—any commandment—one is not operating in the new age, in which neither sin nor the law are relevant.

To be sure, this approach does not eliminate the fact that Paul seems to deal differently with some aspects of the law than others; cf. E. P. Sanders, *Paul, the Law, and the Jewish People* (Minneapolis: Fortress Press, 1983), 162 (hereafter cited as *PLJP*). It seems obvious, for example, that Paul would consider behavior contrary to the commandment "You shall not kill" to be an indicator of sin, whereas he would not consider behavior contrary to the commandment "You shall be circumcised" to be an indicator of sin. Perhaps a way to deal with this difficulty is to think in terms of life in the new age as the *transcending* of sin. In the new age, sin is left behind, including not only certain kinds of behavior (murder, idolatry, etc.; cf. Gal 5:19–21; 1 Cor 6:9–10), but also those barriers which had previously marked out the people of God from "Gentile sinners" (cf. Gal 3:28; 5:4; 6:15).

[24] Cf. Stephen Westerholm, *Israel's Law and the Church's Faith: Paul and His Recent Interpreters* (Grand Rapids: Eerdmans, 1988), 201.

behind; to the extent that one *does* need these instructions, however, one has *not* left sin behind. Rather than providing the means to effect righteousness, therefore, even Paul's own instructions function to measure or describe sin.

The second key point is that fulfilling the law is not the same as keeping it.[25] Obviously, Paul thinks that one who walks in the Spirit will behave in ways that are compatible with many of the prescriptions of the law (Gal 5:22–23). Nevertheless, as we have said repeatedly, to address the problem of sin by keeping the law is to commit oneself to living in the old age, imprisoned under sin. The law can respond to sin only if one lives in the old age where sin reigns; one who lives in the new age in Christ, however, has nothing to do either with sin or with the law (Gal 5:16–18). One who lives in the new age fulfills the law, not by keeping it in response to sin, but rather by being redeemed from sin altogether. In effect, fulfilling the law therefore means *transcending* it.[26] The way to live the life that Paul describes is not to keep the law (or even to keep Paul's own instructions), but rather is to transcend the law by living in the Spirit.[27]

LAW IN GENERAL, OR THE TORAH SPECIFICALLY?

Is Paul's concern in Galatians a concern with the Jewish Torah in particular, or with law as law, that is, with any law that might be given? Based on our reading of Gal 3:1–14, the best answer seems to be "both." Certainly it is clear that it is the Torah specifically, with its call to circumcision, which has given rise to the situation to which Paul is responding in his letter to the Galatians. It seems equally clear that when Paul as a Jew thought about the law being given as a response to sin, he must surely have thought of the Torah specifically.[28] Finally, it seems clear that Paul's problem with the law is not that it requires "doing," in which case the problem would apply equally to any law, not just to the Torah,

---

[25]Cf. Westerholm, *Israel's Law*, 198–218; John M. G. Barclay, *Obeying the Truth: A Study of Paul's Ethics in Galatians* (Edinburgh: T & T Clark, 1988), 126ff.

[26]Cf. the discussion of the discontinuity between fulfillment and promise discussed above, 194.

[27]An analogy might be helpful here. Just as one cannot achieve one's ideal height by climbing the measuring stick, so one cannot fulfill the law by keeping it. The measuring stick *describes* one's height, but does not control it; the law *describes* sin, but does not overcome it.

[28]Again, the use of "Paul as a Jew" here is not intended as a claim to have access to the actual thoughts of Paul, but rather as a convenient shorthand for something like the implied author, or perhaps the expectations readers bring to the text in light of its context (written by a Jew; written with Judaizing opponents in mind; etc.).

since any law requires "doing."²⁹ Since that is not the case, however, one might suppose that the problem is specific to the Torah.³⁰

On the other hand, if the problem with the law is that it is bound to the old age, that means that the problem does not involve any specific feature of the Torah. To be sure, it would come as no surprise if Paul objected to some specific features of the Torah, namely the sociological barriers it poses for his Gentile converts. Based on our reading of Gal 3:1–14, however, it does not seem that Paul's argument focuses on the problem of sociological barriers;³¹ rather his objection is both more profound and more general. The law is bound to the old age; therefore, to take up the law is to step back into the old age. While the sociological barrier between Jews and Gentiles is undoubtedly a *symptom* of the old age (cf. Gal 3:28), Paul is not saying, "Do not take up the law because it will cause sociological barriers, and therefore will draw you into the old age"; rather he is saying, "Do not take up the law because if you do, you must live in the old age, with all that that means—locked under sin, divided from one another, and so on."

If the problem with the law does not involve any specific feature of the Torah, is it therefore the case that Paul would equally object to the use of *any* law as a way to effect appropriate behavior? To put the question another way, is there anything about law as law, law in general, that binds it to the old age rather than the new? Though Paul does not address this question, it seems likely that there is indeed something about law as law that ties it to the old age. Law—any law—is always defined in relationship with transgression, or, in other words, sin. To say it another way, if one lives in the new age—and therefore one no longer has anything to do with sin—then what need is there for any law?

As noted above, the law does continue to speak to believers to the extent that they have not fully escaped the old age, and thus Paul himself gives instructions to the Galatians. Once again, however, neither the law nor Paul's own instructions can actually effect righteouness; they can help the believer measure whether he or she is living under sin, but they cannot actually deal with sin.³² Therefore, while Paul's argument is framed in terms of Torah—and while one could undoubtedly make stronger claims for the Torah, given by God himself,

---

²⁹The problem with the law is that it is bound to the old age; "doing" is not limited to the old age, but rather is expected also of Christians.

³⁰Cf. the position of Sanders and Dunn (see above, 29, 33, 39–40). Because they reject the idea that the problem with the law has anything to do with "doing" (legalism, the "missing premise," etc.), they conclude instead that the problem has to do with some specific feature of the Torah, namely its exclusivity with regard to Gentiles.

³¹Cf. the critique of Sanders' and Dunn's sociological approach, discussed above, 40–42.

³²To paraphrase Gal 3:11, the only ones who truly live righteously are those who live in faith, that is, in the Spirit, in the new age, in Christ.

than for any other law—nevertheless, it seems clear that Paul would have objected to *any* law that might have been given to the Galatians as the way to carry out a righteous life. To keep any law, to live by any law, is to step back into the arena in which law operates, namely the old age of sin. Rather than keeping law, one fulfills it—transcends it—by living in the new age of the Spirit.

One final note along these lines concerns the question of the law for Jewish believers. Some scholars have suggested that Paul's rejection of the law is not only specific to the Torah, but is specific also to Gentiles: Paul continues to believe in law-observance for Jews, even as he vigorously resists any attempt to force law-observance on Gentiles.[33] Based on the reading that has been developed above, this sort of approach does not seem plausible. If the law is a feature of the old age, if living under the law means being imprisoned in the age of sin, then the law is of no more use for Jews than it is for Gentiles as a means to regulate behavior.[34]

LIVING IN THE SPIRIT: A PRACTICAL ETHIC?

The obvious question that must be asked, in light of the preceding discussion, is whether and how one can actually do what we have described. Is it practical to live in the Spirit, with no regard for the law? Is it anything more than semantic gymnastics to claim that in living by the Spirit, one does not keep the law, but nevertheless fulfills it? Is it possible for one to use the law to *describe* righteousness without in some very real sense using it to *prescribe* one's actions? In short, if we rule out the law, or even some portion of the law, how can living in the Spirit actually and practically suffice for producing proper Christian behavior?

LIVING BY THE SPIRIT: INADEQUATE ANSWERS

Scholars have offered a number of answers to the question of how living by the Spirit results in proper Christian behavior. One of the most common of these

---

[33]Cf., e.g., Lloyd Gaston, "Paul and the Torah," in *Paul and the Torah* (Vancouver: University of British Columbia Press, 1987), 15–34.

[34]To be sure, this does not mean that Jewish Christians must set out to break the law; presumably they are likely to continue to observe the Sabbath and avoid certain foods, etc., simply as a matter of habit. As Paul says about circumcision in Gal 6:15, so also he seems to say about such practices in Rom 14: neither observing or ignoring certain days, neither eating or avoiding certain food, matters at all in Christ. As an action, even circumcision is a matter of indifference; if one practices circumcision or food laws, etc., as an effort to *keep* the law, however, one has stepped back under the law, and therefore under sin. I take this to be the point of the dispute at Antioch. Eating or not eating certain foods was not the issue; the issue was Cephas' concern to keep the law, as evidenced by his separation from the Gentiles.

answers is that the Spirit empowers Christians to keep the law.[35] There are, of course, variations on this answer, such as the following: while no one is able to achieve *salvation* by keeping the law (because no one can keep it perfectly, or because attempting to keep the law inevitably results in self righteousness, or so on), those who are saved by faith can keep the law as it was actually *intended* to be kept (not in self righteousness, nor as a means of earning merit, but rather as a response to God's grace, or so on).[36]

Other answers to this question have been suggested, though not always explicitly or clearly. For example, Hans Hübner seems to suggest that the Spirit not only enables proper observance of the law, but also provides Christians with a new and qualitatively different understanding of what the law really requires; this new understanding is centered on the love commandment:

> Thus *it is only at the level of argument involving faith that there is demonstrated the impossibility for those outside the bounds of faith of 'doing' the love which is required by the Law* . . . . *Quantitative fulfillment is not possible because the Torah contains stipulations which must be 'qualitatively fulfilled* . . . . The man presupposed in Gal 3.10 vainly imagines in his flesh, his σάρξ, that he can 'do' the Law and in his illusion loses himself in the quantity he has to produce, and because he does not know that true fulfilment of the Law is possible and real only as a fruit of the Spirit, he deceives himself in seeking to obey a quantitative standard. He understands the fulfilment of this standard as solely *his* work but does not know that his activity, because love is something which belongs to God, can take place only as an outcome of the activity of the Spirit of God in man.[37]

Yet other scholars seem to suggest that Paul understands the Spirit as a new guide for moral behavior. Rather than a static law, the Spirit provides dynamic guidance that makes correct behavior self-evident for the believer.[38] John M. G. Barclay's comments are illustrative:

---

[35]This answer goes back to Luther; cf. Westerholm, *Israel's Law*, 11.

[36]Cf. Thomas Schreiner, *The Law and Its Fulfillment: A Pauline Theology of Law* (Grand Rapids: Baker Books, 1993), 145–78; Robert H. Gundry, "Grace, Works, and Staying Saved in Paul," *Biblica* 66 (1985): 12, 19; Sanders, *PLJP*, 74, 83, 147; Frank Thielman, *From Plight to Solution: A Jewish Framework for Understanding Paul's View of the Law in Galatians and Romans* (Leiden: E. J. Brill, 1989), 34–36, 47–86.

[37]Hans Hübner, *Law in Paul's Thought: A Contribution to the Development of Pauline Theology*, trans. J. C. G. Greig, Studies of the New Testament and Its World (Edinburgh: T & T Clark, 1984), 41.

[38]Cf. Barclay, *Obeying the Truth*, 115; E. P. Sanders, *Paul and Palestinian Judaism* (Philadelphia: Fortress Press, 1977), 513.

[The spirit] must be their standard of obedience ... [στοίχειν] seems to indicate that the Spirit is an order or rule to which the Galatians should align themselves.[39]

Paul saw the divine indicative in peculiarly dynamic terms—it was not simply a matter of what God *had* done (in election, etc.) but what he *continued to do* in and for the believer .... By describing Christian ethics in terms of 'walking in/by the Spirit' Paul could convey this sense of *constant* divine power and direction without, however, diminishing the urgency of his moral directives.[40]

Presumably he was confident that the Spirit would show them how to 'do good to all men' ....[41]

Unfortunately, none of these answers seems entirely satisfactory. Least satisfactory of all is the most common answer. If Christians can and should do the law once they are enabled by the Spirit, why is Paul so concerned if the Galatians—who are already believers, who have already received the Spirit (Gal 3:2–5)—take up the law?[42] Moreover, how is this view any different than the existing Jewish understanding that law observance is possible only with God's help?[43] Similarly, Judaism itself commonly summarized the law in terms of love; thus it seems difficult to make the case that the Spirit points Christians to a qualitatively different understanding of the law based on love.[44] Finally, if the Spirit substitutes for the law in providing a rule or guide for obedience, it is hard to see how this differs substantially from the law given by God. Even if this rule or guide is dynamic rather than static, it still would have the character of law, that is, as a response to transgression.[45]

---

[39] Barclay, *Obeying the Truth*, 155.

[40] Ibid., 227.

[41] Ibid., 231.

[42] Cf. Sanders, *PLJP*, 147: "If the basic thing 'wrong' with the law is that humans are unable to fulfill it, there is no reason to have those in the Spirit, who have been given the ability, fulfill only part of it [i.e., not including circumcision, food laws, days]." Sanders' point, of course, is that it is *not* the case that the problem is human inability to fulfill the law.

[43] Cf. Martyn, *Galatians*, 262.

[44] Cf. Thielman, *From Plight to Solution*, 52–53.

[45] Cf. Barclay, *Obeying the Truth*, 115–16, who describes the Spirit and the law as alternate ways to deal with the flesh. In effect this seems to bind the Spirit, like the law, to the old age, i.e., the age of the flesh—the Spirit must constantly respond to the flesh, instead of transcending it.

Living *in* the Spirit

Once again, the matrix "where to live" provides a helpful insight into this issue. In a sense, the issue can be summed up by saying that the answer is "living *in* the Spirit" rather than "living *by* the Spirit." Our reading of Gal 3:1–14 suggests that, rather than offering an alternative *means* for us to live rightly, Paul is urging us to live in a different place, a different age; rather than offering an alternative way to deal with sin, he is urging us to live where sin does not exist. In other words, living *in* the Spirit does not empower us to resist sin, nor does it give us a new commandment, nor does it even give us moment by moment guidance for dealing with sin; rather, living *in* the Spirit means we are not living in the old age, and therefore we do not sin—or perhaps better, sin has no meaning for us.[46]

At first glance, this answer may seem like an invitation to libertinism. If one is not following *some* sort of rule, some sort of guide, some sort of standard of behavior, then how can one hope to avoid sin? To talk about *avoiding sin* reveals the problem: since sin is defined in terms of the law (or a rule, or guide, or standard of behavior) and vice versa, one cannot live by any sort of law (or guide, or rule, or standard of behavior) without living in the arena in which sin is an active possibility. As we have said repeatedly above, to live in the law is to live in the old age (and therefore under sin). At the same time, however, to live in sin is equally (and even more obviously) to live in the old age (and therefore under law). To live in the Spirit, in the new age, is to leave both sin and law behind. To put the issue in a way similar to Gal 6:15, neither sin nor the avoidance of sin counts for anything; what matters is living in the new age, in the Spirit.

Even if it is not an invitation to libertinism, this answer may seem to be unrealistically mystical, or perhaps simply naïve. Are we supposed simply to hope that we will mysteriously find ourselves living rightly once we become believers? Surely this is inadequate, or at least impractical for those who still must deal with the old age.[47] Or is it? Is there any sense in which living in the Spirit actually and practically works to produce appropriate behavior even for believers who have not yet experienced the fullness of the new age?[48]

---

[46]Cf. Betz, *Galatians*, 33: "Paul's ethics is, in the final analysis, quite simple: The Christian is asked to let the 'fruit of the Spirit' happen. The 'virtues' are there to manifest themselves and the Christian is enabled to allow this. As they occur, evil and its chaos have no room." Betz's analysis of Pauline ethics is very helpful, but it does not explore the mechanism on which Paul's simple ethics rests, namely that one lives in the new age, and therefore leaves sin behind.

[47]Indeed, the Galatians may well be turning to the law precisely because they were struggling with inappropriate behavior; see above, 46.

[48]It could be the case, of course, that Paul really is unrealistic and naïve. Just as a reading of the text which results in an incoherent or inconsistent Paul is likely to prove

An analogy may be helpful at this point. Consider the following question: what is the best way to avoid an affair? One might draw up a strict set of rules: do not flirt with co-workers; do not "check out" attractive passers-by; and so on. One might instead look for a more positive approach, one that actively seeks to do good rather than to avoid evil; for example, one might attempt to love one's spouse as fully and completely as possible. Alternately, one might decide that any particular set of rules or guidelines, positive or negative, may not be able to anticipate every possible situation; instead, one may arrange access to a hot-line offering instant advice whenever needed. Unfortunately, none of these approaches is fool-proof; no matter how long one succeeds in avoiding an affair, it always remains a possibility.[49]

There is a much simpler way to avoid having an affair, a way moreover that is guaranteed to work. One simply takes one's spouse wherever one goes. As long as one is with one's spouse, one will not have an affair. In fact, neither having an affair nor avoiding an affair is even relevant. When one is with one's spouse, "affair" ceases to have meaning. To be sure, one will undoubtedly be fulfilling many of the rules for avoiding affairs[50]—but if one has to start *keeping* those rules, one must not be with one's spouse, because as long as one is with one's spouse, the rules are superfluous.[51]

In the same way, Paul says the following:

> Walk in the Spirit, and you will not fulfill the desires of the flesh. For the flesh desires contrary to the Spirit, and the Spirit is contrary to the flesh; these are incompatible with one another, in order that you might not do whatever things you wish. If you are led by (in?) the Spirit, you are not under the law (Gal 5:16–18).[52]

---

less than satisfying, however, so also with a reading which leaves us with an impractical ethics.

[49]The fact that one must constantly, diligently follow the rules (or the advice from the hotline, assuming one always remembers to call) means that an affair always remains possible.

[50]Though quite possibly not all—for example, one may be able to flirt while with one's spouse.

[51]One might extend the analogy to describe a good marriage. Is a good marriage created by carefully following a marriage manual, or by truly relating to one's spouse? If a couple is truly relating, then they have a good relationship, regardless of whether they even know what the marriage manual prescribes. On the other hand, the prescriptions in the marriage manual (and the extent to which one finds it necessary to consult these prescriptions) may help to identify (but not correct) areas in which the couple is failing to relate.

[52]Gal 5:17b presents some difficulties. Is Paul saying that whatever the *flesh* might desire, the Spirit prevents? Or is he suggesting something similar to Rom 7, that the flesh prevents us from doing the things that we know and want to do? Whatever solution one

Walking in the Spirit not only rules out the desires of the flesh, but also removes one from the sphere of the law. Walking in the Spirit therefore fulfills the law, but does not involve keeping the law.

TASKS REMAINING

In spite of the importance of Gal 3:1–14, especially with respect to issues concerning Paul and the law, the current investigation has remained relatively narrowly focused. Even in this chapter, when our attention has turned from the specific details of how the citations function in this passage to consider some of the implications for issues in Pauline theology, our attention has remained primarily on Galatians. Before ending the current investigation, therefore, it may be useful briefly to sketch out some of the ways the results of this investigation could be extended and/or corroborated in future investigations.

One obvious way to extend the results of this investigation would be to see whether the conclusions reached above, concerning the law and its place in the life of believers, can be extended to other letters of Paul. For example, would the matrix "where to live" shed some light on the difficulties of the letter to the Romans? Would the understanding of life in the Spirit developed above be consistent with the message of a letter such as 1 Corinthians, with all of its practical parenetic material?

To answer these questions in any detail is of course impossible within this brief conclusion; nevertheless, a few general remarks may be in order. First, it is not clear whether or how one could derive the matrix "where to live" from any of Paul's other letters, since the problems and opportunities posed by the citations in Gal 3:1–14 are unique to this passage. On the other hand, it does seem that this matrix might serve as a useful "intertext" to bring to the reading of any of Paul's letters. To the extent that Paul's letters reflect an apocalyptic understanding of Christ as the one whose death and resurrection inaugurates the new age, it would seem appropriate to ask how the believer interacts with the old age and new age; this is a key focus of the matrix "where to live."

Second, and more specifically, the implications of this matrix for understanding the problem of the law seem likely to be compatible with at least some of what Paul says in Romans. To take only a few examples, the discussion of Adam and Christ as the two τύποι would easily fit with a discussion of the two ages (Rom 5).[53] Likewise, the discussion of two righteousnesses, one from the law and the other from God, seems to fit neatly with the idea of the law less as a

---

chooses, the basic point seems clear: Flesh and Spirit are incompatible; to live in one rules out the other.

[53] Note especially that death, sin, and law are all associated with Adam.

CONCLUSION

means to gain life, and more as a closed system (Rom 10).[54] Also, the emphasis on dying with Christ (Rom 6) and walking in the Spirit (Rom 8) parallels much of what we have developed above.

Similarly, the implications of this matrix for understanding life in the Spirit seems likely to be compatible with much of Paul's parenesis. In Romans 14:9–20, for example, it is striking how much of Paul's instruction is given as adjectives and participles—forms which can carry an imperatival nuance, but which lend themselves well to description as opposed to prescription.[55] Equally striking are Paul's instructions concerning πορνεία in 1 Cor 6:12–20, in which he does not quote a law against immorality, but rather a verse that speaks of union. His point seems clear: to be joined with Christ is to rule out any union with a prostitute.[56]

Another obvious way to extend the results of the current investigation would be to apply the same sort of analysis to other citations as we applied to the citations of Gal 3:1–14, particularly with respect to their logical and/or rhetorical function. While it is doubtful that any other passage would offer the same degree of complexity of interwoven citations that we found in Gal 3:1–14 (with the possible exception of Rom 10:5–21), it seems obvious that every use of citation, no matter how apparently simple, has some sort of function within its context. Not only might it be worthwhile to explore the way(s) various texts interact with the presupposition of authority and applicability invoked by the use of citation, but also it might be useful to explore how many of Paul's citations actually function as proof, and how many serve another purpose, perhaps including some purposes not described above.

Finally, of the various intertextual insights and techniques which were used to investigate Gal 3:1–14, the one that bore the most fruit, in ways that were not anticipated prior to conducting the investigation, was the search for and use of the presupposed, anonymous intertexts that shape the way a reader (and perhaps also even an author) interacts with a passage.[57] Not only was it surprisingly easy to identify a wide variety of presuppositions for this passage —although not all of these would necessarily prove to be of great significance[58]—but also the exploration of just two presuppositions led to a great deal of insight into the

---

[54]The law does produce a righteousness, just as one can live within the law. The problem is that the righteousness of the law is limited to this age, i.e., by responding to sin (cf. Rom 7).

[55]Perhaps the well-known phenomenon of Paul's mingled indicative and imperative fits in here as well.

[56]These few, brief examples hardly scratch the surface of possible ways to explore Paul's other letters in light of the matrix, "where to live," but hopefully they have at least shown that such an exploration might prove profitable.

[57]See above, 145–74.

[58]Cf. above, 146.

passage. Based on this experience, it seems likely that an investigation of the presuppositions of other passages might lead to worthwhile results.

Conclusion

Strictly speaking, intertextuality is not a new phenomenon; what is new in an intertextual approach is the attention that is focused on the ways that meaning arises from the interaction of a text with numerous other texts. In the case of Gal 3:1–14, attending to the difficult interactions of the citations and the anonymous intertexts presupposed by such interactions results in new insights into the meaning and significance of Paul's argument. The key result is the insight that Paul's argument centers on the intertextual matrix, "where to live." Christians are to carry out life in the new age, not in the old age under sin and law. Both the intertextual approach and the findings of this investigation hold promise for further investigations into Paul's letters.

Appendix
῞ΟΤΙ ... ΔΗΛΟΝ ... ῞ΟΤΙ IN HELLENISTIC LITERATURE

Using the Thesaurus Linguae Graecae CD-ROM D and Silver Mountain TLG Workplace™ 8.0 software, searching Greek literature from the third century B.C.E. through the first century C.E., a total of fifty-three examples were found in which ὅτι both preceded and followed δῆλον (within a span of twenty-five words before and after δῆλον), not counting Gal 3:11. Of these, twenty-one seem to be false matches, usually because *both* occurrences of ὅτι have a matching δῆλον. Of the remaining thirty-two examples, three clearly associate the δῆλον with the preceding ὅτι, and twenty-nine associate the δῆλον with the following ὅτι. The details are provided below.

EXAMPLES IN WHICH ΔΗΛΟΝ GOES WITH PRECEDING ῞ΟΤΙ

All of the following make clear the connection between the δῆλον and the preceding ὅτι by way of a μέν ... δέ construction. Note that the two examples from Philo are identical, matching the second ὅτι with ῥᾴδιον ἰδεῖν, a phrase that is more or less synonymous with δῆλον. Similarly, the example from Dio Chrysostomus appears to match the second ὅτι with ἔτι μοι δοκεῖ τοῦ πρώτου φανερώτερον.

Dio Chrysostomus, *Orationes* 31.39:

> οὐκοῦν **ὅτι** μὲν τὰ γιγνόμενα ὀρθῶς καὶ μηθὲν ἔχοντα ἄτοπον οὐδεὶς περιστέλλει **δῆλόν** ἐστιν. **ὅτι** δὲ ἥκιστ᾽ ἄν τις φυλάξαιτο τοὺς εὖ πάσχοντας εἰδέναι τίνα τρόπον τῆς χάριτος τυγχάνουσι καὶ τῶν γιγνομένων περὶ τὴν τιμὴν ὁτιοῦν, εἴ γέ τις ἁπλῶς αὐτὸ πράττοι καὶ δικαίως, ἔτι μοι δοκεῖ τοῦ πρώτου φανερώτερον.

Philo, *Arithmetica* (fragments) 23b:

> ὅτι μὲν οὖν τοὺς πρὸ αὐτῆς, παντί τῳ **δῆλον**: **ὅτι** δὲ καὶ τοὺς μετ' αὐτήν, ἐξ ἐπιλογισμοῦ ῥᾴδιον ἰδεῖν.

Philo, *De Plantatione* 123:

> ὅτι μὲν οὖν τοὺς πρὸ αὐτῆς, παντί τῳ **δῆλον**: **ὅτι** δὲ καὶ τοὺς μετ' αὐτήν, ἐξ ἐπιλογισμοῦ ῥᾴδιον ἰδεῖν.

EXAMPLES IN WHICH ΔΗΛΟΝ GOES WITH FOLLOWING ὍΤΙ

In most of the following examples, one or more of the following features clearly indicates that the δῆλον is associated with the following rather than the preceding ὅτι. First, in the majority of examples the initial ὅτι appears to be recitative, following a verb such as λέγω, δείκνυμι, γινώσκω, etc. or an adjective such as φανερός; these examples will be designated by the letter **L** in parentheses following the citation. Second, the δῆλον may be followed by a postpositive conjunction such as γάρ, οὖν, or δέ, or a phrase that functions similarly (e.g., ἐκ τούτων) to show that the δῆλον initiates a new clause; these examples will be designated by the letter **P**. Third, there may be an intervening conjunction, such as καί, εἰ, ἵνα, etc., or one or more intervening clauses, which clearly separates the δῆλον from the preceding ὅτι; these examples will be designated by the letter **I**. Many of the following examples fit into more than one of these categories and will include more than one designation. One example does not fit into any of these categories (Clement of Rome, pseud.); this example is discussed in the text above.

1 Corinthians 15:27 (L):

> ὅταν δὲ εἴπῃ **ὅτι** πάντα ὑποτέτακται, **δῆλον ὅτι** ἐκτὸς τοῦ ὑποτάξαντος αὐτῷ τὰ πάντα.

Apollonius Citiensis, *In Hippocratis de Articulis Commentarius* 20 (L,I):

> καὶ ἤδη μέν τινας εἶδον, οἵτινες ὑπὸ φαυλότητος καὶ τὰ ἔξω κεκλιμένα καὶ τὰ [μὴ] εἰς τοὖπισθεν ἀσκῷ ἐμβάλλειν ἐπειράθησαν οὐ γινώσκοντες αὐτοῖς, **ὅτι** ἐξέβαλλον <μᾶλλον> ἢ εἰσέβαλλον. ὁ μέντοι πρῶτος ἐπινοήσας **δῆλον ὅτι** πρὸς τὰ ἔσω ὠλισθηκότα ἀσκῷ ἐμβάλλειν ἐπειρήσατο.

Chrysippus, *Fragmenta Logica et Physica*, 329 (L,I):

> οὕτω δεικνύοις ἂν **ὅτι** μὴ καλῶς <τὸ τί οἱ ἀπὸ τῆς Στοᾶς γένος τοῦ ὄντος τίθενται>: εἰ γάρ τί, **δῆλον ὅτι** καὶ ὄν.

APPENDIX

Chrysippus, *Fragmenta Logica et Physica*, 339 (I):

ὅτι τισὶ δοκεῖ μὴ εἶναί τι κινοῦν ἀκίνητον, ἀλλὰ πᾶν τὸ κινοῦν κινεῖσθαι—καὶ **δῆλον ὅτι** ταύτης εἰσὶ τῆς δόξης τῶν τε παλαιῶν φυσιολόγων ὅσοι σωματικὴν ἢ μίαν ἢ πλείους ὑπέθεντο τὴν ἀρχήν, καὶ τῶν νέων οἱ <Στωϊκοί>.

Clement of Rome (pseud.), *Epistulae de Virginitate* 1.13.4:

ὅτι δὲ ὁ θερισμὸς πολὺς καὶ οἱ ἐργάται ὀλίγοι, **δῆλον ὅτι** ἐν τοῖς καιροῖς ἡμῶν λιμός ἐστιν τοῦ ἀκοῦσαι λόγον κυρίου.

Dio Chrysostomus, *Orationes* 10.7 (I):

Ἔπειτα, ἔφη, οὐδὲν ἠδίκεις αὐτὸν ἀργὸν ὄντα καὶ ἀμαθῆ τρέφων καὶ ποιῶν **ὅτι** κάκιστον; ἡ γὰρ ἀργία καὶ τὸ σχολὴν ἄγειν ἀπόλλυσι πάντων μάλιστα τοὺς ἀνοήτους ἀνθρώπους. οὐκοῦν ὀρθῶς συνῆκεν ὑπὸ σοῦ διαφθειρόμενος, καὶ ἀπέδρα δικαίως, ἵν' ἐργάζηται **δῆλον ὅτι** καὶ μὴ σχολάζων τε καὶ καθεύδων καὶ ἐσθίων χείρων ἀεὶ γίγνηται.

Dio Chrysostomus, *Orationes* 34.4 (I):

ὅτι μηδενὸς αὐτὸς δέομαι παρ' ὑμῶν, ἀλλὰ τῆς ὑμετέρας ὠφελείας ἕνεκα ἐσπούδακα. ἐὰν οὖν μὴ ἀνάσχησθέ μου, **δῆλον ὅτι** ὑμᾶς αὐτούς, οὐκ ἐμέ, ζημιώσετε.

Dio Chrysostomus, *Orationes* 50.3 (I):

τῆς δ' οὖν εὐνοίας τῆς πρὸς ὑμᾶς καὶ τῆς πίστεως ἐκεῖνο ὑμῖν γιγνέσθω τεκμήριον, **ὅτι** μήτε ἑταιρείᾳ τινὶ πεποιθὼς μήτε συνήθεις ἐξ ὑμῶν ἔχων τινὰς θαρρῶν εἰσέρχομαι πρὸς ὑμᾶς, καὶ νομίζω μηδενὸς ἔλαττον ἂν ἔχειν, **δῆλον ὅτι** τῇ κοινῇ φιλίᾳ πεπιστευκὼς καὶ τῇ πρὸς ἅπαντας εὐνοίᾳ, μή γε ἰσχυρὸς ἢ φοβερὸς εἶναι δοκῶν ἢ βουλόμενος ὡς διὰ τοῦτο θεραπεύεσθαι.

Dio Chrysostomus, *Orationes* 80.3 (L,P):

Σόλωνα μέντοι καὶ αὐτὸν εἰρηκέναι φασὶν ὡς [**ὅτι**] αὐτῷ μὴ ἀρέσκοντα εἰσηγεῖτο Ἀθηναίοις, ἀλλ' οἷς αὐτοὺς ὑπελάμβανε χρήσεσθαι. **δῆλον** οὖν **ὅτι** πονηροὺς ἔγραφε νόμους, εἴπερ τοὺς ἀρέσοντας πονηροῖς ἔγραφεν.

Dionysius Halicarnassensis, *Antiquitates Romanae* 5:66.1 (L,P):

Τοιαῦτα τοῦ Οὐαλερίου λέγοντος καὶ πολλῶν τὴν γνώμην ἐπαινούντων Ἄππιος Κλαύδιος Σαβῖνος ἐν τῷ προσήκοντι κληθεὶς τόπῳ τἀναντία παρῄνει διδάσκων, **ὅτι** τὸ στασιάζον οὐκ ἐξαιρεθήσεται τῆς πόλεως, ἐὰν ψηφίσωνται χρεῶν ἀποκοπάς, ἀλλ᾽ ἔτι πονηρότερον ἔσται μεταχθὲν ἀπὸ τῶν πενήτων εἰς τοὺς εὐπόρους. **δῆλον** γὰρ δὴ πᾶσιν ὑπάρχειν, **ὅτι** χαλεπῶς οἴσουσιν οἱ μέλλοντες ἀποστερεῖσθαι τῶν χρημάτων πολῖταί τ᾽ ὄντες καὶ ἐπίτιμοι καὶ πάσας ἐστρατευμένοι τὰς ἐπιβαλούσας ὑπὲρ τῆς πόλεως στρατείας, οὐδ᾽ ἀξιοῦντες ἃ κατέλιπον αὐτοῖς οἱ πατέρες καὶ αὐτοὶ φιλεργοῦντες καὶ σωφρόνως ζῶντες ἐκτήσαντο δημεύεσθαι τοῖς πονηροτάτοις καὶ ἀργοτάτοις τῶν πολιτῶν.

Epictetus, *Dissertationes ab Arriano Digestae* 1.1.5 (L,I):

τί γάρ ἐστιν ἄλλο τὸ λέγον **ὅτι** χρυσίον καλόν ἐστιν; αὐτὸ γὰρ οὐ λέγει. **δῆλον ὅτι** ἡ χρηστικὴ δύναμις ταῖς φαντασίαις.

Epictetus, *Dissertationes ab Arriano Digestae* 1.9.1 (L,I):

Εἰ ταῦτά ἐστιν ἀληθῆ τὰ περὶ τῆς συγγενείας τοῦ θεοῦ καὶ ἀνθρώπων λεγόμενα ὑπὸ τῶν φιλοσόφων, τί ἄλλο ἀπολείπεται τοῖς ἀνθρώποις ἢ τὸ τοῦ Σωκράτους, μηδέποτε πρὸς τὸν πυθόμενον ποδαπός ἐστιν εἰπεῖν **ὅτι** Ἀθηναῖος ἢ Κορίνθιος, ἀλλ᾽ **ὅτι** κόσμιος; διὰ τί γὰρ λέγεις Ἀθηναῖον εἶναι σεαυτόν, οὐχὶ δ᾽ ἐξ ἐκείνης μόνον τῆς γωνίας, εἰς ἣν ἐρρίφη γεννηθέν σου τὸ σωμάτιον; ἢ **δῆλον ὅτι** ἀπὸ τοῦ κυριωτέρου καὶ περιέχοντος οὐ μόνον αὐτὴν ἐκείνην τὴν γωνίαν, <ἀλλὰ> καὶ ὅλην σου τὴν οἰκίαν καὶ ἁπλῶς ὅθεν σου τὸ γένος τῶν προγόνων εἰς σὲ κατελήλυθεν ἐντεῦθέν ποθεν καλεῖς σεαυτὸν Ἀθηναῖον καὶ Κορίνθιον;

Euclid, *Elementa* 10.9 (L,P,I):

Δέδεικται ἐν τοῖς ἀριθμητικοῖς, **ὅτι** οἱ ὅμοιοι ἐπίπεδοι ἀριθμοὶ πρὸς ἀλλήλους λόγον ἔχουσιν, ὃν τετράγωνος ἀριθμὸς πρὸς τετράγωνον ἀριθμόν, καὶ **ὅτι**, ἐὰν δύο ἀριθμοὶ πρὸς ἀλλήλους λόγον ἔχωσιν, ὃν τετράγωνος ἀριθμὸς πρὸς τετράγωνον ἀριθμόν, ὅμοιοί εἰσιν ἐπίπεδοι. καὶ **δῆλον** ἐκ τούτων, **ὅτι** οἱ μὴ ὅμοιοι ἐπίπεδοι ἀριθμοί, τουτέστιν οἱ μὴ ἀνάλογον ἔχοντες τὰς πλευράς, πρὸς ἀλλήλους λόγον οὐκ ἔχουσιν, ὃν τετράγωνος ἀριθμὸς πρὸς τετράγωνον ἀριθμόν.

Euclid, *Opticorum Recensio Theonis* 220.11 (L):

καὶ ἐπεὶ δεῖ δεῖξαι, **ὅτι** ἔλασσον φαίνεται τὸ ΑΒ τοῦ ΔΖ, **δῆλον, ὅτι** πρότερον δεῖ δεῖξαι, ὅτι ἡ ὑπὸ ΒΕΑ γωνία ἐλάσσων ἐστὶ τῆς ὑπὸ ΖΕΔ γωνίας.

Heron, *Definitiones* 123.1 (L,P):

πρὸς δὲ τοὺς ἀντιθέντας τῷ ὅρῳ τούτῳ καὶ λέγοντας, **ὅτι** μόνα λόγον ἔχει πρὸς ἄλληλα, ἃ δύνανται πολυπλασιαζόμενα ἀλλήλων ὑπερέχειν, οὐδὲν δὲ οὕτως ὁμογενὲς ὡς σημεῖον σημείῳ, **δῆλον** ἄρα, **ὅτι** πολυπλασιαζόμενον τὸ σημεῖον ὑπερέξει τοῦ σημείου, πρὸς δὲ τούτους ῥητέον, ὅτι τὸν κατὰ μεγέθη προσπολυπλασιασμὸν οὐκ ἐπιδέχεται σημεῖον.

Heron, *Stereometrica* 2.27.1 (L):

θὲς εἰς τὸν ἥλιον ῥάβδον ἴσην δίπηχυν πλησίον τοῦ δένδρου ἢ κίονος καὶ ἰδέ, πόσην σκιὰν ποιεῖ, καὶ νόμιζε, **ὅτι** ἐποίησε τὴν σκιὰν ποδῶν: **δῆλον, ὅτι** διπλασίονα ἀναλογίαν ἔχει ἡ σκιὰ πρὸς τὴν ῥάβδον.

Heron, *Stereometrica* 2.67.1 (L,I):

ὅθεν φανερόν, **ὅτι** πᾶσα πυραμὶς τρίτον μέρος ἐστὶ τοῦ πρίσματος τοῦ τὴν αὐτὴν βάσιν ἔχοντος καὶ ὕψος ἴσον. ἐκ δὲ τούτων **δῆλον, ὅτι** πᾶσα πυραμὶς ἐπὶ οἱουδηποτοῦν σχήματος βεβηκυῖα γ΄ μέρος ἐστὶ στερεοῦ παραλληλεπιπέδου τοῦ τὴν αὐτὴν βάσιν ἔχοντος καὶ ὕψος ἴσον.

Josephus, *Contra Apionem* 1.102 (L,P,I):

λέγει γάρ, **ὅτι** ὁ μὲν Σέθως ἐκαλεῖτο Αἴγυπτος, Ἁρμαῒς δὲ ὁ ἀδελφὸς αὐτοῦ Δαναός. Ταῦτα μὲν ὁ Μάνεθως. **δῆλον** δέ ἐστιν ἐκ τῶν εἰρημένων ἐτῶν τοῦ χρόνου συλλογισθέντος, **ὅτι** οἱ καλούμενοι ποιμένες ἡμέτεροι δὲ πρόγονοι τρισὶ καὶ ἐνενήκοντα καὶ τριακοσίοις πρόσθεν ἔτεσιν ἐκ τῆς Αἰγύπτου ἀπαλλαγέντες τὴν χώραν ταύτην ἐπῴκησαν ἢ Δαναὸν εἰς Ἄργος ἀφικέσθαι.

Josephus, *Contra Apionem* 2.13 (L):

ἀκοῦσαι δέ φησι τῶν πρεσβυτέρων, **ὅτι** Μωσῆς ἦν Ἡλιοπολίτης, **δῆλον ὅτι** νεώτερος μὲν ὢν αὐτός, ἐκείνοις δὲ πιστεύσας τοῖς διὰ τὴν ἡλικίαν ἐπισταμένοις αὐτὸν καὶ συγγενομένοις.

Josephus, *Contra Apionem* 2.267 (I):

νῦν γὰρ τὴν ἱέρειαν ἀπέκτειναν, ἐπεί τις αὐτῆς κατηγόρησεν, ὅτι ξένους ἐμύει θεούς· νόμῳ δ' ἦν τοῦτο παρ' αὐτοῖς κεκωλυμένον καὶ τιμωρία κατὰ τῶν ξένον εἰσαγόντων θεὸν ὥριστο θάνατος. οἱ δὲ τοιούτῳ νόμῳ χρώμενοι **δῆλον ὅτι** τοὺς τῶν ἄλλων οὐκ ἐνόμιζον εἶναι θεούς.

Philo, *De Specialibus Legibus* 1.274 (L,I):

ὁ δὲ χρυσοῦ μὲν τοῦ καθαρωτάτου κατεσκεύασται, ἵδρυται δ' ἐν ἀδύτοις εἴσω τοῦ προτέρου καταπετάσματος, ὃς οὐδενὶ τῶν ἄλλων ἐστὶν ὁρατὸς ὅτι μὴ τοῖς ἁγνεύουσι τῶν ἱερέων καὶ γέγονε πρὸς χρείαν τὴν τῶν θυμιαμάτων. ἐξ οὗ **δῆλόν** ἐστιν, **ὅτι** καὶ βραχύτατον λιβανωτὸν παρ' ἀνδρὸς ὁσίου τιμιώτερον ὁ θεὸς νομίζει μυρίων θρεμμάτων, ὅσα ἄν τις ἱερουργῇ μὴ σφόδρα ἀστεῖος ὤν.

Plutarch, *Παροιμίαι αἷς Ἀλεξανδρεῖς ἐχρῶντο* 145.2171 (I):

Εἰ τοῦ ὄντος ἡ εὕρεσις πάντως, **ὅτι** καὶ θεωρημάτων· καὶ ποῦ οὖν ὄντων; ἢ **δῆλον ὅτι** ἐν ψυχῇ.

Plutarch, *Pyrrhus*, 14.10 (P,I):

"**ὅτι** δὲ τούτων κρατήσασιν ἡμῖν οὐδεὶς ἀντιστήσεται τῶν νῦν ὑβριζόντων πολεμίων, τί ἂν λέγοι τις;" "οὐδέν" ὁ Κινέας εἶπε· "**δῆλον** γὰρ **ὅτι** καὶ Μακεδονίαν ἀναλαβεῖν καὶ τῆς Ἑλλάδος ἄρχειν ὑπάρξει βεβαίως ἀπὸ τηλικαύτης δυνάμεως."

Severus Iatrosophista, *De Instrumentis Infusoriis seu Clysteribus ad Timotheum* 30 (P,I):

ὅτι δὲ ἀλήθειά ἐστι τὸ εἰρημένον, ἐξ αὐτῶν τῶν κατὰ τὴν τέχνην ἔργων δυνήσῃ μαθεῖν· πρὸς γὰρ τὰς διαβροχὰς καὶ τὰ καταπλάσματα πλέον ἀγριαίνεται τὸ πάθος. **δῆλον** δὲ, **ὅτι** χύσιν ὑπομένοντος τοῦ χυμοῦ, μεγεθύνεται τὰ συμπτώματα.

Strabo, *Geographica* 10.2.17 (L):

ἐπεὶ οὖν κατὰ τὰ Τρωικὰ Σάμος μὲν καὶ ἡ Κεφαλληνία ἐκαλεῖτο καὶ ἡ Σαμοθράκη ' οὐ γὰρ ἂν Ἑκάβη εἰσήγετο λέγουσα **ὅτι** τοὺς παῖδας αὐτῆς "πέρνασχ' ὅν κε λάβοι ἐς Σάμον ἔς "τ' Ἴμβρον", Ἰωνικὴ δ' οὐκ ἀπῴκιστό πω, **δῆλον ὅτι** ἀπὸ τῶν προτέρων τινὸς τὴν ὁμωνυμίαν ἔσχεν.

Strabo, *Geographica*, 1.2.28 (I):

ὅτι δ' ὁ ποιητὴς ὁμόλογος τούτοις, καὶ ἐκ τῶνδε **δῆλον ὅτι** ἡ μὲν Ἰθάκη κεῖται "πρὸς ζόφον"· ὅπερ ἐστὶ πρὸς ἄρκτον, "αἱ δέ τ' ἄνευθε πρὸς ἠῶ τ' ἠέλιόν τε."

Strabo, *Geographica*, 8.3.6 (L,P):

τοῦτό τε οὖν εἴρηκε σκέψεως δεόμενον καὶ περὶ τῆς Οἰχαλίας **ὅτι** φησὶν οὐ μιᾶς οὔσης, μίαν εἶναι πόλιν Εὐρύτου Οἰχαλιῆος· **δῆλον** οὖν **ὅτι** τὴν Θετταλικήν, ἐφ' ἧς φησιν "οἵ τ' ἔχον Οἰχαλίην, "πόλιν Εὐρύτου Οἰχαλιῆος."

Theon, *Progymnasmata* 83 (L,P,I):

ἐπὶ μὲν οὖν τῆς αἰτιατικῆς ἀναμφισβήτητόν ἐστιν, ἐπὶ δὲ τῶν ἄλλων πτώσεων φανερόν, **ὅτι** προσθέσει ἄρθρων οὐκέτι ἀμφίβολος γίνεται ἡ λέξις· εἰσὶ δὲ Αἰγύπτιοι οἱ Κολχοί· **δῆλον** γὰρ γέγονεν, **ὅτι** περὶ Κολχῶν λέγει, ὥς εἰσιν Αἰγύπτιοι.

Tryphon I, *Fragmenta* 16.8 (L,I):

φησὶ γάρ, **ὅτι** ἐπηκολούθησεν αὐτῷ, καὶ **δῆλον ὅτι** παρὰ [τὸ] ἕπω ἥφθη ἢ εἵφθη ὤφειλεν εἶναι ὁ ἀόριστος καὶ κατὰ διαίρεσιν ἐγίνετο ἑάφθη, ὡς τὸ ἤγη ἐάγη, ἤλη ἐάλη, ἥλω ἑάλω, τῆς δασείας ἐπὶ τὴν ἀρχὴν χωρούσης, ὡς ἔθος.

False Matches

The examples listed below are those which do not represent a valid match for the pattern ὅτι ... δῆλον ... ὅτι. Although the Greek text has not been included in this list, the reason that the match is not valid is given in parentheses. The letter **D** alone indicates that the δῆλον does not appear to go with either ὅτι, while the letters **DODO** or **ODDO** indicate that both occurrences of ὅτι have a matching δῆλον, with the order of the letters indicating the pattern. The letters **OD** or **DO** indicate that the following or preceding ὅτι is too remote (e.g., in another sentence or paragraph) to be taken with the δῆλον.

Chrysippus, *Fragmenta Logica et Physica*, 121 (DODO)

Chrysippus, *Fragmenta Logica et Physica*, 329 (ODDO)

Chrysippus, *Fragmenta Logica et Physica*, 376 (DODO)

Dio Chrysostomus, *Orationes* 31.104 (D)

Dio Chrysostomus, *Orationes* 31.54 (OD)

Dio Chrysostomus, *Orationes* 7.116 (D)

Dio Chrysostomus, *Orationes* 80.4 (DODO)

Dionysius Halicarnassensis, *Antiquitates Romanae* 6.44.2 (D)

Epictetus, *Dissertationes ab Arriano Digestae* 1.17.t (DO)

Euclid, *Phaenomena* Pr.58 (DODO)

Flavius Arianus, *Fragmenta* 2b,156,F.175b.73 (DODO)

Harpocration, *Lexicon in decem oratores Atticos* 207 (OD)

Heron, *Metrica* 1.4 (DODO)

Matthew 26:72 (D)

Philo, *De opificio mundi* 25 (DODO)

Philo, *Quod omnis probus liber sit* 60 (ODDO)

Polybius, *Historiae* 10.2.13 (D)

Posidonius, *Fragmenta* 26.156 (OD)

Posidonius, *Fragmenta* 2a,87,F.85.51 (OD)

Strabo, *Geographica* 10.2.17 (DODO)

Strabo, *Geographica* 3.5.8 (OD)

BIBLIOGRAPHY

Aichele, George, and Gary A. Phillips. "Introduction: Exegesis, Eisegesis, Intergesis." *Semeia* 69/70 (1995): 7–18.

Balentine, Samuel E. "The Interpretation of the Old Testament in the New Testament." *Southwestern Journal of Theology* 23 (1981): 41–57.

Barclay, John M. G. *Obeying the Truth: A Study of Paul's Ethics in Galatians*. Edinburgh: T & T Clark, 1988.

Barker, Stephen F. *The Elements of Logic*, 3rd ed. New York: McGraw-Hill, 1980.

Barr, James. "Paul and the LXX: A Note on Some Recent Work." *JTS* n.s. 45 (1994): 593–601.

Barrett, C. K. "The Allegory of Abraham, Sarah, and Hagar." In *Essays on Paul*, 154–69. Philadelphia: Westminster Press, 1982.

Barthes, Roland. "De l'oeuvre au texte." *Revue d'Esthétique* 24 (1971); ET "From Work to Text." In *Image Music-Text*, trans. Stephen Heath, 155–64. New York: Hill and Wang, 1977.

———. "The Death of the Author." In *Image-Music-Text*, trans. Stephen Heath. New York: Hill and Wang, 1977), 142–48.

———. *S/Z*. Translated by Richard Miller. New York: Hill and Wang, 1974.

Beker, J. Christiaan. "Echoes and Intertextuality: On the Role of Scripture in Paul's Theology." In *Paul and the Scriptures of Israel*, ed. Craig A. Evans and James A. Sanders, 64–69. JSNTS 83. Sheffield: JSOT Press, 1993.

———. *Paul the Apostle: The Triumph of God in Life and Thought*. Philadelphia: Fortress Press, 1980.

Belleville, Linda L. "Under Law: Structural Analysis and the Pauline Concept of Law in Galatians 3:21–4:11." *JSNT* 26 (1986): 53–78.

Bengel, J. A. *Gnomon Novi Testamenti*. Tübingen: Philipp Schramm, 1742; ET *Gnomon of the New Testament*. Edinburgh: T & T Clark, 1860.

Betz, H. D. "In Defense of the Spirit: Paul's Letter to the Galatians as a Document of Early Christian Apologetics." In *Aspects of Religious Propaganda in Judaism and Early Christianity*, ed. Elisabeth Schüssler-Fiorenza, 99–114. Notre Dame, Ind: University of Notre Dame, 1976.

———. "Spirit, Freedom and Law: Paul's Message to the Galatian Churches." *SEÅ* 39 (1974): 145–60.

———. *Galatians: A Commentary on Paul's Letter to the Churches in Galatia*. Hermeneia. Philadelphia: Fortress Press, 1979.

Bonsirven, Joseph-Paul. *Exégèse rabbinique et exégèse paulinienne.* Paris: Beauchesne, 1939.
Boyarin, Daniel. "Inner Biblical Ambiguity, Intertextuality, and the Dialectic of Midrash: The Waters of Marah." *Prooftexts* 10 (1990): 29–48.
———. "The Song of Songs: Lock or Key? Intertextuality, Allegory, and Midrash." In *The Book and the Text: The Bible and Literary Theory*, ed. Regina M. Schwartz, 214–30. Cambridge, MA: Basil Blackwell, 1990.
———. *Intertextuality and the Reading of Midrash.* Bloomington: Indiana University Press, 1990.
Braswell, Joseph P. "The Blessing of Abraham versus 'the Curse of the Law': Another Look at Gal. 3:10–13." *WTJ* 53 (1991): 73–91.
Brauch, Manfred T. "Perspectives on 'God's Righteousness' in Recent German Discussion." In *Paul and Palestinian Judaism* by E. P. Sanders, 523–42. Philadelphia: Fortress Press, 1977.
Brawley, Robert L. "An Absent Complement and Intertextuality in John 19:28–29." *JBL* 112 (1993): 427–43.
Bring, Ragnar. *Commentary On Galatians.* Translated by Eric Wahlstrom. Philadelphia: Muhlenberg Press, 1961.
Bruce, F. F. "The Curse of the Law," *Paul and Paulinism: Essays in Honour of C. K. Barrett.* Edited by M. D. Hooker and S. G. Wilson. London: S.P.C.K., 1982.
———. *The Epistle to the Galatians.* NIGTC. Grand Rapids: Eerdmans, 1982.
Bruns, Gerald L. "Midrash and Allegory: The Beginnings of Scriptural Interpretation." In *The Literary Guide to the Bible*, ed. Robert Alter and Frank Kermode, 625–46. Cambridge, MA: Harvard University Press, 1987.
———. "The Hermeneutics of Midrash." In *The Book and the Text: The Bible and Literary Theory*, ed. Regina M. Schwartz, 189–213. Cambridge, MA: Basil Blackwell, 1990.
Buis, Pierre. "Deuteronome 27:16–26: Maledictions ou Exigences de l'Alliance?" *VT* 17 (1967): 478–79.
Bultmann, Rudolf. "Christ the End of the Law." In *Essays, Philosophical and Theological*, 36–66. London: SCM, 1955.
———. "The Significance of the Old Testament for Christian Faith." In *The Old Testament and Christian Faith*, ed. Bernhard W. Anderson, 8–35. New York: Harper & Row, 1963.
———. *Theology of the New Testament.* Translated by K. Grobel. New York: Charles Scribner's Sons, 1951, 1955.
Burton, Ernest De Witt. *A Critical and Exegetical Commentary on the Epistle to the Galatians.* ICC. Edinburgh: T & T Clark, 1921.
Caneday, Ardel. "'Redeemed from the Curse of the Law': The Use of Deut 21:22–23 in Gal 3:13." *Trinity Journal*, n.s., 10 (1989): 185–209.
Cavallin, H. C. C. "'The Righteous Shall Live by Faith': A Decisive Argument for the Traditional Interpretation." *Studia Theologia* 32 (1978): 33–43.
Clayton, Jay, and Eric Rothstein, eds. *Influence and Intertextuality in Literary History.* Madison: University of Wisconsin, 1991.

———. "Figures in the Corpus: Theories of Influence and Intertextuality." In *Influence and Intertextuality in Literary History*, ed. Jay Clayton and Eric Rothstein, 3–36. Madison: University of Wisconsin, 1991.
Cohen, Aryeh. *Rereading Talmud: Gender, Law, and the Poetics of Sugyot*. Brown Judaic Studies 318. Atlanta: Scholars Press, 1998.
Cohn-Sherbok, Daniel M. "Paul and Rabbinic Exegesis." *Scottish Journal of Theology* 35 (1982): 117–32.
Cosgrove, Charles H. "Arguing Like a Mere Human Being: Galatians 3:15–18 in Rhetorical Perspective." *NTS* 34 (1988): 536–49.
———. *The Cross and the Spirit: A Study in the Argument and Theology of Galatians*. Macon, GA: Mercer University Press, 1988.
Cousar, Charles B. *Galatians*. Interpretation. Louisville: John Knox, 1982.
Cranfield, C. E. B. "St. Paul and the Law." *SJT* 17 (1964): 42–68.
———. *A Critical and Exegetical Commentary on the Epistle to the Romans*, 6th ed. Edinburgh: T & T Clark, 1975–1979.
Cranford, Michael. "The Possibility of Perfect Obedience: Paul and an Implied Premise in Galatians 3:10 and 5:3." *NovT* 36 (1994): 242–58.
Culler, Jonathan. "Presupposition and Intertextuality." In *The Pursuit of Signs: Semiotics, Literature, Deconstruction*, 100–118. Ithaca: Cornell University, 1981.
———. "Riffaterre and the Semiotics of Poetry." In *The Pursuit of Signs: Semiotics, Literature, Deconstruction*, 80–99. Ithaca: Cornell University, 1981.
Dahl, Nils A. "Contradictions in Scripture." In *Studies in Paul: Theology of the Early Christian Mission*, 159–77. Minneapolis: Augsburg, 1977.
Dana, H. E., and Julius R. Mantey. *A Manual Grammar of the Greek New Testament*. New York: MacMillan, 1927.
Dodd, C. H. *According to the Scriptures: The Sub-structure of New Testament Theology*. London: Nisbet, 1952.
Donaldson, T. L. "The 'Curse of the Law' and the Inclusion of the Gentiles: Galatians 3:13–14." *NTS* 32 (1986): 94–112.
Draisma, Sipke, ed. *Intertextuality in Biblical Writings: Essays in Honour of Bas van Iersel*. Kampen: J. H. Kok, 1989.
Dunn, James D. G. "The New Perspective on Paul." *BJRL* 65 (1983): 95–122. Reprinted in idem, *Jesus, Paul, and the Law: Studies in Mark and Galatians*, 183–214. Louisville: John Knox, 1990.
———. "The Theology of Galatians: The Issue of Covenantal Nomism." In *Pauline Theology*, vol. 1, ed. Jouette M. Bassler, 125–46. Minneapolis: Fortress, 1991.
———. "Works of Law and the Curse of the Law (Galatians 3.10–14)." *NTS* 31 (1985): 523–42.
———. *Jesus, Paul, and the Law: Studies in Mark and Galatians*. Louisville: John Knox, 1990.
———. *Romans*. WBC 38A&B. Dallas: Word, 1988.
Ebeling, Gerhard. *The Truth of the Gospel: An Exposition of Galatians*. Translated by David Green. Philadelphia: Fortress, 1985.
Ellis, E. Earle. *Paul's Use of the Old Testament*. Edinburgh: Oliver & Boyd, 1957; reprint Grand Rapids: Baker Books, 1981.

Emerton, J. A. "The Textual and Linguistic Problems of Habakkuk ii 4–5." *JTS* n.s. 29 (1977): 1–18.
Evans, Craig A. "Listening for Echoes of Interpreted Scripture." In *Paul and the Scriptures of Israel*, ed. Craig A. Evans and James A. Sanders, 47–51. JSNTSS 83. Sheffield: JSOT Press, 1993.
Evans, Craig A., and James A. Sanders, eds. *Paul and the Scriptures of Israel*. JSNTSS 83. Sheffield: JSOT Press, 1993.
Feuillet, A. "La citation d'Habaccuc ii.4 et les huit premiers chapîtres de l'Epître aux Romains." *NTS* 6 (1959–60): 52.
Fishbane, Michael A. "Inner Biblical Exegesis: Types and Strategies of Interpretation in Ancient Israel." In *Midrash and Literature*, ed. Geoffrey H. Hartman and Sanford Budick, 19–37. New Haven: Yale, 1986.
———. *Biblical Exegesis in Ancient Israel*. Oxford: Clarendon Press, 1985.
Fitzmyer, J. A. "Habakkuk 2:3–4 and the New Testament." In *To Advance the Gospel: New Testament Studies*, 242. New York: Crossroads, 1981.
Flatt, J. F. von. *Vorlesungen über den Brief an die Galater und Epheser*. Tübingen: L. F. Fues, 1828.
Frow, John. "Intertextuality and Ontology." In *Intertextuality: Theories and Practice*, ed. Michael Worton and Judith Still, 45–55. Manchester: Manchester University Press, 1990.
Fuller, Daniel P. "Paul and 'The Works of the Law.'" *Westminster Theological Journal* 38 (1975): 28–42.
Fung, Ronald Y. K. *The Epistle to the Galatians*. NICNT. Grand Rapids: Eerdmans, 1988.
Funk, F. X., and F. Diekamp, eds. *Patres Apostolici*. Vol. 2, 3rd ed. Tübingen: Laupp, 1913.
Gaston, Lloyd. "Paul and the Torah." In *Paul and the Torah*, 64–79. Vancouver: University of British Columbia Press, 1987.
———. "Paul and the Law in Galatians 2 and 3." In *Paul and the Torah*, 64–79. Vancouver: University of British Columbia Press, 1987.
Gaventa, Beverly R. "The Singularity of the Gospel: A Reading of Galatians." In *Pauline Theology*, vol. 1, ed. Jouette M. Bassler, 147–59. Minneapolis: Fortress, 1991.
Gignac, Alain. "Citation de Lévitique 18,5 en Romains 10,5 et Galates 3,12." *Église et Théologie* 25 (1994): 367–403.
Graham, Susan Lochrie. "Intertextual Trekking: Visiting the Iniquity of the Fathers Upon 'The Next Generation.'" *Semeia* 69/70 (1995): 195–219.
Green, William Scott. "Doing the Text's Work for It: Richard Hays on Paul's Use of Scripture." In *Paul and the Scriptures of Israel*, ed. Craig A. Evans and James A. Sanders, 58–63. JSNTS 83. Sheffield: JSOT Press, 1993.
Gundry, Robert H. "Grace, Works, and Staying Saved in Paul." *Biblica* 66 (1985): 1–38.
Guthrie, Donald. *Galatians*. NCBC. Grand Rapids: Eerdmans, 1973.
Hammerton-Kelly, Robert G. "Sacred Violence and the Curse of the Law (Galatians 3:13): The Death of Christ as a Sacrificial Travesty." *NTS* 36 (1990): 98–118.
Hanse, Hermann. "ΔΗΛΟΝ (Zu Gal 3:11)." *ZNW* 34 (1935): 299–303.
Hansen, G. Walter. *Abraham in Galatians: Epistolary and Rhetorical Contexts*. JSNTSS 29. Sheffield: JSOT Press, 1989.

———. *Galatians*. Downers Grove, IL: InterVarsity Press, 1994.
Hanson, A. T. *Studies in Paul's Technique and Theology*. London: SPCK, 1974.
———. "The Origin of Paul's Use of *paidagogos* for the Law (Gal 3:24)." *JSNT* 34 (1988): 71–76.
Harnack, Adolf von. "Das Alte Testament in den Paulinischen Briefen und in den Paulinischen Gemeinden." *Sitzungsberichte der Preussischen Akademie der Wissenschaften*, Philosophisch-historische Klasse (1928): 124–41.
Hays, Richard B. "Jesus' Faith and Ours: A Re-reading of Galatians 3." In *Conflict and Context: Hermeneutics in the Americas*, ed. Mark Lau Branson and C. René Padilla, 257–268. Grand Rapids: Eerdmans, 1986.
———. "On the Rebound: A Response to Critiques of *Echoes of Scripture in the Letters of Paul*." In *Paul and the Scriptures of Israel*, ed. Craig A. Evans and James A. Sanders, 70–96. JSNTSS 83. Sheffield: JSOT Press, 1993.
———. "The Letter to the Galatians." In *2 Corinthians, Galatians, Ephesians, Philippians, Colossians, 1 & 2 Thessalonians, 1 & 2 Timothy, Titus, Philemon*, 181–348. *The New Interpreter's Bible*, vol. 11. Nashville: Abingdon, 2000.
———. "The Righteous One as Eschatological Deliverer." In *Apocalyptic and the New Testament: Essays in Honor of J. Louis Martyn*, ed. J. Marcus and M. L. Soards, 191–215. JSNTSS 24. Sheffield: JSOT Press, 1989.
———. *Echoes of Scripture in the Letters of Paul*. New Haven: Yale University Press, 1989.
———. *The Faith of Jesus Christ: An Investigation of the Narrative Substructure of Galatians 3:1–4:11*. SBLDS 56. Chico, CA: Scholars Press, 1983.
Heiligenthal, Roman. "Soziologische Implikationen der paulinischen Rechtfertigungslehre in Galaterbrief am Beispiel der 'Werke des Gesetzes.'" *Kairos* 26 (1984): 38–53.
Hempel, Carl G. *Philosophy of Natural Science*. Englewood Cliffs, NJ: Prentice Hall, 1966.
Hofmann, J. C. K. von. *Die Heilige Schrift des neuen Testaments zusammenhängend untersucht*. Nördlingen: C. H. Beck, 1863.
Hollander, John. *The Figure of Echo: A Mode of Allusion in Milton and After*. Berkeley: University of California Press, 1981.
Hong, In-Gyu. "Does Paul Misrepresent the Jewish Law? Law and Covenant in Gal. 3:1–14." *NovT* 36 (1994): 164–82.
———. *The Law in Galatians*, JSNTSS 81. Sheffield: JSOT, 1993.
Hooker, Morna D. "Interchange in Christ (Gal. 3:13, 2 Cor. 5:21, et al.)." *JTS* 22 (1971): 349–61.
———. "Paul and 'Covenantal Nomism.'" In *Paul and Paulinism: Essays in Honour of C. K. Barrett*, ed. M. D. Hooker and S. G. Wilson, 47–56. London: SPCK, 1982.
———. "ΠΙΣΤΙΣ ΧΡΙΣΤΟΥ." *NTS* 35 (1989): 321–42.
Howard, George. "On the Faith of Christ." *HTR* 60 (1967): 459–84.
———. *Paul: Crisis in Galatia. A Study in Early Christian Theology*. SNTSMS 35. Cambridge: Cambridge University Press, 1979.
Hübner, Hans. "Pauli Theologiae Proprium." *NTS* 26 (1980): 445–73.

———. *Das Gesetz bei Paulus: Ein Beitrag zum Werden der paulinischen Theologie.* FRLANT 119. Göttingen: Vandenhoeck & Ruprecht, 1978; ET *Law in Paul's Thought: A Contribution to the Development of Pauline Theology.* Edited by John Riches. Translated by James C. G. Greig. Edinburgh: T & T Clark, 1984.
Jaffee, Martin S. "The Hermeneutical Model of Midrashic Studies: What It Reveals and What It Conceals." *Prooftexts* 11 (1991): 67–75.
Jenny, Laurent. "La Stratégie de la forme." *Poétique* 27 (1976): 257–81.
Jervis, L. Ann. "'But I Want You to Know . . .': Paul's Midrashic Intertextual Response to the Corinthian Worshipers (1 Cor 11:2–16)." *JBL* 112 (1993): 231–46.
Jobes, Karen H. "Jerusalem, Our Mother: Metalepsis and Intertextuality in Galatians 4:21–31." *WTJ* 55 (1993): 299–320.
Johnson, H. Wayne. "The Paradigm of Abraham in Galatians 3:6–9." *Trinity Journal* 8 (1987): 179–99.
Johnson, John F. "Paul's Argument from Experience: A Closer Look at Galatians 3:1–5." *Concordia Journal* 19 (1993): 234–37.
Jung, Peter. "Das paulinische Vokabular in Gal 3:6–14." *ZKTh* 74 (1952): 439–449.
Keesmat, Sylvia C. "Exodus and the Intertextual Transformation of Tradition in Romans 8.14–30." *JSNT* 54 (1994): 29–56.
Klein, Gottlieb. *Studien über Paulus.* Stockholm: Bonniers, 1918.
Koch, Dietrich-Alex. "Der Text von Hab 2 4b in der Septuaginta und im Neuen Testament." *ZNW* 76 (1985): 68–85.
———. *Die Schrift als Zeuge des Evangeliums: Untersuchungen zur Verwendung und zum Verständnis der Schrift bei Paulus.* BHT 69. Tübingen: J. C. B. Mohr; Paul Siebeck, 1986.
Kristeva, Julia. *Desire in Language: A Semiotic Approach to Literature and Art.* Edited by Leon S. Roudiez. Translated by Thomas Gora, Alice Jardine, and Leon S. Roudiez. New York: Columbia University, 1980.
———. *Σημειωτική: Recherches pour une sémanalyse.* Paris: Du Seuil, 1969.
Kümmel, Werner Georg. *Römer 7 und die Bekehrung des Paulus.* Leipsig: J. G. Hinrichs, 1929.
Lambrecht, Jan. "Gesetzesverständnis bei Paulus (Gal. 3:10–14)." In *Das Gesetz im Neuen Testament*, ed. Karl Kertelge. Quaestiones Disputatae 108. Freiburg: Herder, 1986.
Lasine, Stuart. "Jehoram and the Cannibal Mothers (2 Kings 6.24–33): Solomon's Judgment in an Inverted World." *JSOT* 50 (1991): 27–53.
———. "The Ups and Downs of Monarchical Justice: Solomon and Jehoram in an Intertextual World." *JSOT* 59 (1993): 37–53.
Lewy, Immanuel. "Puzzle of Dt. 27: Blessings Announced, but Curses Noted." *VT* 12 (1962): 207–11.
Lieu, Judith M. "Reading in Canon and Community: Deuteronomy 21:22–23, a Test Case for Dialogue." In *The Bible in Human Society: Essays in Honour of John Rogerson*, ed. M. Daniel Carroll, David J. A. Clines, and Philip R. Davies, 317–34. JSOTSS 200. Sheffield: JSOT Press, 1995.
Lightfoot, J. B. *Saint Paul's Epistle to the Galatians.* London and New York: MacMillan, 1896.

Lindars, Barnabas. *New Testament Apologetic: The Doctrinal Significance of the Old Testament Quotations*. Philadelphia: Westminster, 1961.
Longenecker, Richard N. *Biblical Exegesis in the Apostolic Period*. Grand Rapids: Eerdmans, 1975.
———. *Galatians*, WBC 41. Dallas: Word Books, 1990.
Lührmann, Dieter. *Galatians: A Continental Commentary*. Translated by O. C. Dean. Minneapolis: Fortress, 1992.
Lull, David John. *The Spirit in Galatia: Paul's Interpretation of* Pneuma *as Divine Power*. SBLDS 49. Chico, CA: Scholars Press, 1980.
Luther, Martin. *A Commentary on St. Paul's Epistle to the Galatians: Based on Lectures Delivered by Martin Luther at the University of Wittenberg in the year 1531 and First Published in 1535*. Translated by P. W. Watson. London: James Clarke, 1953.
———. *Luther's Works*, vols. 26–27. Edited by J. Pelikan. St. Louis: Concordia, 1963–1964.
MacArthur, John F. *Galatians*. Chicago: Moody, 1987.
Martyn, J. Louis. "A Law-Observant Mission to Gentiles: The Background of Galatians." *Scottish Journal of Theology* 38 (1985): 307–24.
———. "Apocalyptic Antinomies in Paul's Letter to the Galatians." *NTS* 31 (1985): 410–424.
———. "Events in Galatia: Modified Covenantal Nomism versus God's Invasion of the Cosmos in the Singular Gospel. A Response to J. D. G. Dunn and B. R. Gaventa." in *Pauline Theology*, vol. 1, ed. Jouette M. Bassler, 160–179. Minneapolis: Fortress, 1991.
———. "The Textual Contradiction Between Habakkuk 2:4 and Leviticus 18:5." In *Theological Issues in the Letters of Paul*, 183–190. Edinburgh: T & T Clark, 1997.
———. *Galatians*. AB 33A. New York: Doubleday, 1997.
Meyer, Heinrich August Wilhelm. *Critical and Exegetical Handbook to the Epistle to the Galatians*. Translated by G. H. Venables. New York: Funk & Wagnalls, 1884.
Michel, Otto. *Paulus und seine Bibel*. Darmstadt: Wissenschaftliche Buchgesellschaft, 1972.
Miller, Owen. "Intertextual Identity." In *Identity of the Literary Text*, ed. Mario J. Valdés and Owen Miller, 19–40. Toronto: University of Toronto Press, 1985.
Montefiore, C. G. *Judaism and St. Paul*. London: Max Goschen, 1914.
Moo, D. J. "'Law,' 'Works of the Law,' and Legalism in Paul." *WTJ* 45 (1983): 73–100.
Moore, George Foot. "Christian Writers on Judaism." *HTR* 14 (1921): 197–254.
Morgan, Thaïs E. "Is There an Intertext In This Text?: Literary and Interdisciplinary Approaches to Intertextuality." *American Journal of Semiotics* 3 no. 4 (1985): 1–40.
Moyise, Steve. "Intertextuality and the Book of Revelation." *ET* 104 (1993): 295–98.
Mussner, Franz. "Gesetz—Abraham—Israel (in Galatians)." *Kairos* 25 (1983): 200–222.
Neusner, Jacob, and William Scott Green. *Writing With Scripture: The Authority and Uses of the Hebrew Bible in the Torah of Formative Judaism*. Minneapolis: Fortress, 1989.
Noth, Martin. "'For All Who Rely on Works of the Law Are Under a Curse.'" In *The Laws in the Pentateuch and Other Studies*, trans. D. R. Ap-Thomas, 108–117. Edinburgh: Oliver & Boyd, 1966.

O'Day, Gail R. "Jeremiah 9:22–23 and 1 Corinthians 1:26–31: A Study in Intertextuality." *JBL* 109 (1990): 259–67.
Oepke, Albrecht. *Der Brief des Paulus an die Galater*. THKNT 9. Berlin: Evangelische Verlagsanstalt, 1964.
Pfister, Manfred. "Konzepte der Intertextualität." In *Intertextualität: Formen, Functionen, anglistische Fallstudien*, ed. Ulrich Broich and Manfred Pfister, 1–30. Tübingen: Niemeyer, 1985.
Pyper, Hugh S. "Judging the Wisdom of Solomon: The Two-Way Effect of Intertextuality." *JSOT* 59 (1993): 25–36.
Räisänen, Heikki. "Galatians 2.16 and Paul's Break with Judaism." *NTS* 31 (1985): 543–53.
———. "Legalism and Salvation by the Law." In *The Pauline Literature and Theology*, ed. S. Pedersen, 63–83. Teologiske Studier 7. Göttingen: Vandenhoeck & Ruprecht, 1980.
———. "Paul's Theological Difficulties with the Law." In *Papers on Paul and Other New Testament Authors*, ed. E. A. Livingstone, 301–20. *Studia Biblica* 1978, vol. 3. JSNTSS 3. Sheffield: JSOT Press, 1980.
———. *Paul and the Law*. Wissenschaftliche Untersuchungen zum Neuen Testament 29. Tübingen: J.C.B. Mohr, 1983.
Ramsay, W. M. *A Historical Commentary on St. Paul's Epistle to the Galatians*, 2nd ed. London: Hodder and Stoughton, 1900.
Riffaterre, Michael. "Compulsory Reader Response: The Intertextual Drive." In *Intertextuality: Theories and Practice*, ed. Michael Worton and Judith Still, 56–78. Manchester: Manchester University Press, 1990.
———. "The Making of the Text." In *Identity of the Literary Text*, ed. Mario J. Valdés and Owen Miller, 54–70. Toronto: University of Toronto Press, 1985.
———. *Semiotics of Poetry*. Bloomington: Indiana University, 1978.
———. *Text Production*. Translated by Terese Lyons. New York: Columbia University, 1983.
Roberts, Alexander, and James Donaldson, eds. *Ante-Nicene Fathers*. Peabody, MA: Hendrickson, 1994.
Sanders, E. P. "Patterns of Religion in Paul and Rabbinic Judaism: A Holistic Method of Comparison." *HTR* 66 (1973): 455–78.
———. *Paul and Palestinian Judaism*. Philadelphia: Fortress Press, 1977.
———. *Paul, the Law, and the Jewish People*. Minneapolis: Fortress, 1983.
Sanders, James A. "Habakkuk in Qumran, Paul, and the Old Testament." In *Paul and the Scriptures of Israel*, ed. Craig A. Evans and James A. Sanders, 98–117. JSNTS 83. Sheffield: JSOT Press, 1993.
———. *From Sacred Story to Sacred Text: Canon as Paradigm*. Philadelphia: Fortress, 1987.
Schlier, Heinrich. *Der Briefe an die Galater*, 10th ed. Kritisch-exegetischer Kommentar über das Neue Testament 7. Göttingen: Vandenhoek & Ruprecht, 1949.
Schoeps, H. J. *Paul: The Theology of the Apostle in the Light of Jewish Religious History*. Translated by Harold Knight. Philadelphia: Westminster, 1961.
Schreiner, Thomas R. "Is Perfect Obedience to the Law Possible? A Re-Examination of Galatians 3:10." *JETS* 27 (1984): 151–60.

———. "Paul and Perfect Obedience to the Law: An Evaluation of the View of E. P. Sanders." *WTJ* 47 (1985): 245–278.
———. *The Law and Its Fulfillment: A Pauline Theology of Law*. Grand Rapids: Baker Books, 1993.
Schweitzer, Albert. *Paul and His Interpreters*. London: Adam & Charles Black, 1950 [1912].
———. *The Mysticism of Paul the Apostle*. New York: Seabury, 1931.
Scott, James M. "'For as Many As Are of Works of the Law Are Under a Curse' (Galatians 3.10)." In *Paul and the Scriptures of Israel*, ed. Craig A. Evans and James A. Sanders, 187–221. JSNTSS 83. Sheffield: JSOT Press, 1993.
———. "A New Approach to Habakkuk II 4–5A." *VT* 35 (1985): 330–40.
———. "Paul's Use of Deuteronomic Tradition." *JBL* 112 (1993): 645–65.
Seybold, Klaus. "Habakuk 2,4 und sein Kontext." In *Zur Aktualität des Alten Testaments*, ed. Siegfried Kreuzer and Kurt Lüthi, 99–107. Frankfurt: Peter Lang, 1992.
Smiles, Vincent M. "The Gospel and the Law in Galatia: Paul's Response to Christian Separatism and the Threat of Galatian Apostasy." Ph.D. diss., Fordham University, 1988.
Smith, D. Moody, Jr. "Ο ΔΕ ΔΙΚΑΙΟΣ ΕΚ ΠΙΣΤΕΩΣ ΖΗΣΕΤΑΙ." In *Studies in the History and Text of the New Testament in Honor of Kenneth Willis Clark*, ed. Boyd L. Daniels and M. Jack Suggs, 13–25. Studies and Documents 29. Salt Lake City: University of Utah Press, 1967.
———. "The Pauline Literature." In *It is Written: Scripture Citing Scripture. Essays in Honour of Barnabas Lindars, SSF*, ed. D. A. Carson and H. G. M. Williamson, 265–91. Cambridge: Cambridge University Press, 1988.
Sommer, Benjamin D. "Exegesis, Allusion, and Intertextuality in the Hebrew Bible: A Response to Lyle Eslinger." *VT* 46 (1996): 479–89.
Stanley, Christopher D. "'Under a Curse': A Fresh Reading of Galatians 3:10–14." *NTS* 36 (1990): 482–511.
———. *Paul and the Language of Scripture: Citation Technique in the Pauline Epistles and Contemporary Literature*. SNTS 74. Cambridge: Cambridge University Press, 1992.
Stendahl, Krister. "The Apostle Paul and the Introspective Conscience of the West." In *Paul among Jews and Gentiles*, 78–96. Philadelphia: Fortress, 1976.
Still, Judith, and Michael Worton. "Introduction." In *Intertextuality: Theories and Practice*, ed. Michael Worton and Judith Still, 1–44. Manchester: Manchester University Press, 1990.
Stockhausen, Carol K. "2 Corinthians and the Principles of Pauline Exegesis." In *Paul and the Scriptures of Israel*, ed. Craig A. Evans and James A. Sanders, 143–64. JSNTSS 83. Sheffield: JSOT Press, 1993.
———. *Moses' Veil and the Glory of the New Covenant: The Exegetical Substructure of II Cor 3:1–4, 6*. Rome: Pontificio Instituto Biblico, 1989.
Thielman, Frank. *From Plight to Solution: A Jewish Framework for Understanding Paul's View of the Law in Galatians and Romans*. Leiden: E. J. Brill, 1989.
Tschuggnall, Peter. "'Das Wort ist kein Ding': Eine theologische Einübung in den literaturwissenschaftlichen Begriff der Intertextualität." *ZKTh* 116 (1994): 160–78.

Valdés, Mario J., and Owen Miller, eds. *Identity of the Literary Text*. Toronto: University of Toronto Press, 1985.

Vielhauer, Philipp. "Paulus und das Alte Testament." In *Studien zur Geschichte und Theologie der Reformation*, ed. Luise Abramowski and J. F. Gerhard Goeters, 33–62. FS Ernst Bizer. [Neukirchen-Vluyn]: Neukirchener Verlag, 1969.

Voelz, James W. "Multiple Signs and Double Texts: Elements of Intertextuality." In *Intertextuality in Biblical Writings: Essays in Honour of Bas van Iersel*, ed. Sipke Draisma, 27–34. Kampen: J. H. Kok, 1989.

Vorster, Willem S. "Intertextuality and Redaktionsgeschichte." In *Intertextuality in Biblical Writings: Essays in Honour of Bas van Iersel*, ed. Sipke Draisma, 15–26. Kampen: J. H. Kok, 1989.

Vos, J. S. "Die Hermeneutische Antinomie bei Paulus. Galater 3:11–12; Römer 10:5–10." *NTS* 38 (1992): 254–70.

Weber, Beat. "Philipper 2,12–13: Text–Kontext–Intertext." *Biblische Notizen* 85 (1996): 31–37.

Westerholm, Stephen. *Israel's Law and the Church's Faith: Paul and His Recent Interpreters*. Grand Rapids: Eerdmans, 1988.

Wilckens, Ulrich. "Was heißt bei Paulus: 'Aus Werken des Gesetzes wird kein Mensch gerecht'?" In *Rechtfertigung als Freiheit: Paulusstudien*, 77–109. Neukirchen-Vluyn: Neukirchener, 1974.

———. "Zur Entwicklung des paulinischen Gesetzesverständnisses." *NTS* 28 (1982): 154–90.

Wilcox, Max. "'Upon the Tree'—Deut 21:22–23 in the New Testament." *JBL* 96 (1977): 85–99.

Williams, Sam K. "The Hearing of Faith: *akoe pisteos* in Galatians 3." *NTS* 35 (1989): 82–93.

———. "Again *Pistis Christou*." *CBQ* 49 (1987): 431–47.

Wolde, Ellen van. "Texts in Dialogue with Texts: Intertextuality in the Ruth and Tamar Narratives." *Biblical Interpretation* 5 (1997): 1–28.

———. "Trendy Intertextuality?" In *Intertextuality in Biblical Writings: Essays in Honour of Bas van Iersel*, ed. Sipke Draisma, 43–49. Kampen: J. H. Kok, 1989.

Worton, Michael, and Judith Still, eds. *Intertextuality: Theories and Practice*. Manchester: Manchester University Press, 1990.

Wrede, Wilhelm. *Paul*. Lexington: American Library Association Committee on Reprinting, 1962 [1908].

Wright, N. T. *The Climax of the Covenant: Christ and the Law in Pauline Theology*. Minneapolis: Fortress, 1991.

Zahn, Theodor. *Der Brief des Paulus an die Galater*. Leipzig: Deichert, 1922.

Ziesler, J. A. *The Meaning of Righteousness in Paul: A Linguistic and Theological Inquiry*. SNTSMS 20. Cambridge: Cambridge University Press, 1972.

INDEX OF MODERN AUTHORS

Aichele, George, 103, 104, 107, 112
Barclay, John M. G., 29, 43, 46–56, 183, 184, 197, 200, 201
Barker, Stephen F., 152, 159
Barrett, C. K., 33, 78, 137
Barthes, Roland., 98, 100, 105, 106
Beker, J. Christiaan., 1, 4, 49, 56, 64, 84, 88, 144
Bengel, J. A., 163
Betz, H. D., 1, 2, 6, 11, 22, 46, 61, 62, 66, 69, 75, 77, 82, 91, 96, 133, 135, 136, 137, 151, 191, 202
Boyarin, Daniel, 63, 98, 115–17, 118, 122, 123
Brauch, Manfred T., 20
Brawley, Robert L., 97, 113, 123
Bring, Ragnar, 18, 72, 81
Bruce, F. F., 12, 18, 67, 69, 72, 137, 192
Bruns, Gerald L., 63
Bultmann, Rudolf, 2, 4, 16–18, 28, 52, 72
Burton, Ernest De Witt, 18, 22, 66, 69, 71, 83–85, 162, 163, 192
Caneday, Ardel, 158
Cavallin, H. C. C., 79, 139, 171
Clayton, Jay, 99, 101, 105, 111, 123
Cohen, Aryeh, 115
Cosgrove, Charles H., 2, 3, 5
Cousar, Charles B., 5, 18, 69
Cranfield, C. E. B., 22, 63, 71, 72, 81
Cranford, Michael, 19, 67, 68, 72, 95

Culler, Jonathan, 8, 99, 102, 105, 106, 110, 122–23, 126, 128–30, 131, 145–47
Dahl, Nils A., 80, 84, 89–93, 122
Dana, H. E., 160, 161
Diekamp, F., 165
Donaldson, James, 165
Draisma, Sipke, 101, 112
Dunn, James D. G., 4, 23, 30–33, 35, 36, 39–42, 49, 53, 71, 72, 73, 84, 166, 175, 177, 178, 191, 198
Ebeling, Gerhard, 6, 18, 72, 81, 82, 95, 158
Ellis, E. Earle, 57, 62, 63
Emerton, J. A., 171
Evans, Craig A., 62, 70, 97, 109, 134
Fishbane, Michael A., 97
Flatt, J. F. von, 163
Frow, John, 99, 106
Fuller, Daniel P., 18, 68, 71, 72, 84
Fung, Ronald Y. K., 67
Funk, F. X., 163, 165
Gaston, Lloyd, 69, 199
Gaventa, Beverly R., 49, 53, 175
Gignac, Alain, 2, 84, 133, 134
Graham, Susan Lochrie, 98
Green, William Scott, 98
Gundry, Robert H., 25, 32, 33–36, 39, 42, 67, 81, 95, 200
Guthrie, Donald, 18
Hanse, Hermann, 163, 164, 165
Hansen, G. Walter, 4, 18, 69, 136

Hanson, A. T., 57, 63
Harnack, Adolf von, 1
Hays, Richard B., 2, 5, 40, 44, 53, 57, 58, 59, 61, 62–64, 69, 79, 89, 90, 91, 93, 95, 97, 98, 107, 108, 109, 112–15, 117, 118, 122, 134, 142, 143, 157, 161, 163, 182, 184, 185, 190
Hempel, Carl G., 157
Hofmann, J. C. K. von, 163
Hollander, John, 114
Hong, In-Gyu, 38
Hooker, Morna D., 33, 53, 56
Howard, George, 53, 68, 69, 71, 80, 178, 190
Hübner, Hans, 17, 54, 68, 71, 80, 81, 191, 200
Jaffee, Martin S., 115, 116, 117
Jenny, Laurent, 110
Jervis, L. Ann, 97, 115, 117–18
Jobes, Karen H., 97, 117, 119–20
Keesmat, Sylvia C., 97, 113, 117–118
Klein, Gottlieb, 89
Koch, Dietrich-Alex, 57, 58, 60–61, 133, 134, 137, 171
Kristeva, Julia, 98, 99, 100, 102, 105
Kümmel, Werner Georg, 16
Lasine, Stuart, 109, 111, 115, 119
Lightfoot, J. B., 67, 69
Lindars, Barnabas, 58, 64
Longenecker, Richard N., 12, 21, 22, 63, 66, 67, 69, 133, 136, 160, 161, 162, 192
Lührmann, Dieter, 95, 134, 144
Luther, Martin, 4, 12, 13–16, 17, 18, 20, 21, 24, 52, 67, 142, 195, 200
MacArthur, John F., 18
Mantey, Julius R., 160, 161
Martyn, J. Louis, 12, 45, 49–56, 61, 69, 78–79, 80, 85–88, 90, 91, 92, 95, 96, 133, 134, 135, 137, 139, 146, 150, 161, 166, 171, 175, 176, 180, 182, 185, 191, 192, 193, 196, 201
Meyer, Heinrich August Wilhelm, 163
Michel, Otto, 57
Miller, Owen, 99, 100, 102, 106
Montefiore, C. G., 16

Moore, George Foot, 16
Morgan, Thaïs E., 99, 100, 101, 102, 105, 106
Moyise, Steve, 115
Neusner, Jacob, 97
Noth, Martin, 4, 38, 70
Oepke, Albrecht, 18
Pfister, Manfred, 99
Phillips, Gary A, 103, 104, 107, 112, 192
Pyper, Hugh S., 120
Räisänen, Heikki, 17, 18, 32, 40, 44, 62, 93–94, 151, 173
Ramsay, W. M., 65
Riffaterre, Michael, 8, 98, 116, 122–28, 130, 131, 132, 142, 148, 149, 172
Roberts, Alexander, 165
Rothstein, Eric, 99, 101, 105, 111, 123
Sanders, E. P., 3, 4, 5, 6, 12, 16, 18, 20, 23–45, 47, 48, 52, 54, 55, 56, 62, 64, 68, 71, 72, 74–75, 77–78, 83, 88, 135, 137, 139, 141, 142, 151, 159, 169, 173, 176, 178, 182, 183, 196, 198, 200, 201
Sanders, James A., 62, 70, 97, 98, 134
Schlier, Heinrich, 17, 71, 72
Schoeps, H. J., 16, 18, 67, 68, 89–90, 93
Schreiner, Thomas R., 3, 4, 12, 18–19, 21, 22, 33, 67, 68, 72, 81, 178, 182, 200
Schweitzer, Albert, 12, 20, 26, 56
Scott, James M., 70, 134, 171
Smiles, Vincent M., 18, 134
Smith, D. Moody, Jr., 58, 59, 60, 61, 65, 79, 139, 140, 170, 171
Sommer, Benjamin D., 103, 109, 112
Stanley, Christopher D., 57, 58, 59, 60–61, 65, 75–78, 80, 133, 134, 136, 137, 138, 139, 147, 179, 180
Stendahl, Krister, 16
Still, Judith, 99, 131
Stockhausen, Carol K., 62
Thielman, Frank, 4, 13, 27, 33, 37–38, 39, 45, 70, 200, 201
Tschuggnall, Peter, 97

Valdés, Mario J., 99
Vielhauer, Philipp, 62, 64
Voelz, James W., 103
Vorster, Willem S., 102, 103, 111
Vos, J. S., 80, 86, 88, 91–93, 95
Weber, Beat, 98
Westerholm, Stephen, 12, 13, 14, 16, 21, 22, 33, 35–37, 38, 41, 45, 47, 134, 196, 197, 200
Wilckens, Ulrich, 18, 19–20
Wilcox, Max, 60
Williams, Sam K., 53
Wolde, Ellen van, 101, 102, 103, 106, 107, 123
Worton, Michael, 99
Wrede, Wilhelm, 12
Wright, N. T., 12, 70, 163
Zahn, Theodor, 163, 164
Ziesler, J. A., 20

www.ingramcontent.com/pod-product-compliance
Lightning Source LLC
Chambersburg PA
CBHW020647300426
44112CB00007B/280